Past and Present Publications

Desolation of a City

Past and Present Publications

General Editor: T. H. ASTON, *Corpus Christi College, Oxford*

Past and Present Publications will comprise books similar in character to the articles in the journal *Past and Present*. Whether the volumes in the series are collections of essays – some previously published, others new studies – or monographs, they will encompass a wide variety of scholarly and original works primarily concerned with social, economic and cultural changes, and their causes and consequences. They will appeal to both specialists and non-specialists and will endeavour to communicate the results of historical and allied research in readable and lively form. This new series continues and expands in its aims the volumes previously published elsewhere.

Volumes published by the Cambridge University Press are:
Family and Inheritance: Rural Society in Western Europe 1200–1800, edited by Jack Goody, Joan Thirsk and E. P. Thompson
French Society and the Revolution, edited by Douglas Johnson
Peasants, Knights and Heretics: Studies in Medieval English Social History, edited by R. H. Hilton
Towns in Societies: Essays in Economic History and Historical Sociology, edited by Philip Abrams and E. A. Wrigley
Desolation of a City: Coventry and the Urban Crisis of the Late Middle Ages, Charles Phythian-Adams

Volumes previously published with Routledge & Kegan Paul are:
Crisis in Europe 1560–1660, edited by Trevor Aston
Studies in Ancient Society, edited by M. I. Finley
The Intellectual Revolution of the Seventeenth Century, edited by Charles Webster

The frontispiece, from a photograph taken by Colin Brooks, shows the physical relationship between municipality (St Mary's Hall), church (St Michael's) and society (contemporary domestic architecture) at the ritual centre of late medieval Coventry.

Desolation of a City

Coventry and the Urban Crisis of the Late Middle Ages

CHARLES PHYTHIAN-ADAMS

Senior Lecturer in the Department of English Local History
University of Leicester

CAMBRIDGE UNIVERSITY PRESS

Cambridge
London   New York   New Rochelle
Melbourne   Sydney

Published by the Press Syndicate of the University of Cambridge
The Pitt Building, Trumpington Street, Cambridge CB2 1RP
32 East 57th Street, New York, NY 10022, USA
296 Beaconsfield Parade, Middle Park, Melbourne 3206, Australia

First published 1979

Phototypeset in V.I.P. Times by
Western Printing Services Ltd, Bristol

Printed in Great Britain at
The Pitman Press, Bath

Library of Congress Cataloguing in Publication Data
Phythian-Adams, Charles.

Desolation of a city.

(Past and present publications)

Bibliography: p.

Includes index.

1. Coventry, Eng. – Social conditions.
2. Coventry, Eng. – Economic conditions.
3. Cities and towns – England – Case studies.
I. Title. II. Series.
HN398.C68P59   309.1'424'87   79-9967
ISBN 0 521 22604 X

297006

FOR MY MOTHER
IN MEMORY
OF MY FATHER

Contents

Tables

Tables in the appendices

Illustrations

Maps

Figures

Plates

Preface

So protracted and discontinuous has the development of this book been, that for the author it emerges at the last somewhat like the ageing Falstaff – 'Surfeit-swell'd, so old, and so profane'. Originally projected as an Occasional Paper for the Department of English Local History at the University of Leicester, it has grown by stages from a slim monograph that was just completed in December 1967, when almost to the day a vast quantity of relevant new material came unexpectedly to light (see appendix 1). At about the same time, the need arose for the author to widen his field of original research considerably in order to be able to lecture at post-graduate level over a broader chronological range. The much more complex analysis that the new evidence made both desirable and possible had thus to be deferred, and it was not until 1974 that a substantially enlarged version was finally completed. By now too lengthy to be an Occasional Paper but yet short of full book length, a technical monograph of this kind was not a commercial proposition even for a university press at that time of deepening economic crisis. Had it not been for the kindness and encouragement of Mr Keith Thomas in the following year, therefore, and at whose prompting the manuscript was submitted to the Editorial Board of *Past and Present*, the impetus to persevere with its publication, in an academic as opposed to popular form, might well have been lost altogether. As a direct result of both the interest then shown, and the constructive suggestions made by the readers, the book has now been completely re-shaped and enlarged for a third time, though not necessarily along the lines they may have expected.

For those scholars who I know have wished to make use of the rare quantitative evidence which is analysed here, these delays will have been tedious. I hope I may be forgiven, however, for having resisted the temptation to break up the analysis into a series of short articles in which these essentially static numerical data would have had to be divorced from an appreciation of the local background circumstances whence they emanated. Whatever the imperfections of this study, it does at least attempt to provide an integrated *moving* picture in which all kinds of evidence are essentially inter-related on contrasted chronological and analytical planes.

The debts I have incurred however discontinuously over so many years are inevitably legion. The foremost is to Professor W. G. Hoskins who originally set me on the Coventry trail, and even made available to me his extracted version of the 1522 assessment at a time when easy access to Coventry from Oxford was peculiarly difficult. Academically, I have profited greatly from the rather special ethos and environment of the Department of English Local History here at Leicester both under his direction and under that of Professor Alan Everitt. Each at different times, moreover, has shown a forbearance bordering on the saintly in their office as editor of the Occasional Paper series.

At Leicester, likewise, I have been frequently helped with information and advice from my other colleagues: Richard McKinley – an inexhaustible source, Michael Laithwaite, Harold Fox and especially David Hey who even gallantly read and constructively criticised one of the more tortured early versions of this study. Margery Tranter has once again kindly made the time to draft one of my maps as well as acting as an occasional sounding-board. I would also like to record my lasting gratitude to the late Jim Dyos, Professor of Urban History at Leicester, whose continuing kindness, encouragement and interest were never-failing with regard to the fluctuating publishing fortunes of this book. To the University of Leicester as a body, I am further obliged. A short term as Research Fellow in this Department, followed by a grant from the University Research Board, and the opportunity to use the university's (sometimes wilful) punched card sorting machine have all contributed to the prosecution of this project. Colin Brooks of the University's Central Photographic Unit kindly visited Coventry with me to take the pictures used in this book. In more ways than one, this is very much a product of 'the *Leicester* school' of local history.

At Coventry, in the days when Mr Alan Dibben was Archivist and Mr David Smith Assistant Archivist at the City Record Office they and their colleagues – Pat Barlow and the late Mr Norris, a superlative restorer of manuscripts – gave unstintingly of their time and help. Considering the virtually uncatalogued state of the records when I first went to Coventry in 1964, the fact that the research for this book was largely completed at the time when I was most at liberty to do it, owes much to the zeal of these two archivists. My other obligation at Coventry is to the Company of Cappers and

Feltmakers and Miss J. Compton, who courteously made available to me, not only their earliest records but also a place in which to study them. That this was an office of *The Coventry Evening Telegraph* at the time of the student riots in Paris, and hot copy was thus continually landing on my desk, gave an added piquancy to the weary labour of transcribing the Cappers' earliest, and very bulky, account book. More recently, I have been helped both by Mr David Rimmer and his staff at the City Record Office, and by Dr Levi Fox and Mrs Marion Pringle at the Shakespeare Birthplace Trust at Stratford-upon-Avon.

With regard to interpretation, I have benefited much from the reactions of those who have patiently listened to papers on some of the themes of this book at conferences (the Urban History Conference in 1971; the Anglo-American Conference in 1972; and the *Past and Present* Conference in 1975), as well as at seminars in Oxford, Cambridge, Sheffield, Keele, the Institute of Historical Research, and at one for Open University staff. If I have unconsciously absorbed the views of others in the process, and have therefore not acknowledged the fact here, I trust this may be viewed rather as a compliment than otherwise.

And yet my greatest debts are more personal: to John Eyre, for his original intellectual stimulation on so many matters; to the late Rev Anthony Hardcastle for a lengthy and learned communication on the age of confirmation; to Mrs Marjorie Annand, for an extended loan of that rare volume, *Dr Troughton's Sketches of Old Coventry*; and to Mr Peter Laslett who long ago gave a complete stranger a whole afternoon's tutorial on matters to do with early listings. Those friends that have sought with, I fear, only varying success to dispel the cloudier aspects of my thinking on various points, and who have thereby given more encouragement than they may have realised, include Malcolm Airs, Peter Clark, Alan Macfarlane, David Palliser, Peter Phillipson, Paul Slack, Wendy Warren, Kevin Wilson, and particularly Colin Bourn, who has been especially patient.

Others still have actually slaved in the cause. Dorothy Brydges typed and re-typed some indescribable drafts as well as the finished product. Julia Kerr spent hours helping to cross-check my figures. Of even greater assistance at an early critical moment was Jill Bourn, whose massive practical help and impetus with regard to correlating evidence, and coding and sorting the punched cards, were probably more responsible than any other single factor for ensuring that the more elaborate analysis of the new material that became necessary was ever completed. For all of these friends, if their's was the effort, mine alone are the faults and inaccuracies which inevitably must linger even after such care has been taken and kindness freely given.

C.V.P-A.:
The Department of English Local
History
The University of Leicester

September 1978

Abbreviations

Access.	Accession
Ag.H.R.	*Agricultural History Review*
B.A.S.T.	*Birmingham Archaeological Society Transactions and Proceedings*
Bodl.	Bodleian Library, Oxford
B.L.	British Library
Cal. Charter Rolls	*Calendar of the Charter Rolls Preserved in the Public Record Office*
Cal. Pap. Regs.	*Calendar of Entries in the Papal Registers Relating to Great Britain and Ireland*
Cal. Pat. Rolls	*Calendar of the Patent Rolls Preserved in the Public Record Office*
Cappers' accs.	Cappers' accounts
C.R.O.	Coventry Record Office
E	Exchequer Records, P.R.O.
Econ. H.R.	*Economic History Review*
Harl.	Harleian MSS.
H.M.C. *Middleton*	Historical Manuscripts Commission: *Report on the Manuscripts of Lord Middleton, Preserved at Wollaton Hall, Nottinghamshire*, ed. W. H. Stevenson (H.M.C., Cd. 5567, H.M.S.O., 1911)
hhs.	Households
L.B.	*The Coventry Leet Book or Mayor's Register Containing the Records of the City Leet or View of Frankpledge A.D. 1420–1555 with Divers Other Matters*, transcribed and ed. by Mary Dormer Harris (Early English Text Society, cxxxiv, cxxxv, cxxxviii, cxlvi, 1907–13)
L.M.	'A list of the Mayors & Sheriffs *etc*. of Coventry', Bodl., 31431, MS. Top. Warwickshire d. 4
L. & P.	*Letters and Papers Foreign and Domestic of the Reign of Henry VIII*

P.C.C.	The Prerogative Court of Canterbury (with reference to wills now in P.R.O.)
Pers.	Persons
P.R.O.	The Public Record Office
Reader, 4–8	Reader MSS., Bodl. MSS. Top. Warwick c. 4–8.
Sharp, *Antiquities*	Thomas Sharp, *Illustrative Papers on the History and Antiquities of the City of Coventry ... from Original and Mostly Unpublished Documents*, reprinted with corrections, additions and a brief memoir of the author by W. G. Fretton (Birmingham, 1871)
Sharp, *Dissertation*	Thomas Sharp, *A Dissertation on the Pageants or Dramatic Mysteries Anciently Performed at Coventry, by the Trading Companies of that City; Chiefly with Reference to the Vehicles, Character and Dresses of the Actors* (Coventry, 1825)
SP	State Papers Domestic, P.R.O.
Statutes of the Realm	*The Statutes of the Realm* (Record Commission, London, 1810–28)
Valor	*Valor Ecclesiasticus Temp. Henr. VIII Auctoritate Regia Institutus*, 6 vols., ed. J. Caley and J. Hunter (Record Commission, 1810–34), iii (1817)
V.C.H.	*Victoria County History*

Ward abbreviations

BG	Broad Gate
BL	Bailey Lane
BP	Bishop
E	Earl
G	Gosford
JW	Jordan Well
MP	Much Park
SM	Smithford
SP	Spon
XC	Cross Cheaping

Overleaf: Map 1
Late Medieval Coventry (see Appendix 5)

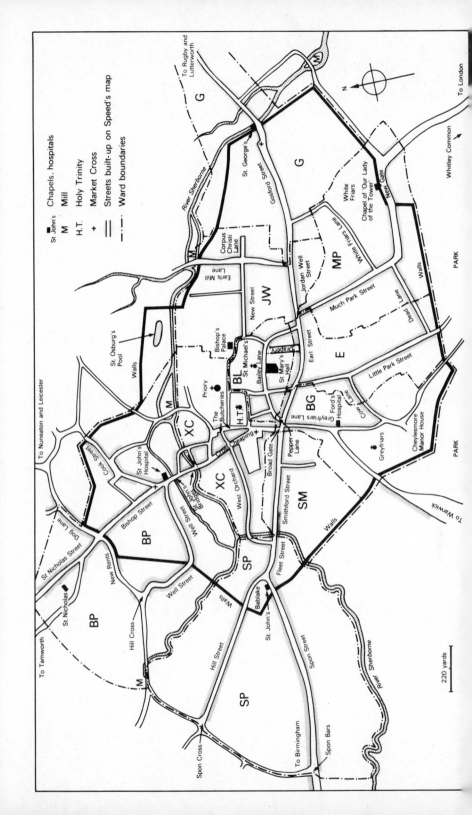

Introduction

There are a number of ways in which social historians delimit their subjects. One is to concentrate on a 'class' of society and to look at it over time in a regional or national context. Another is to take a specific theme like literacy, criminality or sexual *mores*, and to investigate that, often in predominantly quantitative terms. A third, and perhaps the longest established approach, that nevertheless still seems to lack the lustre of fashionable respectability which both 'class' and topical investigations attract, is that of the local historian in his study of a particular community. An anthropologist may spend six months or a year on one Pacific island and much of a career writing about it; a new breed of 'urban' historian may devote himself to the analysis of a single nineteenth-century city; but there is still a residual suspicion in some quarters that a detailed historical study of one 'pre-industrial' English community bears a somewhat pedestrian, even amateur taint, and is valuable essentially only insofar as it is a source for wider and hence more 'significant' generalisation.

This book is written, however unsuccessfully, in a contrary spirit. It seems to me that investigations of particular 'classes' or themes, valuable as they undoubtedly are, invariably concentrate on only one facet of society. By definition they have to view society selectively and hence to some extent from without. A community study too will inevitably be selective but far less so, and it also provides the opportunities at least both to examine a society from within and to identify its local peculiarity. Above all, it permits the investigation of as many facets of life and society as the evidence allows. It thus becomes possible to evaluate the inter-action of both separate social themes and of differing social groups through a more objective perspective. If the concept of 'total history' is unrealisable, there is, nevertheless, a need for studies which examine communities as 'wholes' – a rather different proposition.

That need is becoming ever more marked in the field of urban history. Over the last few years, Mr Peter Clark and Dr Paul Slack have between them laid the foundations of a typology of English towns in the period 1500–1700, which characterises 'the urban

1

hierarchy' in terms of differing functions and sizes.[1] This valuable
preliminary exercise now requires testing at the level of specific
studies for the different types of town concerned. In particular we
need to know more about both late medieval urban social organisation and also the manner in which towns emerged economically and
socially out of the middle ages, into the era of the 'pre-industrial'
town.

It is indeed remarkable that with the partial exception of Sylvia
Thrupp's masterpiece on *The Merchant Class of Medieval London*,[2]
there exists in print not one close study of an English urban *society*
as a whole at the end of the middle ages. There are essentially
municipal histories of medieval towns, and there are important
modern studies in the round of individual sixteenth-century towns.
In the latter, however, attempts to characterise *pre*-Reformation
urban society tend to be limited, on the one hand, to analyses of the
distribution of wealth in the 1520s, and especially urban elites and
the poor in that regard; and, on the other, to occupational structures
as derived from the evidence of freemen's admissions.

A major, but not wholly convincing, explanation for this state of
affairs, might be that auxiliary documentation is lacking. For a
small, but significant number of key towns, however, and amongst
which Coventry is only one, this is in fact untrue. Nevertheless, if for
no other reason, the unusually informative series of records with
which Coventry is endowed does make it an appropriate object of
study during the crucial years of the early sixteenth century when its
social organisation may be characterised in some detail, and the
distortion of this framework under severe pressure may be partially
measured.

An   investigation   into   such   matters   involves   necessary
methodological assumptions of which the reader should be aware.
In looking at a society under strain, it is clearly necessary to distinguish between what was 'normal' and what was 'abnormal'. This
may be especially difficult when, as in this case, a good deal of the
evidence (though far from all) derives from a period of intense
short-term   crisis,   and   the   subsequent   years   of   accelerating

---

[1] Peter Clark and Paul Slack, 'Introduction', in Peter Clark and Paul Slack (eds.),
Crisis and Order in English Towns 1500–1700: Essays in Urban History (London,
1972), pp. 4–6 – a classification which is further developed by the same authors in
their *English Towns in Transition 1500–1700* (Oxford, 1976), chaps. 1–5.

[2] Sylvia L. Thrupp, *The Merchant Class of Medieval London 1300–1500*
(Michigan, 1962).

economic decline. Problematic as this may be, however, it is here that the historian may claim one advantage over his anthropological colleagues. A longer time-scale under investigation does permit a more confident assessment of what was 'typical'. Indeed, since strain at this period is most usually first displayed by either the shortage or the failure of individuals to fill various social positions, rather than by changes in the pattern of positions itself, it does seem quite possible to distinguish between normality and otherwise at Coventry before institutional change results.

Rightly or wrongly, therefore, this analysis is based on two premises. First, that to understand social structure (as a framework of social positions and relationships, *infra* p. 72), it is necessary to view it as a process over a period of roughly one generation. Instead of taking a single moment in time (as subsidy returns or early listings of inhabitants force us to do), it is essential to reconstruct the average life-cycle: the normal processual passage of individuals through a changing pattern of social roles. Here, the 'generation' concerned has been arbitrarily taken to comprise that which was born, flourished, or died in the period 1500 to 1530, and especially during the first two decades of that period. For certain purposes, when precisely contemporaneous evidence is lacking, however, I have had to look either forwards or further back. Where this is so, the fact is drawn to the reader's attention.

A second premise concerns the necessity for a multi-dimensional approach to social structure. It is surely impossible to characterise a medieval society simply by evaluating its activities in separate economic, political, religious and similar categories. As far as possible we need to seek for the manner in which these factors and many others inter-connected and over-lapped: that is, to look at the formal and informal contexts in which medieval citizens inter-related. If this involves in some cases a statement of what seems obvious in one sphere, it is only then that a valid picture of the balance between *different* spheres of activity may be assessed. Clearly, however, it will be impossible wholly to fulfil this ideal. Although Coventry is peculiarly well documented for this period, there are, nonetheless, considerable areas of social life where the information is either scanty or non-existent – most seriously for the incidence of various forms of social deviance.

Given these assumptions then, this study will focus on Coventry society as an example of what may have been happening in different ways and in different degrees to similar provincial cities or other major towns at the end of the middle ages. An introductory survey of English towns, and some comments on their varying fortunes at the beginning of the sixteenth century will therefore trace the general urban context in which the fate of Coventry should be judged. In part II, a discussion of the long-term decline of Coventry, culminating in a critical period of short-term crisis between 1518 and 1525, then provides the dynamic circumstances in which an understanding of the city's social structure has to be placed. The analysis which follows in part III, thus involves a change of tempo from macro-time to micro-time: it concentrates on the more permanent institutional and processual features of the social structure largely before the period of crisis. In so doing, it also seeks to appraise the ideal of late medieval urban community before the framework was distorted. Part IV (and the essential appendices that complement it) is inescapably more detailed. In it are measured the incidence of depopulation which the city was experiencing in the early 1520s; the degree to which the population structure was consequently affected – as represented in the only census of a medieval city yet known in this country; and, finally, the increasing strains which subsequently deformed the social system. The book ends with an attempt to evaluate the nature of Coventry's experiences in the wider context of what the author would take to have been a period of general urban crisis for large numbers of important English towns during a much ignored period in the history of English communities.

This survey will then have served some purpose even if it goads others into disagreement about the approach slopes to one of the major watersheds in the cultural, social and economic history of the nation. The wider generalisations that might be made from this analysis, however, are in large part dependent on its validity as a community study.

Part I

An urban panorama

' . . . And where you say we have never a good towne in England, onely
London, I pray you what is Barwike, Carlile, Duresme, Yorke, Newcastell,
Hull, Northampton, Norwyche, Ippeswyche, Colchestre, Coventre, Lych-
feld, Exetoure, Brystowe, Salisbury, Southampton, Worsetour, Shrowes-
bury, Cantorbury, Chychestre, with thousandes more of cyties and townes
in Englande, Wales, and Irlande, whiche, yf they were in Fraunce, shulde be
called good townes?'

> (From *The Debate between the Heralds of England and France by
> John Coke*, 1549, *Tudor Economic Documents*, ed. R. H. Tawney
> and Eileen Power, 3 vols. (London, 1924), iii, p. 7.)

The urban landscape of England in the twilight of the middle ages has been but fitfully lit by modern historians. Those surveys that have been made, understandably tend to concentrate for the most part on the 'wealth' of the leading forty towns or so in the 1520s. In doing so, however, the numbers, functions and sizes of those other places with claims to an urban status are apt to be ignored. Even a survey as brief as this must therefore seek to place the leading cities of England in their wider urban context.

The point at which quasi-urban settlements faded into the rural spectrum is clear enough. The vast majority of simple market centres were too small – perhaps one of only two points in the urban hierarchy where size was critical in defining urban qualities. A 'simple' market town like Lutterworth in southern Leicestershire for example, which has been studied in depth by Dr J. D. Goodacre, boasted no more than 116 dwellings in 1509 and only the rudiments of urban economic activity. Apart from its modest weekly market and its Drapery – used largely by itinerant cloth merchants – the place was not much different in character from a swollen open-field village.[1] Such a town, to judge from its number of taxpayers in the 1523 subsidy, was probably representative of perhaps three quarters of those centres that had marketing rights.

Above this level there were possibly two or three hundred small towns with economic functions that set them apart from either rural market centres or industrialised villages. The distinction has been well drawn by Dr John Patten in his study of a heavily industrialised hundred of Suffolk. There, the leading market town of Sudbury (pop. *c*. 1,200) boasted over twice the numbers of different trade types, as the simple market town of nearby Nayland (pop. *c*. 520). Rather less than a third of the occupied population of the former was employed in textiles; rather more than two thirds in the latter.[2]

[1] J. D. Goodacre, 'Lutterworth in the Sixteenth and Seventeenth Centuries: a Market Town and its Area' (University of Leicester Ph.D. thesis, 1977).

[2] J. H. C. Patten, 'Village and Town: an Occupational Study', *Ag.H.R.*, xx (1972), p. 9; W. G. Hoskins, *The Age of Plunder: the England of Henry VIII 1500–1547* (London, 1976), pp. 94–5. For the earlier functions of such places *v*. R. H. Hilton, 'The Small Town as Part of Peasant Society', in his *The English Peasantry in the Later Middle Ages* (Oxford, 1975), lecture V.

The distinction then depended not only on size and the more vigorous market at Sudbury, but also on its more broadly based occupational structure.

These were the towns which caught the attention of Leland in nearly every shire for the 'quickness' of their markets or the nature of their industries. A number of them, moreover, developed 'urban' institutions like the ruling gilds of Birmingham or Stratford, or the Craft fellowships to be found at Loughborough.[3] Above all, they were markedly larger than the simple market towns like Lutterworth or Nayland. Some of them, indeed, had achieved a prosperity or size that now rivalled towns of a once greater importance in earlier times. It was at this level in particular that those centres that were declining on the scale like Boston, Bridgwater, Stamford and Bridgnorth, met those that were newly vigorous, as table 1 demonstrates. Even with some allowance made for inefficiency in the calculation of these estimates drawn from a number of different dioceses, it seems clear that while towns at this level might

Table 1. *Numbers of families in 25 small towns in 1563*[4]

Boston	471	Walsall	290
(Wirksworth	470)	Kidderminster	260
(Manchester	414)	Loughborough	256
Ellesmere	374	Grantham	252
(Darlington	355)	Glastonbury	246
(Chesterfield	351)	Hitchin	245
Richmond	340	(Preston	243)
(Knaresborough	340)	(Uttoxeter	240)
Bridgwater	333	Bridgnorth	228
(Wolverhampton	323)	Pershore	216
Stratford-upon-Avon	320	Stamford	213 +?
Evesham	311	Birmingham	200 +?
Wisbech	292		

Note: The *more* obvious cases of towns in the midst of large encircling parishes have been placed in brackets.

[3] I am obliged to Dr J. D. Goodacre for this information about the Loughborough Crafts. Stratford had 'more than a dozen', *Minutes and Accounts of the Corporation of Stratford-upon-Avon and Other Records 1553–1620*, ed. Edgar I. Fripp (Dugdale Society, i, 1921–3), p. xlii.
[4] B.L. Harl. MSS. 594, 595, 618.

contain between two and four hundred families, the majority boasted fewer than three hundred. A number of these towns have their population sizes inflated to an unknown extent by the inclusion of people who lived in the parochial countrysides surrounding them, and who were often concerned with rural industries. The urban element in these populations, particularly in the north, may thus have been markedly smaller than that shown. The lower range of sizes however is not likely to be much altered thereby except towards the bottom of the list. Had the relevant information survived nationwide, even the most celebrated towns of this type, Lavenham and Totnes, would have been limited to some place in the higher reaches of this table. The former had 199 taxpayers in the 1523 subsidy, the latter 220.[5]

It is a truism to remark upon the tiny sizes of such places (few can have contained more than 1,500 souls – the equivalent of a large comprehensive school today) but it does remind us that it was the number and the distribution of such towns rather than their physical size that was significant. It also serves to underline that there were other towns too at about this level that had functions over and above those described. County towns that never appear in rankings by wealth include Dorchester, Taunton, Hertford, Chelmsford, Bodmin (or Launceston) and Lancaster (or Preston), none of which is likely to have much exceeded a population total of 2,000 and most of which would have been very much smaller. Similar county towns for which the 1563 estimates survive, also emphasise their unimpressive sizes. As in the upper reaches of the list in table 1, only

Table 2. *Numbers of families in eight small county towns in 1563*

Derby	507	Stafford	298+
Carlisle	450	Appleby	237 (including chapelries)
Warwick	410	Bedford	191
Buckingham	351	Huntingdon	119?+

[5] J. D. Sheail, 'The Distribution of Taxable Population and Wealth in England as Indicated in the Lay Subsidy Returns of 1524/5' (University of London Ph.D. thesis, 1968) gazetteer – and for all references to the subsidy, *infra*. I am particularly indebted to Dr Sheail for kindly permitting me to quote so extensively from his work.

Derby in this group may have just exceeded 2,000 people.[6] Bedford and Huntingdon (where the evidence may be incomplete), from both of which had emanated loud complaints of decline in earlier times, may have contained fewer than 1,000.[7] The margin between the population of a prosperous market town and that of the modest country town was thus very slight, though there can be no mistaking the shift into a different urban category.

Included in this table, but invariably excluded from rankings by wealth, is the cathedral city of Carlisle. This town, of trivial pretension when set against such places as Norwich, was nonetheless the dominant centre of a topographically secluded area. It therefore prompts a couple of points about urban functions and geography in late medieval England.

First, while it is the presence of a relatively large permanent population that is most often singled out as an unambiguous mark of developed urbanism at this period; was such permanence in fact a true measure of urban status? Even leaving aside the continuing demands of agriculture at this level, it seems likely that the urban quality of both senior market towns and the modest county towns was more a function of periodicity: as in much earlier centuries, these towns were *foci* in time.[8] It was the extent of the rural crowds at weekly markets and seasonal fairs that transformed such places into recognisable urban centres, rather than the meagre totals of their resident populations. Similarly at, and even above these levels, the staging of ceremonies (Stratford, for example, had its St George's Day procession);[9] the attraction of shrines to pilgrims (as at Glastonbury); or the demands of justice – whether the Assizes, Quarter Sessions or the ecclesiastical courts: all served to underline this transient quality of contemporary urbanism. Some frontier towns, like Carlisle, may have acted as temporary refuges for the

[6] Simply for the sake of argument, I am assuming a mean household size of four persons throughout this discussion (*infra*, pp. 244–5). Even if this multiplier is too low when discussing 1563, the results may not be too far out for the 1520s.

[7] J. Godber, *History of Bedfordshire* (Luton, 1969), p. 117; *Cal. Pat. Rolls, 1446–52*, p. 36; *Cal. Pat. Rolls, 1494–1500*, p. 369. *Cal. Charter Rolls, 1341–1417*, p. 179; *Cal. Pat. Rolls, 1441–6*, p. 79; cf. *Rotuli Parliamentorum: ut et Petitiones, Placita in Parliamento*, ed. J. Strachey, 6 vols. (London, 1767–77), ii, p. 371.

[8] Charles Phythian-Adams, 'Jolly Cities: Goodly Towns. The Current Search for England's Urban Roots', *Urban History Yearbook 1977*, pp. 36–9.

[9] *Minutes and Accounts of the Corporation of Stratford-upon-Avon*, ed. Fripp, pp. xix–xx.

leading families and the heads of religious houses in the locality.[10] In two other cases further up the hierarchy, the incidence of university terms was simply an extended version of the same characteristic.

This easily forgotten first consideration suggests a second. In assessing what was urban at this period, it is tempting to take an arbitrary cut-off point in terms of size – perhaps at the level of three or four thousand, and then to infer that only the very largest acted as provincial capitals. That the nine greatest provincial cities exerted a far-flung economic influence is not to be doubted, and it is equally true that a majority of them were also the centres of either dioceses or counties or both. Conversely, however, far from every region was blessed with a major city; while three such centres – Colchester, Bristol and Coventry, were not even shire towns. It is evident in fact, that unless we are to define a provincial 'centre' in purely economic terms, the vast majority of such places were not large cities at all. Over half the county towns of England had populations of less than 4,000, and most of these probably contained fewer than 2,000. They acted, nonetheless, as the unrivalled administrative and sometimes ecclesiastical *foci* of their regional, or often more correctly, *sub*-regional hinterlands.

In looking at the upper reaches of the urban hierarchy, therefore, a national view, useful as it may be, is of limited value. It helps us to guess where impermanent factors yielded first place to more constant functions, and it serves to identify the areas in which urban life was most fully developed. Beyond that, it is necessary to turn to the regional dimension.

In identifying the largest towns of provincial England, contact is unfortunately partially lost with the main source of evidence so far invoked – the 1563 returns of families. Instead, reliance has to be placed on the greatest numbers of taxpayers found in any one instalment of the 1523 subsidy. Luckily, although the direction of overall population movement in such towns between 1523 and 1563 is not yet established (though it was more probably, downward than upward),[11] some comparison between the two sources at critical points is possible (table 3). It is nevertheless essential to view

[10] B. C. Jones, 'The Topography of Medieval Carlisle', *Transactions of the Cumberland and Westmorland Antiquarian and Archaeological Society*, new ser., lxxvi (1976), p. 79.

[11] Charles Phythian-Adams, 'Urban Decay in Late Medieval England', in Philip Abrams and E. A. Wrigley (eds.), *Towns in Societies: Essays in Economic History and Historical Sociology* (Cambridge, 1978), pp. 170–3.

Table 3. *The largest towns in late medieval England*[12]

		Approx. size	Nos. of taxpayers in 1520s	1563 families
(A)		*Over 10,000*		
	1.	Norwich	1,423	—
		Over 6,000		
	2.	Bristol	1,101	—
	3.	York	871	—
	4.	Salisbury	570+?250=820?	—
	5.	Exeter	807+?	—
	6.	Colchester	785	—
?7.		Canterbury	784	—
	8.	Newcastle	—	1,545
	9.	Coventry	713	1,500–1,600 (1523)
(B)		*c. 4–5,000*		
	10.	Bury St Edmunds	645	—
?11.		St Albans	463+? 177=?640 max.	—
?12.		Lincoln	625	459+100
	13.	Hereford	611	—
	14.	Oxford	542 (incl. university)	—
	15.	Reading	523	—
	16.	Cambridge	523	—
	17.	Worcester	499	1,025
?18.		King's Lynn	—	—
	19.	Great Yarmouth	497	—
?20.		Ipswich	412+?	—
		c. 3–4,000		
	21.	Northampton	477	—
?22.		Gloucester	*c.* 466	952
	23.	Chester	—	927
	24.	Crediton	433	—
	25.	Newbury	414	—
?26.		Shrewsbury	—	815
?27.		Durham	—	752
(C)		*Over 2,000*		
	28.	Leicester	401	591
	29.	Lichfield	391	'400'
	30.	Ely	382	400 (max.)
	31.	Southampton	'365'	—
	32.	Chipping Walden	362+	—
	33.	Winchester	330	—
	34.	Hadleigh	311	—
	35.	Plymouth	310	—
	36.	Beccles	307	—
	37.	Chichester	301	—
	38.	Nottingham	295	—
	39.	Tiverton	289	—
	40.	Wymondham	287	—
	41.	Bodmin	285	—
	42.	Hull	279	—

Note: In the cases of some large towns, the figures may be misleadingly inflated by the inclusion of rural populations living in the urban counties concerned.

the results in very broad terms: in particular, the varying penetration of the subsidy returns into the wage-earning class in each town has not yet been the subject of comparative study. Until that is done, these results represent only a very rough guide. It would certainly be premature to place any credence on the precise order in which they are listed. Allotting approximate population sizes on the basis of this evidence is similarly risky, and particularly towards the bottom of the list. The largest town hitherto discussed, for example, has been Derby with only 232 taxpayers but 507 families – figures that are hard to square with their equivalents at Leicester. Other places, and hence their order on the table, may be equally distorted by either the penetration of the subsidy, or by the incidence of depopulation between the two dates in some cases, or by population growth in others. All this table seeks to do, therefore, is to provide a rough comparative perspective.

If figures in the 1563 column provide the surer yardstick of population totals, and also furnish a link with the previous discussion, then the hierarchy of urban sizes becomes broadly apparent. Above the level of the prosperous market centre with perhaps 300 households, was a band of towns containing up to 600. It contained not only newly important centres like Tiverton and Hadleigh (the totals for which may be inflated by their parochial hinterlands), but also modest county towns like Derby, Nottingham and Leicester, and declining towns like Winchester, Southampton,

---

¹² Sheail *op. cit., passim*; B. L. Harl. MSS., 594, 595, 618. For Gloucester in 1562 *v.* M. D. Lobel and J. Tann, 'Gloucester', in *Historic Towns, i,* ed. M. D. Lobel and W. H. Johns (London and Oxford, 1969), p. 12 – a figure which may be partly inflated by the inclusion of the city's immediate hinterland. Like all first attempts at ranking, this table will be subject to considerable revision in the light of local research. The undoubtedly exaggerated placing of Canterbury here, for example, does not agree with Mr Peter Clark's estimate of 3,000 people (based on 766 tax-payers), even though his figure looks a little low, Peter Clark, *English Provincial Society from the Reformation to the Revolution: Religion, Politics and Society in Kent 1500–1640* (Hassocks, 1977), p. 8. I have deliberately excluded the 1563 total for Canterbury (B.L. Harl. MS., 594, fos. 64–65v.) since, as is the case elsewhere in Kent, all the figures given for individual parishes are rendered in suspiciously rounded terms which look as though they have been deliberately forced to add up to a hypothetical '700' families. For Shrewsbury, Mr W. Champion kindly informs me, a locally preserved return of 1525 indicates 522 tax-payers (excluding the Abbey Foregate) which is best compared with an adjusted figure of 742 in 1563 when certain rural areas are also included. Given the inclusion of Lichfield and Ely at the lower end of the table, finally, it is clear that allowances ought also to be made in 1563 for some towns with no recorded evidence from the 1520s, e.g. Boston and Carlisle (*supra,* tables 1 and 2).

Bridgwater and Hull. Both the economies and the sizes of these places were limited. Some, like the midland group of county towns were sited relatively close to each other, none of them appearing pre-eminent. Others lay in the shadow of a larger centre still as in their different ways did Lichfield, Hull and even Southampton.

The distinction may be a fine one, but in terms of both functions and sizes, a significant contrast is provided above this level. Both Crediton (again probably an exaggerated total) and perhaps Newbury are ambiguous cases, but for the rest, from Durham upwards to Bury St Edmunds, these are substantial towns, by the standards of the day. All were either of marked regional importance or possessed sophisticated urban economies – usually both. There are large areas of uncertainty with regard to the exact ranking of some East Anglian towns in particular, but wherever they may be precisely placed they clearly warrant inclusion in this broad and identifiable category. Compared with the prosperous market towns, this group as a whole comprised conspicuously urban concentrations of population ranging from a probably inflated total of about 750 families in the case of Durham, itself a major ecclesiastical centre for an under-populated region, through to perhaps 1,250 families. The artificiality of any mid-way cut-off point in this sequence on the table, is thus very apparent.

The significant break in the sequence, in fact, comes further up. Bury has been placed rather higher on the list than some would allow: Dr Patten credits it with a population of only 3,550, and situates it lower down his list than both King's Lynn and Great Yarmouth.[13] Whatever the truth of the matter, few are likely to claim that its population, or even that of Lincoln (which seems to be under-estimated by Sir Francis Hill for this period)[14] were in excess of 5,000 persons. It is thus peculiarly fortunate that the contemporary census of Coventry in 1523, which is to be discussed in detail later in this book, is available to confirm the lower population limits

[13] J. H. C. Patten, 'Population Distribution in Norfolk and Suffolk during the Sixteenth and Seventeenth Centuries', *The Institute of British Geographers*, lxv (1975), p. 49.
[14] Francis Hill, *Tudor and Stuart Lincoln* (Cambridge, 1956), p. 88. Were the numbers of Lincoln's subsidy-*payers* inflated by some of its county-population or by the inclusion of an excessive proportion of wage-earners? Since it is impossible to accept that this city, of all places (*v*. n. 15, *infra*), was ruthlessly taxed throughout, it could well be that Lincoln experienced depopulation over this period on a scale comparable with, or even in excess of, that at Coventry, *infra*, p. 284.

of the leading urban category on the table. On this basis it seems certain that the top nine provincial cities were in a class by themselves, even the smallest of them having about a thousand inhabitants more than their nearest rivals further down the list. Of these nine, three were major ports, three were further up navigable waters, and three were situated inland. Five of the total were both county towns and diocesan sees. Only two, Bristol and Norwich, are likely to have contained 9,000 inhabitants or more. Together they comprised nodal economic centres for every area of the kingdom except the north-west, and the east midlands. In the latter case the same function was decreasingly fulfilled by the rapidly declining city of Lincoln, the fifth largest provincial city in 1377.[15]

Yet although these nine centres were undoubtedly provincial capitals in the economic sense and regional capitals in a social sense, and even though they were geographically dispersed, the admittedly ambiguous case of Lincoln in this context serves to correct inferences that may be drawn from elementary rankings of either populations or wealth. None of these cities (apart perhaps from York)[16] can have exerted much social influence – as opposed to casual contact – beyond their own wide regional hinterlands. Given the realities of the local topography and communications, that role was performed in many areas by towns that did not belong to the top levels of the hierarchy. To the north-west, certainly Carlisle and Chester; to the west, possibly Shrewsbury, and probably Hereford, Worcester and Gloucester; to the south-west, Plymouth or Bodmin; in the southern midlands, perhaps Oxford and St Albans; to the south, Chichester; in East Anglia itself, Bury for Suffolk and Lynn for the fens: all these, and doubtless others (Northampton, for example) probably acted as undisputed regional capitals. Their status in fact was determined less by their sizes or even wealth, but more by their unrivalled positions as historically significant administrative or ecclesiastical centres and above all their geographical situations in relation to the communications system, to smaller urban competitors, and to local densities of rural population.

---

[15] *Ibid.*, pp. 19–23; cf. Francis Hill, *Medieval Lincoln* (Cambridge, 1965), pp. 253–6, 270–3, 278–81, 285–8; W. G. Hoskins, *Local History in England* (London, 1959), p. 176.

[16] D. M. Palliser, 'York under the Tudors: the Trading Life of the Northern Capital', in Alan Everitt (ed.), *Perspectives in English Urban History* (London and Basingstoke, 1973), pp. 39–59. This admirable discussion of what is, methodologically, an extremely difficult subject has not received the attention that it deserves.

Within regions the economic balance as between types of town might gradually alter, though their social functions may have been more enduring. Between regions, when these are defined from an urban viewpoint, the pace of economic change was pitiless. The English towns that emerged most successfully from the demographic and economic upheavals of the later middle ages reflected a profound change of emphasis in the geographical balance of the contemporary urban system.

The year 1377 provides an arbitrary point of comparison with the situation in the earlier sixteenth century, and as in the case of all such fixed points itself represents no more than a transitional moment in a period of change.[17] Such a comparison nonetheless epitomises the shift which may be substantiated from other evidence, provided it is made with due regard to the imprecision of the ranking in table 3.

On this basis there can be no doubting the absolute decline of a series of towns sited on, or looking towards, the eastern sea-board.[18] Of the leading 31 towns in 1377 – Boston (9th), Beverley (10th), Hull (24th), Scarborough (30th) and Stamford (31st) – only Hull and possibly Boston were still just represented in the top 42 in the early sixteenth century. Further inland, York had been toppled from undisputed first to third place, and Lincoln from fifth to roughly twelfth; while Leicester (16th), Nottingham (28th), Newark (32nd) and Derby (37th), all decisively fell in rank during these 150 years. That the economic diminution of some dozen major towns (Pontefract, 35th in 1377, should probably also be included although the early sixteenth century information is inadequate for the comparison), was as much to do with the fundamental transition from wool to cloth exports, as with demographic factors, is hardly to be doubted. The effects were nevertheless demographically disastrous. Rounded *minimal* estimates for the worst casualties, based on the poll-tax-payers (multiplied by two to allow for both under-fourteens and evasions), suggest that Boston and Stamford boasted some 5,750 and 2,500 inhabitants respectively in

[17] Hoskins, *op.cit.*, p. 176. While there are clearly dangers in a comparison between tax records of a different kind, and hence exaggerations in the changes of ranking positions have to be guarded against, those cases where promotion or demotion were most marked, do seem to be broadly borne out by other evidence. Cf. Phythian-Adams, 'Urban Decay', *loc.cit.*, *passim*.

[18] *Ibid.*, p. 168.

1377. By 1563, however, it is difficult to inflate either population to more than 2,000 for the former or 1,000 for the latter (*supra*, table 1). Even King's Lynn, which marked the southern-most point in this string of midland and eastern towns, was undoubtedly demoted from its seventh place in the leading nine of the late fourteenth century, though its position in table 3 might well be too low. Its population in 1377 may have been in the region of 6,500, but if Dr Patten's estimate is correct, this total had fallen to 4,500 by 1524/5.[19] The relative, and in some cases absolute, demise of a major sector of the late medieval urban system is thus incontrovertible.

A smaller and more self-contained area of the west midlands was similarly affected. Gone were the days when Shrewsbury (ranked 17th in 1377) boasted a population in excess of 4,000, with nearby Ludlow thirty-third in importance, and Bridgnorth perhaps not much inferior. Further south, even Gloucester (15th in 1377), with a population a third as big again as Northampton in the late fourteenth century, had shrunk to a point where it may even have been smaller than the latter. Its fifteenth-century complaints of 300 houses in decay have to be taken seriously.[20] By the early sixteenth century, even Bristol was in the doldrums.

Other areas which had been adversely affected over longer periods also stand out. In Somerset, both the pleas of desperation from the localities concerned, and the contemporary observations of Leland, bear witness to the economic and demographic demise of Ilchester and Bridgwater. Along the south coast, the Cinque Ports had long been relegated to obscurity, while by the early sixteenth century the medieval flowering of Southampton was over.

Inland there can be no doubting the growing vulnerability of Canterbury while the longer-term decline of Oxford's staple industry is hardly a matter of question. In addition to the county towns already mentioned, the stagnation of Warwick was of more than a century's standing; Bedford and Huntingdon had been reduced to the level of market towns (*supra* table 2). Even Cambridge had shown signs of strain. For neither university town was the erection of growing centres of learning on the rubble of former streets an

---

[19] Patten, 'Population Distribution in Norfolk and Suffolk', *loc.cit.*, p. 49.
[20] *Cal. Pat. Rolls, 1446–52*, pp. 70–1; *Calendar of the Records of the Corporation of Gloucester*, ed. W. H. Stevenson (Gloucester, 1893), no. 59; Lobel and Tann, 'Gloucester', *loc.cit.*, pp. 10–11.

unmitigated blessing, let alone an immediate compensation for the loss of wealth-creating citizens.

By contrast to this panorama of widely experienced urban decay, the points of growth were urban centred only in an ambiguous sense. The prime example is East Anglia with Essex, an area which already contained three of the most populous nine towns in 1377 – Norwich, King's Lynn and Colchester. The difference between then and the early sixteenth century was thus mainly a matter of emphasis, and was due in large part to the disappearance of so many eastern sea-board oriented towns from the upper levels of the hierarchy. No new *major* urban centres make their appearance in the list. The most successful developments like Hadleigh aspire no higher than the level of a modest county town; while the Lavenhams and Long Melfords simply epitomise the more successful type of prosperous market town. If Norwich, Colchester and perhaps Ipswich sustained or even improved their *relative* ranking positions, it needs to be remembered that Lynn was in difficulties by the Tudor period, and that Great Yarmouth had been experiencing ever more pressing problems of silting, as well as the decimation of its fishing fleet since the fourteenth century.[21] By the early sixteenth, even Norwich was under pressure.

If East Anglia and Essex were unquestionably the most heavily urbanised areas at this period, the same pattern of, at most, urban stability set against the varying relative strengths of the prosperous, but modestly sized, market towns is most marked elsewhere.[22] To the north, Leeds, Halifax and Wakefield were the unpretentious urban rivals to a vulnerable York; in the north-west, Chester looked to places like Manchester or even Kendal; to the west, Worcester still towered above the industrialised market centres of Evesham, Droitwich, Kidderminster and Bromsgrove; to the south-west, Exeter, the only unambiguous example of urban success since 1377 (when it ranked 23rd), dominated Crediton, Tiverton and Totnes; in the south-east, Canterbury's economic influence may have been to some extent eroded by Maidstone, Faversham and Cranbrook;[23]

---

[21] Since East Anglia is apt to receive over-much attention in the context of urban prosperity at this time, it is worth emphasising the unambiguous decay of Great Yarmouth, Phythian-Adams, 'Urban Decay', *loc.cit.*, p. 165, n. 33.

[22] *Supra*, n. 21.

[23] Faversham boasted 525 tax-payers in the subsidy, while Maidstone was *taxed* at over four times as much as the former. All three towns, however, were credited with suspiciously rounded totals of 300 families in 1563, B.L. Harl. MS. 594, fos. 70v., 71,

even *parvenu* Reading looked westwards *via* Newbury towards such market centres as Hungerford and Marlborough. When set against both the decline of the old east midland urban system, and the withering of so many other centres over an extended period, the 'success' stories of Exeter, Newcastle, Reading and perhaps Newbury, together with a late revival of Chester, hardly suggest that what was happening over the last 150 years or so of the middle ages was simply a matter of a shifting balance between the different regional parts of an established *urban* network. On the contrary, the picture is one of marked national imbalance, not only as a result of major geographical changes of emphasis, but also as between significantly different levels in the urban hierarchy. If a small number of important centres with both maritime outlets and industrialised *rural* hinterlands successfully survived the general reduction in demand for urban products which surely characterised the national demographic collapse of the later middle ages, such towns were under no threat from emergent urban rivals. The places that both sustained and conceivably enhanced their positions were those more prosperous market or industrialised centres, whose urban functions depended heavily on periodicity; and whose populations represented anything from less than a half to no more than a fifth of those in the major towns. Even taken collectively, these market centres – with their heavy dependence on adjacent *rural* industries (especially in *pastoral* areas) – can hardly be taken as compensation for the decline of so many towns of a truly *urban* significance. When taken singly, probably only Birmingham was to shift markedly into a superior urban category over the following century. At a time when nearly all towns were anyway suffering greater or lesser reductions of population, this widely experienced imbalance represented decentralisation with a vengeance.

The nodal point of the provincial urban network in the later middle ages was Coventry. Through it, from the north-west, came lambskins from Ireland *via* Chester *en route* to London; and back to Chester, Coventry carters carried local goods in return.[24] Dublin

75. Cf. Clark, *op.cit.*, pp. 9, 30. For Cranbrook, *v.* A. Butcher, 'The Decline of Canterbury 1300–1500', unpublished paper submitted to the Urban History Conference, 1971, p. 44.

[24] *L. & P., Addenda*, i (1), no. 385; K. P. Wilson, 'The Port of Chester in the Fifteenth Century', *Transactions of the Historic Society of Lancashire and Cheshire*, cxvii (1965), pp. 5, 14.

merchants belonged to the Trinity Gild in the fifteenth century and to the Corpus Christi Gild in the sixteenth.[25] From Bristol came French wines, spices, even artillery, and possibly dye-stuffs; to it, probably *via* Coventry went alabaster panels from Nottingham.[26] From the ports of the Wash came 'fish and other Baltic wares': while merchants of Boston and Lynn belonged to the two great Coventry gilds.[27] To and from Southampton the carriers also plied bringing with them to the city the woad which made Coventry blues so renowned.[28] With the capital, the city's mercers and grocers had close connections.[29] Through Chester, Southampton, Bristol, King's Lynn, Boston and above all London, there can be little doubt that Coventry exported most of its cloth.[30] Even York purchased Coventry cloth, and even Carlisle citizens joined the city's two fraternities.[31] In the midlands, Coventry was involved in toll disputes not only with Bristol, but also with Gloucester and Nottingham.[32] To the banquets of the Corpus Christi Gild frequently came citizens of Worcester, Shrewsbury and Ludlow; Nottingham, Leicester and Lichfield; as well as from smaller centres still like Birmingham, Evesham, Pershore and Stratford.[33]

In size and importance Coventry towered over its nearest urban neighbours. Ranking nationally as third in population to only York and Bristol in 1377, it was then more than twice the size of either Oxford, Gloucester or Leicester; three times as big as both Northampton and Nottingham; and four times the sizes of Derby and Lichfield. Its diocese, which, with the last named city, it dominated, extended as far as Cheshire, Staffordshire and Derbyshire. Its char-

[25] *The Register of the Guild of the Holy Trinity, St. Mary, St. John Baptist and St. Katherine of Coventry*, ed. Mary Dormer Harris (Dugdale Society, xiii, 1935), pp. xxi–ii; C.R.O. A6, *passim*.

[26] Dormer Harris (ed.), *op.cit.*, p. xxi; E. M. Carus-Wilson, *Medieval Merchant Venturers* (London, 1967), pp. 5, 7–8, 258.

[27] Eleanora Carus-Wilson, 'The Medieval Ports of the Wash', *Medieval Archaeology*, vi-vii (1962–3), p. 198; Dormer Harris (ed.), *op. cit.*, p. xx; C.R.O. A6, *passim*.

[28] Olive Coleman, 'Trade and Prosperity in the Fifteenth Century: Some Aspects of the Trade of Southampton', *Econ. H.R.*, 2nd ser., xvi (1963–4), pp. 13–16.

[29] Dormer Harris (ed.), *op.cit.*, p. xxi; cf. Thrupp, *The Merchant Class*, p. 335 *sub* 'Coventre'; p. 369 *sub* 'Tate'; Carus-Wilson, *loc.cit.*, p. 200, n. 91.

[30] Carus-Wilson, *loc.cit.*, pp. 198–9.

[31] Palliser, 'York under the Tudors', *loc.cit.*, p. 51; Dormer Harris, *op.cit.*, p. xx; C.R.O. A6, fos. 251v.–252.

[32] *L.B.*, pp. 549–52, 592, 594–5, 599–600; Levi Fox, 'The Coventry Gilds and Trading Companies with Special Reference to the Position of Women', *B.A.S.T.*, lxxviii (1962), p. 14, n. 2.

[33] E.g. C.R.O. A6, *passim*.

ter of incorporation (1345) was the first in English municipal history, and since 1451 the city and its immediate hinterland had been a county unto itself.[34] Since 1465–9 it had been, with York, Norwich and Bristol, one of only four provincial mint towns.[35] Even in 1507 it stood third only to London and York when it acted as surety for the proposed marriage of the king's daughter to the Emperor's grandson.[36]

Coventry's pre-eminence in the midlands was epitomised both economically and socially by its ecclesiastical status. For its last episcopal incumbent, the Benedictine priory church was 'my principal see and head church', and close by to it stood the palace of the Bishops of Coventry and Lichfield.[37] From at least 1498, the city had usurped the place of Northampton as the periodic *venue* for provincial chapters of the Black Monks.[38] The minster itself piously preserved in a case of copper and gilt, the head of the martyred virgin, St Osburg who, being widely venerated in the midlands, was thus both the object of regional pilgrimage and the subject of a brisk souvenir trade.[39] Yet even more renowned perhaps, was a shrine to 'our Lady of the Tower' in the city wall, which was visited by travellers *en route* to or from London. Its importance was sufficient to warrant inclusion in a single breath with Doncaster and Walsingham by one obdurate heretic in 1485.[40]

The great Benedictine priory, one of the wealthiest in the midlands, which in palmier days had controlled much of the town, was only one religious house amongst a number that were significant in Coventry's economy.[41] Within the city, there were houses of Carmelites and Franciscans; outside it was a Charterhouse. More important still, there can be no doubting the seventeenth-century view of both Dugdale and the indefatigable town clerk, Humfrey

---

[34] *L.B.*, pp. 748–9.   [35] *V.C.H. Warks.*, viii, pp. 166–7.
[36] *L.B.*, pp. 609–18.   [37] *L. & P.*, xiv (1), no. 57.
[38] *L.B.*, pp. 588–9; *Documents Illustrating the Activities of the General and Provincial Chapters of the English Black Monks 1215–1540, iii* (Camden Society, 3rd. ser., liv, 1937), p. 262. For similar provincial chapters of both Franciscans and Carmelites at Coventry, *V.C.H., Warks.*, ii, pp. 104–5.
[39] *L. & P.*, xiv (1), no. 69; Mary Dormer Harris, *Dr Troughton's Sketches of Coventry* (Coventry and London, n.d.), p. 7.
[40] E.g. H.M.C. *Middleton*, pp. 334, 354, 357; Dormer Harris, *Dr Troughton's Sketches*, p. 6.
[41] R. H. Hilton, *A Medieval Society: the West Midlands at the End of the Thirteenth Century* (London, 1966), p. 27. For the disputed earlier history of Coventry, *infra*, p. 118 n. 1.

Burton (from whose researches the former may have benefited), as to the importance of 'the great helps & meanes in trades & otherwise that Coventrey had in former times before the dissolucions of Monastories', and nine of which the latter specified.[42] Above all they probably acted as important suppliers of wool for the city's textile industry. The Prior's sheep flock on the pastures around the city alone numbered 400 in 1480, while it can hardly be doubted that the wool-crop from the nearby Cistercian houses of Combe, Stoneleigh and Merevale also found its way to Coventry.[43] The heads of all these houses, as well as those of the Augustinian priories of Kenilworth and Maxstoke were often wined and dined by city's Corpus Christi Gild while most, if not all, were simultaneously members of the senior gild of the Holy Trinity. To the banquets of these two wealthy fraternities also came the heads of other religious houses from further afield – from Evesham, Pershore, Winchcombe, Tewksbury and Wenlock to name but some of the monastic connections the city could boast in a network which covered the west midlands.[44] It would be naive to suppose that such visits were fired by purely spiritual or even gastronomic considerations alone. Many were from outside the diocese of Coventry and Lichfield. They underline, nevertheless, the extent of Coventry's influence as a provincial centre.

But if Coventry was still the undisputed urban giant of the midlands in the earlier sixteenth century, reference back to table 3 will show that the gap between it and Oxford, Northampton, Gloucester and even Leicester, had been by then substantially narrowed. Since all these towns, however, had themselves experienced decay over at least the preceding century, the most that may be inferred from this is that in the Tudor period Coventry was simply declining at a greater rate than the others. None of them could rival Coventry in either size or pretensions in the 1520s. It is therefore necessary to probe rather more deeply into the problem of Coventry's position in its regional context at this time in order to gauge its reduced importance in the urban system. The accompanying map (map 2), which is almost wholly based on the sizes of towns recorded in the 1563 returns, illustrates the distribution of urban centres in the midlands above the level of the simple market town. With the partial excep-

[42] For Dugdale's view, *infra*, p. 236; for Burton's, C.R.O. A35 unfol.
[43] *L.B.*, p. 438; Hilton, *op.cit.*, pp. 82–4.
[44] C.R.O. A6, *passim; Register of the Guild*, ed. Dormer Harris, pp. 101–12.

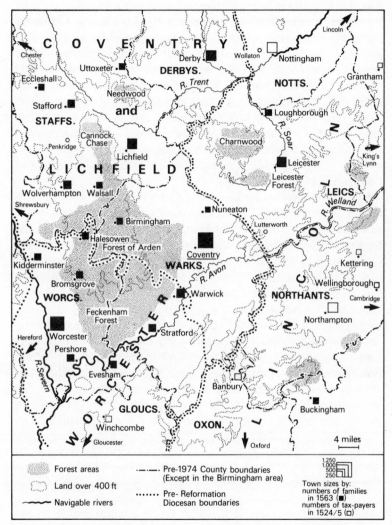

Map 2   The position of Coventry in relation to all Midland towns containing 200 or more families in 1523–63

tion of Coventry itself, the *relative* importance of the towns so plotted will not have been vastly different in 1500 even though their population totals may have changed in the interim.

Geographically, the area defines itself. To the north, Uttoxeter marks the southernmost point of the Pennine barrier between east and west; to the south are the Cotswolds, and to the east their continuation *via* the Northampton uplands into the elevated parts of eastern Leicestershire. Physically, the centre of the area is dominated by the Birmingham plateau and the 'forest' country which largely characterised it and its environs: Arden, Feckenham and further north Cannock Chase. Another area of forest characterised the ancient geological series of the Charnwood area to the north-west of Leicester, while due west of that town was the forest of Leicester itself.

These physical features, soil types and the major river systems largely determined the pattern of rural settlement, only a broad summary of which is necessary here. North-east of Charnwood, the Soar valley with its natural access to the Trent, comprised a densely settled area, as did the Welland valley some distance to the east of Coventry. A great tract of country that was but sparsely populated, however, separated these areas from the city, and stretched from Coventry towards Leicester forest and Charnwood, and thence broadly westward towards Eccleshall. The south-eastern corner of Staffordshire and the north-eastern part of Warwickshire in particular had both been exceptionally subject to the processes of village desertion in the later middle ages, while western Leicestershire, like the moorland and southern upland areas of north Staffordshire had always been lightly populated.[45] The main exception to this highly generalised picture was a concentration of almost 400 families near

[45] For rural areas, *v.* C. T. Smith, 'Population', in *V.C.H., Leics.*, iii, pp. 138–9; D. M. Palliser, *The Staffordshire Landscape* (London, 1976), pp. 83–5 and map; Maurice Beresford, *The Lost Villages of England* (London 1954), p. 231. On map 2 and throughout this discussion, the population figures are derived from B.L. Harl. MSS. 594 (for Derbyshire, Shropshire, Staffordshire and much of Warwickshire), 595 (for Worcestershire, and the rest of Warwickshire), 618 (for Leicestershire, Lincolnshire and Buckinghamshire). For towns in those counties not comprehended in 1563, I have had to depend on the numbers of tax-payers in the subsidy: Northampton and Nottingham (*supra*, table 3); Wellingborough (188 tax-payers); Kettering (142); Winchcombe (129). Banbury only boasted 97 tax-payers, and in so dubiously qualifying for inclusion, thus illustrates the inevitable artificiality of this exercise. For some justification in this case, *v.* P. D. A. Harvey, 'Banbury', in M. D. Lobel and W. H. Johns (eds.), *Historic Towns, i*, (London and Oxford, 1969), pp. 5–7.

the Watling Street in the parishes of Mancetter, Nuneaton and Attleborough.

Only a little more densely settled than this under-populated region, were the 'felden' area of Warwickshire south of the Avon, the central lowland areas of Staffordshire and the south-eastern corner of Worcestershire, with their patterns of nucleated villages and common fields.[46] As is well known, however, with the partial exception of the Avon valley, the balance of population between the 'felden' areas of Warwickshire and the large woodland parishes of Arden had tipped decisively in favour of the latter during the early medieval period.[47] Even at the close of the middle ages, therefore (and in marked contrast to the 'forest' areas of north-west Leicestershire, where woodland remained ringed rather than invaded by settlement), the densest areas of population were to be found some miles west of Coventry, and most noticeably on the Birmingham plateau. Over a substantial swathe of territory that straddled the county boundaries of Warwick, Worcester and Stafford, and in an area broadly delimited by, and including, Walsall and Sutton Coldfield to the north; Wolverhampton and Halesowen to the north-west; Alvechurch and Tanworth to the south-west; Henley-in-Arden and Rowington to the south; and Berkswell to the east; there probably resided at least 3,500 families in 1563.[48] Small as this total may seem in modern terms, and dispersed as the population was, this region nevertheless then contained more people even than Norwich, the largest provincial city in the land; and over twice as many inhabitants as Coventry in 1523. The six parishes that roughly comprised the core of this area (Aston, Birmingham, Yardley, King's Norton and West Bromwich) alone boasted more families (1,059) than the city of Worcester in 1563 (1,025).

When these factors are set against the contemporary pattern of river and road communications, a number of features that deter-

---

[46] A broad impression of the variegated nature of this region may be gleaned from a generalised map of its field-systems in B. K. Roberts, 'Field Systems of the West Midlands', in A. R. H. Baker and R. A. Butlin (eds.), *Studies of Field Systems in the British Isles* (Cambridge, 1973), p. 204.

[47] J. B. Harley, 'Population Trends and Agricultural Developments from the Warwickshire Hundred Rolls of 1279', in Alan R. H. Baker, John D. Hamshere and John Langton (eds.), *Geographical Interpretations of Historical Sources: Readings in Historical Geography* (Newton Abbot, 1970), pp. 60–1.

[48] Outside this area and to the immediate south-west of Coventry, Stoneleigh contained 108 families and Kenilworth 110.

mined Coventry's place in the regional urban system stand out. Although it had originated within it, by this period the city lay on the eastern-most edge of the central woodland area. As such it was very much on the periphery of the most densely populated zone.[49] The most natural physical approach to Coventry was from the south-west, *via* the Avon valley, although the river was not navigable beyond Stratford.[50] In this context it belonged geographically to a string of towns which stretched along this line and beyond it – *via* Evesham, Stratford, and Warwick and culminating perhaps at Nuneaton (though this centre with only 188 households in 1563 barely qualifies for inclusion on the map). Further to the south-west urban spheres of influence probably overlapped. Evesham, Pershore, Bromsgrove, Kidderminster and perhaps Halesowen looked to Worcester in terms of mutual economic self-interest with regard to both their textile industries and, in the last three cases, their outlets *via* the navigable Severn.[51] To the south-east, Coventry's records betray little contact with Northampton which, it must be assumed, consequently exerted its own independent sphere of influence. To the north-east, the facts of geography and population distribution ensured that while Leicester roughly marked the edge of Coventry's economic influence, that town as well as Loughborough, Derby and Nottingham were oriented towards the navigable Trent, as must have been Uttoxeter too. Only to the north, east and south, therefore did Coventry look towards regions that were both barely urbanised (except for a scattering of simple market towns) and correspondingly under-populated when compared with the forest area and its distinctive pattern of prosperous market centres.

An inland provincial city of Coventry's importance fulfilled three

[49] To judge from the place-name Weston-in-Arden, some miles to the north-east of Coventry, and the numerous local place-names suffixes in -*leah*, Coventry emerged as a woodland town in the first instance.

[50] There was also, of course, an important road-route indicated on the Gough Map that may be roughly correlated with the Anonymous map of Warwickshire (P. D. A. Harvey and Harry Thorpe, *The Printed Maps of Warwickshire 1579–1800* (Warwick, 1959), plate 2), and which cuts through the forest of Arden.

[51] Evesham, Droitwich, Kidderminster and Bromsgrove all combined with Worcester to secure the passage of the 1533 act (*Statutes of the Realm*, 25 Henry VIII, cap. 18). The sphere of Worcester's market-influence is excellently mapped by Alan D. Dyer, *The City of Worcester in the Sixteenth Century* (Leicester, 1973), p. 69, though the author argues that the towns of Worcestershire strictly limited that city's economic range (*ibid.*, p. 68). The unanswerable question in our present state of knowledge is: which cities supplied the distributive traders in these lesser centres?

major economic functions. As a manufacturing centre exporting textiles as far afield as Iceland, the Baltic and Portugal, its significance has already been broadly indicated. As a major distributional centre for products reaching the midlands from the ports through which it traded, it was also of outstanding importance. Short of a massive investigation into the earliest probate inventories throughout the entire region (a task which it has been impossible to undertake), however, it is only possible to guess that Coventry's distributive traders must have been largely responsible for supplying similar dealers in the smaller urban centres of the central midlands. Overlapping with this second function was a third which involved customers visiting the city from both the countryside and other towns – a matter for which some local evidence is forthcoming.

Recognisances of debt for visitors from places outside Coventry are recorded in the statute merchant rolls that survive for the earlier sixteenth century, though unfortunately none is earlier than the period of short-term crisis.[52] Nevertheless, from the 180 references to such places (and involving both debtors and creditors), a suggestive pattern does emerge, and this is baldly summarised in table 4. Only a broad comparison is indicated here. But even taking the 'forest' area in a much wider sense than that described above (i.e. thus including the ring of less densely populated parishes that

Table 4. *Numbers of references to various places in different statute merchant transactions at Coventry*

Warwickshire forest area	40 max. (including Kenilworth)	N.E. Warks and Felden	61 (including Warwick)
Staffordshire	8	Leicestershire	21
Cheshire	1	Northamptonshire	9
Salop	8	Oxfordshire	2
Worcestershire	5	Gloucestershire	2
	—		—
	62		95

Other mentions: London (12); Lincolnshire (2); Herefordshire, Buckinghamshire, Somersetshire, Derbyshire, Nottinghamshire, Rutland, Lancashire, Durham, Northumberland (one each).

[52] C.R.O. E6: membranes for 12, 13, 14, 25, 26, 27, 34, 37, 38 Henry VIII; '1551'; 6 Edward VI; 1 Mary; Philip and Mary 1 & 2, 2 & 3, 3 & 4, 4 & 5; 1, 2, 3, 4, 5 Elizabeth.

circumscribed the east and south of the already generously defined
Birmingham plateau), and then arbitrarily adding to it places
further to the west and north-west, it is evident that Coventry was
not mediating equally between two separate geographical zones.
Overwhelmingly its customers were drawn from the other parts of
Warwickshire, from Leicestershire and from the more or less contiguous parts of Northamptonshire – from those areas in fact which
did not contain urban centres of a more developed type than the
simple market town. Indeed, when the 'forest' area in question is
restricted as originally (above) to the parishes of the densely populated Birmingham plateau alone, visitors from only 14 places are
recorded. Difficult as it is to interpret the precise nature of statute
merchant transactions by this date, there do remain some grounds
for believing that the urban facilities provided by Coventry were
equally well met for the rural populations concerned by the major
market centres of the plateau area – Birmingham, Wolverhampton,
Walsall and perhaps Halesowen. All of these could look more
conveniently to the easier communications with the Severn, Worcester and supplies from Bristol. All were situated on the very edge
of, or even beyond, Worcester's immediate sphere of influence. All
could operate effectively on a periodic basis.

The vast majority of those concerned in these recognisances of
debt were described as *armiger, generosus*, yeoman or, less frequently, husbandman. Urban connections, however, were not lacking. Merchants, mercers or grocers were mentioned from London,
Leicester, Banbury and Birmingham as well as from the simple
market centres of Atherstone and Market Harborough. Shrewsbury was represented by a draper, Stamford by a tailor and Stafford
by a freemason. From Warwick came a tanner and a corvisor.
Superficial as this evidence is, it does no more than confirm even in
outline what might reasonably be expected *vis-à-vis* the linkages
between towns provided by the distributive trades in particular.

But if Coventry probably acted as both a major distributional
centre in the midlands and as a focus for important markets and fairs
for its rural hinterland particularly to the south and east, the use of
major towns by the wealthiest and most mobile rural purchasers for
their normal needs at this period is still a much neglected subject.
Evidence drawn only from such urban centres themselves is apt to
exaggerate the consistency of customer loyalties. When regarded
from the outside, it is clear that there was a considerable freedom of

choice which, not surprisingly, was widely exercised. The theoretical provincial dominance of Coventry is thus best measured against the purchasing activities of substantial families within and on the edge of its potential economic range. For the Poultney's estate at Misterton in Leicestershire (some 18 miles east of Coventry and bordering on Lutterworth to its west), for which the detailed accounts survive (when it was in wardship), there were connections with Coventry's clothiers and weavers insofar as the wool crop was concerned. But for the purchase and sale of beasts, the estate looked much further afield: to Yorkshire, Northampton and London, as well as to Coventry and Birmingham. Other commodities like fish came from Leicester, and rope from Stourbridge.[53] Similarly for the Willoughbys of Wollaton Hall just outside Nottingham, whose business brought them often enough to Coventry, the city was convenient essentially for scarce commodities only: oranges (which incidentally they also purchased at Birmingham); aniseed, almonds, sugar, white soap and prunes (which they similarly procured on another occasion at the Lenton fair at Nottingham); pomegranates, liquorice, rice and white paper. It was to a goldsmith in Birmingham, not to one at Coventry, that they sent their salt for repair in 1524; and from Birmingham that a carter brought a load of wine in 1526. The fairs they most regularly patronised in the 1520s were those of Lichfield and Stourbridge, as well as those of Nottingham, Derby and Penkridge. In the 1540s, they also attended fairs at Mansfield, Chesterfield, 'Adylton', Newark and even Birmingham: never Coventry.[54]

The moral of this negative evidence is not without significance in underlining the economic functions of Coventry as a major centre by this period. First, the city's attractive power over regional customers was limited. To the north-east, easy communication ended essentially at Leicester, with which town Coventry had many close linkages.[55] For both Nottingham and Derby, however, the road system more easily connected with Lichfield and Birmingham, in each of which towns scarce commodities and services were available. Coventry may well have acted as a source of supply for both the latter, but its economic influence can have stretched only to a limited extent so far as Nottingham and Derby. Secondly, while the city already doubtless acted as an entrepôt for livestock brought

[53] Information kindly furnished by Dr J. D. Goodacre.
[54] H.M.C. *Middleton*, pp. 376, 382, 386, 372. [55] *Infra*, pp. 139, 150, 154, 269.

from the north and west (as mentions of drovers from Shrewsbury testify); it nevertheless lay third along a well-worn route *via* Penkridge fair and Birmingham. Similarly to the south, the ancient Welsh road which channelled cattle from Wales through the midlands passed well to the south of the city. Further south still it was through Stratford-upon-Avon that the traffic of imports from Bristol passed more conveniently *en route* for either Northampton or Banbury.

By the close of the middle ages, Coventry's regional economic significance, in fact, was limited on the one hand by the communications system: in particular by its distance from navigable waterways and its vulnerability to the changing fashionability of land routes for different purposes; and, on the other, by the long-term evolution of periodically available services amongst its small competitors in the densely populated region to its west. If the distributive trades of the city may well have profited from this latter development in the short term, it is still true that the supply of these centres was much easier *via* the navigable Severn, and Kidderminster in particular. Moreover, Coventry was not the county town, while its anyway divided diocesan influence ranged north-westwards over the very area in which it seems to have exercised least economic influence. It is thus difficult not to conclude that the greatness of late medieval Coventry depended to an excessive degree on its role as a major textile-manufacturing centre. On that role essentially depended the city's nodal position in the rapidly changing urban system of late medieval England. When that role was eroded, Coventry's fate as a leading provincial centre was sealed.

Part II

Desolation of a city

'CAPPER: . . . this city which was heretofore well inhabited and wealthy (as you know everyone of you) is now for lack of occupiers fallen to great desolation and poverty.
MERCHANTMAN. So be the most part of all the towns of England, London only excepted.'

> (*A Discourse of the Commonweal of this Realm of England: Attributed to Sir Thomas Smith*, ed. Mary Dewar, The Folger Shakespeare Library, University Press of Virginia, 1969, p. 18.)

> Greate De(ar)th and much idelnes,
> lytle money and much sickness
> gret pryd and smale Riches,
>   How can these agree?
>   x x x x
> Many gammers and few archers,
> gay cortyars and yll warryers
> many craftesmen and halff beggers
>   both in townes and cyty.

> (From the ballad 'Nowe a Dayes', c. 1520. Tawney and Power (eds.), *op. cit.*, iii, pp. 19–20.)

1. *The tempo of decline*

If Coventry was still flourishing in 1450, a hundred years later the glittering prosperity of the city had not merely dulled; it had vanished. During the years around 1550, indeed, it is no exaggeration to state that Coventry's fortunes sank to the nadir of their recorded history. The manner of this eclipse of one of the major cities of England is thus of more than local interest alone. Until much more work has been done on both the national and regional incidence of demographic decline and the changing structure of the textile industry, however, the wider causes of this process may only be indicated tentatively. Here it will be necessary to concentrate more particularly on the pace and the nature of the city's internal decline in order to provide the context in which its late medieval social structure may be examined. Above all, since the claims made by urban contemporaries as to the severity of demographic decline in fee-farm petitions and the like are still apt to be viewed somewhat sceptically, it is essential to establish unambiguously the rapidity and the extent of both long- and short-term depopulation in this comparatively well-documented case.

The reconstruction of demographic trends in the later middle ages is a notoriously precarious undertaking. There can, however, be little doubt that between 1334 and 1377, during which time a comparison between Dr Glasscock's and Professor Hoskins' approximate rankings of provincial towns shows Coventry shooting up from twelfth or even nineteenth place to third, the population was also rapidly expanding despite the Black Death.[1] On the basis of the 4,817 'adults' totalled in the latter year, J. C. Russell estimated a population of 7,226.[2] But although, as is discussed below,[3]

---

[1] R. E. Glasscock, 'England *circa* 1334' in H. C. Darby (ed.), *A New Historical Geography of England* (Cambridge, 1973), p. 184; Hoskins, *Local History in England*, p. 176. For the short-term impact of the Black Death *v.* an important unpublished paper read to the Dugdale Society by E. and A. Gooder, 'Coventry at the Black Death and Afterwards' (1965). I am most grateful to the authors for letting me have a copy of this.

[2] J. C. Russell, *British Medieval Population* (Albuquerque, 1948), p. 142. A population of 5,000 has been estimated for 1280, i.e. *before* the fourteenth century expansion, Hilton, *A Medieval Society*, p. 196.

[3] *Infra*, p. 243, though at a time of demographic growth, it is probable that the proportion of children was higher.

his estimate for children at this period is probably a good deal more plausible than some would admit, there can be no doubt whatsoever that his failure to allow for omissions, exemptions, and evasions produces an unrealistically minimal figure. A maximum, however, can also be obtained by invoking Professor Postan's surmise that under-counting etc. may well have amounted to 25 per cent of the total.[4] On this basis the population would have been some 9,634 persons, a figure which would seem nearer the mark than Russell's. A total in the region of 9,000 plus might thus be a reasonable guess. Since there is no reason to suspect that the population abruptly ceased to grow in 1378, it may be suggested with some confidence that it continued to increase thereafter while economic circumstances were still propitious. Certainly the probability of growth by, and/or during the early years of the fifteenth century receives confirmation from the visual evidence. Messrs. Jones and Smith have recently elucidated the adaptation of the 'Wealden house type' to cramped urban conditions at Coventry. They have traced 40 examples of this exotic species (28 definite and 12 probable) on or towards the outskirts of the old city, and they have dated them 'probably to the first half' of the fifteenth century.[5] The authors conclude: 'We suppose that the streets where Wealden houses stand were being built up closely for the first time, whatever else may have stood there earlier; and that the town's prosperity favoured the growth of speculative building in several places where land was still available, or cheap enough, for intensive development.'[6] Such a description seems to fit a population that was already bursting out of those very walls which it was then building to contain itself, and a period that witnessed the enlargement of St Michael's into one of the most spacious parish churches in the realm.[7] The probability of

[4] M. M. Postan, 'Medieval Agrarian Society in its Prime: England', in M. M. Postan (ed.), The Cambridge Economic History of Europe, 2nd edn, (Cambridge, 1966), pp. 561-2. By adopting the highest possible estimate for omissions, any exaggeration may be to some extent counter-balanced by the point made in n. 3 supra.

[5] S. R. Jones and J. T. Smith, 'The Wealden Houses in Warwickshire and their Significance', B.A.S.T., lxxix (1960-1), pp. 29-30.

[6] Ibid., p. 33. For other examples of fifteenth-century methods of adapting housing to cramped street-frontages towards the eastern side of the city, v. W. A. Pantin, 'Medieval English Town-house Plans', Medieval Archaeology, vi-vii, (1962-3), pp. 220-1.

[7] E. Gooder, Coventry's Town Wall, Coventry and N. Warwickshire History Pamphlets, iv, revis. and enlarg. edn (1971), passim; Nikolaus Pevsner and Alexandra Wedgwood, The Buildings of England: Warwickshire (Harmondsworth, 1966), p. 250.

continuing increase after 1377 is further supported by a cautious estimate based on a list of contributors to a present for the king in 1434, since the lowest sum involved, 4d., could indicate a penetration similar to that of the 1523 subsidy. Even a conservative calculation from this premise suggests a population of 9,824 in 1434, so a ceiling of some 10,000 inhabitants would therefore seem a distinct probability, and could even be too low.[8]

This, however, may well have represented the high point of the city's medieval population: the year 1439 was marked by a massive subsistence crisis of the kind to be discussed below, and thereafter the evidence suggests decline.[9] Already in 1442, the Leet was agitating over the failure of landlords to rebuild houses they had pulled down, on pain of a crushing £10 fine for every ten shilling's rent, an ordinance that had to be repeated three years later.[10] Evidently tenants were simply not available to fill these empty houses. That the city government was apprehensive of this situation deteriorating may be seen in 1457 when it forbade the masters of crafts to sue their members in spiritual courts, a practice which 'yf hit contynued be liklyhode wold cause moche people to voide oute of this Citie'.[11] The same problem doubtless lay behind the prior's complaint in 1451 that the Earl's part of the city was not worth an eighth of the £88.6s.8d. farm which he paid annually for it.[12] As Miss Dormer Harris has remarked, by 1466, when he was £550 in arrears for this farm, 'his tenants in the city must therefore have been backward in paying the rent due to the priory treasury'.[13] Within two years the corporation was in similar straits when it owed £800 for *its* farm – the equivalent of sixteen years' arrears.[14] By 1473 the situation had so far deteriorated that the Leet was forced

---

[8] *L.B.*, pp. 160–9 which gives a total of 1,228 persons. The 1524 subsidy instalment (P.R.O. E179/192/125) embraced about 45% of all households estimated minimally for *1523* and whether or not these may be securely identified with those enumerated (*v. infra* p. 190). If in 1434 the proportion included is taken to be higher – at 50% – and the mean household size to be only four persons (cf. *infra* p. 245), the total suggested should not be too unrealistic as a minimum estimate.

[9] L.M., fo. 8 r.; *infra* p. 59. [10] *L.B.*, p. 199.

[11] *Ibid.*, pp. 302–3.   [12] *Cal. Pat. Rolls, 1446—1452*, p. 502.

[13] Mary Dormer Harris, *Life in an Old English Town* (London, 1898), p. 127.

[14] *Ibid.*, p. 126. For the frequency of plague up to 1468 *v. Cal. Pap. Regs.; xii, 1458–1471*, p. 644. This reference does *not* indicate an epidemic in 1468 as has been supposed elsewhere. Given the date at which the 'Jesus-mass' was probably initiated (*infra* p. 118 n. 2), the most recent visitation is more likely to have been 1464–5, J. N. W. Bean, 'Plague, Population and Economic Decline in the Later Middle Ages', *Econ. H.R.*, 2nd ser., xv (1962–3), p. 429.

to reverse its previous policy on decayed housing, and insist that any building 'beyng in doute to fall' should be immediately demolished on pain of £5 for each default and the same quarterly thereafter.[15] No one any longer laboured under the illusion that such houses ought usefully to be re-built.

But if the 1470s began inauspiciously, they ended in disaster. In 1479 the citizens were grievously smitten by a virulent pestilence. Should the city annals be believed, some 3,300 of the inhabitants then died within the town, and a further suspiciously round and inflated figure of 1,150 within its franchises during an epidemic of what Professor Shrewsbury has elswhere diagnosed as probably cholera.[16]

Most fortunately, from about this stage it is possible to gauge the scale and the trends of the housing situation. As a base-line there survives for 1485–6 a rental of one of the city's largest property owners, the Trinity Gild. At that date about 135, out of some 387, houses and cottages belonging to the fraternity were standing empty, the vast majority having been so for over a year. Nearly a third of its properties and 22 per cent of its possible total rental were thus affected by vacancies.[17] From two to three years later it is possible to construct a continuous histogram (figure 1) of rents lost to the Gild of Corpus Christi also as a result of vacant housing, which covers a period of exactly forty years.[18] Although the number of properties involved was somewhat smaller than that of the senior gild – a mere 43 tenements, 44 cottages, 6 chambers, 2 stables, 1 mayor's parlour, 3 closes, a garden and a field (and therefore contained an in-built bias against the generally more numerous cottage properties in the city) – the similarities between the two sets of rents in both cases where some sort of comparison can be made,

[15] *L.B.*, p. 386.
[16] B.L. Harl. MS. 6388, fo. 23v.; J. F. D. Shrewsbury, *A History of Bubonic Plague in the British Isles* (Cambridge, 1970), pp. 148–9.
[17] *The Records of the Guild of the Holy Trinity, St Mary, St John the Baptist and St Katherine of Coventry, II*, ed. G. Templeman (Dugdale Society, xix, 1944), pp. 48–69, 70–5; excluding the gaol, the framing yard, 'divers leyes', a garden, and counting together a chamber above another as one dwelling; and including estimates of a round 15 and 20 cottages for Dead Lane and Rood Lane respectively – cf. pp. 55 and 72, pp. 65, 66 and 74. In calculating the total possible rental for *houses*, the potential income from fields and the first four entries of the five specified in the previous sentence have been deducted from that given on *ibid.*, p. 69, n. 1. Some of the vacancies were, of course, temporary.
[18] C.R.O. A6, *passim*.

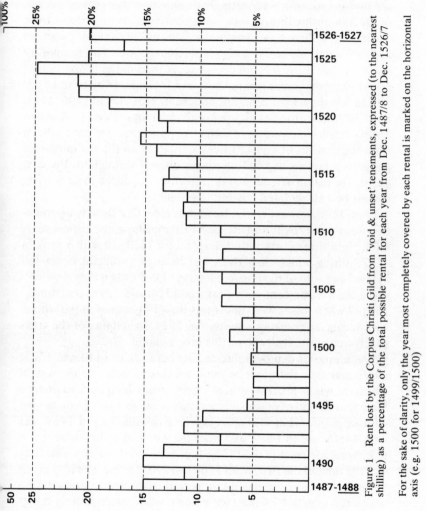

Figure 1   Rent lost by the Corpus Christi Gild from 'void & unset' tenements, expressed (to the nearest shilling) as a percentage of the total possible rental for each year from Dec. 1487/8 to Dec. 1526/7

For the sake of clarity, only the year most completely covered by each rental is marked on the horizontal axis (e.g. 1500 for 1499/1500) between 1485–6 and 1488, and in 1524–5,[19] are so marked that there is little need to question the trends they betray. In the case of the former period it would seem that the reduction in rents lost by the junior gild, which surprisingly distinguishes the closing decade of the fifteenth century, was but a continuation of a trend from earlier years when, according to the Trinity Gild's rental, vacancies had accounted for an even higher percentage loss. This temporary recovery, however, was not complete. Although the proportion of rents lost by the junior gild fell between 1490 and 1498 from 15 per cent to less than 3 per cent, it is noticeable that only in 1496, 1498, and 1500 did it drop below 5 per cent of the total. Even so, it would appear that conditions were such as to encourage a revival at least from the ravages of 1479. If Leet legislation on the demolition of dangerous houses in 1473 had been obeyed throughout the city, clearly the extent of a demographic recovery deduced from housing cannot be extrapolated beyond that date.

From 1500, however, it is abundantly clear that the city's population was again rapidly and inexorably diminishing, the critical years falling into three fairly well-defined steps: 1501–10 with a peak in 1507, during which time rents lost through vacancies never fell below 5 per cent of the possible total; 1511–20 when they regularly exceeded 10 per cent with peaks in 1514 and 1518; and finally 1521–7 when losses were never less than 17 per cent of the whole, with vacancies reaching a summit in 1524, the climax of the crisis which comprises the core of this investigation.

The tempo of demographic decline between c. 1440 and 1525, which may now therefore be outlined, clearly indicates the way in which the whole process gathered momentum. It comprised firstly a forty year period of reasonably gradual decay to 1480, interspersed with moments when the process was accelerated as in 1439, the later 1460s and in 1479, and from the worst of which there was a temporary recovery in the 1490s. In the second stage, covering only half the time of the first, from 1500 to 1520, decline was very much more rapid, and culminated in a period of disastrous crisis during which the situation of the 1480s was reached again and then sur-

[19] *Ibid.*, fos. 147v.–148v., 246v.–247v. – the only two early Corpus Christi Gild rentals to survive, with trifling differences between them. Templeman, *op.cit.*, pp. 81–94, misdates the Trinity Gild rental for Master Nethermill's year to probably 1528 (*ibid.*, p. 93 n. 3). Nethermill was Master on 19 January 1525, C.R.O. A7 (a) p. 79. His term of office would have begun on the previous 18 October – cf. Templeman, *op cit.*, pp. 152 159.

passed, with definitely more permanent and far-reaching consequences for the future. The actual magnitudes of decay, however, at
least during the later stages of the process, must await further
discussion.

2. The hastening of decline

With the tempo of decline broadly established it is possible to turn to the question of its causation – a far from straightforward matter. Indeed, it will be as well to begin by eliminating some of the more obvious reasons which are sometimes put forward in general discussions of urban decay. Coventry, for example, was hardly a case of a city being overtaken by urban rivals even though its provincial pre-eminence had been reduced. Nor was it a matter of a radical redistribution of regional wealth; if anything, Warwickshire may have improved its position in this respect.[1] It was not, furthermore, a simple question of commercial infiltration by London merchants: the evidence of both the statute merchant rolls and membership of the two Gilds makes it quite clear that, on the contrary, London played but little part in the city's affairs.[2] Neither need the well-known re-alignment of England's export trade during the fifteenth century have affected an inland city so centrally placed as Coventry which could turn to any port it chose for its outlet. Finally, the increasing competition of the local rural textile industry, such as it was, seems to have been an effect not a cause of decline. Not until 1514 is anything heard of this problem in either the Leet Book or the regulations of the Weavers, both of which sources only betray an increasing sensitivity on the subject thereafter.[3] The related question of compensatory over-regulation within the city therefore does not arise. What then *were* the reasons for Coventry's downfall?

An answer to this can only be attempted on the basis of a distinction between the first and second stages of the city's decline. For while both were connected, new factors, which had originally played little or no part in the earlier period, had clearly begun to operate influentially by the later. In the case of the former, however, it is easier to generalise than to provide concrete evidence from local sources. It needs no emphasising, for example, that the

[1] R. S. Schofield, 'The Geographical Distribution of Wealth in England, 1334–1649', *Econ. H.R.*, 2nd ser., xviii (1965), pp. 504, 506.

[2] *Supra*, p. 27; C.R.O. A6, *passim; Register of the Guild of the Holy Trinity*, ed. Dormer Harris, pp. 101–12.

[3] *Infra*, p. 48. The Tanners, however, were claiming a monopoly of *retailing* hides within eight miles of the city in 1495, C.R.O. Transcription of the Ancient Minute Book of the Fellowship of Tanners, original fol. lv.

city was greatly dependent on textiles and clothing; in addition to the males working in the industry, spinning occupied a legion of women while an unknown multitude of workers serviced the industry – the cardmakers, the sheargrinders, the makers and menders of looms and wheels, quite apart from the necessary supportive victuallers.[4] But it can only be postulated that the resulting vulnerability to the fluctuations of a particular industry became critical when for a generation 'the cloth trade as a whole was greatly depressed from 1448 to 1476'.[5] That this *was* so would seem almost certain, but it seems impossible either to ascertain figures for local output or to establish the depressed state of the relevant crafts since their records begin too late for this purpose and Coventry did not keep a Freemen's register. All that can be said is that there are some scraps of information which seem to indicate the decay of the key craft of dyeing, in whose hands lay the city's reputation for 'Coventry blues'. For apart from all else, supplies of its basic ingredients at least from Southampton were totally dislocated during this period. Not only did the Genoese importation of alum – the mordant for madder – collapse between 1443/4 and 1459/60, but as from 1477/8, the supply of Toulouse woad seems to have dried up also, and whether compensatory lines of supply then opened up is far from clear.[6] It can have been no accident therefore that this period

---

[4] *V.C.H. Warks.*, viii, p. 155, *L.B.*, p. 658.

[5] H. L. Gray, 'English Foreign Trade from 1446–1482', in Eileen Power and M. M. Postan (eds.), *Studies in English Trade in the Fifteenth Century* (London, 1933), p. 25. For the decline in the number of master weavers *v. infra* p. 48–9. An overall proportional comparison of occupations, between 1450 and 1522, is not possible, because journeymen were largely excluded in the former year, *L.B.*, pp. 246–52.

[6] A. A. Ruddock, *Italian Merchants and Shipping in Southampton 1270–1600* (Southampton Record Series, i, 1951), pp. 88, 213 (I owe to one of my Readers the suggestion that the importation of Tolfa alum by Florentine merchants might have filled one of these needs, but this must remain a matter for textile historians); Olive Coleman, 'Trade and Prosperity in the Fifteenth Century: Some Aspects of the Trade of Southampton', *Econ. H.R.*, 2nd ser., xvi (1963–4), p. 11; *The Brokage Book of Southampton 1443–1444, i*, ed. Olive Coleman (Southampton Records Series, iv, 1960), p. xxxiii; *idem, ii* (Southampton Records Series, vi, 1961), pp. 321, 324. With regard to woad, it is worth repeating the later testimony of Sir Thomas Smith in 1549, to the effect that 'I have heard say that the chief trade of Coventry was heretofore in making blue thread and then the town was rich even upon that trade in manner only; and now our thread comes all from beyond the seas, wherefore that trade of Coventry is decayed and thereby the town likewise' (*A Discourse of the Commonweal*, ed. Dewar, p. 124). Quite apart from the evidence cited here and *infra*, p. 88 n. 49, this statement seems to bear out the long-term decline of this industry despite a possible short-term revival in the later sixteenth century (cf. Joan Thirsk, *Economic Policy and Projects: the Development of a Consumer Society in*

seems to have witnessed the erosion of the once proud Dyer's monopoly of their craft. There are hints for example that the Drapers were undercutting the Dyers by providing some of the necessary equipment themselves and hiring poorer dyers to use it, for, in 1473/4, all the dyers seem to have agreed not to work on drapers' premises. In a somewhat cryptic regulation they enacted 'that no dyer in Coventre, man nor woman, shall neyther shoote, woadde, nor madder to any Draper, or drapers, in the said cytie, any maner of Cloathe, but that it be coloured upp *before* it passe or goe oute of his, her, or their house' (my italics).[7] If, as is likely, this was the mysterious undertaking mentioned in the Leet Book, then it was further cemented by solemn oaths, and it explains the reaction of the Leet jury, which contained a hard core of drapers when, in the following year, it annulled an unspecified and illegal ordinance made by the dyers.[8] Undoubtedly the fellowship was fighting a losing battle, because in 1495/6 it had to enact that no one without 'a fatte and a leade of his owne' could be master of the craft – a revealing indication of declining prosperity.[9] By 1516 they were even having to fend off the Hatters who seem to have been elbowing in on at least part of the process. In that year the masters agreed that 'no dier . . . from that daye fforward schold not wode no hatts to no man, nor colore no hatts to no man, but that [the] dier colour them up clen, or the[y] pase his honds, for any more coloryng to be doone them'.[10] It was probably no coincidence that the mayor in 1519 was the last dyer to hold that office for over a generation.[11]

But if the running down of the textile industry was surely a major factor in the long-term decline of medieval Coventry, its effects were undoubtedly intensified by its co-incidence with those dynastic broils, the implications of which for English towns Dr Bridbury was inclined to minimise.[12] Of any accompanying dislocation of internal trade nothing is known, but Coventry's geographical position alone ensured it an embarrassing place at the very centre of hostilities,

Early Modern England (Oxford, 1978), pp. 114, 121: I am especially grateful to Dr Thirsk for letting me see this important work in proof). By 1606, however, it was said that 'the said Commoditie is now counterfeited in *London, Manchester*, and divers other places . . . and there put off and sold in the name of *Coventrey* thridd to the great abuse of the people and the hindrance of the sale of that thridd', C.R.O. A3(b), p. 40.

[7] Reader 4, fo. 116v.   [8] *L.B.*, p. 418.
[9] Reader 4, fo. 116v.   [10] *Ibid.*, fo. 118r.
[11] Templeman, *op. cit.*, appendix I and L.M. *passim*.
[12] A. R. Bridbury, *Economic Growth: England in the Later Middle Ages*, 2nd edn (London, 1975), pp. 101–2.

while its as yet barely tarnished prosperity made it a dazzling potential prize. Though not sacked like Carlisle and Stamford, it suffered financially as did Leicester, York, Hull, and Norwich.[13] The cream of the city's prosperity was syphoned off in subsidising fortifications, armour, soldiers, extravagant royal entertainments, loans and eventually when it sided with the losers, the inevitable massive fine for the redemption of its liberties. Warfare and its attendant consequences cost the city well over £2,000 between 1449 and 1485, when increasingly it could ill-afford to pay: the worst years falling between 1469 and 1471 during which time it had to find £600 to finance Warwick and then pacify the king.[14]

If the first stage of Coventry's decline may thus be explained in large measure by the combination of lowered returns from a stagnant textile industry and the simultaneous diversion of capital to economically unproductive martial enterprises, neither should it be forgotten that the period was both ushered in by a subsistence crisis – the worst since the great famine of 1315–16 according to Thorold Rogers – when wheat rose to 3s. a locally adjusted bushel and bread was being baked from peas, beans and barley as a result; and concluded with a major epidemic.[15]

The *fin de siècle* recovery which occurred too quickly for it to have been due to the typical reaction of a 'pre-industrial' population to excessive mortality, was therefore remarkable (fig. 1). The rapidity with which housing was re-occupied, indeed, implies immigration on a sizable scale, and may be partly explained by the marked upswing in cloth exports and the improved ratio of wages to prices which distinguished the last five years of the century.[16] Numbers may thus have been made up locally by the return of an ever-fluid

---

[13] *Cal. Pat. Rolls, 1461–7*, p. 82; Alan Rogers, 'Medieval Stamford', in Alan Rogers (ed.), *The Making of Stamford* (Leicester, 1965), pp. 39, 34; *V.C.H. Leics.*, iv, pp. 7–8; H. Heaton, *The Yorkshire Woollen and Worsted Industries*, 2nd edn (Oxford, 1965), p. 47; *V.C.H. Yorks: E. Riding*, i, pp. 23–6; B. Green and R. M. R. Young, *Norwich – the Growth of a City* (Norwich, 1964), p. 18.

[14] *L.B.*, pp. 236, *et passim*: cash for loans, gifts, troops etc. alone must have cost about £1,700, an exact calculation not being possible since there are too many additional unknowns. Not only has normal taxation been excluded from this total, but so too has the cost of the walls. Between 1430 and 1499, there was built roughly three times the length erected between 1499 and 1534, during which latter period the cost was £1,443, Gooder, *Coventry's Town Walls*, pp. 4, 58.

[15] J. E. Thorold Rogers, *A History of Agriculture and Prices in England*, 8 vols. (Oxford, 1866–1902), iv, p. 233; L.M. fo. 8r.

[16] E. M. Carus-Wilson and O. Coleman, *England's Export Trade, 1275–1547* (Oxford, 1963), p. 139; E. H. Phelps Brown and Sheila Hopkins, 'Seven Centuries of

labour force rather than by a more steady and stable increase in small masters across the economy.

It was indeed also a period which saw the take-off and meteoric rise of the capping industry, the numbers of masters in which practically trebled between 1496 and 1550.[17] Although an apparently all-inclusive list of Crafts providing armed men in 1450 does not even mention the occupation,[18] by 1496, not only were the Craft's ordinances admitted for the first time, and their earliest account book about then opened, but one of their number already held the office of mayor for the first time in their history. Three other cappers were to follow suit in the succeeding three decades, for head-gear was rapidly becoming one of the city's major exports.[19] In 1517 some of the wealthiest mercers and grocers in the city were being incorrectly described in a royal pardon as hatters and cappers of Coventry, including Richard Marler, 'one of the three or four richest merchants in provincial England'.[20] By 1531, the fellowship, 'now beying in nomber meny welthy and honest persones' was taking from the Cardmakers and Saddlers not only their Corpus Christi pageant but also a leading share in their chapel.[21] The success of this one trade, however, hardly compensated for the decline in the city's staple industry. It can have provided direct employment for at best no more than ten per cent of all households in the city at this period.[22]

For in practice the overall revival of Coventry was illusory: by the second stage of decay the permanent damage had already been done. From the 1490s onwards, it becomes increasingly clear that the diminution of population, particularly in the privileged sectors of society, had itself become a cause of further decline.

This fundamental erosion of the employing class may be observed at all levels. By 1494, for example, it was being already publicly admitted by the Leet that those Crafts which had borne the costs of the Corpus Christi plays 'at the begynnyng of such charges were

the Prices of Consumables, Compared with Builders' Wage-Rates' in E. M. Carus-Wilson (ed.), *Essays in Economic History*, 3 vols. (1962), ii, p. 94.

[17] *Infra*, p. 102.   [18] *L.B.*, pp. 246–52.

[19] *L.B.*, pp. 572–4. The mayors in question were John Dove, 1496; Thomas Padlond, 1504; John Saunders, 1510; Nicholas Heynes, 1525.

[20] *V.C.H. Warks.*, ii, p. 265; W. G. Hoskins, *Provincial England: Essays in Social and Economic History* (London, 1963), p. 73.

[21] *L.B.*, p. 708.

[22] A rough estimate which probably errs on the side of generosity even when allowances are made for the unknown numbers of females involved.

more welthy, rich & moo in nombre then nowe be, as oppenly appereth', a complaint which was echoed more specifically by the Tanners in 1507.[23] Even in the absence of a Freemen's register, the deterioration of the situation may be followed with some precision, for the crux of the matter was recruitment, a vexed problem which was rooted ultimately in the price of admission to the Craft fellowships. Not that this was a straight-forward question, however, for it had three distinct aspects: the recruitment of apprentices; the encouragement of these once qualified to set up shop in the city; and the attraction of stranger craftsmen. In all three cases it was becoming increasingly clear that matters were not as they should have been.

It is possible that civic policy may have been partly responsible for discouraging apprentices. In what was probably an attempt to combat the power of the Crafts, which alone had the power to admit masters, the mayor in 1494 enforced an unobserved ordinance of such antiquity that it does not even appear in the earlier pages of the Leet Book, to the effect that all apprentices thenceforth should be sworn to the franchises and registered at the cost of one shilling at their indenturing.[24] This extortionate fee brought down on its author 'many a Curse, I wene', as a piece of critical doggerel nailed to St Michael's church door unoriginally put it, and no doubt contributed to the shortage apparent in later years.[25] By 1510 the state of the city's finances was such that the mayor was then obliged to consult eight substantial men from each ward *weekly* on, amongst other matters, how 'profite myght ryse vnto the Comen Weele of the Citee as haue be made afore-tyme, as of receyuing of prentyses & such other'.[26] In 1519, the civic indenturing fee had to be halved.[27]

Quite as serious in their implications, however, were the varying admission fines payable by natives and strangers to each Craft on setting up. In 1496 native apprentices of the Cappers had to find 13s. 4d. while strangers were obliged to pay twice that amount.[28] Both Smiths and the Carpenters, by contrast, demanded £1 from their own apprentices, while the Barbers asked the same sum of strangers.[29] It was naturally common practice for strangers to pay

[23] *L.B.*, p. 556; C.R.O. access. 24, fos. 4v., 5r.   [24] *L.B.*, p. 560.
[25] *L.B.*, p. 567.   [26] *L.B.*, p. 630.
[27] *L.B.*, pp. 666–7.   [28] *L.B.*, p. 574.
[29] *L.B.*, pp. 585, 281; C.R.O. A5, fo. 2; *L.B.*, p. 225.

considerably more than the natives: strangers to the Tanners' Craft were charged three times as much as the local men in 1514, while most remarkably of all, the Weavers when still enjoying the full flood of prosperity in 1452–3 expected only 26s. 8d. from their own apprentices but the staggering sum of £60 from outsiders.[30] Where the evidence survives, however, it does seem that strangers were allowed to ply their trades for a year and a day before their higher fines were demanded.[31]

It is against these facts that the significance of later Leet legislation must be measured. Anxiety over the recruitment of masters is first apparent in the stern action taken by the city government to protect the rights of strangers in 1508, the year following the first peak of vacancies on the histogram in the second stage of Coventry's decline. From the fact that the Leet now had to clamp down hard on Crafts which extorted admission fines from strangers *before* the end of their first full year, it may be inferred that the companies were trying, successfully, to discourage the potential competition of strangers in a shrinking economy.[32] It was not, however, until 1514, another peak year for vacancies, that positive action was taken to encourage more local apprentices to set up in the city. To judge from the language of the ordinance, the Tanners' admission fines were then substantially reduced: those on native apprentices to 6s. 8d., and those on strangers to £1. At the same time, all Crafts were to submit their books to the governing body 'and if there ffynes be to moch to moderate them'.[33] The outcome of this was apparent four years later, by when the situation had deteriorated critically. Admission fines were then ruthlessly reduced all round, in many cases by a half or even more. It was now declared that apprentices of every Craft were to pay but 6s. 8d. only, the Mercers and Drapers on being indentured, and all the rest on setting up shop until 'the Cite be encreased to more welthynes then it is now'. Simultaneously a new note of plaintive warmth towards strangers was sounded: they were 'to Com and welcom', and their charges too seem to have been drastically reduced if those recited above are any guide. All strangers were now to pay a mere 10s. to their Craft, half at the end of their first full year and the rest a year later.[34] In a city where only a century earlier the sole interest evinced in strangers had been to

[30] *L.B.*, p. 641; C.R.O. access. 34: Weavers 2a, fo. 4v.
[31] *L.B.*, p. 574 – cf. p. 281.   [32] *L.B.*, p. 623.
[33] *L.B.*, p. 641.   [34] *L.B.*, p. 655.

protect their persons from objects hurled by the citizens,[35] this *bouleversement* of traditional protectionist attitudes was truly remarkable.

More deeply disturbing still, however, was the glaring shortage of really substantial citizens, the essential pivots around which medieval urban economies, large and small, ultimately revolved. That over a quarter of the tax due in 1523–7 from a city so important and so large as Coventry should have been paid by only three men was symptomatic of this scarcity.[36] For though Coventry was excluded from the operation of the 1511–12 statute, its main thesis – the widespread shortage of merchants to take civic offices in particular, and the new dependence that was having to be placed on the hitherto mistrusted victuallers (like Coventry's hostel-keeping mayor of 1487) – could find ample illustration in the increased reluctance of leading citizens to serve locally.[37] Once again, the earliest hints date back to the 1490s when, in 1495, the Leet had to go so far as to threaten a £5 penalty on anyone who attempted to secure the exemption of potential officers.[38] Just how serious the situation was becoming, may be gauged from the fact that, in 1507, three ex-mayors secured relief from ever serving a second term, a comparatively well-established custom in the preceding century.[39] As a result the mayor of that year was the last in many decades to accept a second term voluntarily. Precedents were therefore flung to the winds in the following two years, when the council house was clearly desperate for suitable candidates. Instead of choosing men who had just vacated the post of Master of the Corpus Christi Gild within the previous year or two as was customary, the electors were forced in 1508 to adopt Richard Smythe who, though Master as long before as 1490, had evidently evaded the mayoralty since, and, in 1509, Richard Marler who had never even served as Master. In both years there were recent Masters available.[40] In 1508, furthermore, the city government was both scandalised by the refusal of one Roger a Lee to accept the Chamberlainship, although he had

---

[35] *L.B.*, p. 27.
[36] Hoskins, *Provincial England*, p. 73: without these men, two of whom had anyway died by 1527 (P.C.C. 37 Bodfelde, 20 Porch), the city's national ranking would of course be lowered.
[37] *Statutes of the Realm*, 3 Henry VIII, cap. 8; *L.B.*, p. 533.
[38] *L.B.*, p. 568.
[39] *L.B.*, p. 606; Templeman, *op. cit.*, appendix I.
[40] *L.B.*, p. 619, C.R.O. A6, fos. 19–27; *L.B.*, p. 624.

already procured the postponement of that office three years prior, and also fearful of 'the parlous example, that he hath shewid to other in like cas so to do'.[41] Reluctance to serve, in fact, was only the culminating manifestation of a longer, invisible process. In more prosperous times, such men would never have had to be asked.[42]

These cases of office-evasion comprise only the first hints as to a situation that was to develop into a serious problem over the following three decades. The implications of this however may only be assessed with a knowledge of the city's medieval social structure and its working, which is the object of the analysis in part III. In the meantime it is only necessary to state that the major discouragement to office-holding was its expense.[43] The threat of office, moreover, also comprised a disincentive to urban residence as a direct consequence. There is no reason to question the testimony of one such Coventry citizen who was a self-confessed evader of office when he wrote to the king in 1533 that

> the charges of the Citie be so great that euery man feareth theme so that when a man haith goten eny good to fynde his lyvyng for feirre of office which be so chargeable that he sueth to an abbey fore a Convent Sealle orelles goeth to a farme in the contre & ther occupieth boithe his occupacion & husbondry to the great hynderaunce of the Citie & the undowyng of the poore husbondman.[44]

That this widely experienced decentralisation of urban occupations was becoming a contributory factor in the decline of the city's staple industry is hardly to be doubted. If 1514 was the first year in which the city attempted to supervise what was going on in its hinterland by insisting on all country-woven cloth being inspected; four years later the flow of work to the country had to be stemmed altogether.[45] In 1518 the clothiers were instructed both to 'put no cloth to wevyng in-to the countre but to ther own neighbours within this Cite', and also to 'put no cloth to ony walker to full but if he will will burle it & wranghalf it within the Cite'.[46]

Such action was not a moment too soon. Between 1450 and 1522–3, the number of Coventry's own master weavers had fallen

---

[41] *L.B.*, pp. 619–21.   [42] *Infra*, pp. 250–2.   [43] *Infra*, pp. 262–5.
[44] P.R.O. SP1/141, fo. 57r. This document is clearly misdated in *L. & P.* xiii (2) no. 1198. Cf. P.R.O. SP 1/74, fo. 16.
[45] *L.B.*, 639.
[46] *L.B.*, pp. 661, 659. In view of the point made below, it is notable that neither of these fulling processes seem to have been to do with milling.

by a third – from a minimum of 57 to about 37.[47] Indeed, if anything, the authorities were probably either dilatory or merely helpless in their attempts to staunch and supervise the flow of work away from the city. In 1518, for example, it was admitted that cloth masquerading as Coventry cloth was being sold in London simply because it was not authentically sealed by the city, 'which is a gret[er] slaunder to the Cite than hit deserueth by a gret partie'.[48] Not until 1539, by when it was too late, were country weavers obliged to be members of the City fellowship if they were to be given work by the inhabitants.[49] By Elizabeth's reign the situation must have been critical, for a late recension of the Weavers' ordinances then sought to impose a 'trybute' of four times the Craft's usual quarterage payment on those weaving within the liberties, and even forbade the supply of yarn to those living within four miles of the city.[50]

The same threat of country competition was felt by the city's fullers, as the regulation with regard to the finishing of cloth in 1518 quoted above clearly indicates. Whatever may have been the case during the high medieval period, by the sixteenth century it is difficult to find any evidence for fulling *mills* within the city. Those recorded in Elizabeth's reign were all devoted to the grinding of corn, while a number of fullers who belonged to the Corpus Christi Gild in the earlier sixteenth century came from places situated either on, or just over, the county boundary of Coventry to the south – from Baginton, Stoneleigh and Ryton on Dunsmore.[51] After 1518, the repeated efforts made to keep fulling within the city – in 1530, 1531, 1536 (on two occasions) and in 1538 – do no more than emphasise the failure of this policy against an irreversible trend towards locations that were better sited on watercourses away from the city.[52]

If the causes for Coventry's decline are more difficult to document than the fact of it, the decay of the city's major industry on

[47] *L.B.*, pp. 247–8. C.R.O. access. 100/17/1: Weavers 11 shows the masters' quarterage payments (1s. *p.a.* each, according to the first book of ordinances, fo. 2) totalling 36s. 8d. for the latter year. The account is in fact dated St Osborne's (i.e. Osburga's) day, 1523 O.S. This local saint's day was 23 Jan. (*v.* C.R.O. access. 100: Weavers 8, under 25 Henry VIII), and so the account refers to the craft year, July 1522–3.   [48] *L.B.*, p. 657.   [49] *L.B.*, p. 738.
[50] C.R.O. access. 100: Weavers 2c – an unsorted collection of draft ordinances. Regulations concerning search by the Craft officers within the liberties were written into C.R.O. access. 34: Weavers 2a, fo. 13, in 1543.
[51] C.R.O. A24, pp. 8, 18, 19, 44, 61; C.R.O. A6, *passim.*
[52] *L.B.*, pp. 704, 707, 723, 724, 727.

which its provincial pre-eminence depended is beyond question.
The extent to which this was due to the competition of other cloth
producing regions in Yorkshire, Lancashire, East Anglia, the Cotswolds or Devon is a matter for textile historians. Until the role of
urban centres in that connection is analysed on a national scale for
this period, it is only possible to re-assert the unequivocal evidence
for the decay of Coventry by 1518 in terms of a declining population, a reduced entrepreneurial and employing class, the fear of
rural competition, and the reluctance of outsiders to settle in the
city. With a state of affairs as serious as this, the helplessness of
Coventry in the face of the savage short-term crisis which now
engulfed it is thus hardly surprising. By suddenly and simultaneously magnifying practically all the factors hitherto rehearsed, and
adding to them overwhelming external forces quite outside local
control, these years of disaster decisively sounded the knell of the
medieval city.

3. Crisis 1518-25

The economic content of this crisis was compounded of four ingredients: a local slump, high food prices, a national trade depression, and the sudden subtraction from the city of huge capital sums. That the effects of this formidable combination were exacerbated still further by a pre-existing shortage of specie is probable. The paucity of coinage in circulation has been noted generally by Dietz and fully supported at a more detailed, but admittedly rural, level by the findings of Professor Hoskins.[1] At Coventry the shortage and its implications were being recognised both before and at the very beginning of the crisis. In 1514 clothmakers were specifically enjoined to pay 'for the spynning of euery weight in redy money'.[2] Weavers' charges in 1518 were similarly payable 'in money', while a publicly commended loan to poor cloth-makers included not only wool but significantly also £20 'in redy money for bycause the spynners and the weauers schall haue redy money for their true labour, and to gyue theym as they may lyue'.[3] It can have been no coincidence that, within a year or so, two bequests were also catering to this need for cash in advance. Not only did John Haddon leave £100 to be divided into annual cash loans amongst beginners of his old fellowship, the Drapers, but he bequeathed a further £100 to as many 'good honest Comyners of all occupations which be thryvyng and honest that will bring good suretie', as could purchase 'xxti stone woll' apiece each year.[4] Even the more prosperous clearly needed to be helped over this shortage. In like fashion the other bequest, also from a draper, amounted to £26.13s.4d. 'in money' which was to be divided triennially between 'tenne honeste personnes that mak cloth'.[5]

The effects of such short supply on an urban community where few had the subsistence insurance of farm produce to fall back on,

---

[1] F. C. Dietz, *English Public Finance 1485–1641*, 2nd edn, 2 vols. (London, 1964), i, p. 96, n. 37; W. G. Hoskins, *The Midland Peasant* (London, 1957), pp. 175–6, and *Provincial England*, pp. 140–1.

[2] *L.B.*, p. 640.

[3] *L.B.*, pp. 660, 658–9. This offer, by a 'man nyghe unto this Cite', is unlikely to have been made by John Haddon, who was sitting at this very Leet (*ibid.*, p. 654), and whose own loan was couched in somewhat different terms.

[4] P.C.C. 17 Ayloffe.   [5] P.C.C. 27 Ayloffe.

might be extremely serious. If an employer could not purchase raw materials, then his employees obviously could not earn a living; if he did tie up his money in raw materials, he might find it difficult to pay wages in cash. Thus, in the absence of a proper system of credit,[6] the continued economic well-being of an urban community depended entirely on the immediately available cash resources of the employer class in general, and of the merchant, 'the provider of capital *par excellence*' in particular. As Professor Supple has pointed out in the context of the similar circumstances of dearth and depression exactly a century later, moreover, 'the impairment of the supply of ready money was likely to lead to widespread dislocation'.[7] It may therefore be suggested that at Coventry, where specie was already short – a situation brought about in part by long-term economic decline – a critical proportion, if not all, of the little available slack was suddenly absorbed firstly in soaring food prices, and then in the payment of brutally heavy 'loans' and taxes, at the precise moment that a short-term but severe trade-depression was reducing the supply even further.

The components of crisis

Coventry was no exception to the general morbidity of these years, so before turning in detail to the specifically economic factors in the crisis, it will be as well to examine the spasmodic contribution made by epidemics. The absence of parish registration at this period naturally makes an assessment of the incidence of disease and its diagnosis peculiarly difficult. But an exceptional number of deaths amongst the more prosperous strata of the community, those who were theoretically immune from starvation or fatal diseases consequent on malnutrition, does provide some indication; and this information may be gleaned in rough and ready fashion from mortuary payments to a craft fellowship or religious fraternity. In the accompanying table the payments refer accordingly to years beginning in July and August with respect to the Weavers and the Cappers and on the *previous* 8 December for the Corpus Christi

---

[6] The only surviving membranes from the Statute Merchant Rolls at this time – those for 12/13 and 14 Henry VIII mm. 32a–32c, show such transactions at a very low ebb, C.R.O. E6.

[7] B. E. Supple, *Commercial Crisis and Change in England, 1600–1642* (Cambridge, 1964), p. 13.

Table 5. *Numbers of persons for whom mortuary payments are recorded 1517–27*

	Weavers	Cappers	Combined Crafts	Corpus Christi Gild	
1517–18	—	8	—		
				1518	1
1518–19	—	0	—		
				1519	13
					(including one couple)
1519–20	—	10	—		
		(including 5 members of the city's elite)			
				1520	2
1520–1	—	2	—		
				1521	9
					(including 2 couples)
1521–2	—	4	—		
				1522	5
1522–3	3	1	4		
				1523	0
1523–4	7	?3	?10		
				1524	3
1524–5	6	9	15		
				1525	17
					(including 2 couples)
1525–6	0	11(?6)	?		
				1526	7
					(including 4 Londoners)
1526–7	4	7	11		

Gild.[8] Though the sample be tiny, and in the case of the Gild inevitably distorted by the presence of extra-mural members, the results are nevertheless not unrevealing.

If the Cappers' figures, for example, may only hint at sickness in 1517–18, there is more positive evidence for 1519. The figure of 13 deaths, all from April 1519 for the Gild, should probably be read in conjunction with Stow's famous statement that in 1518 'About the feast of Lammas began the sweating sickness . . . After this, to wit in the winter was a great death of pestilence, almost over all Englande in everie town more or less' – an epidemic which Shrewsbury opines

[8] C.R.O. access. 100/17/1: Weavers 11, *passim*; Cappers accs., *passim*; C.R.O. A6, *passim*. For a discussion of the problems involved in this kind of analysis *v.* Charles Phythian-Adams, 'Records of the Craft Gilds', *The Local Historian*, ix (1971), p. 272.

to have been influenza.[9] The overlap of the possibly inflated Cappers' figures which begin in July 1519 (for that year), moreover, might support the view that by this stage a fresh factor was at work. For despite the evidence for wet weather, on 4 July, it was said that 'the plage Rayneth sore' in the city (a comment that might embrace any serious epidemic).[10] Yet another little peak seems to be visible in the Gild's figures for 1521 – a bad year in London for which Shrewsbury, in view of the high social strata affected, unconvincingly diagnoses famine-fever.[11] Fortunately the evidence for 1525 seems somewhat firmer. In this year the Gild's figure of 17 deaths appears to be borne out by the combined total derived from the Cappers and Weavers for 1524–5 which ends in July/August of that year. Since 'the dethe' was said to be in the city on 13 August 1525, it seems very probable that the continuing high figures of the Cappers for 1525–6 reflect a summer plague visitation in the former year.[12] Thus even if it is impossible to claim disease as a major contributory factor in the crisis on the basis of this fragile evidence, it will be as well to remember its malignant presence, particularly in 1519 and 1525, when the figures for population are discussed below.

Epidemics were quite outside human control, but 1518, the first year of the crisis, saw the city to all intents and purposes in the grip of a local slump which was the direct result of long-term decay in the textile industry combined with three successive years of soaring wool prices.[13] To judge from the histogram (figure 1), houses were being increasingly vacated as from the previous year, a process which persisted for a further twelve months thereafter. One ordinance of 1518, indeed, was to be specifically enforced 'tyll the Cite be better inhabyt'.[14] As early as April a series of measures for the true making of cloth had to be approved with exhortations to speedy action thereupon 'Or els the Cite wol-be so far past that it wol-be past remedie to be recouered to eny welth or prosperite'.[15] Looms were standing idle: the loan of 200 stone of wool and ready money to

[9] John Stow, *The Annales of England . . . untill this present year of 1601* (London, 1601), p. 852; Shrewsbury, *op.cit.*, p. 162.
[10] *Infra* p. 55; P.R.O. SP1/232, fo. 152.
[11] Shrewsbury, *op.cit.*, p. 163.   [12] B.L. Bibl. Cotton Titus B1, fo. 81v.
[13] 1515–17 inclusive: Peter Bowden, 'Agricultural Prices, Farm Profits and Rents', in Joan Thirsk (ed.), *The Agrarian History of England and Wales, iv, 1500–1640* (Cambridge, 1967), p. 841.
[14] *L.B.*, p. 661.   [15] *L.B.*, pp. 656, 656–61.

poor cloth-makers being fervently commended, 'by Godes grace, to some other good men . . . so that the Cite schal-be better occupied by the love of Jhesus, Amen'.[16] Under- or un-employed craftsmen were loitering away the hours 'levyng ther besynes at home that they shuld lyve by', and playing at bowls or quoits instead.[17] Efforts by the journeymen to take cooperative action within their crafts had to be severely quashed.[18]

At this unfortunate moment a fresh factor began to bite, for the harvest crisis which reached its peak in 1520 was one of the most severe in the century. Although Professor Hoskins' graph of harvest fluctuations vividly charts the national progress of disaster – showing the 1519 harvest as 'deficient', 1520 as a year of 'dearth', and the 1521 harvest as 'bad'[19] – local detail serves to re-adjust the timing and intensity of the crisis as experienced at Coventry. The price evidence unambiguously puts the start of it as early as the 1518 harvest, a fact which may explain the clause in the will drawn up by John Haddon in March 1519, leaving £20 'to lye in a stokk within saint Mary Hall to by corne with at such tyme that corne Risith, to bryng the markett down, as farr as this said some of xxli. will extend'.[20] His action was timely in view of the meteorological depression which gripped the country as from the following May. As the city annals put it, 'then was the weate sommer that men might not know winter for summer by the greene trees. The raine beganne one Hocksewsday [sic] and continued til Christmas'.[21]

---

[16] *L.B.*, p. 659.   [17] *L.B.*, p. 656, 661–2.   [18] *L.B.*, p. 656.

[19] W. G. Hoskins, 'Harvest Fluctuations and English Economic History 1480–1619', *Ag.H.R.*, xii (1) (1964), p. 39. Cf. C. J. Harrison, 'Grain Price Analysis and Harvest Qualities, 1465–1634', *Ag.H.R.*, xix (2) (1971), pp. 135–55, and 152 in particular. It may be that definitions of harvest quality (based on percentage differences from 31 year moving averages) are in danger of obscuring this matter. On the basis of Dr Bowden's figures, Dr Harrison defines the 1520 harvest as merely 'bad', but from the viewpoint of contemporaries both the wheat and rye harvests in that year were the worst for at least the preceding 70 years. Apart from in 1517, oats cost more than in any other year covered by the index; while barley prices were at their highest since 1482. It is thus clear that the harvest crises of the 1520s and the price rise they usher in, are largely responsible for inflating the long-term moving average, against which qualities are being measured. Prior to 1520, prices had remained remarkably stable. It is, therefore, more meaningful to compare Dr Bowden's base of 100, calculated for the half century 1450–99, with his average for 'all grains' in 1520, which amounts to no less than 193: 25 points higher than its only serious rival (1482) for the whole period since and including 1450. This was 'dearth', and a serious one at that. Peter Bowden, 'Agricultural Prices', *loc.cit.*, pp. 814–16.

[20] P.C.C. 17 Ayloffe.

[21] L.M., fo. 16a, r.; Hock Tuesday was on 3 May in 1519.

With the 1519 harvest, therefore, Coventry wheat prices reached a level which, when attained at Exeter in the following year, has been there described as 'the highest *average* . . . since 1316'.[22] It was thus understandable that by early October, the Leet was preferentially enforcing the right of the City to purchase corn on market day before 'foreigners'; was forbidding forestalling; and was prohibiting the sale of malt 'out of the Towne when it is of the price of v*s* and aboue'.[23]

A year later, as the accompanying table illustrates, the situation had deteriorated critically. The comparative evidence, indeed, demonstrates that the dearth achieved even more serious proportions locally than Professor Hoskins' general graph indicates.

Table 6. *'Harvest' prices 1516–24*[24]

	Wheat per bushel								Pigs		Geese	
Year	Exeter				Lincoln		Coventry		Coventry			
	Max.		Min.									
	s.	d.	s.	d.	s.	d.	s.	d.	s.	d.	s.	d.
1516		—		—		7½	1	7		—		—
1517		11½		9½		—		—		4½		*c.* 5
1518	1	0½		10	1	0½	1	5		6		6
1519	1	4	1	0		—	1	9		*c.* 5¼		*c.* 6½
1520	1	9	1	7	1	11¼	2	3		4½		*c.* 4
1521	1	9	1	7		11¼	1	1		—		*c.* 4¼
1522	1	1		11		7½		8		5½		4¾
1523		—		—		—		10		*c.* 7		*c.* 5¼
1524		10	1	0		8¼	1	5		*c.* 4½		*c.* 5

[22] Hoskins, *loc.cit.*, p. 33, my italics. [23] *L.B.*, p. 666.

[24] *Exeter*: I am obliged to Prof. W. G. Hoskins' good offices in arranging for Mrs M. M. Rowe, of Exeter City Library, to list (and voluntarily kindly check) Dr R. C. Easterling's unpublished table of prices against the Mayors' Court Rolls. The prices, in each case here, relate to the best and lowest qualities of wheat for the first date recorded after Michaelmas in every year.

Lincoln: Michaelmas prices calculated from J. W. F. Hill, *Tudor and Stuart Lincoln*, pp. 222, 30.

Coventry: Wheat and other commodities purchased for the Carpenters' Craft Harvest dinners, C.R.O. access. 3: A5, fos. 66, 68, 69v., 74v., 76v., 83r., 87v., 91v., 95; the cost of grinding, at what seems to have been the standard charge of one penny (*L.B.* pp. 130, 760), has been deducted from the wheat prices which specifically include this. The numbers of pigs purchased range between two and seven, and geese between eight and twenty-five. Prices are calculated to the nearest farthing.

Even when due allowances are made, as needs they must, for difficulties in comparing the official prices at Lincoln and Exeter with a once yearly purchase of grain of an unknown quality by the Coventry Carpenters, the data are still instructive. The generally higher price of wheat at Coventry, for example, need occasion no surprise: at Newcastle, indeed, it actually reached 2s. 6d. a bushel in 1521.[25]

Coventry's geographical position, furthermore, made it peculiarly vulnerable at such times, since the grain surpluses locally available for urban markets in former years had probably been considerably reduced over the previous century by enclosure for sheep or cattle farming. The hundred of Knightlow, in which the county of Coventry was physically situated, closely followed by its southerly neighbour, Kineton hundred, was the hardest hit in the whole of Warwickshire. Not only did Knightlow contain the highest percentage of deserted villages in the county, but it suffered most between 1488 and 1517.[26] Though Leadam's figures should not be treated as gospel truth,[27] they do indicate the gravity of the local situation. Over the period covered by the 1517 commissioners, some 88.8 per cent of the land concerned in Warwickshire was converted to pasture, a greater proportion than in any other midland county.[28] Some of it became unproductive parkland at the hands of the local gentry or rich merchants like John Bonde, who ironically found himself mayor of the city at the peak of the dearth.[29]

Coventry, in fact, was exceptionally exposed to the dangers of

For considerable debts incurred by religious houses at Coventry and Kenilworth as a result of emergency grain-purchases apparently during the harvest year 1520–21, v. *Bishop Blythe's Visitations c. 1515–1525*, ed. Peter Heath (Collections for a History of Staffordshire, 4th ser., vii, 1973), pp. 85–6, 70.

[25] R. Welford, *A History of Newcastle and Gateshead*, 3 vols. (London, n.d. – 1887) ii, p. 5.

[26] M. W. Beresford, *The Lost Villages of England* (London, 1954), p. 231; Maurice Beresford, 'A Review of Historical Research (to 1968)', in Beresford and Hurst (eds.), *Deserted Medieval Villages*, p. 39, table IX, shows Warwickshire as the worst hit mainland county in the *present* state of knowledge; and the county's adjusted ratio rises from 2.3 to 2.9 desertions per 1,000 acres when the forest of Arden is excluded, *ibid.*, p. 38. *The Domesday of Inclosures*, ed. I. S. Leadam, 2 vols. (Royal Historical Society, 1897), ii, p. 390.

[27] E. Kerridge, 'The Returns of the Inquisition of Depopulation', *English Historical Review*, lxx (1955), pp. 212–28. It is claimed for Warwickshire, however, that 'the 1517 Inquiry reported many evictions, substantiated by the later proceedings in the court of Exchequer', Beresford, *op.cit.*, p. 388.

[28] Leadam, *op.cit.*, p. 41.   [29] *Ibid.*, ii, pp. 389, 400.

crop disasters. To the immediate west was the forest of Arden, the settlements in which were hardly renowned for their grain sur-pluses.[30] The 'champain' half of Warwickshire on the other hand had not only to supplement Coventry's needs – Warwick bakers called twice weekly[31] – but had also to feed Alcester, Stratford upon Avon and the county town itself. To the west was Worcestershire, the granary of Bristol whose officers scoured its countryside in times of dearth.[32] If further to the south was the Cotswold sheep and corn country, to the east and south-east and within the borders of War-wickshire itself, the representatives of London were also search-ing.[33] To the north-east were concentrated hungry mouths at Leicester. Urban competition for the precious grain must have been intense at such moments; in the case of Coventry it may often have been desperate. For, above all else, the town was one of the few major centres which was not situated on a navigable inland water-way: the Avon could not take craft above Stratford.[34] While other cities might thus depend ultimately on imported corn, it may well be doubted whether much – or any such – successfully completed the over-land journey to Coventry. It is therefore probably significant that in the similar crisis of the 1590s it was not to imports from the Baltic, but to the market town of Lutterworth in southern Leicester-shire, that the city turned for supplies in its hour of need.[35] Doubt-less it was this very problem of provision in the 1520 dearth which finally prompted the city government, as late as May 1522 (when corn prices were falling), to insure against the future by over-riding traditional common pasture rights, which became available annu-ally on 1 August, by enacting that 'the Tenauntes of all the same Comen Growndes last taken yn to be seuerall schall yerly plowe & sowe all or halffe the same Growndes or els to fforfet ther takes and leses'.[36]

---

[30] V. H. T. Skipp, 'Economic and Social Change in the Forest of Arden, 1530–1649', in Joan Thirsk, ed., *Land, Church and People: Essays presented to Professor H. P. R. Finberg, Ag.H.R.*, xviii (1970), supplement, p. 91.

[31] *L.B.*, p. 717.

[32] Robert Ricart, *The Maire of Bristowe Is Kalendar*, ed. Lucy Toulmin Smith, (Camden Society, new ser., v, 1872), p. 49.

[33] *L. & P.*, iii (2), no. 2,015.

[34] T. S. Willan, *River Navigation in England 1600–1700* (Oxford, 1936), map I.

[35] C.R.O. A14(a), p. 240. There were clearly established procedures for assessing the supply of Warwickshire grain at such times, cf. the civic census of grain in the surrounding hundred of Knightlow (? 1555–6), C.R.O. A.94.

[36] *L.B.*, pp. 679–80.

Everything points in fact to famine during the harvest year which began in 1520. The wheat for the holy-cake in both parishes was strictly rationed, and it was laid down that 'noder to make cake nor bun beside the haly-cake'.[37] Close surveillance of the victualling trades was now extended from the Bakers and the Fishmongers to include also the Butchers who, like the other two fellowships, now had one of their two keepers chosen annually by the mayor himself.[38] Most notably, the situation was so grave as to require an emergency investigation into both 'what stores of all maner of corne, and what nombre of people was then within the said cite, men, women and children etc.' and simultaneously the number of all the common brewers and bakers with their weekly requirements of grain. Not long after the harvest, on 10 October, it was discovered that to sustain the counted population of 6,601, the brewers needed, weekly, 146 quarters, 1 bushel of malt, while the bakers required 132 quarters of wheat, not to mention peas and rye, both of which constituted the poor man's crust in times of dearth quite apart from their employment as horse fodder. A simple calculation reveals that *if* all the grain resources reported in the city had been pooled, and *if* supplies had ceased thereafter, then the brewers would have had sufficient malt and barley to last them into the following February. The bakers, on the other hand, would have had barely enough grain to last them a fortnight. Matters may indeed have been pitiable by Friday 21 December, when the mayor and his friends tactfully imported 97 quarters and 6 bushels 'of all maner of greyn' – scarcely sufficient to keep the bakers busy for five of the twelve days of Christmas, let alone the brewers.[39] It can thus have been no coincidence that by the following midsummer the price of a sextary of ale which had been long officially 'fixed' at 1s. 8d. was then being sold for 2s.; even barley was now in dangerously short supply.[40]

Throughout the dearth, prices of foodstuffs other than grains, however, seem to have behaved in a contradictory manner which can only be partly ascribed to the imperfections of the source (see table 6). If 1518, the beginning of the harvest crisis, was the second

[37] *L.B.*, p. 669.
[38] *L.B.*, p. 669 – an order which was flagrantly disregarded in 1523, B. L. Harl. MS. 7571, fo. 33r.
[39] *L.B.*, pp. 674–5.
[40] *L.B.*, p. 678, C.R.O. access. 3: A5, fos. 79r., 82v.

worst year for geese and pig prices, the peak of the dearth in 1520 was accompanied by the lowest prices for both these commodities. In 1523, by contrast, when corn prices were low, the prices of pigs, and to a lesser extent geese, once again rose markedly. Thus if the Coventry evidence bears out Dr Bowden's suggestion that since the supply of poultry was plentiful, a bad harvest would bring prices down in this respect, his other tentative point – that pig prices usually maintained their level at such times – is scarcely substantiated on this particular evidence.[41] An interesting hint at the impact of wet weather on dairy livestock, however, is to be gleaned from the two surviving milk prices, which show the price of a gallon soaring from 1¼d. in 1519 to 6d. in 1521. In general it would seem that temporary reductions in some areas hardly compensated for the increase in the price of bread. On the contrary, it is probably more relevant to note that the fickle movements of prices served rather to extend the subsistence crisis in ways which indices of corn prices cannot reveal. If 1519 was the worst year for geese prices, 1520 was worst for wheat, 1521 perhaps for milk and 1523 for the price of pigs. The medieval housewife may well have felt that saving on one commodity at such times was immediately cancelled out by a price increase on another. The savage intensity of the subsistence crisis can thus hardly be questioned.

But if wretched weather was responsible for the food shortage, there can also be little doubt that a practically continuous period of rain from May to December in 1519, and probably thereafter too, was also a contributory factor to the national trade depression of these years. The influence of weather on the supply of wool has been described by Dr Bowden. Lambing averages succumbed easily to bad winters, while prolonged wet weather not only raised the sheep mortality rate through the rot, but also reared a serious obstacle at shearing time, when the dryness of the fleece was a *sine qua non.*[42] As Dr Bowden has further suggested, moreover, bad harvests and high food prices inevitably dictated the suspension of clothing purchases as a form of saving. A widespread contraction of demand thus inexorably provoked unemployment in the textile industry.[43]

[41] Peter Bowden, 'Agricultural Prices', *loc.cit.*, p. 629. His index also demonstrates that the average prices of all cattle in 1519 and 1520 then reached a record level since 1450, *ibid.*, pp. 823–4.

[42] P. J. Bowden, *The Wool Trade in Tudor and Stuart England* (London, 1962), pp. 16, 22–3.   [43] Bowden, 'Agricultural Prices', *loc.cit.*, p. 629.

Such a situation was of course intensified when, as in this case, it was not confined to England. These were disastrous years of dearth in the Netherlands, and there was famine in Castile and Portugal, the peak of the subsistence crisis in Europe generally not being reached until 1521.[44] At this unfortunate moment, furthermore, the Emperor's foreign policy moved into an aggressive phase. Huge sums were diverted from trade in the form of loans to finance war with France. In one year, 1520, Charles V's debt at Antwerp alone practically doubled – from half to about 1m. *livres*. His creditors were primarily merchants.[45] And much the same was true of France where from the *taille* alone Francis I raised 1,591,184 *livres* in 1520–1.[46] Demand for English cloth thus contracted simultaneously both at home and abroad.

These 'years of crisis'[47] for the English textile industry – 1520–2, and 1523 should also be added – have not received the attention they deserve from economic historians. National cloth exports which had risen by practically 40,000 cloths to nearly 100,000 between 1498–9 and 1519–20, sagged suddenly to almost the late fifteenth century level in 1521–2.[48] At Bristol, probably one of Coventry's more important outlets, the worst year, 1522–3, represented the lowest point for cloth exports since the fourteenth century.[49]

Following so soon after the local slump of 1518, Coventry was obviously peculiarly vulnerable to the winds of fortune. Even the Cappers were claiming 'not to bee ocupyd' in October 1523.[50] Early the following year, four of the richest citizens felt that the severity of the situation merited the considerable contribution of some £125

[44] C. Verlinden, 'Crises Économiques et Sociales en Belgique à l'Époque de Charles-Quint', *Charles-Quint et Son Temps* (Paris, 1959), p. 180; R. Mousnier, *Les XVIe et XVIIe Siècles* (Paris, 1961), p. 97; Peter Bowden, 'Agricultural Prices', *loc.cit.*, p. 852.

[45] M. F. Braudel, 'Les Emprunts de Charles-Quint sur la Place d'Anvers', *Charles-Quint et son Temps*, p. 194.

[46] R. J. Knecht, *Francis I and Absolute Monarchy*, Historical Association pamphlet, general series, lxxii (1969), p. 11.

[47] G. D. Ramsay, *The Wiltshire Woollen Industry*, 2nd edn (London, 1965), p. 65.

[48] Carus-Wilson and Coleman, *England's Export Trade 1275–1547*, p. 139.

[49] E. M. Carus-Wilson, *Medieval Merchant Venturers*, 2nd edn (London, 1967), pp. 5, 7, 8; Carus-Wilson and Coleman, *op.cit.*, pp. 142–3. In 1522 and 1523 wool prices also slumped in sympathy, Bowden, 'Agricultural Prices', *loc.cit.*, p. 841.

[50] B.L. Harl. MS. 7571, fo. 33v. – misdated in *L. & P.*, iv (3), appendix 1; the entries pertaining to the mayoralty of Thomas Banwell (1524–5) precede those for Julian Nethermill's year (1523–4).

between them 'to goo to a Comen Welthe for makynge of Clothe',[51] presumably an attempt at providing employment on a civic basis during the emergency and at a time when the Weavers were again complaining at receiving truck wages.[52] For only a serious unemployment situation would have emboldened the Leet to abrogate the established protectionist rights of Crafts such as the Cappers, who had always (and as recently as 1520) restricted the number of apprentices *per* master to two, by now legislating that 'euery Craftes-mane within this Citie shall fromehensfurthe take as meny prentises & Journeman as they woll accordyng to the liberties of this Citie, eny acte or caue tofore maid to the contrary notwithstandynge'.[53] The context of this order was made explicit in 1525 when it was stated categorically that 'moche idlenes & pouertie is greatelie encreassed within this Citie'.[54]

But dearth and depression were not the end of Coventry's troubles. The *coup de grâce* was administered by the king of England himself as he plunged into vain-glorious war on the heels of his imperial colleague. For the financing of this particular adventure involved a crippling burden of taxation, the grant of which was bitterly opposed both in Parliament and without. One contemporary indeed observed that it could not be remembered 'that euer there was geuen to anyoone of the . . . kinges auncestours half somoche at oone graunte',[55] while even Thomas Cromwell feared that the subsidy would withdraw all the money from the realm into the royal treasury.[56] So far were the localities out of sympathy with central government that the payment of the anticipation in 1523 aroused deep suspicion at Coventry. The Marquis of Dorset had to write specially to reassure the mayor that bills under the privy seal would indeed be made out to every contributor when the cash was delivered, 'which order ye shall not nede to mistrust for my said lord [Wolsey] hath soo expressely writen unto me for he saith that order is taken for all the hoole Realme which he cannot breke for oon shire aloone'.[57]

[51] *Ibid.*, fo. 31r.   [52] *L.B.*, p. 689.

[53] *L.B.*, pp. 573, 670; p. 687 – probably a direct outcome of the 1523 census, *infra* pp. 207–15.

[54] *L.B.*, p. 690.   [55] B.L. Bibl. Cotton Titus B1, fo. 117r.

[56] Dietz, *op.cit.*, p. 96, n. 37; cf. *Suffolk in 1524: Subsidy Returns*, ed. S.H.A.H. (Suffolk Green Books, x, 1910), pp. ix–x.

[57] C.R.O. A79, vol. i, p. 596: dated Tuesday after Holy Rood day, which almost certainly refers to 3 May 1523. Letters under the Privy Seal promising repayment are dated 19 May, C.R.O. B60.

In view of the substantial sums involved the desire for an unambiguous acknowledgement of royal indebtedness was understandable. Some time after August 1522, the city was assessed of its wealth in lands and goods, and on 3 October the first exaction was taken. 116 of the wealthiest inhabitants, and the two great fraternities – the Trinity and Corpus Christi Gilds – between them contributed the massive total of £1,009.[58] In November, a further five persons contributed £36, and in the following May or before, all those with lands worth between £1 and £20, or with goods valued at £5–£20, 194 persons in all, paid a further £150.[59] But even this was only to anticipate. The first instalment of the subsidy itself amounted to £463 in 1524; and the second to a further £386 a year later.[60] Between 1522 and 1525, therefore, the city contributed no less than £2,044 to the royal treasury. The sheer magnitude of this colossal sum may only be fully comprehended when it is measured against the city's normal annual tax quota – a mere £50.[61] However unrealistic this figure may have been when Coventry was prosperous; in straitened circumstances, it could certainly not afford to pay, as it now had to, the equivalent of over 40 annual instalments in fewer than four years.

It can thus have been no accident that open opposition to royal taxation at Coventry anticipated the situation at industrial Lavenham and elsewhere in East Anglia. Not only, as will be seen,[62] was conspiracy uncovered in 1523, but the local situation was so serious that Warwickshire as a whole seems to have successfully obtained remission from the Amicable Grant even *before* the uproar in the south-eastern counties of 1525. A royal letter, dated 28 April (almost a fortnight prior to the East Anglian affair) admits that in the county the people's 'powars & abilities be not correspondent & egall to their good willes . . . nor ther be able to make un to us payment of the sayed graunte with owt their extreme detryment & excessiue hinderaunce', and speaks of 'wayes of moderacion' instead.[63] In view of Wolsey's efforts to hold out for contributions to the grant, such a concession represents a remarkable indication of the extent to which the gravity of the local situation had forced itself onto the attention of central government.

[58] C.R.O. B58.   [59] C.R.O. B59; B60.

[60] P.R.O. E179/192/125; E179/192/130: the figure of £386 has been obtained by deducting the total for the foreigns from the tax paid by the county of Coventry as a whole.   [61] *L.B.*, pp. 533–5, 584, 741.

[62] *Infra* p. 253.   [63] C.R.O. A79, i, p. 55.

The chronology of depopulation

Analysis of the constituent factors in this prolonged crisis thus seems to indicate two major peaks: 1520–1 as the worst year for dearth, and 1523–4 at the culmination of the trade depression and just after the heaviest royal exactions had been taken. A year by year examination of the evidence for population movements appears to confirm this outline of sustained disaster and to emphasise its worst moments.

1520–1: The histogram (figure 1) shows that the proportion of rents lost to the Gild through vacated houses rose suddenly during this year from under 14 per cent to nearly 19 per cent of the possible total rental. In the context of the dearth it is thus tempting to seek the explanation in the parallel circumstances of the 1590s. A contemporary when recording the events of 1597, 'the third deare yeare', recounted the high price of corn, butter, cheese and eggs, and then concluded 'and all other victuall so extreame deare that many good householders sold up all they had and were faine to begge'.[64] It can hardly have been coincidence, therefore, that in April 1521 an official distinction between the deserving and undeserving poor was made for the first time in the city's history, and a decade in advance of central government thinking. Select beggars were now licensed to carry pouches bearing the city's arms, 'the signe of the Olyfaunt', while the remainder were commanded to depart within a night and day.[65] In the same year, membership of the humble Carpenters' fellowship dropped by 12.5 per cent.[66]

1521–2: Rent losses again rose perceptibly to 21 per cent of the possible total rental of the Corpus Christi Gild. A penetrating indication of the general scene of desolation, moreover, may be gained from the financial state of the largest property owner in the city. The assessors in the early autumn of 1522 discovered that, though the Priory's possessions were valued at £346, no less than £220 of this total or 63.6 per cent, was lost because of 'houses ther

[64] L.M. fo. 29v.

[65] *L.B.*, p. 677: the keeper of the Mill Lane gate was apparently also made responsible for 'the beggars' in 1521, C.R.O. A7(a), p. 63; G. R. Elton, 'An Early Tudor Poor Law', *Econ.H.R.*, 2nd ser., vi (1953), p. 56. The indexes in Phelps Brown and Hopkins, *loc.cit.*, pp. 193–4, show consumables at their highest price level since 1370, and builders' wage rates at their lowest since 1371.

[66] C.R.O. access. 3: A5, *passim*: based on a running analysis of membership as described in Phythian-Adams, 'Records of the Craft Gilds', *loc.cit.*, p. 271.

lyeng voied & in dekay'.[67] Significantly, there is also evidence from this year that immigrants were either refusing to settle or unable to set up shop in the blighted city. By May 1522 it had become clear that stranger craftsmen, who had been allowed two years to pay their substantially reduced admission fines of 10s. in 1518, were not paying their second 5s. instalment, for it was now enacted that sufficient sureties were to be found for that sum.[68]

1522–3: The histogram for this year indicates stability at the high level of vacant housing achieved in the previous twelve months, and there was even a small recovery in the total membership of the Carpenter's Craft.[69] It was perhaps this pause in the process of headlong decay which now encouraged the city fathers to take a second census with the obvious intention of measuring the extent of the demographic damage. As counted in June 1523, the figures revealed a drop of some 900 people on the 1520 total, a fall of 13.7 per cent within three years. Since, however, as will be shown below, it seems clear that at least two of the wards were under-counted in the earlier year, this crude proportional fall may have been higher still. Simultaneously the enumerators counted 565 'vake' or 'vakond' houses in the city, a figure which represented 26 per cent of all 'houses' (vacant houses plus all households).[70] Whatever the exact orders of magnitude involved, however, the need to take a second census so soon after the first certainly supports the view that a radical drop in the total population had taken place in the interim.

1523–4: The events of this year demonstrated how hopelessly optimistic the city government had been to assume that the crisis was over. The Gild's rent losses from vacant housing now increased to all but a quarter of the total rental. In the four years since 1520,

[67] C.R.O. A.96, fo. 91.

[68] *L.B.*, p. 679. In July 1523, the Craft of Shermen and Tailors 'hadd pleyn Aunswer by the Counseill', when they pleaded unsuccessfully for a return to the pre-1518 scale of fines for apprentices and others, B.L. Harl. MS. 7571, fo. 32.

[69] C.R.O. access. 3: A5, *passim*, and fo. 89. It is impossible to pin the start of the pause precisely, but slight evidence on empty housing in C.R.O. access. 100: Weavers 8 (unfol.) is suggestive. For three successive years, each beginning on 25 July, rent losses were as follows: 1520–1, total receipts from rents ('vakes a loude'): £8.19s.0d., 'vakes': £1.5s.0d.; 1521–2, receipts: £8.0s.3d., 'vakes': £1.10s.8d. (four dwellings); 1522–3, receipts: £8.1s.0d., 'vakes': £1.19s.2d. (ten dwellings, three of which had been vacant the previous year although temporarily re-occupied for the year in question. Only one had been empty for the whole year). Considerable mobility is thus implied (cf. *infra*, p. 303–4), but half the grand total had been vacated within the six months prior to 25 July 1523. Depopulation may thus not have been slowing down until the summer or early autumn.   [70] *Infra* pp. 196–8.

moreover, the Carpenters' Craft had fallen in numbers by 25 per cent.[71] So importunate had mendicants become, that a special officer was perforce appointed to ensure that 'no beggar of this Citie fromhensfurthe shall begge within the two parishe Churches of this Citie in tyme of Goddes seruice vsed ther'.[72]

1524–5: Though rent losses were now down by 5 per cent on the peak of the crisis, vacancies accounted nevertheless, for one fifth of the Corpus Christi Gild's total rental – a level which was still higher than that of 1520–1 during the worst of the dearth. In the same year – probably one of plague – the Trinity Gild was also losing almost 24 per cent of its larger gross rental from empty houses, a higher figure than its losses in 1485–6 when a third of its properties had been vacant.[73] Trouble over admission fines, moreover, underlined the rapid turn-over of potential citizens and strangers in particular. In 1525 it was 'now compleyned & enfourmed at this lete that meney of the said persons, so settyng vp ther craftes, do depart the Citie before thende of the said first yeire, & before eny peny of the said fyne of tene shelynges be payed'.[74] Strangers in fact were not even staying for one year before hastily moving on. Not only was the city being exploited as a result, but its own newly fledged apprentices must have been placed at a distinct disadvantage. After 1518, strangers were paying 5s. at the *end* of their first year and a further 5s. before the end of their second. The city's ex-apprentices, how-ever, were liable for a down payment of 6s. 8d. at the *beginning* of their first year – a particularly invidious state of affairs if strangers moved on before even half their fines were paid.[75] Accordingly in the spring of 1525 it was laid down that not only were strangers to pay their first 5s. at the *beginning* of their first year, and the second at the end of the *same* year, but also that native apprentices were now to pay their 6s. 8d. in two easier instalments – 3s. 4d. at setting up and 3s. 4d. at the end of their first year. Everyone was specifically obliged to find two sufficient sureties to be bound to the Master of each Craft concerned.[76]

---

[71] C.R.O. access. 3: A5, *passim*. For the drop in the Craft's apprentices *v. infra*, p. 215

[72] *L.B.*, p. 687.

[73] Templeman, *op.cit.*, pp. 84–93. For the correct dating of this incomplete rental *v. supra* p. 38 n. 19. No deduction from the total charge may be made in this case for fields and chief rents, but, if the sum of these had remained constant since 1485–6, the proportion of the rental lost through vacancies would rise to 27%.

[74] *L.B.*, p. 691.   [75] *L.B.*, p. 655.   [76] *L.B.*, p. 691.

This then was the culmination of a crisis which, as will be discussed in detail at a later stage in this study, shook the medieval city to its very foundations in demographic, economic and social terms. The severity of its impact, indeed, marks a major turning-point in the city's development. Before discussing the nature of this portentous change, however, it is essential to turn now to the character of the society which was to be thus affected. In doing so it is necessary to step aside from this diachronic analysis of the city's failing fortunes, and to examine the more enduring features of Coventry's socio-economic organisation which only a synchronic investigation can elicit.

Part III

Anatomy of a city

'The past is a foreign country: they do things differently there.'

(L. P. Hartley, *The Go-Between*, Harmondsworth, 1971, p. 7.)

... How could communities,
Degrees in schools, and brotherhoods in cities,
Peaceful commerce from dividable shores,
The primogenitive and due of birth,
Prerogative of age, crowns, sceptres, laurels,
But by degree, stand in authentic place?
(W. Shakespeare, *Troilus and Cressida*, I, iii.)

I Substantial housing in Pepper Lane, Bailey Lane ward, as it survived into the nineteenth century (Troughton drawings: C.R.O.)

4. *Introductory*

The 'desolation' of Coventry was so rapid and so dramatic that it prompts an obvious question: why was there not a revolution? In a city where, even in 1520, the population was packed together within the walls at a density of roughly 35 persons to the acre; in a society where a tiny percentage of privileged people held a disproportionate share of the total wealth; and in a community where unemployment, poverty and depopulation were familiar experiences; are we to assume that the threat of arms alone sufficed to keep the populace in order? Unrest and conspiracy there certainly were, as we shall see, but there is no evidence for revolutionary programmes involving social upheaval. In other words, not only were the leaders of society trusted – men like Julian Nethermill, at whose behest as mayor perhaps the 1523 census was taken, or Ralph Swillington, the Recorder – but above all, and admittedly in the short term only, the institutions of society held firm.

If then the second part of this book was concerned with economic and demographic change, it will be pertinent to concentrate now on the strength of continuity in the social fabric, and to test the quality of its communal muscle. To do so, it will be essential to view society as far as possible as a whole, an exercise that is not often practicable for urban historians of this period for want of source material. It is then peculiarly fortunate that Coventry is blessed with a remarkable series of records that allows us to catch intimate glimpses of late medieval urban society before its medieval character was finally eroded. The most unusual of these sources is the 1523 enumeration which will be analysed in part IV. To discuss this record in isolation and the strains that it reveals, however, would be to give a misleading impression of both the living society which it freezes into immobility within its folios, and of the enduring social structure of the city, only one facet of which does it delineate. This part, therefore, will concentrate not only on the 'household', but also on as many other aspects of contemporary social organisation as the documentation permits.

For many historians, the term 'social structure' has been restricted in its usage, being applied most commonly to the stratifications of 'class' or wealth. With regard to the late medieval period,

71

this has meant in practice that for those towns where other documentation is thin, too much reliance has had to be placed on the evidence of the 1523 lay subsidy, its assessment and collection. When, as in this case, the evidence is embarrassingly rich, there is thus no excuse for not attempting a more ambitious reconstruction.

To do so it will be necessary to use the term 'social structure' in a sense that is more akin to that of the social scientists. Given that no historical analysis can possibly probe as deeply as a modern investigation, however, the term here will have to be employed somewhat crudely. Stripped of jargon, it may perhaps be most simply defined as a description of the contemporary system of social positions and the socially prescribed relationships between the individuals occupying those positions. During his life, every individual pursued his own path through the structure of these positions, many of which, like those of husband, father, craftsman and citizen, might be occupied simultaneously, and none of which, obviously, was occupied for a whole life-time. All such positions, however, were defined by particular contexts. Some of them were formally recognised social groups: the household, the craft fellowship, a religious gild or the institutions of civic government. Others comprised informal groupings of people into common situations like the extended family, neighbourhoods or recognisable stratifications of wealth. It will be the aim of succeeding chapters, then, to discover how the biological life-cycle of the individual was related to the *social* process and how the occupancy of several key positions simultaneously helped to inter-connect the various groups and groupings concerned.

Faced with such clinical statements of intent, the reader may reasonably be forgiven his premonitory frissons of apprehension at the prospect of a parade of social skeletons bereft of individuality, life and culture. To this it is only possible to rejoin that it is a *whole* community that is to be dissected, and that at the least both the rhythms of life and the cultural context are inseparable from such an analysis. Indeed, the reconstruction that follows is based on three assumptions that are very relevant in this respect. First, an understanding of the anatomy of a community cannot be divorced from the pulse of its everyday routines. Secondly, and especially so at the period in question, no social analysis of an institution can concentrate only on its overt *raison d'être*: relationships at work, for example, were carried over into religious, military, recreational and other spare-time activities. Both social groups and social groupings have therefore to be viewed in the round and in their cultural contexts. Lastly, it is assumed that the contemporary use of language provides us with the most intimate link with the past which is available to us. In seeking to understand this, we can come as close as is possible to bridging the gap between the present and the past which it is the historian's mission to effect. It is only by appreciating the pre-conceptions that lie behind contemporary usages, and not be super-imposing modern terminologies like 'class', that the English historian can hope to evaluate at least some of the nuances which characterised the 'foreign' cultures even of our own long-since dead.

5. The working context

To the outsider, including the historian, the vibrance, vitality and individual character of a town may be gauged from the every-day bustle of its streets. The daily and weekly round – the normal rhythms of life itself, represent the heart-beats of an urban community. For late medieval citizens, however, these were very different from our own experience. In an age when the only artificial illumination available to the mass of people was gained from fire-light or tallow-dips, the length of the working day depended essentially on the hours of day-light, which naturally varied from winter to summer. At Coventry, the year had been artificially divided a century earlier between 'yeme' or winter (from 1 November to 2 February) – when the city waits played more frequently and for longer than in any other quarter – and the remaining nine months.[1] Confusion may have arisen, however, when this division was re-defined by Michaelmas (29 September) and the movable feast of Easter.[2] Nor is it clear how quickly or to what extent the transition from hours of variable length (according to the season) to those of regular length was effected as the city churches added clocks to their towers.[3]

During the first half of each quarter-year for four nights a week, and for five in winter, the waits piped and trumpeted their ways through different parts of the city. Normally beginning at 2 a.m., but at midnight in winter, they only ceased playing at 4 a.m., when most citizens were waking up.[4] For it was at this time that the day-bell in each of the two parish churches was then rung by the deacons.[5] Indeed, the fourteenth century, so-called 'Dyers' ' bell in St John's Bablake was still being rung at 4 a.m. in the first half of the nineteenth century.[6] At day-bell, the night-watch stood down, the city gates were opened, and the conduits were unlocked.[7] Not long after, most of the inhabitants were rising from their rest. Unemployed carpenters, tilers, masons, dawbers and labourers for

[1] L.B., pp. 43, 807, 777; Poole, *Coventry: its History and Antiquities* (London and Coventry, 1870), p. 56.   [2] L.B., pp. 21, 673.
[3] *'The* clok' (my italics) was to 'be duly kept' in 1468, L.B., pp. 388, 335.
[4] Poole, *op.cit.*, p. 56.   [5] L.B., p. 338; Sharp, *Antiquities*, p. 122.
[6] Sharp, *Antiquities*, p. 152.
[7] L.B., pp. 253, 254, 208, (cf. C.R.O. A3(b), pp. 56, 78), 632.

example had to appear with their tools at the city's central cross-roads at 5 a.m. in hope of work.[8] Journeymen cappers too, who had had their working hours lengthened in 1520, were also expected to start at 5 a.m. in their masters' houses.[9] By this time, therefore, much of the adult male population would have been coming onto the streets, a fact which accounts for the prohibition against mastiff dogs being allowed to roam at large after this hour in summer (but 7 a.m. in winter).[10]

In winter, by contrast, and possibly all the year round for those higher up society, the working day may not have begun until 6 a.m. Later inscriptions (but the earliest recorded) on the bells of St Michael's and St John's may well recite an older tradition:

I ring at six, to let men know
When too and from theair worke to go. 1675.[11]

Certainly journeymen cappers had not been expected to start until 6 a.m. in 1496, and this continued to be the case in the winter months, even in 1520.[12] Similarly, at the end of the sixteenth century, each master carpenter was instructed not to work out of his house 'befor he goeth to his dayes worke . . . at sixe of the clock in the mornynge'.[13] That time also makes sense of two relevant Leet ordinances. One, agreed during the crisis in October 1520, laid down that the city gates were not to be opened *until* 5 a.m., presumably to allow enough time for residents in the suburbs to walk to their places of work.[14] In an effort to avoid time-wasting recreation, moreover, the Leet also forbade the playing of bowls near the Charterhouse (outside the city) before 6 a.m.[15] – a further indirect indication that this was the normal time for many to begin work. Throughout the year, by contrast, the mayor's day began somewhat later – at 7 a.m. when he was escorted to church.[16]

From such beginnings, the medieval working day extended for twelve to fourteen hours. If the 1495 statute was observed, however, the day was broken by set times for meals, which for many employees were provided by their masters. During most of the year, half an hour was allowed for breakfast, an hour for 'dinner', and half an hour for 'noon-meat'. Only between mid May and mid August

[8] *L.B.*, p. 807.   [9] *L.B.*, pp. 574, 673.   [10] *L.B.*, p. 623.
[11] Sharp, *Antiquities*, pp. 66, 152.   [12] *L.B.*, pp. 574, 673.
[13] C.R.O. access. 3: A5, fo. 2v.   [14] *L.B.*, p. 669.
[15] *L.B.*, p. 656.   [16] *L.B.*, p. 662.

was a siesta permitted, for which purpose the dinner-break was extended to 1½ hours. It may well be wondered, however, whether this last restriction, which was aimed in particular at what was obviously a widespread custom of 'longe tyme sleping at after none' throughout the year, was very effective, particularly in a city where unemployment and under-employment were rife.[17] It was nevertheless a long day. In both summer and winter, journeymen cappers did not finish until 7 p.m., though clearly these hours were not tightly observed.[18] Others may have finished an hour earlier, as indeed had the cappers themselves in 1496.[19] The carpenters were also said to leave work at 6 p.m. in 1598, while significantly the ban on bowling was re-imposed at this time.[20] It is noteworthy that it was only from 7 p.m. in winter and 8 p.m. in summer that mastiffs were once again let roam, by which time many of the menfolk would have returned home.[21] The 1520 emergency regulation also laid down that the gates should be shut by 8 p.m., so that by then, even in normal circumstances, most extra-mural dwellers would probably have been expected to be back in their homes.[22]

As it had begun, the day ended correspondingly early. At 8 p.m., the second deacon of Holy Trinity (and no doubt his counterpart in St Michael's) sang Curfew before searching the church 'lest ther be any person lyeng in any sete or corner', and then locked the door.[23] The clerks of both parish churches had also to ring curfew each night.[24] In normal times, at 9 p.m., the watch having been assembled and sworn, the conduits and the city gates were locked.[25] At that time too, the lanterns which had hung outside the doors of innkeepers and of the more substantial householders since dusk on moonless winter nights were then extinguished.[26] The only permissible outside activity (apart from the waits and the watch) after that hour, was the disposal of unsociably smelly fish-water.[27]

Such in outline was the shape of the average urban day, which in its turn should be set against the usual rhythm of the week. This pattern was dictated more by the victualling requirements of the town, than by the demands of manufacturing, since every day saw at least one market. It was this feature more than any other, perhaps,

[17] *Statutes of the Realm*, 11 Henry VII, cap. 22, sec. iv.
[18] *L.B.*, pp. 673, 693.　　　[19] *L.B.*, p. 574.
[20] C.R.O. access. 3: A5, fo. 2v.; *L.B.*, p. 656.　　　[21] *L.B.*, p. 623.
[22] *L.B.*, p. 669.　　　[23] Sharp, *Antiquities*, p. 123.
[24] *L.B.*, p. 338.　　　[25] *L.B.*, pp. 256, 253, 208, 254.
[26] *L.B.*, pp. 234, 777.　　　[27] *L.B.*, p. 632.

that most overtly marked off the complexity of a city economy from the simplicity of the market town since industrial activities took place in houses, back-yards or even outside the city.

The corn market on Monday, was followed on Tuesday by a meat market and the sale of hides, and on Wednesday by a visit of the Warwick and country bakers.[28] This mid-point in the week was also an important Council House day, when the mayor and aldermen usually met and received petitions. Thursday witnessed further meat sales.[29] Friday and Saturday, however, were the climax of the working week, for the activities of the former, the main marketing day, spilled over into Saturday. On Friday morning, the mayor was escorted to Jesus Mass in St Michael's church before repairing, in his capacity as clerk of the market, to the Cross Cheaping, where, by 9 a.m., he should have inspected the fish there laid-out for sale on this fish-eating day.[30] Friday was probably also the most important corn market day of the week, while the city was again visited by the Warwick and country bakers.[31] Probably because of the crush, carts bearing hurdles, wood, charcoal and sea-coal were then forbidden in the streets, having presumably brought in their loads the previous day.[32] On Fridays too, the great covered cloth-market, the Drapery, was then the only venue for large cloth sales.[33] In the evening, the inhabitants of Cross Cheaping – the chief open-market area – had to collect the muck and sweepings left during the day for removal on the Saturday.[34]

Meanwhile, the butchers had been preparing for Saturday's meat market. Probably bull-baiting (which was held to improve the tender qualities of the meat),[35] as well as slaughtering and scalding, took place on Thursdays and Fridays, prior to the sale of hides on Saturday morning.[36] The markets for both meat and sea-fish opened at 7 a.m.; while those for bread and corn began two hours later.[37] As

[28] *L.B.*, pp. 780, 223, 717, 799.

[29] *L.B.*, pp. 71, 571, 599, 653; 26, 585, 780.

[30] *L.B.*, p. 662: for 'Jesus Mass', *infra* p. 118 n. 2; *L.B.*, pp. 29, 646–7.

[31] *L.B.*, pp. 223, 717, 799.   [32] *L.B.*, pp. 28, 739.

[33] *L.B.*, pp. 100, 104.   [34] *L.B.*, p. 624.

[35] I am indebted to my colleague, Dr Claude Luttrell for this information and the loan of his two interesting articles 'Baiting of Bulls and Boars in the Middle English "Cleanness"', *Notes and Queries*, cxcvii (1952), pp. 23–4; cci (1956), pp. 398–401. At Coventry, it was compulsory to bait bulls before slaughter, *L.B.*, p. 58.

[36] *L.B.*, pp. 694, 715. The scalding-house was in Palmer's Lane (*L.B.*, p. 232), near both the Butchery area and the Bull ring (*L.B.*, p. 83). cf. *L.B.*, pp. 271, 279.

[37] *L.B.*, pp. 651, 665–6; C.R.O., access. 18, A110, rule 15 quoting an otherwise lost Leet ordinance of 1529.

many as three to seven hours were allowed for preferential sales to Coventry citizens, before outsiders were admitted.[38] However, no sea-fish other than fresh cod could be sold after 2 p.m., at which time the gutters were to be washed down, while the sellers of clout leather were expected to pack up at 4 p.m.[39] The market would have probably closed soon after.

For those not concerned with the market, most of Saturday was still a working day. Both the tilers and the cardmakers would have already been at their place of work seven or eight hours by 1 p.m. when, as on vigil evens, they were forbidden to continue working.[40] They may not have been representative, however. Holy Trinity's first deacon was to 'ryng noon' every Saturday or holy even – possibly a signal to stop work.[41] Certainly the master weaver was prohibited from working his broad loom on vigil Saturday afternoons, and likewise his narrow loom 'excepte that he may fall his worke by thre of the clocke then next folowing'.[42] The later time, however, is probably nearer the truth with regard to ordinary Saturdays. The cappers, for example, were forbidden to mill caps 'on the Saterday after evunsong' (which *began* at 3 p.m.) 'nor the Sonday tyll evunsong be don'.[43] This makes better sense of the rule that weavers' journeymen were not to be paid until 'the Satturday at nyght' – thus indicating that they (and their masters) then normally worked for more like a full day.[44] Saturday, indeed, was clearly pay-day, for it was then that the Common Serjant also had to wait upon the Chamberlains to see their workmen paid.[45] It thus seems likely that this was the only week-day when the workman would have had both the money and, after his evening meal, perhaps the leisure, to patronise his local ale-house for an extended period. It was, finally, on Saturdays too, that the streets before every tenement had to be swept prior to inspection by the Common Serjeant on Sunday afternoon and Monday.[46]

For those in manufacturing at least, Sunday was largely a day of rest. A journeyman weaver who remained unpaid on Saturday, for example, was expected not to complain until the following Mon-

---

[38] *L.B.*, p. 666.
[39] *L.B.*, pp. 651, 680, 555; C.R.O. access. 241, orig. fo. 2.
[40] Reader 4, fos. 217v., 95v.   [41] Sharp, *Antiquities*, p. 122.
[42] C.R.O. access. 34: Weavers 2a, no. 19.
[43] *L.B.*, p. 640; Sharp, *Antiquities*, p. 123.
[44] C.R.O. access. 34: Weavers 2a, no. 22.
[45] *L.B.*, pp. 622–3.   [46] *L.B.*, pp. 23, 30, 587.

day,[47] though, as we have seen, cappers were allowed to mill caps after Sunday evensong.[48] It is also clear that many of those who had received their wages then had recourse to the city's inns and ale-houses. In 1539, such visits for 'brekefastes or drynkynges at Matyns, high masse or evensong tymes on the Sondays or holydayes'[49] were forbidden. No doubt many masters' fellowships, like the Drapers, attended church services in a body with their apprentices in attendance;[50] and certainly the city's rulers marked the day with dignity. The mayor processed to church for matins and evensong, while the aldermen were expected to wear their scarlet robes.[51] However, under a contemporary gloss 'Sonday market', the Leet had to lay down in 1493 that no fletcher or any other craftsman was to open his shop or sell anything upon Sunday 'in tyme of dyuyne seruice' – a clear indication that trading continued over the week-end.[52] Certain personal services were also allowed. A smith was then obliged to shoe the horses of strangers, while a barber could shave (under licence from the mayor) 'a seke man or a weyfareng man that comethe to this Citie that hathe nede to-be shavon'.[53] Nevertheless for most of the population, Sunday was the one day of the average week in which extended recreation could be taken. In summer at least, it was doubtless then, that many enjoyed the 'shutyngs, rennynges, daunsynges, bowelyng aleyes and other their disportes' on Whitley Common a mile to the south of the city.[54]

Even a survey as bald as this, which ignores seasonal rhythms and the annual cycle of feasts, fasts and extended festivities, indicates immediately that the tightness of the social structure, which is now to be discussed, was reflected in the organised communal rhythm of everyday living. The *minutiae* of life in pre-Reformation society were determined in a manner more akin to that of a school or the forces in the modern world – not least, perhaps, because the waking hours of the week were so continuously occupied that, in normal times, there were few occasions when malcontents could regularly congregate in any number and so threaten the social order. The place of every individual in such a society was correspondingly much more precisely defined.

[47] C.R.O. access. 34: Weavers 2a, no. 22.   [48] *L.B.*, p. 640.
[49] *L.B.*, pp. 739; cf. p. 812.   [50] Reader 4, fo. 93.
[51] *L.B.*, pp. 662, 812–13.   [52] *L.B.*, p. 547.
[53] *L.B.*, pp. 185, 226.   [54] C.R.O. F.4; *L.B.*, p. 508.

6. *Formal groups (i) The household*

This consideration of every-day routines leads naturally into a review of the arena in which most of life was carried out – the house and the workshop. In particular it underlines the fact that a fully employed journeyman at least, cannot have been free to spend more than four to five *waking* hours at most each weekday in his own home. Not only did he labour most of his day at his master's house, but even when he was at home he was severely limited in the amount of work he was allowed to do there. Journeymen cappers in 1520 were only permitted 'to ffreshe and scower old Bonettes in ther own howsys'.[1] Similarly, a healthy journeyman cordwainer in 1577 was not allowed even to cobble, except when 'mendynge of his owne shoes, bootes or slyppers, or of his wyfe, children or famelye'.[2] For the urban journeyman the so-called 'domestic system' meant work outside his own home. There was thus a fundamental division, not often commented upon by historians, between, on the one hand, those whose dwellings were deserted daily by the menfolk, and probably any others of their families who were old enough to go out to work; and on the other hand, those homes where the inmates both lived and worked together with, in some cases, daily outside additions.

This division was recognised by contemporaries who drew a distinction between householders and cottagers. The former term was usually restricted in its meaning. In 1536, for example, it was laid down by the Leet that 'euery householder of this Citie, which is not associat to some Crafte, shal-be associat & bere with some Craft before Whitsontyde next' – a statement which was later glossed in the margin as 'Euery ffreeman to hold off some Company.'[3] An agreement between the Cappers and the Cardmakers in 1531 was even more specific in speaking of 'euery householder or Shop-keper of euery of the seid companyes',[4] while, in 1577, the Cordwainers' rules explicitly referred to the currier who was 'an howseholder or occupier for hymselfe, and not a Journeyman nor a covenaunte servaunte'.[5]

---

[1] *L.B.*, p. 673.

[2] C.R.O. access. 14: A98, rule no. 16. For a sweeping exception to this generalisation with regard to metal-workers cf. *L.B.*, p. 185 (1436).   [3] *L.B.*, p. 724.

[4] *L.B.*, p. 709.   [5] C.R.O. access. 14: A98, rule no. 15.

Contemporaries in fact assumed that a household comprised a larger entity than that living in a cottage, basically because the former included, or could include either in-servants or out-servants. Regulations prohibiting the sweeping of muck into the river Sherbourne laid penalties on 'euery housholder that is offendeth by hymself, his wyff, his seruaunt, or otherwise'.[6] The obligations of cottagers were correspondingly slighter. In raising money for the repair of the conduits, for example, a distinction was drawn between those inhabitants 'hauyng & openyng a hall durre', who paid 1d. quarterly, a shop paying a half penny, and every cottager who paid likewise.[7]

This distinction was reflected in the housing itself. Cottages can have consisted of little more than one chamber, though we do hear of one case where there was possibly a chamber also above.[8] Even the simplest houses, on the other hand, included a hall with one solar. In most cases, a workshop fronted onto the street, and the hall could only be reached through it.[9] The living and working areas of houses in fact had to be larger to accommodate more people. Familial groups containing living-in servants were over twice as big on average as those that did not, though it is clear that even some cottages contained in-servants.[10]

It is in these domestic contexts, therefore, that the life-cycles of both males and females should be understood. The years of childhood, however, are something of a mystery. In whatever way one reads the figures that are discussed in detail in part IV, it is clear that there were proportionately fewer children in the population of

---

[6] *L.B.*, p. 721.

[7] *L.B.*, p. 586. Cf. pp. 517, 552. No doubt many 'shops' so described were simply subdivisions of larger buildings. They appear to have been usually let with chambers 'above' and/or even 'under' them, e.g. C.R.O. C183, 187. That some distinction was also drawn between householders and cottagers with regard to their respective rights of common is implied in the customs of the neighbouring manor of Stoneleigh (*c.* 1392), where it is stated that 'vbicumque tenentes manerii communicant cum aliis vicinis per certa loco et ipsi per certa loco communicabunt cum eisdem vt ipsi de Coventre exceptis cotagiariis de Couentre qui terram in campis non habent habent communam in solo manerii', *The Stoneleigh Leger Book*, ed. R. H. Hilton (Dugdale Society, xxiv, 1960), p. 101.

[8] Templeman (ed.), *The Records of the Guild of the Holy Trinity*, pp. 66–7, *sub* Palmer Lane.

[9] A number of such houses from different parts of the city are currently being reconstructed in Spon Street, with suggested plans of room-functions attached. For more detailed analyses cf. the studies cited *supra*, p. 34, nn. 5 and 6.

[10] *Infra*, p. 239, table 29.

Coventry in the 1520s than was to be the case in most places at a later date in pre-industrial times.[11] In those homes where there were children, they were most often numbered in only ones or twos, so there can be no doubting the heavy incidence of infant and child-mortality. Strong affection for babies there must have been: the well-known Coventry carol speaks fondly of the 'yongling' Jesus – a term which probably reflects widespread usage.[12] Nevertheless, children did not achieve their own social *persona* until adolescence. In only one ward of the city in 1523 did the enumerators even bother to give a sex to the children counted, let alone catalogue their names. Significantly, too, the terminology used in this single case is very revealing. Instead of describing children as boys or girls, the enumerator often called them manikins or womankins – little men or little women – that is in terms which were indicative of what they were to become, rather than what they were.[13] Similarly, the male victims of the massacre of the Innocents, in one of the Corpus Christi pageants, were described as 'man-chyldur' and not as boys.[14] This use of language fully bears out the observations of Philippe Ariès to the effect that at this time children were viewed as potential adults and were therefore dressed as such. It was not until much later that the costumes of European children reflected their actual age.[15]

Childhood, which in the poorer houses at least must have been in practice almost a fatherless experience, ended only when the child left home, at about which time he or she may have been also confirmed. The age of confirmation is not known directly, but by the time a child had gone into service he or she was expected to have taken their first communion. The 1523 census specifically distin-guished between men and their wives, 'houseling people' and chil-dren, and closer inspection shows that the communicants in ques-

[11] *Infra*, pp. 233–5
[12] *Two Coventry Corpus Christi Plays*, 2nd edn, ed. Hardin Craig (Early English Text Society, extra series, lxxxvii, 1957), p. 32. Cf. p. 46 where Mary addresses the infant Jesus as 'my darlyng Dere,/My myrthe, my joie, and al my chere!'.
[13] Broadgate ward. This anyway seems the best interpretation to put on the words rendered as 'menkynnys' or 'menskynnes' and on 'wemenkynnys'.
[14] Craig, *op.cit.*, p. 29. When the Broadgate enumerator did not use the terms described in the preceding note, he too referred to 'menchyld[re]n' or to 'weme[n]chyld[re]n'.
[15] Philippe Ariès, *Centuries of Childhood*, translated by Robert Baldick (London, 1962), p. 50.

tion were the servants.[16] Whether a boy went into service earlier than a girl we do not know, but it seems very probable as well as logical that, for the former, service began at about the age he went into tithing – a system of thus ensuring good behaviour amongst the males of twelve years and over in each ward.[17] It appears likely that only in the wealthier households did boys remain at home after that age. In the middle of the sixteenth century it was declared that a draper could apprentice his own son at 14, but that others might only be indentured at 16. The same may have been true of the Mercers, the Dyers and, in view of their heavily male labour-intensive trade, the Butchers.[18]

Once again the contemporary use of language is instructive. In the Corpus Christi play about the Disputation in the Temple, Christ, whose age at this point was traditionally taken to have been twelve, was alternately described not only as child, but also as 'son', 'page' and 'lad'. In the Gosford enumeration of 1523 serving 'lads' were distinguished from 'maids'.[19] Not only were adolescents thus recognised for what they were, but, in the case of males, a further description was used to cover the whole age-group between apprenticeship and marriage. In the earliest Drapers' ordinances, for example, an indenturing fee was only to be taken by a master if he 'Takyth any yong man to be hys prentes yf he kepe the seyd yong man In hys house and shope the space of vj wekes.'[20] The age-range of this social categorisation was made explicit in a rule passed by the Carpenters in 1561, which laid down that 'nother maryed man nor yonge man (was) to be bound as prentis excepte he keppe hym in his own house at meate, drynke, and lodgynge'.[21] References to 'the yonge men that arre & be to begyn and sett up' and to the rule 'that no yong man unmarryed take any prentys till he haue occupied iij years at the least', are further corroborations of this definition.[22]

The duration of this period in a young man's life is however very

---

[16] *Infra*, appendix 1, and p. 229. n. 8. It may be wondered whether children attended church at all before confirmation.

[17] For a probable tithing list, *infra* pp. 229–30.

[18] Reader 4, fo. 93; *infra*, p. 228.

[19] Craig, *op.cit.*, pp. 68, 56, 57; C.R.O. w. 1405.

[20] C.R.O. access. 154: Drapers 1c, fo. 2.

[21] C.R.O. access. 3: A5, fo. 184.

[22] C.R.O. access. 14: A99 (*sub* 1566), fo. 9; access. 154: Drapers 1c, fo. 64. For 'yong beginners' cf. P.C.C., 17 Ayloffe, 6 Alenger.

hard to determine. The age at which an apprenticeship was undertaken, the number of years indentured, and in the cases of those
who went on to become master craftsmen eventually, the length of
time endured as a journeyman before setting up shop, were all
variable. Only the Drapers' rule already quoted indicates the age at
which apprenticeship away from home was expected to begin – at
sixteen, but this wealthy fellowship may not have been typical of
other Crafts. More definitely, the length of apprenticeship also
fluctuated. At one end of the scale, the humble Carpenters' Craft
expected this to last only five years; though a seven years stint was
required by the middling Crafts of the Weavers, Cappers and Hat-
makers; while at the upper end of the occupational structure, both
the Drapers and the Grocers appear to have demanded a nine year
apprenticeship.[23] With regard to any time spent by some as a journeyman before setting-up shop, the evidence is all but non-existent.
Such as it is, it simply confirms what we would expect – an unknown
number of craftsmen did experience such a transitional stage in
their lives.[24]

Of two matters, however, we can be certain. First, this was a
late-marrying population. Hajnal's ultra-cautious criterion by
which to prove the existence of this 'European marriage pattern'
from census results is 'if over 30 per cent of women 15 or over are
single'.[25] At Coventry in 1523, when all female servants (many of
whom were very probably *under* 15) and 96 unspecified females
(some of whom were clearly widows) are included, the percentage is
as high as 43 per cent. There is thus a safe enough margin, even
when allowances have been made for the factors just specified as
well as for the under-representation of children in six wards, within
which to admit the prevalence of late marriage in the city: in

[23] C.R.O. access. 3: A5, fo. 1; C.R.O. access. 34: Weavers 2a, fo. 3v.; *L.B.*, p. 573
(but cf. Cappers' accs., fo. 27 for apprenticeships of eight and nine years); *L.B.*,
p. 561; Reader 4, fo. 93; C.R.O. access. 15: A99, fo. 2v. (1551). It should be
emphasised that there was, of course, little alternative to taking up an apprenticeship. There were two schools for grammar in the city (one under the aegis of the
corporation, the other a gild school at Bablake), but neither can have been very large.
Almonry schools catered for a further fourteen scholars at the Priory and twelve at
the Charterhouse (*V.C.H. Warks.*, ii, pp. 318–21). For apprenticeships concluding
by the age of 21 *v*. P.C.C., 27 Alenger (1541); and by the age of 24, P.C.C., 23
Wrastley (1552).
[24] *Infra*, p. 144.
[25] J. Hajnal, 'European Marriage Patterns in Perspective', in D. V. Glass and
D. E. C. Eversley (eds.), *Population in History* (London, 1965), p. 136.

non-European areas, 'well under 20 per cent of women aged 15 or over are single'.[26]

Secondly, it is clear that the majority of men did not set up house, cottage or shop until they were married. Only a tiny minority of household heads in 1523 were 'single men' (61 out of 1,302 house-holders), and of these at least a third were widowers to judge from the fact that their homes contained children.[27] Where there was a delay before marriage, moreover, bachelor master cappers at least appear to have been betrothed within at most four years of setting-up shop.[28]

At the poorest levels of society, indeed, it would have been difficult to set up house at all without the contribution a girl would bring to her marriage, and wealthy citizens were convinced of the need for subsidies to this end. In 1501 Sir Robert Tate, a mercer of London though the son of a Coventry man and husband to a Coventry woman, left £33 for this purpose.[29] Similarly William Pysford in 1517 bequeathed 'unto xiij pour maidens towards their mariages xiij li that is to sey to every of them xxs'.[30] Perhaps this was an indication of the dowry a poor girl might be expected to find, for John Haddon too left £60 for 60 maidens 'to be gyven in houshold stuff as it shalbe thought most nedfull'.[31] It may be wondered indeed, whether wealthy householders took upon themselves to provide portions for their long-serving servants. Isabel Waide, for example, bequeathed £1 and a black gown to each of her women servants at 'theyre mariages'.[32]

Further up society, the wealth of the potential husband and wife were of vital importance in securing parental consent and hence in determining the timing of a marriage. When in 1508 Roger a Lee refused to be chamberlain of the city on the grounds of expense, it was discovered that 'the seid Roger had with his wif, oon John Pachette's doughter, in redy money & plate xxxli., and also it was right well knowen that he hadde right largely of his owne, or els the seid John Pachet wold not haue maried his doughter to hym'.[33]

---

[26] *Ibid.*, p. 136. For the overall breakdown of Coventry's population by household status *v.* appendix 3(a). Children are discussed on pp. 223–5, *infra.*
[27] For variations in household composition *v.* table 15 *infra.*
[28] Cappers' accs. *passim.*
[29] W. K. Jordan, *The Charities of London 1480–1660* (London, 1960), p. 405.
[30] P.C.C. 9 Ayloffe.   [31] 17 Ayloffe and cf. 22 Adeane.
[32] P.C.C. 27 Alenger.
[33] *L.B.*, p. 619. At this level of society, the greater merchants were of course intent

Marriage in fact represented the most important single step in an individual's career. Not only did it mark the late transition to a socially superior age-group from menial dependency in a household that was not necessarily that of a person's origin, but it also signalised the creation of a new domestic unit that was familial, economic and social in its implications. The pledging was thus both private and public. In the first stage a contract *per verba de praesente* was agreed between the parties, and as such was considered binding. Thus, when in 1521 William Byrd and Margery Pysford of Coventry were so contracted, their's was held to be a true marriage even though there had been no church wedding. When, therefore, Margery subsequently contracted a marriage 'de facto' and was wedded to William Morton in the chapel of Temple Grafton some miles from Coventry, she was then stated to be living in adultery with her 'husband'.[34]

The second stage in establishing a marriage, the actual wedding, was thus crucial in setting a public seal on the contract. As such it was held in the open-air: the porch of St Michael's church, for example, was known as 'the wedyng doore'.[35] The ceremony, moreover, was more than a family affair. Weddings were attended, on pain of fine for absenteeism, by all masters in the relevant fellowship: the Pinners, Tilers and Coopers; the Bowyers and Fletchers; the Cardmakers and Saddlers, the Curriers and Cordwainers; Smiths and Goldsmiths; Bakers, Weavers and Cappers; and the Dyers, Drapers and Mercers.[36] Members of the more humble Craft of Masons were, however, excused on work-days, though the journeymen organisations of the Dyers, Weavers and Tanners attended the weddings of their members.[37] With regard to the Tanners, indeed, all the journeymen too had to attend the marriages of masters, though their officers only were present at the weddings of out-brethren.[38]

on creating a propertied family line. Julian Nethermill's (now destroyed) tomb in St Michael's (1539–40) was one of the very earliest known in the country to portray the dead man kneeling in company with both his wife and all his children, Eric Mercer, *English Art 1553–1625*. The Oxford History of Art, 11 vols. (Oxford, 1962), vii, pp. 218–27.   [34] *L. & P.*, iv (3), no. 6127.   [35] P.C.C. 15 Thower.

[36] B.L. Harl. MS. 6466, fo. 7; *L.B.*, p. 206; C.R.O. access. 14: A98, rules nos. 8 and 15; *L.B.*, p. 685; C.R.O. access. 8: A110, rule no. 3; C.R.O. access. 34: Weavers 2a, fo. 2v.; Cappers' accs., fos. 24, 36, 59; Reader 4, fos. 116v., 92; C.R.O. access. 15: A99, fo. 2.

[37] *L.B.*, pp. 206, 694; C.R.O. access. 100: Weavers 2c; access. 241, orig. fo. 3.
[38] *Ibid.*, fo. 2v.

For a woman, marriage was the basic means of recognition by a craft fellowship: both the Butchers and the Tilers described their members as brothers and sisters.[39] Nevertheless, a wife's economic status derived solely from her husband's. It is notable that the 1523 census does not record the name of a single wife when her spouse was present: instead the words 'et uxor' are tagged on to the husband's name in each case. Only a handful of girls are known to have served short apprenticeships of a mere three years in previous centuries; none in the *early* sixteenth century.[40] Moreover, any 'sole woman' under 40 was specifically forbidden from setting up house by herself and was required instead either to share a chamber or to go into service until she was married.[41] Untrained at marriage, many women thus had to be instructed in their husbands' crafts where this was allowed, and to that extent would have had to accept at least temporarily a status not unlike that of a servant. Members of the Cappers' fellowship, for example, were, to 'teche noo poyntes of the Craft to noo person save to his prentiz and his wyf'.[42] But if some Crafts like the Cardmakers did allow a wife's participation,[43] yet others forbade the involvement of wives altogether. The Carpenters ordained that no man was to show the Craft's counsel 'to his wyfe, or to one other body, man, woman, or' chylde'.[44] Similarly, the draper, John Haddon, expressly forbade 'my wyf in any wise to entmedle' with his stock of cloth after his death.[45]

Certain tasks might also be held to be improper. The Weavers considered that for a master to set 'his wyffe or his doughter or ony woman servaunt to weyve in the brode loom . . . is a geyn all goode

---

[39] Reader 4, fos. 100, 218v.

[40] Levi Fox, 'The Coventry Gilds and Trading Companies', *loc.cit.*, p. 21. For reasons discussed *infra*, p. 88, it seems that Dr Fox might have been premature in inferring that 'spinsters' etc. may have undergone apprenticeships at this period. Those women who are recorded as practising trades (e.g. *ibid*., p. 23), frequently turn out to have been widows on closer inspection. Payments for sisterhood membership in a craft, particularly when made in company with the husband do not necessarily prove economic activity. The tiny number of female apprentices recorded in the late sixteenth century (*ibid*., pp. 21–2) may reflect a recent shift in the position of women, on which *v*. pp. 272–3, *infra*.

[41] *L.B.*, p. 568, a regulation that lowered the age-limit from 50 as laid down three years earlier, *L.B.*, p. 545. To judge from the context of the 1492 ordinance, this was part of a campaign against harlots in the city (cf. *L.B.*, p. 552).

[42] *L.B.*, p. 673.

[43] 'No maister not his wyfe, jorneyman, nor prentiz' was to work at certain tasks on specified holidays, Reader 4, fo. 95v.

[44] C.R.O. access. 3: A5, fo. 1.   [45] P.C.C. 17 Ayloffe.

order and honeste' – no doubt because they would have had to hitch up their dresses to operate the treadles.[46] The early seventeenth-century ordinances of the Bakers which, so they claimed, incorporated rules going back to the sixth year of King John, were also concerned to protect the decency of womenfolk and through them their men's own statuses. No wife was to 'carrye any breade to any Taverne, Inne, or alehowse, unlesse it be by urgente occasion, that her husbande or servaunte be oute of the waye, or ells have no servaunte to do it for them, And then to carry the same eyther in some handbaskett, or in their apprones pryvelye, but not in skepps or mawltsyves, or openly.'[47]

Nonetheless, it is likely that it was amongst the victualling or related trades (apart from the butchers) that women had the greatest independence. As elswhere, there were fish-wives and ale-wives, and at least one woman was known as a cake-baker, while others were candle-makers.[48]

In the poorer sections of society at least, most wives would have had to work at home while their husbands were out: it would have been essential to supplement the men's wages. Indeed it is clear that thread-making,[49] spinning and knitting – all female activities – involved considerable numbers. Without them, the textile and clothing industries would have collapsed. Standards of spinning were therefore maintained on a ward basis. Wool and yarn were weighed at the spinners' houses, the clothmaker being responsible for bringing faulty workers to the alderman for public punishment.[50] A wife's economic role at this level of society was consequently more independent of her daily absent husband, than that of her socially superior equivalent who pursued her own tasks under the same roof as her husband throughout the entire day.

[46] C.R.O. access. 34: Weavers 2a, fo. 4.

[47] C.R.O. access. 8: A110, rule no. 23.

[48] L.B., pp. 646, 688, 801, 723, 555.

[49] For some of the difficulties associated with assessing the importance of this industry, supra, p. 41, n. 6. Much of the problem clearly has to do with the fact that it was largely a female activity at the manufacturing end of the process and is thus inadequately evidenced in the sources. Cf. L. & P. i(1), 438; and C.R.O. access. 18: A96, passim, where in a survey of the whole city not one thread-maker is mentioned.

[50] L.B., pp. 658, 672–3, 707. An indication of the numbers that must have been involved may be derived from the scale of specific bequests: e.g. 100 pairs of cards and 100 'payre of whelys to spin' to 100 poor women (P.C.C. 22 Adeane); or to 100 poor women, 100 pair of cards and 30 wheels (P.C.C. 9 Ayloffe). Cf. P.C.C. 20 Porch.

The exact balance of the relationships between husband and wife in the domestic sphere is difficult to determine, but in the circumstances just outlined at the householder level, friction could not have been far away. It was thus probably no accident that economic roles at this level of society tended to be differentiated and that modes of address appear to have been highly formalised. A marked feature of the Corpus Christi plays, the texts of which were deeply rooted in the norms of contemporary behaviour, is the manner in which spouses not only addressed each other by their christian names, but also as 'husband' or 'sir', or 'wife' or 'dame'.[51] It can hardly be doubted that this was common practice at least in the presence of other people, though the use of christian names in wills might suggest that greater informality was the case in private. Within the semi-public confines of a servant-keeping household after all a wife would have had to sustain her considerable authority before the servants. In the case of the Tanners, both the master and the dame had the power to tell the keepers of the Craft whether or not a servant should be employed elsewhere.[52]

There is no need to rehearse the legal helplessness of wives at this period, but to infer from this that they were totally down-trodden and lacked influence within their own homes would be to caricature past reality. The need for cuck-stools 'to punysche skolders and chidders' shows beyond doubt that some husbands, despite their theoretical authority, required the assistance of society in controlling their wives.[53] Rough justice operated in an age when wives might beat their husbands, in a manner often illustrated on medieval misericords. Of necessity, a woman's main weapon remained her tongue. Nothing is more convincing in this connection than the rueful humour of the Weavers' Corpus Christi play, and its appeal to a commonly shared experience amongst its male audience:[54]

[51] Craig (ed.), *Two Coventry Corpus Christi Plays*, pp. 46–8, 50–1. Marital tension and mutual distrust are implicit in for example Julian Nethermill's expressed testamentory wishes regarding his last wife's actions after his death: 'and in case that the said Margerie . . . do take recover or haue duryng her liff her dower in the same lands and tenementes and wolnot releas her title and right thereof' to his son by an earlier marriage 'Then I woll that all my said legacies and bequests to her before . . . shalbe voide.' He directed his body to be buried beside his previous wife. P.C.C. 6 Alenger.
[52] C.R.O. access. 241, fo. 2v.   [53] *L.B.*, pp. 59, 186, 188.
[54] Craig (ed.), *op.cit.*, p. 48 and cf. p. 68, where the general point is repeated. The extract, however, also hints at social taboos on marriage between disparate age-groups.

JOSOFF . . .
How sey ye all this cumpany
Thatt be weddid asse well asse I?
        I wene that ye suffur moche woo;
For he thatt weddyth a yonge thyng
Mvst fullfyll all hir byddyng,
Or els ma he his handis wryng,
Or watur his iis when he wold syng;
        And that all you do know.
MARE. Why sey ye soo, sir? Ye be to blame.
JOSOFF. Dame, all this cumpany wyll say the same.
Ys itt not soo? Speyke, men, for schame!
        Tell you the trothe ase you well con!
For the that woll nott there wyffis plese
Ofte-tymis schall suffur moche dysees;
Therefore I holde hym well at es
        Thatt hathe to doo with non.

The formal division of male/female roles was reflected in the
social field. Women's parts in the Corpus Christi plays were taken
probably by 'young men': in 1524 we read *à propos* the Weavers'
pageant 'our lady – Rychard byrskow; Anne – Thomas Sogdyn'.[55]
Women probably sat separately in church – St Michael's at least
contained 'seats for lifes to women only' from 1564/5, while a
ceremony like that for the Purification of women was an all-female
affair.[56] With the possible exception of the Carpenters' Craft,
moreover, wives did not usually attend the frequent dinners and
drinkings held by the Crafts.[57] Even when the Queen presented
twelve bucks to the governing body, these were divided *inter alia*
between the mayor and his brethren on the one hand, and 'the
Mairasse & hir Sisters' on the other.[58] Wives were clearly debarred
from all Craft and civic offices, and as in economic matters, would
appear to have derived their social statuses from those of their
husbands. Mayors' wives wore the civic scarlet but were excluded
from the formal inauguration of the mayor in St Mary's Hall. Before
the officers transferred themselves to St Michael's church after the
ceremonial oath-taking, 'Old Mistress Maioris attended on by the
Maiors' and Sheriffs' wives & other officers' wives cometh to the

---

[55] C.R.O. access. 100: Weavers 11, *sub* '1524'.
[56] C.R.O. A166: extracts from St Michael's vestry book.
[57] E.g. C.R.O. access 3: A5, fos. 119v., 130.   [58] *L.B.*, pp. 405–6.

new Maior's house, and they fetch new Mistress Maioris to that Church, the new Maioresse, having the right hand place: they being attended on by the Towne Sergant after he hath taken his othe.'[59] What is particularly interesting in both these activities of the Mayoress and her colleagues is that they obviously had a social role to play (however it was derived) and played it as a group quite separately from their husbands. Social demarcation may have been even more sharply differentiated outside the household than that within it.

It is in all these circumstances of rigidly defined economic, domestic and social differences that the significance of the annual Hock Tuesday play must be assessed. In fifteenth-century War-wickshire and elsewhere, it was customary for the men to bind or heave the women on Hock Monday; and in a classic example of role reversal, for the wives to respond in like manner on the following day. At Coventry after 1416, this stylised popular ritual was trans-formed into a play-cum-game which nevertheless retained the popular core of the Hock Tuesday custom. In particular the drama emphasised 'how valiantly our English women for loue of their cuntree behaued themseluez', and how the local Danes (at the time of Ethelred) – and obviously played by men – were 'at the last conflict, beaten doun, ouercom, and many led captiue for triumph by our English weemen'.[60]

By contrast to this emphasis on ritualising the separateness of male and female roles, it is noticeable that widowhood or old age, like childhood, were not marked by social ceremonies which under-lined the relationships between the sexes. For a woman indeed, widowhood was a social version of old age and male/female roles could, to some limited extent, merge. On the death of a husband who had been a master craftsman it was clearly essential for the widow to be able to perpetuate the family business at least until her children went out to service. The widows of tanners, for instance, supervised tanning, while in the Cappers' accounts, such women were specifically described, in rather charming contemporary terms, as 'goodwives'.[61] In eight out of the ten cases concerned

---

[59] C.R.O. A34, fo. 269. There is no reason to doubt that this early-seventeenth-century description accurately reflects ancient tradition.

[60] Charles Phythian-Adams, 'Ceremony and the Citizen: The Communal Year at Coventry 1450–1550' in Clark and Slack (eds.), *Crisis and Order*, p. 69. Poole, *Coventry: its History and Antiquities*, p. 52.   [61] Cappers' accs. *passim*.

between 1523 and 1547 (where the husbands' careers may be also traced), each of these women continued their deceased husband's quarterage payments immediately after his death. The term, 'goodwife', in fact clearly referred to a woman who managed her husband's business, and it is thus significant that in the two exceptional cases amongst the Cappers, the same description was used three or four years *before* the husband's decease. In other words, it was also possible for a woman to take over if, and only if, her husband was too old or infirm. None of these women, however, remains in the record longer than the time it would have taken for their sons to complete their apprenticeships, and there was no question that widows might perpetuate the business by training up apprentices on their own account. In a draconian regulation, involving one of the highest financial penalties in their ordinances, for example, the Weavers ruled 'that ther schall no wyddewe of the seyd Crafte make no prentys, nor no Jorneyman to teche none seyche w[ith] a wyddew, upon the payn of xx^{ti}s. for to be payd as a for seyd that hath byn a vever's [*sic*] wyffe be for tyme'.[62]

Not only was a widow who failed to re-marry thus placed in a disadvantageous position, but there were also major demographic obstacles in the way of taking on a new spouse. In a society where for every 72 males of servant-age or above there were 100 females,[63] a widow needed to be wealthy, or still young and attractive, or both, to achieve a second or third marriage. There were thus nearly nine times as many widows as widowers (in both cases actual *and* presumed) heading households in 1523.[64] Of the unambiguous cases, one in five widows still had children at home, while nearly a third of such households contained servants. These last, however, were the lucky ones. Roughly half the known widows lived alone, many of them in extreme poverty to judge from their *nil* assessments and low rents in the 1522 survey.[65] Indeed, even at the commoner level, a widow was expected to do with less than a widower. At Ford's hospital, where lodging was provided, a couple received 7½d. a week, and so did a surviving widower after the death of his wife. A widow however received only 3½d. on the death of her husband, though two widows who shared were allowed the full sum.[66]

The contrast between the situations of men and women at this

[62] C.R.O. access., 34: Weavers 2a, fo. 3v.   [63] *Infra*, table 13.
[64] *Infra*, tables 14 and 15.   [65] *Infra*, table 15; and C.R.O. A96, *passim*.
[66] P.C.C. 9 Ayloffe.

stage of the life-cycle was thus most marked. For a man, advanced years brought an enhanced status – Shakespeare's 'prerogative of age' – as succeeding chapters will demonstrate. In the meantime, it is sufficient to note that even in a city like Coventry where everything of importance was recorded in writing, considerable weight was still placed on oral tradition. On some important matters, the old could then act as the repositories and the guardians of local custom. Thus in 1472 a sworn declaration with regard to rights of common was attested by 30 old men 'In alsmoche as for oure gret ages be liklyhode wee may not long abyde in this erthely lyfe'.[67] 23 of these were aged over sixty, since this seems to have been the point at which old age was customarily taken to date. The provision of Ford's hospital for the elderly, for example, fixed the bottom age limit at sixty 'or nygh upon that age'.[68] The proviso in this case, however, might be significant, for survival beyond sixty for men may well have been unusual. One contemporary at least saw 'the best age' as between thirty and forty,[69] and evidence from the Cappers' records indicates that on average a man's working life at least was over by forty-five to fifty even in this relatively prosperous craft.[70] It may therefore be relevant to note that seven of the 30 old men mentioned above were in their forties or fifties. The surplus of widows over widowers in the 1523 census is thus not to be accounted for simply in terms of successful re-marriages by the latter. It seems more likely than not that women often outlived their men-folk even at this period despite the risks of child-birth.

At the commoner level, the change in the status of a household unit brought about by death was therefore publicly acknowledged and witnessed. Those that were wealthy enough, paid for the tolling of bells for their friends,[71] while there were clearly established procedures with regard to funerals at different strata of society. At the aldermanic grade, the details of these customary practices are not known,[72] but at the Craft level and, as in the case of weddings, the whole fellowship was involved. It was expected of the Tilers, for example, 'that if ther be ony man of the lyuerey ded, or his wyfe, or his chyld, that they shallen come to gydur to the dyryge and to the masse, and there for to offer at the same owre that thei benne a

---

[67] C.R.O. F4.   [68] P.C.C. 9 Ayloffe.
[69] L.M. fo. 19v.   [70] *Infra*, pp. 230–1.   [71] *L.B.*, p. 585.
[72] P.C.C. 1 Alenger: obits for 'men of worshipe' appear to have employed as many as ten priests, three clerks and two children, C.R.O. C210.

symond for to comen'.[73] The custom then, was not restricted to the masters themselves. The Weavers' accounts record mortuary payments for wives and children, while the Tanners' journeymen even attended the 'Buryings of all in-breethren and sisters and all the Chilldren of euerie Mr of the maistors.'[74] The ceremony began with a procession – the whole Drapers' fellowship for example was accustomed 'to feche and bere the corse to churche' – and probably ended with a drinking or a breakfast.[75]

Tempting though it is to describe such ceremonies as marking the extinction of the social personality, the system of trentals, obits and accompanying drinkings ensured that the memory of the most wealthy at least was constantly re-affirmed in public. It is not often appreciated that obits took place with the pall-covered funeral 'hearse' (a frame for candles which stood *over* the bier) standing before the congregation as a last physical symbol of contact with the person being commemorated.[76] At a lower level of society too, the deceased were similarly apprehended as still standing in relation to the living community. The first deacon of Holy Trinity, for example, was to go 'on All halowe day, at evyn, a mong the pepyll, in the northesyde of the churche, and gedyr money off them, for the ryngars that ryng For all crystyn solls'.[77] In pre-Reformation society, where funerals were frequent and public, the state of death as but a further progression from the life-cycle of the individual was thus also periodically recognised on certain established anniversaries.

This broad outline of the life-cycle viewed from a social as opposed to demographic standpoint raises a number of issues in connection with the household. First, as in later periods, the conjugal family of one couple with or without children was the norm. In the 1523 census only one per cent of all households contained adult relatives of any sort (though it is of course always possible that 'servants' sometimes included kin), and of these nearly half were sons. As these were specifically not included in the count of children (who were only sexed in one ward), they must be presumed to have been of adult or near adult status. More important was the fact that

[73] Reader 4, fo. 217.
[74] C.R.O. access. 100: Weavers 11, *sub* '1523'; access. 241, orig. fo. 3.
[75] Reader 4, fo. 92; P.C.C. 38 Bodfelde.
[76] Templeman (ed.), *The Records of the Guild of the Holy Trinity*, pp. 153, 155;
C.R.O. A6, fo. 338.   [77] Sharp, *Antiquities*, p. 123.

in 1,302 homes there were no more than three recorded multi-generational households, the senior *member* being a presumptive grandmother in each case, while a further three domestic groups included the 'mothers' only of one or other spouse.[78] Indeed, so pronounced is the absence of any residual trace whatever of the developed extended family within the household, that this evidence must be taken to prove absolutely the existence of the elementary family system since at least the late fifteenth century, i.e. much earlier than has been hitherto supposed by some authorities.[79]

Secondly, and by no stretch of the imagination, could this be described as a 'patriarchal' system. There is no evidence for lineage groupings. When a father died the children did not then revert to his kin. On the contrary, they accompanied their mother on her re-marriage and thus became step-children to a new 'father'. The kinship system in fact was a bilateral one which encompassed the relatives of both father and mother without distinguishing them in contrasted kinship terms, and it focused on the conjugal family. Dowries were paid to the husband, not to the husband's father.

The status of the father and the system of patri-nominal surnaming, moreover, should not disguise the realities of the situation in most families. A first marriage involved the cooperative creation of a new home for both husband and wife: only rarely can it have meant the addition of a wife to an already established and functioning household. Within that context, there were, as we have seen, marked differences between the life of the cottager and that of the householder. In the case of the former, the husband and father was absent from home for most of the daylight hours in each week. Even when he was unemployed, he probably stayed away. Sunday drinking apart, it was said in 1547, for example, that

> it is daylye seen that they whiche be of the pooreste sorte doo sytte all daye in the halehouse drynkinge & playing at the Cardes and tables and spende all that they can gett prodigally vpon

---

[78] *Infra*, table 15.

[79] This is not to suggest that the nuclear family appeared everywhere simultaneously nor to deny that it might be periodically subject to extension. For informed comments on the extended family in rural conditions a century earlier *v.* Hilton, *The English Peasantry*, pp. 28–30. For the development of the three-generation family under one roof in similar circumstances *after c.* 1500, *v.* Cicely Howell, 'Peasant Inheritance Customs in the Midlands, 1280–1700', in Jack Goody, Joan Thirsk and E. P. Thompson (eds.), *Family and Inheritance: Rural Society in Western Europe 1200–1800* (Cambridge, 1976), p. 145.

themselfes to the highe displeasure of God and theyre owne ympouershynge, whereas if it were spente at home in theyre owne houses theyre wiffes and childern shulde haue parte thereof.[80] If then a cottager husband was also usually an absentee father, the years in which he might exercise his fatherly authority when he *was* at home were limited by the departure of his children one at a time into service in some other person's household. Not only did such a father thus never exercise a 'patriarchal' domination over a host of adult kin within his household, but his own children would have left it before they even achieved maturity. The conclusion must be that childhood in a cottage was largely characterised by the domination of a mother.

At the householder level, matters may have been rather different. Even here, however, it needs to be borne in mind that the work of many small craftsmen, like the tilers and carpenters, took them away from home for much if not all of each day, while other occupations like dyeing, fulling, currying and smelting involved activities away from the house, even though the craftsmen involved may have returned for meals. It is nevertheless true that for such men, at least the opportunity to apprentice their own sons to themselves was available even though it does not appear to have been necessarily taken up. At the upper end of society, a father's concern for appropriate marriages for his children and the wealth that was his to divest to them were clearly also powerful factors in perpetuating his authority long beyond the time his offspring had departed into service or apprenticeship elsewhere. At this more prosperous level where a wife's activities were largely restricted to the domestic aspects of the home, it is also likely that a husband's authority was correspondingly greater. Nevertheless, it should not be supposed that such women were without status in their own houses. In these cases often large numbers of servants, most of them female, were at least partly under their supervision.

A third factor which should be considered when assessing the significance and character of the household in late medieval urban society, is its longevity in the context of the domestic cycle. The evidence already advanced with regard to the male expectancy of life, suggests that the bald figures calculable from the 1523 census over-simplify the structure of the conjugal units which it describes. It furnishes no guide to variation in the structure of the family. Yet,

[80] *L.B.*, p. 786.

even leaving aside the situation when a husband outlived his wife, it would be likely that these listings of persons and couples with or without children disguise the range of possible family types in a woman's life-cycle. At its simplest there are seven variations:

(1) The new unit of husband + wife (possibly + an elderly mother)

(2) Husband + wife + child or children

(3) On the death of the husband: widow + children

(4) New husband (possibly + his children from a previous marriage) + re-married widow + her children

(5) New husband (? + his children) + re-married widow (+ her children) + the children of the re-marriage

(6) New husband + re-married widow (all of whose previous offspring have departed into service) + the children of the re-marriage only

(7) Either husband or wife, after death of spouse + any child still at home.

Obviously this list does not exhaust all the possible combinations, but it does serve as a reminder that when we speak of the pre-eminence of the nuclear family, we are including not only the basic conjugal unit of parents and children, but also broken families and re-constituted families. When to these variations is added the normal experience of service from around twelve, in one and probably more households other than the parental home before a person was married, then it becomes clear that for many, if not most, individuals the household context must have had a kaleidoscopic quality. To that extent, while the household surely was the basic unit of society, we should never under-estimate the impermanence of its membership nor exaggerate the stability of the relationships it engendered. The household was a changeable unit through which each individual moved in ever-varying capacities and at fluctuating rates of progress.

It may well be that in disease-ridden towns these variations in structure were more marked than in the countryside, but this very point suggests a final consideration *à propos* the household in late medieval urban communities. The status of its head and his spouse, and to some extent the regulation of their economic activities, were fixed by a more permanent body, the Craft fellowship. Their marriages and funerals, even the burial of their children, were matters of involvement for either masters or journeymen in the Crafts concerned. There was thus a very real sense in which the transitory structure of each household was subsumed into the more enduring organisation of the fellowship. For all the reasons so far discussed, therefore, the urban household of this period was rather less significant as a self-contained entity than is often supposed.

7. Formal groups (ii) The craft fellowship

Like the household, the Craft was both an economic and a social institution. Its functions, however, should be distinguished at the outset from those of the socio-religious gilds or fraternities which are to be discussed in the next section. At Coventry, what elsewhere has been described as a craft gild, was known unambiguously only as 'the Company, feliship & Craft'.[1] All such fellowships were involved in religious observances and some even had their own chapels and/or priests. But only one, that of the Shermen and Tailors, was specifically licensed as a gild and thus able, in its corporative capacity, to own lands in mortmain.[2]

There were two kinds of Craft organisation at Coventry: the Crafts proper which contained the masters, and the journeymen fellowships. Evidence for the latter is unfortunately slight, but there is enough to suggest that most if not all companies had such organisations annexed to them. In 1524, the Leet specifically enacted 'that all the Journemen of euery Crafte in this Citie shall brynge in & deliuer ther bokes of ther Caues & actes to Maister Meire',[3] while explicit information is available for the Dyers, Cappers, Weavers, Tanners and Shermen and Tailors.[4] A master's fellowship, therefore, may be most simply defined as an occupational association of 'householders', and a journeymen organisation as an association of cottage household heads and of those few journeymen who lived in their masters' houses.[5] Insofar as the term was recognised, contrasted degrees of 'freedom' in the city were accorded by membership of both types of fellowship.[6]

[1] *L.B.*, p. 707.

[2] *Cal. Pat. Rolls, 1436–41*, pp. 308–9 is a grant dated 9 March 1438 to the tailors and *fullers*. The latter were separated from the former in 1448, *L.B.*, p. 234. For the otherwise unknown fraternity of St Antony (the butchers), *infra*, p. 160, n. 9; and for the 'confratres utriusque sexus fraternitas pannariorum', p. 118, n. 2.

[3] *L.B.*, p. 687.

[4] *L.B.*, p. 694; Cappers' accs., fos. 58, 24v., 31; C.R.O. access. 100: Weavers 2c; C.R.O. access. 241, orig. fo. 3; *L.B.*, p. xxxiii.

[5] Only one ward enumerator distinguished between apprentices and living-in journeymen in 1523, when Muchpark appears to have contained a mere nine of the latter, *infra*, appendix 3a.

[6] Both the 'earliest' uses of the term 'freeman' appear to be no more than later

In terms of numbers, the Coventry Crafts (i.e. when both types of fellowship are combined under their occupational heading) were closer to the total of those at Norwich than those at York.[7] At the funeral of Lady Isabel Berkley in 1506, the bier was preceded by 33 Crafts with 200 torches, the former figure matching closely with other evidence.[8] The companies providing soldiers in 1497 also numbered 33 though this total disguises something of the reality of a situation in which particular fellowships might comprehend many more than one trade.[9] Professor Hoskins, after all, counted no fewer than 90 different occupations in 1522.[10]

The most senior company was the Mercers' which, since the palmy days of the wool-merchant had clearly diversified its activities: its members included grocers (and probably vintners) on the one hand – and hatters on the other.[11] By and large, the other companies fell into clearly identifiable occupational groupings. That for textiles was the most numerous, containing as it did seven fellowships including the Drapers (second only in importance to the Mercers), the once proud Craft of the Dyers and also the Weavers. The Shermen and Tailors, however, while quite possibly still operating separately for trade purposes were, nevertheless, amalgamated as we have seen as the only Craft gild in the city. The Fullers, by contrast, who before 1448 had been joined to the Tailors, may well have split into two groups of Walkers and Cappers, the ordinances

glosses added in the margins of Leet ordinances for 1494 and 1536, *L.B.*, pp. 558, 724 and cf. p. 790. It would seem that it was not until after the middle of the sixteenth century that an organised effort was first made to register retrospectively the membership of the Crafts centrally and, for a period, *en bloc*, C.R.O. A14(a), fos. 842–3, 849–53. For the use of the word 'commoner', *infra*, pp. 128–9. From 1494, however, an effort was made to revive an 'old' custom that apprentices should be sworn to the franchises of the city, *L.B.*, pp. 553, 560. The freemen's oath to the city is first given only in 1595, C.R.O. A3(b), pp. 12–13, but people had been 'sworn' well before this. For later problems of definition, *infra*, p. 271, n. 10.

[7] For a comparative table of towns containing varying numbers of Crafts v. Charles Phythian-Adams, 'The Economic and Social Structure' in *The Fabric of the Traditional Community* (The Open University, course A322, English Urban History 1500–1780, unit 5, 1977), p. 30. D. M. Palliser, 'The Trade Gilds of Tudor York', in Clark and Slack (eds.), *Crisis and Order*, p. 89.

[8] F. Bliss Burbidge, *Old Coventry and Lady Godiva: Being Some Flowers of Coventry History* (Birmingham, n.d.), p. 179.

[9] *L.B.*, pp. 582–3.   [10] Hoskins, *Provincial England*, p. 79.

[11] *L.B.*, p. 545. The earliest account book of the company variously lists the members in 1566 under mercery, grocery, saltery, linnen drapery, haberdashery and small silk wares, and hats, caps, and trimmings thereof, C.R.O. access. 15: A99, fo. 8v.

of which last appear to have been admitted by the Leet only in 1496.[12] The Crafts devoted to the leather trades were six in number: Skinners, Whittawers, Glovers, Tanners, Corvisors and Saddlers, the last of which, though maintaining a separate existence had been united with the Cardmakers and others for some time in order to support a pageant.[13] The victualling trades may also have comprised six fellowships. They included the Fishmongers, Butchers, Bakers and Cooks. The status of the Millers' Craft, however, seems to have fluctuated (having an existence in 1497, yet created a fellowship in 1544),[14] while the Beer-brewers had only a shadowy existence as 'the breusters yelde' – a term which more probably reflects the groupings of victuallers for the collection of quarterly dues.[15] Five companies spanned the metal trades: the Girdlers, Smiths, Wire-drawers, the Cardmakers and Pinners. Again, however, membership was not clear-cut. The Smiths included the Goldsmiths (who nonetheless retained their occupational independence)[16] and, curiously enough, until 1515 when they were created a separate fellowship, the Tallow Chandlers.[17] The Pinners, on the other hand, were combined with the Tilers, who in their turn included the Craft of Plumbers.[18] The four building Crafts comprised the Wrights (otherwise known as the Carpenters' fellowship since 1436, and which, until 1528, also contained the Carvers); the Masons; the Painters (who took over the Carvers from the Carpenters); and finally the Tilers who were also associated with the Coopers and Turners.[19] Of the remaining Crafts, the Bowyers and Fletchers were amalgamated together, having won their independence of the Tilers' fellowship in 1505 apart from a continuing contribution to the latter's pageant;[20] and the list is completed by the Companies of Barbers and Ropers.

[12] *L.B.*, p. 234. The close relationship between Cappers and Fullers is brought out in *L.B.*, pp. 565, 583, 640.

[13] *L.B.*, pp. 205–6. By the sixteenth century they seem to have had their own pageant, C.R.O. access. 241, orig. fol., fos. 4v.–5r.

[14] *L.B.*, pp. 583, 772–3.   [15] *L.B.*, pp. 234, 623, 855.

[16] *L.B.*, p. 685, and cf. pp. 743–6, where the goldsmiths are ignored in the ordinances of the Craft.

[17] *L.B.*, pp. 547, 643.   [18] Reader 4, fo. 218v., *L.B.* pp. 699, 702.

[19] *L.B.*, 185, 695, 743, 306; Reader 4, fo. 218v.

[20] This ordinance is missing from the Leet Book. Craig (ed.), *Two Coventry Corpus Christi Plays*, p. 104. It should be added that there was also an extra-mural fellowship which consisted of the tile-makers of nearby Stoke – within the liberties – an important midland centre for encaustic tiles. Philip B. Chatwin, 'The Medieval Patterned Tiles of Warwickshire' *B.A.S.T.*, lx (1936), pp. 2, 16–17; 13, 23–4; Norma R. Whitcomb, *The Medieval Floor-Tiles of Leicestershire*, Leicestershire Archaeological and Historical Society (1956), pp. 9, 11, 14, 16–17.

But if, as at York, the total number of fellowships might thus fluctuate, so too did their memberships in response to the ebb and flow of economic fortune. In the absence of a freeman's register, it is only possible to be precise about a scattering of Masters' fellowships though indirect evidence is also available. Most exactly, the remarkable growth of the Cappers' fellowship may be traced from around 25 masters in the 1490s to about 70 in 1550.[21] For this period, the latter total almost certainly represented the largest membership for any single Craft, as comparison with Professor Hoskins' ranking of trades in 1522 demonstrates.[22] The 1520 dearth census, for example, counted 43 bakers in the city, while the Carpenters' Craft, which then included Wheelwrights and Carvers, mustered about 40.[23] Calculations from Weavers' quarterage payments, moreover, suggest that this important fellowship had dwindled to around 37 by 1522–3; while a list of master Drapers shows a similar decline by the 1530s when they numbered about 35.[24]

With such figures as a guide, it is also possible to look more broadly at other evidence, for, as will be explained below, the Corpus Christi Gild contained at one time or another practically all middling to prosperous citizens. Analysis of the Gild's register[25] (membership being calculated over the decade 1515–24) therefore isolates minimal figures for the most numerous middling to wealthy Crafts, and probably gives a pretty exact figure for the most prosperous.

Comparison with the largest trade totals in the 1522 assessment[26] also provides corroboratory detail, though this is confused in two ways. Occupational coverage of the wards was uneven, so in this sense these figures too are minimal. On the other hand, the firm evidence for the Cappers shows that many journeymen were also given occupational labels when their wealth was assessed. Unfortunately there is no way of telling how representative they were of journeymen in other Crafts though we may guess that in this respect they were atypical.

Nevertheless, taking all these factors together, this table suggests

[21] *Infra*, p. 212.
[22] Hoskins, *Provincial England*, p. 79.
[23] *L.B.*, p. 675; C.R.O. access. 3:A5, *passim* – on the basis of a running index.
[24] *Supra*, pp. 48–9; C.R.O. access. 154: Drapers 1c, Daffern transcript.
[25] C.R.O. A6, *passim*.
[26] Hoskins, *op.cit.*, p. 79 and C.R.O. access. 18: A96 *passim*.

Table 7. *Comparative figures for the membership of masters in select crafts*

Craft	Members in the Corpus Christi Gild 1515–24		Known totals	Occupational totals in the 1522 assessment	
Mercers*	34	} 40		26	} ?31
Vintners	6			?5	
Drapers	39		35 (1538)	28	
Dyers	18				
Fullers	22				
Cappers	29		54 (1522)	71	
Shermen	30	} 40		38	} 59
Tailors	10			21	
Weavers	33		*c*. 37 (1522–3)	41	
Tanners	11				
Butchers	29			36	
Bakers	23		43 (1520)	37	
Fishmongers	11				
Carpenters	14		*c*. 40† (1520)		

* Including Grocers and Merchants of the Staple.
† Including Carvers, Sawyers and Coopers.

that at least the largest fellowships of masters have been isolated. Of these, the combined Craft gild of the Shermen and Tailors emerges as probably the biggest, closely followed by the Cappers. Below this level were the Mercers, Drapers, Weavers, Butchers, Bakers and Carpenters with memberships hovering in the region of 40 masters. To these should probably be added the Shoemakers, 28 of whom are given occupational labels in 1522, but who number only a maximum of ten members in the Corpus Christi Gild between 1515 and 1524 inclusively. Fellowships with perhaps 20 to 30 members probably included the Dyers and Fullers, and it seems possible that the remaining Crafts in the city were even smaller. An extremely rough calculation on these premises might therefore suggest that the total number of masters in the city is unlikely to have exceeded 800 and may have been well below this total.[27]

With regard to the ratio between masters and journeymen, the information available is even flimsier. What little there is, however, seems to indicate two tentative conclusions. First, when a Craft was

[27] I.e. two Crafts with 60 members; six with 40; two with 30; and 23 with 15.

relatively prosperous, the masters may have exceeded the number of journeymen. In 1547, for example, there were some 63 master cappers, but only 47 journeymen.[28] Conversely, if a Craft was declining, as most were during this period, the opposite tendency may have been true. In 1522–3 master weavers appear to have been outnumbered by about 45 to 37; while in 1536 the ratio was 41 journeymen to 27 or 28 masters.[29] For there would have been logic in this situation. When times were bad, the incentive and the means for newly qualified apprentices to set up shop were lacking. Obviously there were complicating factors here, however, since some trades required more skilled male labour than others. Secondly, at the humblest level, like that of the Carpenters, the distinction between master and journeymen may have been slight and the numbers of journeymen correspondingly few. The presence of journeymen at Craft dinners and then in very small numbers, is only to be found in the Carpenters' accounts, and it is therefore quite possible that in this fellowship there may not even have been a separate journeymen organisation.[30] On a broad view, however, the serious shortage of male labour revealed in the 1523 census, which is to be discussed in part IV, confirms that the apprenticeship system was breaking down at this time.[31] Clearly too few lads had been indentured to replace both the masters and the journeymen over an extended period prior to this date. It thus seems likely in view of the mobility of the journeymen that their numbers in the city as a whole were not as great as the total of masters, many of whom would have been unable to employ even an apprentice, let alone pay the wages of a skilled worker.

The functions of the Craft system

At a period when most of society spent twelve to fourteen hours a day in a six-day week at their place of work, there was an obvious need for an institution which mediated between the community as a whole and the activities of particular occupations within it. The

[28] Cappers' accs. fos. 68, 71.

[29] C.R.O. access. 100: Weavers 11, sub '1523' and '1536': the approximate figures for masters are deduced from quarterage payments as supra, p. 49, n. 47, and those for the journeymen from their payments of groats. The fluctuations implied by these changing ratios indicate considerable instability.

[30] E.g. C.R.O. access. 3: A5, fos. 57v., 64v., 67, 69v.

[31] Supra, pp. 45–6, 62 and infra pp. 209–15.

Craft system, however, had nothing to do with industrial organisation or capital investment. The commercial nexus between different economic interests (as between the Tanners and the Butchers over the sale of hides, for example) and the financial relationship between entrepreneurs and small masters (like the Clothiers and Weavers) existed independently of particular fellowships, and were regulated, if need be, not by them, but by the city government. Within the Crafts themselves, moreover, new rules could only be adopted with the consent of the mayor and his brethren, who not only inspected the books of ordinances periodically, and imposed new regulations, but also regularly took half the fines imposed for their breach.[32] In certain cases, where the assize was at risk, the city government had even greater powers since it controlled the choice of one of the Craft officers each year in the fellowships of Bakers, Fishmongers and Butchers.[33] In the last resort an obdurate fellowship could be disbanded altogether by an Act of Leet.[34] In other words, the real unit of 'industrial organisation' was not the Craft but the City, and it was the civic government (itself composed of the more influential business-men in the city) which (with the exception of the Cappers) appears to have appointed the searchers.[35]

Civic influence was equally important in the case of a Craft's membership, the protectionist attitudes towards which are commonly taken as the hallmark of the Craft system. Only in the retention (but not the fixing)[36] of admission fines were the fellowships wholly free of municipal control. Obviously both the length of an apprenticeship and the number of apprentices permitted to each master had implications for the extent of future competition within the occupation. However, and no doubt usually after consultation with the Craft concerned, it was the city government that could and did adjust these matters when economic circumstances dictated, and even when this was against the wishes of the fellowship.[37] Similarly while locally-qualified apprentices were preferred to stranger journeymen or masters, the latter would not be refused entry provided they could afford the higher admission fines which in any case were being drastically reduced by the Leet, not the Crafts, at this period.[38]

---

[32] *L.B.*, pp. 645–6; 670–3.   [33] *L.B.*, p. 669.
[34] *L.B.*, p. 695.   [35] *L.B.*, p. 663; *L.B.*, pp. 639, 793, 712, 687.
[36] *Supra*, pp. 45–6.   [37] *Supra*, p. 65, n. 68.
[38] *Supra*, pp. 46, 66.

Craft ordinances comprehend not only the constitution of a fellowship but also the acts which provided the basic framework within which industrial relations operated. It is thus not without relevance to assess from this source of evidence how much weight the Crafts themselves placed on their economic functions. In the eight sets of rules that survive for the period c.1425–c.1550,[39] there is an overwhelming pre-occupation with matters of membership, constitutional structure and propriety, and with the containment of disputes. Between them, these questions dominate from a half to two thirds of six of the ordinances concerned, and five-sixths of the rules in a further two. The regulation of economic competition, including the relationship between master and journeyman, was therefore very much subordinated. This is not to deny, of course, that an important function of a Craft was economic, but it does mean that we should free ourselves from pre-conceptions and judge this institution in the wider context of a way of life in which work, residence and much socialising activity all overlapped.

From a social structural viewpoint, therefore, the Craft system performed three basic functions. It was concerned with regulating and composing conflict within households; it was involved in enforcing the rules by which conflict between different households might be contained; and, above all, it related every household, or at least its head, to the wider structure of the community.

Within a household, it was mainly the relationship between master and skilled worker that required regulation. When seeking a job, a local journeyman weaver could of course expect to be employed in preference to a stranger. From 1424 indeed, any masters who took on stranger journeymen were obliged to pay as much as £1 to the Craft.[40] While employed, it was customary for the journeyman to receive a third of the money paid for any cloth he had woven with his master.[41] If his wages were left unpaid he could withhold his labour: 'his loome schall not goo but stond styll'.[42] The journeyman weaver,

[39] Given the problem of precisely dating individual ordinances within a particular series, the following proportions should be treated as no more than broad indicators of emphasis over time. These generalisations are based on: Reader 4, fos. 217–18 (Tilers); ibid. 92–92v. (Drapers); L.B. pp. 670–3 (Cappers and cf. L.B., pp. 572–4); L.B., pp. 743–6 (Smiths, and cf. C.R.O. Daffern transcript of 'Records and Accounts of the Smiths' Company, Coventry 1684–1822'); C.R.O. access. 34: Weavers 2a (Weavers); C.R.O. access. 3: A5, fos. 1–2 (Carpenters); C.R.O. access. 241 (Tanners); C.R.O. access. 15: A99, fos. 2–2v. (Mercers).
[40] L.B., p. 93.   [41] L.B., p. 94.
[42] C.R.O. access. 34: Weavers 2a, no. 22.

however, was not allowed to leave his master 'of hys mynde or make anney debate or brawle'.[43] Until the differences between the two had been composed, he would have risked not finding employment with other masters of the Craft. He had, nonetheless, the right to a reasonable period of notice – a 'laufull warnynge to deeparte' according to 'the order & custome of this Citie' in the case of journeymen dyers.[44] For the Cappers, the eight days notice required of both parties in 1496 was in fact extended to a fortnight in 1520, though in 1544 it was also laid down that a journeyman in this Craft had to work out a full week before leaving.[45] These then were the simple ground-rules to which either masters or journeymen could appeal in case of conflict: the Weavers' ordinances of 1452–3, for example, were specifically confirmed by the journeymen.[46]

Quite as important as the working relationships within the household, were the tensions that might arise between rival households in a society that was dominated by the self-employed. Potential areas of conflict were therefore primarily to do with equal access to skilled labour, to job opportunities and to the market. In the first case, it is clear that in most occupations, the domestic unit was dependent on its skilled workers for its efficient functioning. The ultimate sanction imposed by the Weavers' fellowship on a master who did not pay his quarterage, for example, was to discharge his journeymen[47] – an action that would certainly have crippled any business with more than one loom, and probably the household with only one as well, in view of the heavy work involved in coping with broad-cloths twenty-four yards in length. Access to skilled labour, moreover, was an increasingly worrying matter at a time when trained man-power was in ever shorter supply. A constant refrain in the Craft ordinances, therefore, was the prohibition against poaching servants from another man's household.[48]

Similarly aimed at the need to preserve amity amongst economic competitors were the regulations which sought to share fairly among the masters the work that was available. A weaver could 'take yn no more worke then that he ys abull and may doo in his owne howse' on pain of a heavy £1 fine.[49] Journeymen weavers, moreover, were

---

[43] *Ibid.*, no. 7.   [44] *L.B.*, p. 715.
[45] *L.B.*, pp. 574, 673, 774.
[46] C.R.O. access. 34: Weavers 2a, pre-amble.
[47] *Ibid.*, no. 2.
[48] E.g. C.R.O. access. 241, orig. fo. 3v.
[49] C.R.O. access. 34: Weavers 2a, no. 26.

expressly forbidden to poach work for their masters.[50] Competing
for a job was strictly controlled. A master carpenter could not
under-cut another 'In bargenyng of a warke' unless his colleagues
had already broken-off the negotiation: and if he then took the job,
he had to warn the Master of the Craft, who then passed on the
information to the rest of the fellowship. Any brother requiring help
had, of course, to take another member of the Craft in preference to
a stranger or foreigner.[51] Similarly a master tiler was not to poach
work without consultation nor 'to prefur his werk to noe man'. In
this Craft, each job was restricted to one master and one apprentice
each time, though, in addition, a stranger might be given employment (under licence) by different masters consecutively 'so that he
schall not goo ydull'.[52] Masters in humble fellowships and small
masters in more prosperous Crafts alike all feared the shadow of
unemployment.

Establishing minimum prices was probably simply another aspect
of a similar desire to achieve a fair share of the market. A master
tanner, for example, was specifically forbidden to reduce the price
of the leather that another tanner already 'chepeneth, till he leave it
& forsake it'.[53] Weavers, tilers and plumbers all set minimum prices
for their products and services.[54] In such cases, however, it is fairly
clear that the level fixed had to meet the approval of the city
government.

The Craft system in fact was largely concerned about economic
matters insofar as work was based on the household. It can hardly
be said to have stopped fortunes being made because of protectionist restrictions nor can it be claimed to have had anything to do with
the financing, supply, and providing of raw materials and their retail
as finished products. The Craft fellowship was no more than an
interest group concerned with the industrial *relations* between master and skilled servant, between household and household within
the same occupation, and between either occupation and occupation, or occupation and the city. It protected interests, but not in the
anachronistic and economically retardive manner that has been
accorded to it.

The real measure of a Craft's economic influence, then, lay in its

---

[50] *Ibid.*, no. 20 and cf. *supra*, p. 80.   [51] C.R.O. access. 3: A5, fo. 1v.
[52] Reader 4, fo. 217v.   [53] C.R.O. access. 241, orig. fo. 3v.
[54] C.R.O. access. 34: Weavers 2a, no. 20, *L.B.*, pp. 660, 688–9; Reader 4, fos.
218–218v.

ability to mobilise cooperative action on behalf of its members against other interests. Probably the threat alone was usually sufficient. In the case of amalgamated fellowships for example, considerable pressure might be threatened. It was agreed by the combined Crafts concerned in 1452 'that no Cowper or Pinner, Tyler, Plum[m]er, or Turner, shall worcke wythe eny man that ys indettyd unto eny of the said Craftes, and is not contentyd to paye the same dette, or to take a reasonable daye for the payment of the same'.[55] Similar menaces were uttered by the Dyers and the Curriers,[56] while the threat of a boycott was also a way in which the masters might bring their wage-earners to heel. Journeymen weavers who taught the skill to untrained workmen were not to be employed by any master of the Craft.[57] Spinners and knitters, who worked for journeymen cappers, were similarly threatened by the employers of the latter.[58] Likewise on rare occasions a Craft might actually act *en bloc* against either another fellowship or even the whole city. Thus in 1528, the Tanners refused to pay the price set on hides by the city butchers, though their action was circumvented by the Leet which then allowed the hides to be sold to country tanners instead.[59] On the other hand, chaos might be caused by an influential Craft like the Bakers in 1484, when they reacted to what they felt to be an unfair assize, and 'sodenly departed oute of the seid Cite vnto Bakynton, levying the seid Cite destitute of bred'.[60]

The solidarity necessary for a formal association of household heads meant that the Craft fellowship was in fact as much a social as an economic institution, but it was so only because of the bonds of mutual economic interests. A major binding factor was the secret character of such associations. A Craft was a 'mystery' to be maintained by initiates alone.[61] Indeed, if 'unytie in all fellowshipps and companyes is especially to be kepte and preserved' – as the Cordwainers put in in 1577 – secrecy was fundamental.[62] With the exception of one menial task, no weaver was to 'teche ne soffer to be tawght nother man ne chylde . . . nether his owne son ne cosyn nor none other exsept that he be bounde prentes'.[63] Cappers were

[55] Reader 4, fo. 218v.
[56] *Ibid.*, fo. 117v.; C.R.O. access. 14: A98 (unfol.), 'For debts owynge to the Curriars'.   [57] C.R.O. access. 34: Weavers 2a, added in a later hand, fo. 8.
[58] *L.B.*, p. 672.   [59] *L.B.*, p. 695.
[60] *L.B.*, p. 60.   [61] E.g. C.R.O. Weavers 2c: recensions.
[62] C.R.O. access. 14: A98, rule 6.
[63] C.R.O. access. 34: Weavers 2a, fo. 3v.

expressly forbidden to 'disclose nor vtter no thynges that ought of Right to be secretly kept amonges themselfes whereby any dyssension or debate myght Ryse theruppon'.[64] Conflict was to be avoided, but if it did arise, it was to be contained. Just as the city itself sought to restrict litigation to within its limits, so too all the masters' Crafts (and those of the journeymen also, if the Weavers are any guide)[65] insisted like the Smiths that 'no brother . . . shall sew one another in the lawe to the tyme be he haue asked license of the kepers'.[66] In the case of the Carpenters, anyone who 'sclanders ore telles eny tale be ony of hys bredryn . . . whech he can make no profe by' would be harshly fined by the fellowship.[67]

Social unity was fostered by regular meetings. Apart from the election of officers, most fellowships met together as a body on three other occasions in the year for the purpose of dining together, though the Cappers usually foregathered only twice.[68] Commensality indeed was obviously recognised by contemporaries as an act of social reconciliation: the resolution of a fifteenth-century conflict between two fellowships was to be explicitly sealed by a meal taken together.[69] Even at the modest social level of the Carpenters' Craft, dinners were lavish affairs in which staggering quantities of food and drink were consumed. At their Harvest Dinner in 1524, for example, 33 members and some outsiders were served with seven pigs, $2\frac{1}{2}$ lambs, six joints of beef, 13 chickens and 16 geese, quite apart from a bushel of wheat's worth of bread and additional bread and cakes, and finally $2\frac{1}{2}$ sextaries of ale or, by the standards laid down in 1521, 35 gallons.[70] A feast like this looks like deliberate excess; it cost each craftsman 9d., that is over a day's summer wages even in 1553 when the rates were increased.[71] In addition to blowouts on this scale, were the drinkings on the great processional days in the civic calendar quite apart from those other occasions on which refreshments may have been served to the membership as a body as at marriages and burials. There can thus be no doubting the socialising function of the Craft system.

The fellowships were also closely integrated into important communal activities that had no economic significance. In particu-

[64] L.B., p. 672.

[65] L.B., pp. 294; 302–3; C.R.O. access. 100: Weavers 2c.

[66] L.B., p. 744; cf. C.R.O. accession 34: Weavers 2a, fo. 3.

[67] C.R.O. access. 3: A5, fo. 1v.   [68] Cappers' accs., passim.

[69] L.B., pp. 203–4.   [70] C.R.O. access. 3: A5, fo. 95; L.B., p. 678.

[71] L.B., p. 806.

lar at Coventry it was usually the Crafts, not the wards, that had to provide and maintain the archery butts outside the city, and at least one of which, Barkers' Butts has survived as a street name to this day.[72] A contemporary writing in the 1530s when this function was declining could say 'I haue seen here x or xij companyes goying on' showtying wher as a man now shall seke thorough the Citie or he cane geyt one company to shote half take pense.'[73] It seems likely that at least the younger members of the fellowships thus practised together perhaps on certain Sundays in the year. For when it came to providing soldiers for war, it was usually customary to spread the burden of furnishing man-power between the Crafts. A virtual census of potential military man-power was thus taken in 1450, and the muster and assessment of 1522, although listed by wards, takes care to give the occupations of most of those concerned.[74] The Cappers' accounts, indeed, demonstrate that the muster of men in harness in the latter year took place at the cost of the fellowship, in the Little Park.[75] It was no accident then that the marchings of the King's Watch on Midsummer and St Peter's eves, when the city paraded numbers of men in their military equipment through the streets, were organised essentially on a Craft basis.[76]

In a similar fashion it was the Crafts that upheld the dignity or worship of the city on other special occasions, whether it was a royal visit or a provincial chapter of the Black Monks when the fellowships assembled in their liveries to greet such notables.[77] Likewise the most spectacular day in the civic calendar, the feast of Corpus Christi, was marked both by a major procession partially staged by the Crafts and then by the performance of the plays financed by some of them.[78] Each of the fellowships concerned in the latter, indeed, had pageant-houses in the city where the special wagons used, and the stage-props and costumes, were stored throughout the year.[79] At Corpus Christi, the marchings of the Watch and probably the Fair Friday procession, the reputation of Coventry was at stake. The fellowships were thus intimately identified with the public

---

[72] *L.B.*, p. 572. *V.C.H. Warks.*, viii, p. 24.   [73] P.R.O. SP 1/141, fo. 55.
[74] *L.B.*, pp. 244–52; C.R.O. access. 18: A96.
[75] Cappers accs., fos. 29v.–30r.   [76] Sharp, *Mysteries*, pp. 192–5.
[77] On royal visits, numbers of pageants were usually specially decked out, *L.B.*, pp. 287, 289, 392–3. *L.B.*, 588.
[78] Phythian-Adams, 'Ceremony and the Citizen', *loc.cit.*, p. 63; Craig (ed.), *Two Coventry Corpus Christi Plays*, pp. xi–xix.
[79] E.g. Craig, *op.cit.*, p. xiii, n. 2; C.R.O. A24, p. 8.

image of the city. It was this factor rather than ideals of economic rationalism, therefore, that motivated the amalgamations of some-times disparate trade fellowships, and dictated financial contribu-tions from others, when declining Crafts could no longer afford the lavish expenditure necessary for the furnishing of the Corpus Christi plays.[80]

The need to sustain ceremonial leads to a final feature of the social functions performed by the Craft system. The essence of culture in the late medieval city was that it was visual and public. Nothing was more public than the regular communal processions of the year and their hierarchical ordering. As the Weavers' ordi-nances put it: 'In every procession and all other Congregacions for worschip of the Citte and welthe of the seyd Crafte . . . every man schall goo & sytt in order as he hath byn put in Rule of the seyd crafte.'[81] Office in a fellowship was a status that was thus commun-ally recognised. In particular it was drawn to the attention of a man's neighbours whatever their occupations. For it was to the officer's home that each Craft processed after the swearing-in ceremony – 'when the Maister Commyth home to his house' so the Weavers described it.[82] And it was from a senior Craft officer's house that the processions of each fellowship set out to join the communal occa-sions of Corpus Christi, Midsummer and St Peters. Every dyer, for instance, had to be

> readye when the heade master of the sayde companye sendethe his clerke or somener to gyve his attendaunce on Mydsommer nyghte, to fetche the under master . . . at hys howse, And from thence to goe to the heade master's howse, And there to take suche thynges as shalbe provyded for them. And after that to attende uppon bothe the sayde masters before the maior and his brethren to kepe the kynges watch.[83]

The Craft system was consequently the basic means of achieving social status in the community as a whole. Indeed no man of reason-able substance could hope to escape the obligations of office, the tenure of which was imposed upon the reluctant on pain of fine.[84] Above all, Craft office represented the first rung on the ladder to higher status still.

[80] *Infra*, pp. 212, 216, 264.
[81] C.R.O. access. 34: Weavers 2a., fo. 3v.   [82] *Ibid.*, ordin. 2.
[83] Sharp, *Dissertation*, p. 183. Cf. *ibid.*, p. 22, where a since-lost rule of the Smiths (of 13 Henry VII) indicates that the journeymen also waited on the head master.
[84] E.g. *L.B.*, pp. 670, 743.

The office-holding system, it is important to note, embraced the journeymen fellowships as well. Each of these appears to have had its own summoner, who, if the same practice as that which obtained amongst the masters was observed, would have been the most newly-joined member.[85] More to the point in the context of office that brought status, it seems clear that journeymen fellowships were probably each headed by 'keepers'[86] – usually four in number. The Tanners, for example, had 'ij keepers of the Jurney men and the ij quartor men of the said occupacion', amongst whose tasks it was to attend the weddings and funerals of out-brethren of the Craft.[87] In the case of the Weavers, a precious fragment of the only ordinances of a journeyman fellowship to survive in the city demonstrates that in the mid sixteenth century the organisation was ruled, like the Crafts, by 'xij of the best' of the fellowship. It was they who chose two of the four stewards of the journeymen, the other two being nominated by the 'chefe master' of the Craft. Even at this level, the precedence bestowed by office was publicly underlined, for the whole fellowship had to 'wayte on the stuardes' at for instance weddings and burials.[88]

The number of officers in the fellowships of masters varied. Most commonly, as in Crafts like the Carpenters, Cappers and Weavers, there were two.[89] The Smiths, however, had three,[90] while the leading fellowships of Drapers and Mercers boasted four.[91] Other officials might also be appointed where property was involved: the Weavers for example had their own rent-gatherers and the Cappers, wardens for their 'lands'.[92] Ordinances seem to imply that the annual election was in some cases open to the whole fellowship, but it seems more likely that the choice was in fact restricted as in the case of the Smiths and the Weavers to the senior twelve men of each Craft.[93] A later version of the Mercers' rules also make it clear that the process lay firmly in the hands of the twelve, and that attendance

[85] *L.B.*, p. 656.   [86] Cappers' accs., fo. 58.
[87] C.R.O. access. 241; orig. fo. 2v.   [88] C.R.O. access. 100: Weavers 2c.
[89] C.R.O. access. 3: A5, *passim*; Cappers' accs., *passim*; C.R.O. access. 100/17/1: Weavers 11, *passim*.
[90] *L.B.*, p. 743 – as may the Shermen and Tailors also have done, Craig, *op.cit.*, p. 31.
[91] C.R.O. access. 154: Drapers 1c, *passim*; C.R.O. access. 15:A99, *passim*.
[92] C.R.O. access. 100: Weavers 8; Cappers' accs., fo. 42v.
[93] E.g. the Cappers (*L.B.*, pp. 573, 670) and the Tanners (C.R.O. access. 241, fo. 4). *L.B.*, p. 743 (Smiths); C.R.O. access. 34: Weavers 2a, no. 4; and 2b, folded leaf, second clause.

at the election by the membership was purely for the purpose of assenting to the choice.[94]

The rate of progress through the office-holding structure varied, but only to a degree. In the case of the Carpenters, junior office might be achieved on average six years after setting-up shop while for the more prosperous Cappers the gap was about nine years.[95] There was then a pause. As a result it was fourteen years after setting-up that a successful carpenter became senior officer of the Craft. The date at which weavers became brothers is not known, but the gap between junior and senior office in this Craft was two years longer than in that of the more humble Carpenters.[96] For the Cappers, however, senior office was achieved only two or three years after relinquishing the junior post or some 14 to 15 years since setting-up. There cannot, therefore, be much doubt that even allowing for the fact that we do not know exactly the variable age at which it was most common to set up shop, the approximate age at which senior office was undertaken in these cases was usually around forty. Only in the cases of the Mercers and Drapers was it probably somewhat later, as it was customary for the Head Master in each of these fellowships to have held the civic office of *sheriff* before undertaking the Craft post.[97]

Two by-products of this system are of the utmost significance for our understanding of late medieval urban society. First, when due allowance is made for the low expectation of life amongst craftsmen, and also when the emphasis placed on the youthful categorisation of the age-group that was unmarried is recalled, this was deemed to be an essentially gerontocratic system. The ex-senior

[94] C.R.O. access. 15: A99, fo. 2, for their pre-1551 ordinance no. 1; and fo. 16 for rule 1 in 1593.

[95] Both these results (from C.R.O. access. 3: A5, *passim*, and Cappers accs., *passim*) have been obtained from running indices of attendances along the lines described in Phythian-Adams 'Records of the Craft Gilds', *loc.cit.*, p. 271. With regard to the Capper's figure, probably the more trustworthy of the two results, the mean gap was 8.9 years in 16 fully documented cases, and, of which, 9 achieved office within between 4 and 8 years of setting-up. For a further 23 cases where the dates of their admissions as new brethren were not recorded, the median drops as might reasonably be expected to 7 years.

[96] Calculated from C.R.O. access. 100: Weavers 11, *passim* where only the names of officers are regularly recorded.

[97] The figures for the Cappers are based on 28 cases. The career-cycles of mercers and drapers may be deduced from the fact that many new senior officers in these two companies were already designated 'master'. C.R.O. access. 154: Drapers 1c, *passim*; C.R.O. access. 15: A99, *passim*.

officers of each Craft were termed 'Ancients' or, as in the case of the Smiths, the 'xij of the Eldest & discretest of the feliship'.[98] A mid sixteenth century recension of the Weavers' ordinances plainly stated this ideal of gerontocratic authority when it emphasised that 'honor vnto Euery elder, Auncient And gouerner is due. And thereby both gouernment, Sivilytie and dutie to all degrees is mayntayned.'[99]

Secondly, the system was one of remarkable fluidity. In the early sixteenth century it was almost unknown for junior office to be held more than once by any individual (though, for the very wealthiest, a second term as senior officer might be expected), and so there was a constant flow of individuals moving through the posts in question. The 33 Crafts were thus producing roughly 350 new junior officers per decade. Within each Craft, consequently, there was plenty of opportunity. In 1520, well over 50 per cent of the Master Carpenters had been, were, or were to become Craft officers, while even amongst the more numerous Cappers, the proportion was as high as 44 per cent.[100] In the Drapers' company in 1538, where officeholding opportunities were more numerous, 70 per cent of the membership may be so characterised.[101] The status and the obligations of office were therefore widely experienced by masters, and we may infer that much the same would have been true at the journeyman level.

Not only did membership of a Craft provide the only avenue to true status in the community; but it also served to place a man with regard to his socio-economic standing in general. The division between the handy-craftsmen and the rest, for example, was clear-cut. The former were those who did the roughest work with their own hands for other people in public. Above all they included the building trades: the Carpenters and Tilers, both of which had their own fellowships.[102] The probably short-lived organisation of the rough-masons and dawbers, however, had been suppressed in 1517

---

[98] E.g. C.R.O. access. 34: Weavers 2a, fo. 6; *L.B.*, p. 743.

[99] C.R.O. access. 100: Weavers 2c – a collection of unnumbered loose leaves which represent various attempts at re-drafting the Craft's ordinances. For a more general discussion of gerontocracy, *v.* Keith Thomas, *Age and Authority in Early Modern England*, Proceedings of the British Academy, lxii (1976), pp. 5–10.

[100] Figures based on the indices described in n. 95 *supra*.

[101] C.R.O. access. 154: Drapers 1c, p. 14 for a list where, of 35 individuals, 24 had been or were officers, although the ex-officers are known for only six preceding years.   [102] *Supra*, p. 101.

when they were to revert to the status of 'comen laborers as they were afore'.[103] Above the handy-crafts level, came the broad ruck of the middling fellowships like the Smiths and the Weavers. Standing somewhat apart from these Crafts, however, were the victualling trades, one of whose officers in each case was annually chosen by the Mayor, and none of whom qualified for the posts of civic office unless they were wealthy enough to give up their business for the year in question.[104] To this extent such wealthy Crafts were not fully integrated into the system of status within the city. For service in civic office was the true hall-mark of superior status, and the leading fellowships like the Mercers and Drapers, and decreasingly the Dyers, together dominated the governing echelons of the city through their personnel.[105] The broad spectrum of socio-economic standing was thus displayed every year in the great Corpus Christi procession when the victualling crafts led, and the superior Crafts brought up the rear in the place of honour. At the midsummer processions, indeed, the inclusion of a current civic officer in the Craft concerned appears to have been publicly advertised by the inclusion of a 'Giant' carried by the fellowship in question.[106]

The Craft fellowship in urban society

It is clearly necessary to assess the importance of the Craft system from two view-points: that of society as a whole and that of the individual citizen. In both cases it is misleading to regard it only in an economic light. At a time when dense concentrations of population were exceptional, the Craft fellowship may be seen as the contemporary urban solution to the problem of the potentially self-organisable mass. In structural terms, by institutionalising the

[103] L.B., p. 653.

[104] Coventry was expected from the operation of the 1511–12 act, Statutes of the Realm, 3 Henry VIII cap. 8. Thomas Astleyn, baker, who became sheriff in 1510 (L.B., p. 630); was described as clothier on becoming mayor in 1529 (L.B., p. 696), but he was then to be 'assisted' in assessing the prices of victuals by two of his magisterial colleagues.

[105] Between 1481 and 1530 inclusively, and even discounting five second terms of office by those concerned, fourteen merchants, mercers or grocers occupied the mayoralty, and twelve drapers and five dyers. The occupations of only two mayors are unknown for this period. Templeman (ed.), The Records of the Guild of the Holy Trinity, appendix I, pp. 164–8, a list which has been augmented from L.M. and C.R.O., A6, passim.

[106] Phythian-Adams, 'Ceremony and the Citizen', loc.cit., p. 63.

protagonists of economic competition, the majority of the population was thus subdivided into a hierarchy of small units. The system
provided an ordered and decentralised framework for conflict between household and household, Craft and Craft, and between Craft
and civic government. Within it, the fact that localised status was the
first step to later and wider influence in the city as a whole, ensured
the perpetuation of the system. Through it, conversely, the community gained from the presence of numerous unpaid officials: the
searchers and officers, who were responsible for supervising the
observance of regulations, and *via* whom, in a generally illiterate
age, the economic decisions of the Leet could be communicated to
every citizen.

From the citizen's standpoint, and particularly in view of the
general paucity of both leisure-time and privacy, the Craft fellowship was the basic reference-group in society. Through it, a man and
his wife were admitted to the community. By it, their developing
social standing was established. Under it, the household relations
between master and journeyman and apprentice were regulated.
Because of it, communal obligations like military service and public
ceremonial took on the forms they did, and thus trespassed on a
man's spare time. In its company the citizen worshipped, and by it,
he and his family might well be buried. For every citizen, the Craft
fellowship was much more than the industrial organisation it is so
often taken to be in the text-books. It operated as nothing less than
the transforming agency in a continuous process whereby the life-
cycle of the citizen was related to the working of the urban social
system as a whole.

8. Formal groups (iii) Gilds and councils

The Gilds

The life-cycle of the more successful citizen was also related to the two great socio-religious fraternities of Coventry, the Gilds of Holy Trinity and Corpus Christi. If the origins of both, and thus the nature of their earlier memberships, were to be sought in the historic division between the Prior's and Earl's halves of the city (and hence in the two parishes that broadly fossilised that dichotomy), the social functions of the two gilds had changed radically since those times.[1] In the 150 years that had elapsed since the union of the two jurisdictions of Coventry, these fraternities had been absorbed into the structure of the community as a whole. Their prestige, however, remained undiminished, despite the unsuccessful attempts made by the Craft Gild of St George which had once seriously claimed to compete with them.[2]

---

[1] The earlier history of Coventry has recently been increasingly disputed by: Joan Lancaster, whose views are concisely summarised in *V.C.H. Warks.*, viii, pp. 256–60, and partially modified in her 'Coventry' in M. D. Lobel and W. H. Johns (eds.), *The Atlas of Historic Towns*, ii (London, 1975), p. 6, n. 36; Alan Dibben, *Coventry City Charters*, The Coventry Papers no. 2 (1969) pp. 16–17, n. 14; P. R. Coss, 'Coventry Before Incorporation: a Re-interpretation', *Midland History*, ii (1974), pp. 137–51; and R. H. C. Davis, *The Early History of Coventry*, Dugdale Society Occasional Papers, xxiv (Oxford, 1976). So far have the traditional views on the division between the Prior's and Earl's halves been over-turned, indeed, that the very existence of two rival administrations has been substantially questioned. The present writer, however, is convinced that more attention needs still to be paid to the relationship of the documentation to the actual physical areas of the town concerned ('Jolly Cities: Goodly Towns', *loc.cit.*, p. 38). For the suggestion that the two gilds separately originated in the two 'halves', *v.* Dormer Harris, *Life in an Old English Town*, p. 95.

[2] C.R.O., B.43 (cf. *L.B.*, p. xxxiii and C.R.O. B.47). The Tailors and Fullers were granted a Gild in 1438, *Cal. Pat. Rolls, 1436–41*, pp. 308–9. The Confraternity of Clothiers (i.e. Drapers in this case), approved in 1468, was a rather different type of brotherhood. It had erected an altar dedicated to Jesus in St Michael's and had caused a weekly mass to be said every Friday 'to the end that Almighty God, appeased by the prayers of the faithful, might deliver the said city' from visitation of the plague, *Cal. Pap. Regs., xii, 1458–1471*, pp. 644, 761–2, 772. This 'Jesus Mass' was apparently founded in 1465–6 through the exertions of the mayor John Pinchbeck, who was himself a draper, *L.B.*, p. 373. A similar mass seems to have been started at Holy Trinity at about the time of the 1479 epidemic, Bliss Burbidge, *op.cit.*, p. 222. For the established weekly attendance of the mayor at the St Michael's mass, *supra*, p. 77.

The junior fraternity was the Corpus Christi Gild. Once restricted to the old Prior's half and so to the parish of Holy Trinity, its prime responsibility by 1500 was, as its name suggests, to furnish the ornate procession which annually marked that feast and the high-spot of the city's ceremonial calendar. In addition to the other specified religious occasions on which the fraternity met, it also held two major banquets – a Lenten dinner and a venison dinner – each year prior to 1520 (earlier still it had enjoyed a goose dinner as well), both of which were heavily attended though not with consistent regularity by the brethren. An estimate of membership has thus to be derived from a running index of those appearing in the bulky register of the Gild between 1515 and 1524.[3] From this it emerges that in 1520, when the small minority of temporary absentees are included, the fraternity boasted no fewer than 282 *Coventry* members from all parts of the city – a figure which thus represented practically 40 per cent of the estimated number of resident masters.

These people undoubtedly comprised the more ambitious and prosperous citizens largely from the middling to wealthy Crafts. They embraced three identifiable groups. There were, first, the sons of the city's elite, who, it would seem, had yet to achieve their majorities since their fines were paid for them by their conspicuously absent fathers. In any one year, however, rarely as many as fifteen to twenty of these adolescent offspring from the wealthiest city families attended. More representative, therefore, was the second group. This was composed, if the Cappers are any guide, of actual or aspirant officers of the Craft fellowships. Indeed, from the careers of those members of the Gild between 1515 and 1524 whose biographical details may be confidently matched from the Cappers' accounts,[4] an established social progression may be inferred. Of these 25 cappers, no fewer than 21 joined the fraternity within five years of setting up shop or of their first appearance in the craft accounts, while 17 of these had been admitted within four years. Nine of the 25 later disappear (presumed dead) from the Craft register before they might have held office in the fellowship, but all the rest served at least as junior officers of the Craft, and most did so usually within five years of joining the Gild. Unfortunately it is impossible to derive comparable figures from the Weavers'

---

[3] C.R.O. A6 – for differently entitled dinners e.g. fos. 77, 87, 107.
[4] Cappers' accs., *passim*: for individuals setting up between 1498 and 1523 inclusively.

accounts since these do not begin until 1522–3,[5] and anyway they record the names of none but the officers. Nevertheless, of the 13 weavers mentioned as Gild brothers in 1519 or thereafter, half were due to hold craft office. Others, like William Osgathorpe who was apparently a searcher in 1514,[6] and John Walton who was described as serjeant in 1517,[7] may well have already done so. If these two Crafts were representative, therefore, it seems highly likely that the bulk of the Gild's brotherhood was so comprised. A third and smaller group of members, however, seems to have embraced representatives of the more humble Crafts, those who could afford to join only somewhat later in life. Thus, of the five men specifically described as 'carpenter' in the Gild between 1515 and 1524, four appear to have joined at about the time or even after they took on *senior* Craft office.[8] Not only were such men therefore markedly older than the average on admission, but their fellowships were correspondingly under-represented in the fraternity.

Gild membership was consequently very much a part of the status system in the city. Above all, it brought together those citizens who aspired to *civic* office, since membership of both fraternities at one time or another was expected of the city's elite. In 1496 in defence of the rebellious Lawrence Saunders, who had held the office of sheriff a decade previously, the aldermen were reminded:

> You cannot denygh hit but he is your brother;
> & to bothe Gildes he hath paid as moch as another.

> They that woll be brother to the Gildes or therto pay,
> We have no more to lose, the soth for to say.[9]

It is possible to watch the future elite of the city troop dutifully through the pages of the Corpus Christi Gild register, but in the absence of a similar volume for the Trinity Gild, the relationship between the membership of the two fraternities has to be inferred from the former. However, it does seem clear that it was normal to transfer from the junior to the senior gild at an advanced stage in a successful citizen's career. Of fifteen officers or ex-officers of the Cappers' fellowship, who we know from their account book were still alive in 1520, ten appear to have been no longer attending the meetings of

---

[5] *Supra*, p. 49, n. 47.   [6] *L.B.*, p. 639.   [7] C.R.O. A6, fo. 221v.
[8] One, Thomas Yardley, only achieved junior office, but did so three years before he apparently joined the gild; C.R.O. access. 3: A5, fo. 67v. His christian name is not given at C.R.O. A6, fo. 244v.   [9] *L.B.*, p. 578.

the Corpus Christi Gild after 1519. Of the remainder, one may never have joined, one disappears from the Gild record in 1521, and three exceptionally were yet to hold senior Craft office for a second term a decade or so later. It is unlikely in the extreme that those cappers who no longer attended the Gild, and half of whom were to die within the decade, then failed to join the only other organisation in the city which was specifically concerned with the future of their immortal souls. We may therefore guess, within a fair degree of certainty, that such people had in fact removed themselves to the Trinity Gild. Similarly, in the cases of aspirant civic officers from other fellowships, for which the registers have not survived, it would seem that membership of the Corpus Christi Gild was discontinued at about the time the rank of sheriff was achieved. When such a man attended the odd banquet of the fraternity thereafter, his payment was distinguished in the register as being made simply 'for his dinner'.[10]

The achievement of shrieval rank was the critical step that had to be taken if a citizen was to aspire to both Gild and further civic office. The progression was clear-cut. A year or two before such a man was elected mayor, he became Master of the Corpus Christi Gild, and as such headed the ex-sheriffs and other junior civic officers who each year comprised the junior 'twelve' of the electoral jury of 24. After relinquishing the mayoralty he became immediately, or within the year, Master of the Trinity Gild itself, and took precedence only after the mayor in all meetings of the Council House. In his capacity as Master he headed the senior 'twelve' of the Gild, who not only supervised their own fraternity, but, half of whom it would seem, oversaw the business of the Corpus Christi Gild.[11] There can thus be no doubt in the case of these senior citizens that it was normal to transfer from one fraternity to the other well in advance of becoming mayor.

[10] Presumably this was after the point his subscription had been finally paid.
[11] The precedence of the Master of the Trinity Gild is evidenced not only in the earliest council minutes (B.L. Harl. MS. 7571), but also in *L.B.* where his name invariably seems to head the list of jurors. Templeman, *op.cit.*, appendix I, failed to identify most of the masters in the 1520s and 1530s, when the names may be recovered from C.R.O. A7(a), pp. 75, 79, 83, 90, 94, 98, 103, 112, 123, 127, 134, 143. The existence of a senior twelve has to be deduced from a garbled version of the early rules of the gilds, Templeman, *op.cit.*, p. 178. The number was anyway probably ideal and therefore variable: cf. the nine auditors, *ibid.*, pp. 93–4. A similar group, but of six, appears to have audited the Corpus Christi accounts: C.R.O. A6, fo. 165; cf. fos. 8, 316.

In these circumstances, it seems probable that the structure of Gild membership in the city served to emphasise the social categorisation of age which has been a recurring theme in this analysis. At about the time a man became an ancient of a prosperous Craft, or became eligible for the senior civic and gild offices which would lead to the status of 'alderman', he transferred to the Trinity Gild. In this way, wealth, status and the gerontocratic ideal were fused together in a social institution.

Unlike many primitive societies, however, the division between the age-groups was not completely clear-cut. The cost of admission to the Trinity Gild, probably £5, must have been beyond the means of ex-Craft officers from the humbler fellowships who, like the Carpenters, joined the Corpus Christi Gild later in life than normal.[12] Conversely, it is highly probable that the sons of the city's elite, whose subscriptions to the junior fraternity were paid by their fathers even before they set up shop, advanced more rapidly to membership of the senior Gild than was usually the case. To this extent, then, the social categorisation between age-groups was blurred.

An estimate of the numbers involved in the Trinity Gild is hard to make, though they were clearly much fewer than the junior fraternity. A minimal figure may be derived from the total number of fathers who appear to have paid for their sons to represent them in the meetings of the Corpus Christi Gild. Over the decade prior to 1520, nearly sixty such men appear in the register in this capacity, and most of these were still alive in 1520. How many more were either childless or had daughters only as surviving offspring, it is impossible to say. Nevertheless, it seems unlikely that the Trinity Gild contained many more than a total somewhat in excess of 100 Coventry members.

The councils of the city

At the pinnacle of Coventry's formal institutions were the civic councils which, in a manner beloved of medieval burgesses since the days of the Danes, were each ideally composed of twelve or multiples of twelve members. The division of political responsibilities between these bodies was clearly defined, and differed only in detail

[12] Templeman, *op.cit.*, p. 178.

from that found elsewhere. Here we are concerned primarily with the social implications of membership.

The senior body – where power really resided – was the Council House which, at this time, was restricted to the ex-mayors or aldermen together with the Mayor and the Recorder.[13] These men together comprised the senior 'twelve' (more usually less) of both the annual electoral jury and of the twice yearly meeting of the Court Leet.

The composition of these last two bodies was broadly similar. Each numbered 24, and the junior 'twelve' in both was largely comprised of the ex-sheriffs, ex-wardens and ex-chamberlains, though numbers might be augmented from outside. The pool from which these outsiders was drawn was almost certainly the group of citizens who made up the junior ranks of the 48 – the Common Council of the City, which thus embraced the senior 24 (the electoral jury/Court Leet) plus these 24 others.[14]

Through these bodies lay the path of civic advancement, the entry to which was *via* service as one of the two annually elected chamberlains or wardens. As already indicated, by this stage in a man's career he would already have served as a senior Craft officer, except in the case of the Mercers and Drapers, before being able to qualify for a civic post. Thus of seven cappers whose career-profiles may be followed in detail in the first half of the sixteenth century, all achieved junior office within eight years of being keeper of the Craft, the median interval being five years. All but two of these high fliers did so over twelve years after being admitted to the fellowship, or 15.4 years on average. Five of these seven men progressed even further to the rank of sheriff after a second interval between civic offices that varied between one and twelve years. This key post was thus reached $22\frac{1}{2}$ years on average after setting up shop.

There is no reason to doubt that these rates of progression were representative. For eighteen non-cappers who were to be sheriffs between 1517 and 1544, and whose first appearances in the Corpus Christi Gild may be precisely fixed, it took between ten and 32 years from becoming a brother to achieving the office of sheriff. The close bunching of seven cases indicates that the median interval of 16 to 17 years was most typical. When allowances are therefore made for

[13] B.L. Harl. MS. 7571; the status of ex-mayor was the ultimate distinguishing mark of political standing, *L.B.*, p. 522.

[14] E.g. *L.B.*, pp. 44, 69, 157, 228, 421, 431, 520.

the probability that the average age for setting-up shop is unlikely to have been earlier than 24, and also that a number of years normally separated this event from admission to the Gild, it would appear that the rank of sheriff was not usually occupied until a man was in his middle forties. Only in exceptional cases, like that of Julian Nethermill, could it have been earlier.

It is therefore significant that another considerable interval elapsed before the status of alderman was reached. For the thirty individuals who served as mayor between 1501 and 1534 inclusively, a clear-cut pattern emerges. In 22 cases the years between taking up the shrievalty and relinquishing the mayoralty ranged from eight to twelve, the median being 10. All but two of the remainder took longer than this. The final rung on the office-holding ladder, the Mastership of the Trinity Gild, was consequently not reached until well into a citizen's mid-fifties. With on average a further nine or ten years of service in the Council House ahead of them, the aldermen thus represented the apogee of the gerontocratic system of authority within the city.

9. *Formal groups and the citizen's life-cycle*

Before turning to the problems of social stratification it may be helpful to bring together the themes of the preceding discussion. Above all it is important to inter-relate not only the complex sequence of social positions through which the successful citizen passed, but also the way in which the simultaneous occupancy of such positions helped to inter-connect the formal institutions of medieval urban community. For the sake of argument, it is necessary to take the age of twenty-five as an arbitrary starting point in the cycle. The resulting sequence must therefore be viewed in generalised terms although there is little reason to doubt that it does broadly reflect actuality (see table 8).

Such a reconstruction can be no more than a bald summary of what was normal. It omits, for example, those unusual cases in which senior Craft office or the Mastership of the Trinity Gild was held more than once by the same individual, and it obscures the fact that ex-junior civic officers moved on to the senior Gild. It also excludes the unique case of Richard Marler (a millionaire by the standards of his day), who proceeded from the office of warden to that of mayor within a space of nine years without ever being Master of the Corpus Christi Gild. In no such instance, however, does the individual exception disprove the general rule.

What this summary does do, however, is to reveal the intricate inter-connectedness of a pre-Reformation urban society. The city was so tightly organised that the three major types of formal institution that brought householders together – the fellowships, the gilds and the councils – all inter-locked to produce a graduated system of status in the community as a whole. Admission to the aldermanic elite was possible only after holding a sequence of seven, ever-more responsible official positions, during which time the successful citizen was garnering experience and, though not consequentially, wealth along the way. Short-cuts were exceptional.

Within this social structure, moreover, the two civic gilds together acted as the basic intermediaries between the tiny councils of the city and the ruling bodies of the Craft fellowships. Together they resolved the necessary equations between wealth, influence and,

Table 8. *The career-cycle of the successful citizen through the formal institutions of the city*

(C.C.G. = Corpus Christi Gild   T.G. = Trinity Gild)

Approx. age	Craft fellowship	Gild	Civic office	City Council	
c. 12–24	'Young man'				
c. 25	New brother (Summoner or beadle)				
c. 30		New brother of C.C.G.			
early 30s	Junior Craft Officer				
c. 40	Senior Craft Officer (except Mercers and Drapers)	C.C.G.	Chamberlain/ Warden, Ex-junior civic officer	Junior 24 of Common Council	
mid-40s	'Ancient' of Craft (Senior Craft office for Mercers and Drapers)	C.C.G. T.G.	Sheriff, Ex-Sheriff	Junior 12 of Leet	48
Early 50s	'Ancient' of Craft (occasional searcher)	Master of C.C.G.			
mid-50s		T.G. Master of T.G.	Mayor, T.G. 12 or 6	Council House 12	
Sixties		T.G.	Alderman		

above all, the status that came with advancing years. In doing so they brought together with some sense of common identity, probably in the region of half the master-craftsmen in the city, and in marked contrast to the rest of society which lacked any kind of institutional combination that might have integrated citizens from different occupational groups. Insofar as hierarchy and oligarchy are usually linked in discussions of the late medieval town, therefore, the system at Coventry was, for the upper levels of society, of a very much more diffused type than the stock picture of urban social structure at this period would lead us to believe. In view of the incidence of gilds of a quasi-civic character in so many other important towns, moreover, there is no reason to suppose that Coventry was peculiar in this respect.[1]

[1] Phythian-Adams, 'The Economic and Social Structure', *loc.cit.*, p. 32.

10. *Informal groupings (i) Social stratification*

Before looking at the manner in which the system of official promotion and status fitted into the social stratification of the city, it is essential to take into consideration the social evaluations of contemporaries. A starting point is provided by local sumptuary legislation in 1522, which was primarily concerned with the wearing of different types of furs, satins, silks and velvets on the clothes of three levels of society.[1]

The first of these comprised those of 'the degre of a Scheryffe', the one social stratum at and above which the status of degree or rank was acquired. Only citizens who held, or had held, this office, were accorded the designation 'Master' in the city. It is notable, however, that within this social stratum, a further distinction was made between those who were 'notyd and knowyn in this Cytte to be of the Substans' of £300 and above, and those who were below that level. Even at this level, two factors were at work – official status and, above all, wealth that was publicly perceived.

The second social stratum embraced 'all Comeners within this Cytte' below the rank of sheriff. It is clear, nevertheless, that we ought not to read modern pre-conceptions into this term. 'Commoner' meant no more and no less than a member of the commune or community – those who served together in this capacity. The Weavers' fellowship, for example, held a 'communication' or 'communing together' for their new officers each year.[2] The term should thus be distinguished from the wider meaning of its adjectival use in such phrases as 'the comen people of the Citie'.[3] In 1456, for example, the penalties imposed on any inhabitant sueing another outside the City's courts, included those of being 'discomyned oute of this Cite, to be estraunged from his Crafte that he vseth here, & of all maner Gildes & Bretherhedes of this Cite'.[4] The implication is plain. To be a commoner involved above all being a member of a Craft fellowship. It therefore included the journeymen organisations. Thus in 1450 journeymen wiredrawers were specifically included in a list of

[1] *L.B.*, pp. 680–1.
[2] C.R.O. access. 34: Weavers 2a, fo. 6; cf. C.R.O. access. 100: Weavers 11 for the craft year ending 1535.   [3] *L.B.*, p. 717.   [4] *L.B.*, p. 294.

civic officers 'and euery oder Comener of the seyde Cite, that may bere the coste' of armour.[5] By contrast, when in 1527 the fellowship of journeymen dyers was disbanded, its membership was ordered 'to vse themeselfes as seruauntes & as no Craft or feliship'.[6] To be a commoner of Coventry at this period was, in practice, the equivalent of what elsewhere involved being a freeman.

As with those of the degree of sheriff, however, the sumptuary legislation of 1522 once again also distinguished between those of different scales and types of wealth. On the one hand, commoners who were known to be worth £100 and above were permitted to boast their status with more conspicuous trimmings to their clothing than those that were below this level of wealth. On the other hand, the bye-law further split the commoners of the city. For the third category included any 'seruant man or woman reteyneyd for wages' – a description that must have included for this specific purpose not only in-servants, but also the journeymen.

These divisions of society do no more than serve to outline the manner in which contemporaries broadly evaluated them. The lowest level of all clearly comprised those wholly unprivileged wage-earners who, like the demoted journeymen dyers just quoted, did not belong even to a fellowship. It will be recalled that when, in 1517, the Rough Masons and Dawbers were also disbanded as such, they were to become 'only comen laborers . . . and to take such wages as is lymyte them by the statutes theruppon made'.[7] To these people must also be added impoverished widows and the chronic paupers.

Above this stratum was the broad ruck of the 'Commonalty', which was itself much sub-divided. More clearly marked off from the unprivileged and unorganised wage-earners than is usually acknowledged by historians were the journeymen in their occupational combinations, who, as we have seen, had access to their own official status-system. Next in the hierarchy of commoners were the master craftsmen whose ranks were probably characterised by even greater differences than those which demarcated them from the journeymen. About a half or even more of the membership of a masters' fellowship never aspired to office in it. Many such citizens, we may be sure from the negative evidence of the 1523 census, never employed servants of any kind in their households. More

[5] *L.B.*, pp. 245, 249.   [6] *L.B.*, p. 694.   [7] *L.B.*, p. 653.

likely than not, a considerable proportion of these citizens was consequently employed on a piece-work basis[8] – and perhaps sometimes irregularly – by their more affluent colleagues, and in a manner which barely distinguished them in terms of wealth from the regularly paid journeymen. Within the spectrum of different occupations, moreover, there may have been few clear-cut differences between the incomes and the reflected statuses of, for example, a modest master carpenter and a regularly employed journeyman dyer.

Insofar as it may be measured by the possession of in-servants in 1523,[9] the employing class probably comprised well over a third of all households in the city in times of normality. It must obviously have included also those householders who only engaged out-servants. And yet, not even all of these masters can have aspired to office within their own Crafts, although most must have been members of the two gilds. That small minority aside, however, it was at this social level that citizens aspired to both Craft and civic status. As such these townsmen fell into a socially recognised group which was much concerned with its honour. A master weaver who failed to observe the due order of processional precedence was fined if he had wittingly disobeyed a request to the contrary 'by the Mr or by other oneste men bothe for his onestee And the onestee of the crafte allso'.[10] These people included the 'honest persons . . . that hath boren no office' – in this case, civic office.[11] Above all, these were they who 'take theym-selfes to be honest Comyners'.[12] A man had thus to be *seen* to be an honest commoner and a person of wealth. The best way of being so observed was to be an officer of either a Craft or of the city. This level of society therefore probably included at the very least all the present or past officers of both the Crafts and of the city below the rank of sheriff. Most would have been members of the Corpus Christi Gild. A few others, who had either failed, or had not even attempted to become, part of the city's elite, would nevertheless have been sufficiently prosperous to be members of the Trinity Gild, like those who were worth over £100 in the sumptuary bye-law.

[8] Though in 1544, the Cappers in general were banned from putting out piecework (*L.B.*, pp. 773–4, 781), a regulation that had to be somewhat relaxed in 1549, (*L.B.*, p. 792).   [9] *Infra*, pp. 204–7.

[10] C.R.O. access. 34: Weavers, 2a, fos. 3v.–4.

[11] *L.B.*, p. 649 – and were thus liable to be chosen as constables. Cf. 'the most honest within their warde', *L.B.*, p. 607.   [12] *L.B.*, p. 777.

If the elite of the city may thus be defined as those who held, or had held, the office and rank of sheriff, and 28 of whom were living in 1522, there were others who also qualified to be of their number. Such families might include not only a widow of a late magistrate, like Margery Wardlow, but also the heir of another, like Henry Pysford, who, though assessed on 1,000 marks in 1522,[13] evaded civic office altogether. To these should also be added the three permanent city officials, the Recorder, the Coroner and the Steward. The elite of Coventry in fact comprised a maximum of 40 householders, or about two per cent of all householders in 1520.

Below this level, it becomes increasingly difficult to estimate the proportion of families at each social level. Nevertheless a crude outline in rounded terms may be attempted on the basis of the various estimates already discussed (see table 9).

Table 9. *The social stratification of Coventry c. 1520*

	Approx. no. of households	Social standing
The Magisterial elite	40	Men of 'degree'
Other members of the Trinity Gild	80 ? max.	Honest commoners
Members of the Corpus Christi Gild	260 (excluding minors)	
Small Masters	400	Other commoners
Journeymen	600 ?	
Labourers, out-servants, poor widows, etc.	500 ?	The poor

Of these, obviously the last two categories are the most problematical, and even to the extent that it is impossible to tell with complete confidence which was the larger.[14] It is likely, however, that in relation to the estimated total number of masters, the proportion of journeymen has been pitched too low. In addition, no allowance has been made at and above this level for the widows of former masters and journeymen. We may therefore guess that somewhere between 20 and 25 per cent of the households in the city

---

[13] C.R.O. access. 18: A96, fos. 20v., 57v.   [14] *Supra*, pp. 103–4.

were excluded from even partial membership of 'the community' at this time. In 1500, however, the percentage may have been nearer the former figure, since then the proportion of journeymen is likely to have been somewhat higher than in 1520.[15]

But if perhaps a fifth of all households in Coventry were thus debarred from the real 'community', it is nevertheless difficult to assess the differences in living standards between at least employed labourers and the journeymen. It has been suggested that 'fully two-thirds of the urban population in the 1520's lived below or very near the poverty-line, constituting an ever-present menace to the community in years of high food-prices or bad trade'. Of these two-thirds, in very general terms, half were wage-earners and half were 'without any recognisable means of subsistence'.[16] The reason why these pioneering suggestions fit uneasily with the evidence advanced above is that they are based wholly on the evidence of the subsidy and particularly the assessments of 1522. It will be seen in part IV, however, that the assessment can only be used as a very broad guide in this respect. The new evidence, which the 1523 census reveals, shows beyond doubt that a substantial minority of people credited with *nil* assessments cannot possibly have been total paupers, since their households contained in-servants, or they lived in dwellings worth annual rents in excess of the poorest cottagers.[17] Even allowing for the omission of about 20 per cent of all households in 1522, it is also difficult not to suspect extreme artificiality in assessment of goods generally.[18] Are we to believe that the wage-earners assessed on £2, as most concerned were in 1524, and many of whom may well have been earning 4d. *per diem*, in fact only worked for 120 days or twenty six-day weeks in the year? Chronic under-employment and a probable maximum of eight weeks 'lost' because of compulsory holidays notwithstanding, even 44 four-day

---

[15] For a possible recovery in the size of the labour force at this time, *supra*, pp. 43–4.   [16] Hoskins, *Provincial England*, p. 84.   [17] *Infra*, table 30.
[18] It is clear, in fact, that figures derived from the assessment furnish only a very rough and ready framework for analysis. What for example, are we to make of cases like that of William Thomas who was assessed on nothing in goods but paid a rent of 22s., i.e. over four times as much as an average cottager (C.R.O. access. 18: A96, fo. 18); or that of Roger Bromwhich (a fishmonger and Corpus Christi Gild member) who was assessed on only £2 worth of goods, but paid an annual rent of more than this, i.e. 43s. 4d. (fo. 20)? There are too many cases of this kind for comfort, even though an appreciable number of *nil* assessments were later picked up by the subsidy commissioners in 1524 and usually taxed on £2 worth of goods, P.R.O. E179/192/125.

weeks at 4d. *per diem* works out at practically £3. At 3d. *per diem*, the equivalent figure is £2. 4s., or taking the year as a whole, a weekly income of about 9½d.

If an impoverished householder and his wife could live rent-free on 7½d. per week in Ford's hospital (a sum that had in fact been raised from 5d. in 1517)[19] then a labourer could have managed likewise, and still have been able to pay the 1½d. per week necessary for the 6s. annual rent of a cottage (most cottage rents were 4s. to 5s. *p.a.*). Indeed such a calculation ignores two further factors which together outweigh the extra expense of raising children: that the labourer unlike the poor commoner may well have been fed by his employer on the days when he worked, and that his wife may have earned a little extra from spinning.

Estimates of this nature of course ignore seasonal variations in income due to both different wage-scales and the differential incidence of holy days and extended holidays. If the rates set in 1553 are any guide, however, it was only for the winter months, from the beginning of November to the beginning of February, that the lower rate was customary – and at a time that included only one long break at Christmas. In truth, it is almost certain that the lowest rate never fell below the 3d. per day used in assessing income for the *whole* year in the previous paragraph. Those calculations then surely represent *minima*, and so serve to highlight even further the artificiality of the assessment on wages in the subsidy.

The wages in question moreover relate to the labourers. Even carpenters' journeymen in 1553 were allowed a penny a day more than the labourer:[20] a substantial differential when the chances of more regular employment were greater for the journeyman who had been hired over a longer period. Indeed, journeymen cappers' wages which were fixed in 1496 at 12d. per week represented a take-home pay of 44s. in a notional working year of 44 weeks, and included as well all meals on working days between 6 a.m. and 6 p.m., for the journeymen were not apparently allowed to leave their masters' houses between those times.[21]

None of these considerations, of course, may be taken to imply that the unprivileged wage-earners in late medieval society were living in comfort. It is simply to suggest that before the years of crisis and the decades of inflation that then ensued, the scale of real wages

---

[19] P.C.C. 9 Ayloffe.   [20] *L.B.*, pp. 806–7.   [21] *L.B.*, p. 574.

was at least sufficient to keep a labourer above, and a journeyman well above, the level of true subsistence poverty. In other words, it was the catastrophic impact of repeated years of unprecedented famine prices combined with unemployment alone that reduced the urban labourer to that wretched condition. If the figures for depopulation between 1520 and 1523 are any measure, and they are the best we have, then it is relevant to note that it was not a half, or even a third of the population that was so affected, but a proportion somewhere in excess perhaps of 20 per cent.[22] Among these unfortunates, moreover, were clearly numbers of smaller craftsmen, numerous poor widows and children. The Coventry evidence, therefore, does much to substantiate what may be inferred elsewhere from civic attempts to deal with the situation: that the years of crisis which ushered in the Tudor price inflation also witnessed the making of the Tudor poverty problem. It was these factors which reduced the urban labourer to nearer the subsistence level at a time when his wages were failing to increase correspondingly. Before that time, there is little reason to suppose that his income was not usually sufficient, except in exceptionally bad years, to keep him and his family safe from starvation.

But if the proportions of impoverished labourers and true paupers in late medieval urban society should not be exaggerated, no more should bald estimates of the numbers of households in different social strata blind us to the major role played by the servant-keeping households in blurring these crudely outlined divisions. In 1523, at least, about a quarter of all people in the city were fed and accommodated as in-servants by such households,[23] and it seems highly probable that the vast majority of journeymen were also fed by them on working days. The servant-keeping household was thus a potent instrument of social control: in it, many an offspring of a poor family was held as a form of social hostage. Just as the Craft fellowship served to divide up the different social levels by occupation; so the servant-keeping household split up those within an occupation.

Conversely, the burden of provisioning the vast majority of all adolescent or adult males and perhaps half the women in the entire city imposed severe strains on the institution of the servant-keeping household in times of crisis and inflation. It was truly said that

[22] *Infra*, p. 196.   [23] *Infra*, p. 204.

without the right of pasturing their cattle and horses on the city's common lands, 'the comeners & inhabitauntes ... cannot well liff & meynteyn ther occupacions & menyall seruauntes'.[24] If the heads of such households were thus both privileged and economically influential, they were no less subject to substantial social obligations.

An assessment of both labouring living standards and the practical functions of the servant-keeping household, however, does much to emphasise the yawning chasm that separated many of the privileged citizens from the paupers whose survival depended wholly on their own efforts. Why otherwise did William Pysford in 1517 – the year before the crisis – feel it necessary to bequeath 'in the most coldest seasone of wynter at sundrye tymes a thousand fagotts a yere' for ten years; or John Humfrey in 1532 make similar provision for seven years, or Isabell Wade in 1541 leave money for both bread and faggots to be distributed in every winter for forty years?[25] To the same shivering poor, went numerous other bequests of freeze gowns, shirts, smocks and blankets, all of which vividly indicate the wretched living standards of the recipients.[26]

Yet even at this date it is clear that a harsh distinction was already drawn between the respectable poor and the rest. Those that were to be admitted to Ford's hospital when it was reorganised, for example, were specifically to be of good repute 'and kept housholde and so the worlde fallen from theym'.[27] Again and again in such bequests the same note is struck: the beneficiaries were to be poor householders 'as can be knowen have nede and ben ashamed to aske or begge openly'; 'poore housholders which be ashamed to begge and be no comen beggars'; or those 'which be in pouertie and goo not a begging'.[28] In other words, the objects of such acts of mercy were those commoners whose householder status and personal standards of honour marked them out from the importuning paupers. For the former, society made some permanent provision: Bonde's hospital, for example, was founded specifically for the use of impoverished members of the Trinity Gild; while the 'diminutions of rents' that are so conspicuous in the accounts of both fraternities may well be associated with similar needs.[29] For the

[24] *L.B.*, pp. 719–20.   [25] P.C.C. 9 Ayloffe; 15 Thower; 27 Alenger.
[26] E.g. P.C.C. 17 Ayloffe; 23 Bodfelde.
[27] P.C.C. 9 Ayloffe.   [28] P.C.C. 9 Ayloffe; 6 Alen; 20 Porch.
[29] P.C.C. 22 Adeane. Templeman, *op.cit.*, pp. 35–6, 45 (letter no. 12), 81–4. Similar allowances were made annually in C.R.O. A6, *passim*. Whether the 'mendiv-

paupers, on the other hand, it was becoming a matter of obtaining a licence to beg; of being no doubt 'moved on' by the keeper of the beggars; and of waiting for an issue of bread at the Priory Gate.[30]

ants' also mentioned in the accounts of both fraternities refer to repairs (Templeman, *op.cit.*, p. 36; C.R.O. A6, fo. 321v.) seems unlikely. Surely these were dwellings granted at lowered rents or even rent-free to impoverished gild members. In 1522 it was said that the Trinity Gild paid £7 to 'certeyn mendivauntes whych be brethern and sisters fallen in povertie and geven yerelie to theym in almes towardes ther lyving', C.R.O. access. 18: A96, fo. 92v, cf. *infra*, p. 197, n. 4. The Master of the Corpus Christi Gild annually accounted for 'houses that mendyfauntes holdon' under the same head as 'Diminuc[i]ions' of rents (e.g., C.R.O. A6, fo. 95v. *et supra, et infra*).

[30] *Supra*, p. 64, n. 65. The *Valor*, of course, furnishes no information on alms-giving other than that for which each house was responsible as a result of bequests *etc*. Annual spending in this last respect by the Priory amounted to nearly £20 (after allowing for payments to institutions), p. 512. A measure of what this might mean is furnished by the case of the Coventry Carthusians, amongst whose expenditures on alms was an annual payment of £14.0s.10d. for the daily issue of bread and beer (involving 30 quarters each of rye and malt *per annum*), *ibid*., p. 54.

11. *Justifications of obedience*

In these circumstances, both of crying need and of the evident deathbed consciences of those wealthy enough to meet part of that need, it may well be asked, how did the upper levels of society justify their positions? Within the community, the answer would have followed straightforwardly from a statement of social *mores* made in 1494. This was to the effect that:

The vynte, concorde, & amyte of all Citeez & Cominalteez is principally atteyned & contynued be due Ministracion of Justice & pollytyk guydyng of the same, forseying that no persone be oppressed nor put to ferther charge then he conuenyently may bere, and that euery persone withoute fauour be contributory after his substance & faculteez that he vseth to euery charge had & growyng for the welth & worship of the hole body.[1]

In other words, the responsibilities (and hence the privileges) of both administering justice and giving politic guidance for the welfare of the community, were in effect obligations placed on the shoulders of those best able to bear the cost. Apart from the authority which attended advanced age, two other factors would also have carried weight. One was the relationship of local hierarchy to God; the other was its relationship to the nation.

Perhaps more overtly before the Reformation than after it, the structure of organised religion conspicuously under-pinned the stratification of society. Even in the parish church after Mass every Sunday, the 'Holy Cake' (as opposed to the consecrated bread) was distributed by the deacons 'a-quordyng for every man's degre'.[2] At the public ceremonial procession of Corpus Christi, if gangs of journeymen pulled the pageants through the streets, the Host itself was transported under a canopy borne by four 'burgesses'.[3] Apart from those Crafts that had chapels in the two parish churches – the Mercers, Drapers, Dyers, Girdlers, Smiths, Cardmakers and Saddlers, the Butchers and Tanners; the Shermen and Tailors as well as the Weavers had separate chapels and priests elsewhere in the city,

[1] *L.B.*, pp. 555–6.
[2] Sharp, *Antiquities*, pp. 122–4; *L.B.*, pp. xxx–xxxi.
[3] The number of 'men that dryved' the pageant varied from eight (Cappers accs., fo. 82v.) to ten (*ibid.*, fos. 53, 92) to twelve (fo. 62). C.R.O. A6, fo. 325.

while even the humbler Crafts like the Tilers had special arrangements with the White Friars.[4] For the honest commoners, there existed in addition the gild chapels of St John's Bablake and St Nicholas, periodic attendance at which was a prime obligation of membership in these fraternities. To the meetings of these quasi-regular religious brotherhoods, moreover, an aura of ecclesiastical respectability was lent by the attendance not only of many city priests, but also of abbots and priors from elsewhere as well as the Prior of Coventry himself, and the bishop and suffragan bishop of the diocese. For those that attained the office of mayor, finally, twice-daily processional attendances at St Michael's for matins and evensong on workdays, Sundays and holidays were public demonstrations of official dedication.[5]

The higher a man aspired in fact, the more frequently did he attend church services. Indeed accession to office itself, whether craft or civic, was marked by an act of public worship and the taking of a religious oath.[6] Not only were certain standards of morality consequently expected of men of status, but observance of them clearly helped to legitimise a man's official standing. Cases of fornication and adultery amongst members of the Trinity Gild in the late fourteenth century were harshly dealt with by expulsion from the fraternity;[7] while in 1429, serjeants and other officers might also be dismissed for adultery.[8] The city gaoler, for example, was specifically warned against fornication with a named married woman.[9] In 1492, even men 'of worship', whether ex-mayors, sheriffs or 'other officer or comiener', who were 'sclandered', warned, and then persisted in the 'synnes of avowtre, ffornicacion or vsure', were, if they were ex-mayors, deprived of their aldermanic scarlet and membership of the Council House, and debarred from being Master of the Trinity Gild. The others were 'neuer to procede nor to be called to ferther worship, nor auaunced but vtterly to be estraunged

[4] *V.C.H. Warks.*, viii, pp. 324, 348–9, 332. Reader 4, fo. 218v.; *V.C.H. Warks*, ii, p. 105.

[5] Dormer Harris (ed.), *The Register of the Guild of the Holy Trinity*, pp. 101–12; C.R.O. A6, *passim*; *L.B.*, p. 662.

[6] Phythian-Adams, 'Ceremony and the Citizen', *loc.cit.*, pp. 60–1.

[7] C.R.O. A166 (n.p.) includes transcripts by George Eld from records of the Trinity Gild now lost, which refer to such expulsions in 1377, 1379, 1380 and 1390. Permanent expulsion from the gild was threatened in cases of 'felonye, homycide, lecherye, hasardour, de sorcerye, ou heresye; ne pur comun contekur, ne de nule vice abominable', Templeman, *op. cit.*, p. 177.

[8] *L.B.*, p. 118.   [9] *L.B.*, pp. 279–80.

from all goode company'.[10] If the tradition of Puritan respectability had a long pre-history, it was because the medieval urban elite jealously guarded the dignity or 'worship' of the group, and the 'honeste' or honour of the prosperous individual. That it did so by identifying itself with the contemporary religious order is clear, and even to the extent of furnishing the local priesthood with members of its own families.[11]

A less obvious justification of superior social status was that it acted as the crucial intermediate link between the local community and the nation. For the average commoner, his freedom to trade in the city meant that his base was permanently fixed in Coventry and its network of contacts in the locality. Perhaps more mobile were the itinerant journeymen, whose contribution to the spread of heresy in 1511 is probable,[12] yet it is difficult to say how numerous a body such people represented. Most journeymen, it may be suspected, were as rooted in the city as their masters. It is then just these considerations that lend significance to the geographical and social membership of the two great fraternities. At their meetings the honest commoners, and the elite in particular, could be associated with the system of rank within the society of the nation as opposed to that of the city. The Register of the Corpus Christi Gild, for example, reveals a remarkable degree of contact with the personnel of other municipalities. Towns heavily deputised by such groups at different times included Bristol, Worcester, Evesham, Lichfield, Birmingham, Warwick, Nottingham, Manchester, Boston: even Carlisle and Dublin were represented. Moreover, to judge from surnames, there were clearly kinship connections between such bodies as well; there were Wyggestons and Reynolds at both Coventry and at Leicester; Herrings at Coventry and Carlisle; Wycams at Coventry and Lichfield; and Crampes at Coventry and Worcester, while William Mucklowe of the latter is referred to in one document as also of Coventry.[13] Even the mayor of Coventry in

---

[10] *L.B.*, p. 544.

[11] *Infra*, p. 143. In 1522, named Coventry priests included a Grene, a Wigston and a Marler, C.R.O. access. 18: A96, fo. 97v. In 1535, a Richard Nethermill was vicar of St Michael's, *Valor*, p. 58.

[12] John Fines, 'Heresy Trials in the Diocese of Coventry and Lichfield 1511–12', *Journal of Ecclesiastical History*, xiv (1963), pp. 163–4: how many of those concerned were either journeymen or masters is not clear.

[13] C.R.O. A6, *passim. Ibid.*, fos. 209v., 251v., 236v. Dyer, *The City of Worcester*, pp. 106–8; *L. & P.*, i (1), no. 438. C.R.O. A6, fo. 230v.

1522, Thomas White, appears to have been also a citizen of Bristol.[14] Fraternities of this kind therefore provided useful forums in which common urban problems could be discussed. Indeed the similarity of the wording of certain bye-laws in different towns at much the same time strongly suggests close communication between such communities.[15]

The social world of the urban elite likewise transcended the local community with respect to the gentle society of the region. Not only ecclesiastical dignitaries and numerous rural parish priests, but also gentlemen, esquires, and even the odd knight, attended the meetings of the Corpus Christi Gild. As prince or king, the Trinity Gild had boasted as members, Henry IV, Henry V, Henry VI and Henry VII, as well as a more marked complement of knights and lords than the junior Gild.[16] Through organisations such as these, then, whether at Coventry or elsewhere, the provincial merchant could feel an accepted part of the national system of degree, a situation that was otherwise most marked only when he 'represented' his community in Parliament.[17]

Conversely, it was to the official class that the royal authority symbolised in the city's mace, sword and seals, was delegated downwards. The motto of the city since the days of the Black Prince was 'Camera principis', and royal receptions to the city harped on this:

Welcom, full high and nobull prince, to us right speciall,
To this your chaumbre, so called of Antiquite.[18]

If Coventry was a chamber of the realm, the civic elite saw themselves as the royal porters at its door. They, and they alone, were the mediators between the local community and the awe-full power of the sovereign. The hierarchy of the city was then dictated from

[14] L.M., fo. 16v. Cf. L. & P., i (1), no. 438.
[15] E.g. L.B., p. 687 (1524); York Civic Records, iii, ed. Angelo Raine (Yorkshire Archaeological Society Record Series, cvi, 1942), p. 68 (1519).
[16] C.R.O. A6, passim. For the way in which at least one magnate joined gilds in certain towns with which he had dealings, v. H.M.C. Middleton, pp. 332, 356, 359. Dormer Harris (ed.), op.cit., pp. 13–14; L.M., fo. 152.
[17] J. E. Neale, The Elizabethan House of Commons (London, 1964), pp. 246–7. Thus in 1523, the Recorder – characteristically as the senior member – 'made Relacion' to a meeting of the Council House of 'the acttes & maner of the last parliment as a borges of thys Cytte and had harte thankes therfore & lykewyse Mt. Marler', B.L. Harl. MS. 7571, fo. 32v. It was more usual than otherwise for citizens to become M.P.s after being mayor, T. W. Whitley, Parliamentary Representation of the City of Coventry (Coventry, 1894), appendix i, p. ii. In addition, of course, the Prior of Coventry sat in the House of Lords.   [18] L.B., p. 391.

within by the obligations of wealth; legitimised from without by authority from the Crown; and sanctioned from above, through the means of moral and religious observance, by the Omnipotent.

But what is so noticeable about the system of social stratification, nonetheless, is the manner in which its apparent rigidity was softened by contact between the different levels within the community proper. Hospitality and commensality eased the official status structure. At least one mayor kept open house for the twelve days of Christmas, and was no doubt publicly mocked by his Lord of Misrule. Before 1545, both the mayor and the sheriffs appear to have provided food and wine for the craft officers at the annual marchings of the watch at midsummer and St Peter's respectively. They may even have furnished the gallons of wine in question for the Craft members. Similarly on these occasions, master dyers and master smiths provided drink for the journeymen, while the weavers, in earlier times at least, sat down once a year to a communal meal and drinking with their journeymen. Both new mayors and new craft officers financed, in whole or in part, a meal for the bodies over which they were to hold sway at the time of their inaugurations. In ways such as these, therefore, the every-day tensions inherent in the hierarchical structure were periodically relaxed.[19]

More relevant still, the nature of the hierarchy was made bearable for many by its flexibility. To appreciate this, however, it is necessary to look at social mobility between its various levels, and the opportunities for advancement even within this declining city.

[19] Phythian-Adams, *loc. cit.*, pp. 67, 64–5, 61–2, and *infra*, pp. 263–4. The word 'hierarchy' is in danger of losing the full force of its meaning, so widely is it nowadays used. Contemporary reality, however, is heavily underlined by the language of deference used towards Coventry's elite. Two petitions to the Leet variously address the mayor and his colleagues as 'youre worthynesse', 'your maistershipps', 'worshipfull maisters' and 'full worshipfull men of the gret e[n]quest' (C.R.O. Carpenters 9a & b: late F.10). A versified critique of corporation policies, moreover, implies that it was customary to bid the aldermen a deferential 'good morrow' when passing in the street, *L.B.*, p. 578.

12. *Social mobility*

The study of social mobility within one community over little more than a single generation presents problems that are rather different from those confronting analyses made on a national basis over a number of generations. Above all, lack of knowledge with regard to wealth and occupational status in the parental generation necessitates an approach to the problem which concentrates more on *opportunities* for mobility rather than on either quantifying mobility itself, or assessing whether one group or class of persons was emerging more strongly than before.

At first sight – and when viewed from the top – social movement at Coventry in the pre-Reformation period was largely downward in direction. The wealthier the family, the more children did it produce.[1] Even of those offspring that remained in the city, only a minority could aspire to the highest positions in society. A number of families, moreover, appear to have established short-lived 'dynasties' that dominated the upper echelons of the community. Perhaps as many as twelve families boasted fathers and sons or other apparently close namesakes as mayor between 1495 and 1580. Most such 'dynasties' involved only two generations, but two concerned three, and one family, the Saunders, may have accounted for as many as five mayors between 1510 and 1570. Between them, therefore, these 'families' alone filled about a third of the possible positions amongst the aldermanic elite over this period, and to that extent blocked the way to aspirants from other families. In a declining population over much of this period, those offspring of such 'dynastic' families that did remain in the city at a lower social level than their parents might be expected to have similarly comprised a disproportionate part of the dwindling class of honest commoners.

It is evident nonetheless that matters were not quite so simple. Even great merchant wealth which might serve to launch one son towards the top, was clearly much divided below this level. Testamentary evidence is of course insufficient for the purpose of measuring the fragmentation of fortunes, but it does make clear that the division of wealth amongst widows and more particularly

---

[1] *Infra*, tables 29 and 30.

younger offspring in marriage portions, lands and stock must have made for marked differences in the social levels of the eldest son and his brothers and sisters. In the case of two of the greatest fortunes that are relevant in this respect, and where the wills were drawn up *before* the eldest son had received his share, this contrast is heavily underlined. Thomas Bonde's son John, who later became mayor of the city for example, received £1,000 in addition to the £100 he had already been given. The latter's probably unmarried sister was left only 400 marks, and his younger brother 300 marks 'to fynde hym to scole' in order to be a priest – a not unusual method of forestalling the dissipation of a fortune at this level of society.[2] Similarly John Nethermill (later to become mayor) received from his father, Julian, 1,000 marks and all the latter's lands and tenements (which must have included the manor of Exhall). The widow received 300 marks, a house and its moveables; a younger son 200 marks, and a daughter whose marriage had clearly already been arranged £20 worth of household stuff at her setting up house.[3] In other cases such as the Marlers and the Pysfords, much the same may have been true though the facts are disguised by dispositions made before the wills were drawn up.[4] What also seems clear is that where there was land available, one son might be destined for the farm like John Pysford at Baginton or Michael Joyner at Stoneleigh, while the commercial stock and the house and shop were as far as possible preserved for the son that was to follow in this father's footsteps.[5] In the former case, potential honest commoners thus left the city, while, with regard to daughters, merchant wealth was re-cycled to the use of other 'honest' families by virtue of the marriage settlements. Moreover, the incidence of mortality affected the wealthy too. Richard Marler was preceded to his grave by his second son; both of the sons of William Pysford, who had remained in the city as grocers, survived their father by only two and eight years respectively; Thomas Bonde's youngest son did eventually become a priest, but did not live long enough to see his elder brother become mayor.[6] For all of these reasons, therefore, there was always room for new faces at the top of society. In looking at social mobility over the community as a whole, it will be more relevant to

---

[2] P.C.C. 22 Adeane.   [3] P.C.C. 6 Alenger.
[4] P.C.C. 20 Porch, 9 Ayloffe.
[5] P.C.C. 9 Ayloffe, 23 Wrastley.
[6] P.C.C. 38 Bodfelde; P.C.C. 22 Ayloffe, 37 Bodfelde; P.C.C. 20 Ayloffe.

turn now to the means by which movement was possible in the opposite direction – from the lowest end upwards. How fluid then was the social system? The passage of journeymen to the status of master is perhaps the most difficult to assess. The only usable lists of the former, moreover, are rather late, pertaining as they do to the Cappers in 1546/7, and 1547/8 respectively.[7] Nevertheless the information they provide is suggestive. 46 journeymen were listed in the earlier year and 47 in the latter, there being a number of names that were not common to both lists. Of those in the first list, however, one died within two years, but no fewer than 37 per cent (17) were to become masters over the next eight years, at which point unfortunately there is a decade's gap in the accounts. Similarly in the second list, 17 of the 47 (again including the journeyman who was soon to die) all went on to become masters over the same period, a total that includes four journeymen not mentioned in 1546/7. Put another way, of the 48 new brethren accepted as masters in the Craft between 1546/7 and 1554/5 (when the account breaks off), 21 appear as journeymen in one or other of the two lists that date from only the first two years of that period. Had succeeding lists survived, it might well be that they would have revealed that at least half the masters in the craft had had some experience as a journeyman before setting-up. Only one of these masters, however, appears later to have achieved Craft office, to judge from the inadequate information that survives over the crucial years. It is, of course, impossible to generalise about other Crafts on this basis, but we may guess that the Cappers were not atypical of those occupations whose standing placed them immediately below the level of the wealthy companies of the Mercers or the Drapers.

Ex-journeymen, therefore, may well have comprised the bulk of the membership in a fellowship who did not aspire to Craft office. Of those that did so aspire, however, it is clear that senior office in a fellowship was not undertaken by only a varying minority of those that had got as far as junior office. Between 1506 and 1525, for example, out of the twenty men each in the Carpenters' and Cappers' fellowships, respectively, who then became junior officers, eight or possibly nine proceeded no further in the case of the former, but only six in the latter.[8] The earliest comparable figures

---

[7] Cappers' accs., fos. 68, 71.

[8] C.R.O. access. 3: A5, *passim*; Cappers' accs., *passim*. One of the six cappers,

for the Weavers unfortunately have to be taken from a later period; 1523/4 to 1544/5.[9] In this declining Craft, the result is more akin to the humble Carpenters. Nine or perhaps eight out of the 20 junior officers concerned dropped out of the status race. Thus over a half of the office-holding class in these quite representative fellowships – perhaps a fifth of their entire memberships at any one time – was able to rise and did so to the senior level.

The system in fact was one of fairly constant replacement, the only delaying obstacle to advancement being a tendency for the wealthier ex-senior officers to hold the post twice. Amongst the Cappers, of the known 42 men who held the senior post before 1554/5, fifteen held office a second time, and of these, eight did so after being sheriff. Of 30 known senior posts in the Carpenters' fellowship which were filled between 1504 and 1543, 18 were occupied twice, or in three cases thrice, by the same man. Similarly seven out of 20 senior men in the Weavers' Craft held the top office twice, and one did so three times between 1522/3 and 1560.

But if advancement was thus slowed, there is no evidence that, for this period, the top official positions were monopolised by particular families. To judge from the incidence of namesakes, the Carpenters produced no dynasties in the first third of the sixteenth century. Among the Cappers over a roughly sixty year period prior to 1554/5, only two families seem to have been involved in successive generations. Of the senior Weavers' officers before 1560, four families may have replaced themselves before or after that date. There was therefore as yet no question of family oligarchies dominating senior positions, so the upward movement of new blood in these Crafts was largely uninterrupted. The situation in the senior fellowships of the Mercers and Dyers, however, may have been rather different.[10] Correspondingly of course, room was left by families that either changed occupations, declined in wealth, died out, or left the city. There is unfortunately no way of quantifying the balance between upward and downward mobility on this scale.

It was obviously only possible for a minority to progress from

Robert Crowe, however, went on to become a sort of script-writer and stage-manager of the Corpus Christi plays, Craig, *op.cit.*, pp. 31, 70, 89, 99, 101, 102. Appropriately perhaps, he was rewarded in 1560 by the Drapers 'for pleaying God', *ibid.*, p. 100.

[9] C.R.O. access. 100: Weavers 11. One year is missing from the series, and to produce a comparable total of twenty persons, one junior officer who unusually served twice has been excluded. [10] *Infra*, p. 149.

senior craft office to civic status. Between 1497 and 1540 inclusively, for example, only two weavers and one carpenter reached the junior ranks of the civic officers as either chamberlains or wardens.[11] The Cappers, however, furnish a useful illustration of the opportunities available below the level of the Mercers' and Drapers' Companies. Over the period 1497/8 to 1539/40, 33 cappers held senior office in the Craft; and of these, as many as nine became junior civic officers. Six went on further to become sheriffs; and one, Nicholas Heynes, was briefly mayor in 1525.[12]

At the top of this bourgeois society, in fact, access to the civic status group was strictly controlled by the number of official positions available. Since, at the junior civic level, office was invariably held only once, the system thus admitted forty new men each decade (two wardens and two chamberlains per year) to the upper echelons of the city, thus providing the pool from which the future magisterial elite would be drawn. Therefore as the number of possible official positions dwindled, upward progress became slowed. If 20 new sheriffs were elected each decade, there were usually only ten mayors. At the top, there was a constant process of replacement as the old aldermen died, or in the odd case, departed. The rate of disappearance was very regular: nine aldermen vanished in the first decade of the sixteenth century; twelve in the second; and ten (including one deposition) in the third.[13]

Rather more marked than in the case of the Craft fellowships, moreover, though hardly critical for the upward movement in society, was the uneven incidence of family perpetuation at the top. There was, in truth, little immediate danger of family oligarchies emerging. In 1544, the first year after which the last of the 28 members of the magisterial elite in 1522 had disappeared from the scene, only one of the new elite was a direct descendant of the earlier group.[14] Indeed, taking the original 28 as a whole, 17 of these families appear to have left no later mark at all on the upper ranks of the city. Of the remainder, however, one may have had a descendant as a ward constable, another was succeeded by a peripheral member of the Forty-eight, and three namesakes appear later as

[11] *L.B.*, pp. 667, 605 – John Mors; 651. The carpenter, John Tomson was chamberlain in 1536, C.R.O. A7(a), p. 145.   [12] *Infra*, pp. 252, 254–6.
[13] Only eight men took up the mayoralty for the *first* time between 1500 and 1509. These figures are derived from a running index of Leet attendances in *L.B., passim.* For departure from the city, *infra*, pp. 265–6.
[14] Christopher, son of Thomas Waren, P.C.C. 26 Jankyn.

junior civic officers.[15] Only three families re-emerge as subsequent mayors and aldermen, though to these should also be added the cases of William Marler, Robert Grene junior, and Thomas Bonde. All three of these descendants of the 1522 group appear to have achieved the rank of gentleman. The two former, moreover, did hold office in the city: Marler as sheriff, and Grene as city coroner from as early as 1521.[16]

Clearly then, the opportunities for upward mobility at the top of society simply became, as one would expect, narrower at this level, even though the same families did not dominate the magisterial elite from year to year. Nevertheless, the part played by family ties cannot be ignored either in this connection or in our wider examination of the social structure. This is therefore an appropriate point at which to turn to that much neglected topic – the significance of kinship in late medieval urban society.

[15] John Wall, who is listed amongst the 50 men from the wards chosen to view the city's lands, was obviously of sufficient 'honeste' at least to be chosen as constable (cf. *supra*, p. 130). John Clark attended as a very junior member of the Leet and so may have been a member of the 48. Thomas Heryng (*L.B.*, p. 693), Richard Humphrey (*L.B.*, p. 718) and Richard Dodde (*L.B.*, p. 770) all became wardens.

[16] The three who proceeded from the office of sheriff were Christopher Waren (*L.B.*, p. 727); Thomas Smyth junior (*L.B.*, p. 739); and John Nethermill (*L.B.*, p. 783). Evidence for gentry status: Marler, C.R.O. C214, *L.B.*, p. 707; Grene, *L.B.*, p. 701; Bonde, P.C.C. F19 Dyngley.

13. *Informal groupings (ii) The extended family*

A second type of informal grouping within the community was the extended family. Cutting across and inter-connecting at least the leading personnel of all the formal institutions of society so far discussed, kinship ties are also relevant to the problems of social stratification. Both conceptually and methodologically, however, an analysis of this subject presents considerable difficulties. First, studies of modern urban society have shown, not surprisingly, that, of the relatives an individual may possess, only those dubbed as 'intimate' kin are of social importance; or, to use a blanket definition, those having 'a fairly-well defined set of rights and duties governing their behaviour as kin'.[1] More specifically, such people comprise 'those with whom there was frequent visiting and mutual aid when necessary'.[2] It follows from this, in the second place, that the historian has to seek for *nominated* kin, and these he can find only in wills. Here, unfortunately, there is a danger that, for those of modest means, personal circumstances may have precluded the mention of certain relatives. For this reason, therefore, much of the analysis which follows has been restricted to the wealthiest men in the city, those whose wills were proved in the Prerogative Court of Canterbury, and more particularly, within that number, the wills of 24 ex-sheriffs who died between 1517 and 1547, i.e. roughly a quarter of all the aldermen serving during that period.[3] Unrepresentative of the community as a whole though they may have been, they provide us nevertheless with a fixed yardstick with which to measure the ramifications of the extended family.

[1] W. M. Williams, *A West Country Village: Ashworthy* (London, 1963), p. 168.
[2] Elizabeth Bott, *Family and Social Network* (London, 1957), p. 120.
[3] William Pysford (P.C.C. 9 Ayloffe); Nicholas Burwey (27 Ayloffe); John Haddon (17 Ayloffe); John Hardwen (27 Ayloffe); Hugh Dawes (29 Maynwaryng); Robert Green (17 Bodfelde); John Strong (20 Bodfelde); John Clerk (23 Bodfelde); Richard Burwey (F28 Bodfelde); Richard Marler (20 Porch); William Dawson (19 Jankyn); Thomas Waren (25 Jankyn); William Banwell (3 Thower); John Humphrey (15 Thower); William Wycam (2 Hogen); William Smith (F38 Hogen); John Bond (F19 Dyngeley); Thomas Dodde (1 Alenger); Christopher Wade (32 Dyngeley); Julian Nethermill (6 Alenger); Thomas Banwell (19 Spert); Richard Dodde (6 Alen); Arthur Godriche (20 Alen); William Cotton (51 Alen).

These 24 members of the civic elite – all but four of whom served as mayor – formed a tightly knit group. As somewhat later, at Exeter and Norwich, and to a lesser extent Bristol and Leicester, they were inter-connected by both blood and marriage ties.[4] Six were either brothers or fathers and sons, with the further possibility of a pair of cousins. Seven or possibly nine were connected directly or indirectly by marriage, and one of these, Julian Nethermill, was brother-in-law to two others in the sample. The firmest marriage alliance was that between the Bondes and the Doddes: John Bonde's son and daughter, Thomas and Winifred, having been married to the two children of Thomas Dodde, an ex-mayor of the city, whose surviving son, Richard, was also an alderman. Other marriage connections are obviously disguised by the nature of the evidence. Nevertheless, a further four families were linked by god–parental ties and, finally, ten were connected by either birth or marriage with other past, present or future members of the Leet. All these categories overlap, but only two men (conceivably four) appear to have had no other aldermanic connections that can be traced.

But if familial ties thus reinforced the bonds of shared responsibility within the tiny councils of the city, there was, on a broader view, also a strong community of commercial interest amongst the male members of the extended family of the elite. This was partly due to a tendency for sons to succeed their fathers in the same occupational fellowships. Thus in the Mercers' company (which contained Grocers, Merchants of the Staple, and probably Vintners as well), both William Pysford and Richard Marler had two sons, while Thomas Dodde and Henry Rogers had one each. Among the Drapers, Thomas Bonde, Julian Nethermill and Thomas Banwell all had

---

Kinship ramifications have been further sought in, and genealogies where possible reconstructed, with the help of: 22 Adeane (Thomas Bonde); 3, 14 and 22 Holder (Henry Smyth, John Gilbert, Thomas Lee, Humphrey Grene); 11, 14, 16, 20 and 22 Ayloffe (Thomas Turner, Henry Rogers, Thomas Ford, John Barnbe, William Bond, William Pysford the younger); 13, 16, 18 and 29 Maynwaryng (Thomas Hill, Robert Wheytell, John Hopkins, Thomas Bemyche); 37 and 38 Bodfelde (Henry Pysford, John Marler); 2 Hogen (John Marler); 19 and 25 Jankyn (Joan Lambard, Henry Kylbye); 27 Alenger (Isabelle Waide); 6 and 15 Alen (Richard Dodde, Joan Banwell); 21 and 23 Wrastley (Thomas Bonde, Cuthbert Geyner or Joyner); 24 Mellershe (John Nethermill).

[4] W. T. MacCaffrey, *Exeter 1540–1640* (Harvard, 1958), pp. 253–6; W. G. Hoskins, 'The Elizabethan Merchants of Exeter' in S. T. Bindoff, J. Hurstfield and C. H. Williams (eds.), *Elizabethan Government and Society: Essays Presented to Sir John Neale* (London, 1961), pp. 164–8.

adult sons also in the fellowship, while the Smyth family boasted two brothers and a son of one of them as well. Inter-marriage forged further links. Among the Mercers it seems probable that the Pysfords were allied with the Fords, and, more certainly, with both the Marlers of Coventry and the Wigstons of Leicester – perhaps so comprising one of the most formidable combinations of merchant-wealth in the Midlands.[5] Within the Drapers' fellowship, Julian Nethermill was father-in-law to Christopher Waren, and Hugh Dawes to Thomas Lee. Lastly, godparentage effected at the least a quasi-kinship connection. The draper, John Haddon, or his wife, were godparents to some of the children of both William Wycam and Julian Nethermill; while among the Grocers, Isabell, wife of Christopher Wade, stood godmother to a daughter each of James Rogers and the latter's brother-in-law Richard Humfrey.

A major function of the extended family at this level of society, and in the preservation of its social standing and business efficiency, lay in overcoming liquidity difficulties. Kinship clearly eased the way both in privately securing a loan and with respect to the time taken in repaying it – considerations of no little importance in a society where the only system of credit available involved a semi-public recognisance of short-term debt in the Statute Merchant Roll. Thus the draper William Smyth expressed his gratitude to his brother Thomas by leaving him 100 marks 'over and aboue the detts I do owe unto him borowed at severall tymes'.[6] Other loans to brothers were made by the shoemaker, Thomas Cotton and by Thomas Bonde, who also lent to a presumptive brother-in-law. Probable first cousins so involved included Henry Marler, a priest of Trinity parish, and John Marler. More distant still, £40 debts were owed not only by James Rogers to his father-in-law, but even by John Bonde, an ex-mayor of the city who seems to have bought his way into the gentry *via* a country estate in Lancashire, by 1537–8, and who had borrowed the sum from his son-in-law's uncle.

The bonds of family in fact were not restricted to blood relatives only, but were extended to affines. The marriage alliance was a reality, and may well have simply cemented existing friendships between families. A selection of six fairly full wills,[7] for example,

---

[5] Cf. *Visitations in the Diocese of Lincoln 1517–31*, ed. A. Hamilton Thompson (Lincolnshire Record Society, xxxiii, 1940), pp. xxx, 12.

[6] P.C.C. 38 Hogen.

[7] P.C.C. 27 Ayloffe, 22 Adeane, 19 Dyngeley, 15 Thower, 19 Jankyn, 22 Holder.

demonstrates the spread of relationships involved in those nominated by the testator as feoffees for property, as executors or as overseers. They include a brother, two cousins, three brother-in-laws, a son-in-law, and even a father-in-law. The limits of affinal obligation, however, seem to have been clearly defined. Henry Smyth, for example, appears to have provided a loan, not a gift, for the burial of his own father-in-law.

Affinal responsibility was even invoked in more personal matters to do with the care of surviving children. An uncle, John Nethermill, took it upon himself to find a good position for his nephew, although his apparently widowed sister was still alive. The boy was bequeathed to another of the testator's brothers-in-law, Sir William Garret and his lady 'praynge them bothe for godesake and at this my request to use him as their owne'.[8] In this case, a bequest of £20 to this end no doubt eased the obligations of affinity. Similarly, the supervision of the marriages of relict daughters could concern only other members of the extended family after the death of the parents. Isabell Waide's bequests to her two unmarried daughters were conditional on their heeding the counsel and advice, not only of their elder brother, but also of their brother-in-law 'especyally in theire maryages'.[9]

But if male affines took on kinship responsibilities, the objects of previous assistance as well as actual bequests were nearly always blood relatives. The most deserving of these, where she survived, was of course the widowed mother. The twice-widowed Joan Banwell, for example, was not only deeply grateful to her son, by her first marriage, who was by then resident in London, for 'his goodnes extended towards me continuallye over and above my poor lyving'; she was also indebted for a loan of 20 nobles to her son-in-law Thomas (presumably through a previous marriage of her first husband).[10] By the same token, annuities were settled on the mothers of Isabell Waide and Henry Kilby.

Similar obligations of blood relationships were expressed even more widely. Thomas, sire of the Bonde dynasty, made vast philanthropic arrangements for the poor of Coventry, its suburbs and Warwickshire, 'provided that if any of my kindrede within the iiij[th] or iiij[th] degre be in necesitie that then they and everyche of theym in the almes afore rehersed be proferd and served afore other' – in

[8] P.C.C. 24 Mellershe.   [9] P.C.C. 27 Alenger.   [10] P.C.C. 15 Alen.

itself a suggestive indication of the extent to which contemporarie may have been expected to keep track of extended family relation ships.[11] More particularly, provision might be made, as in the case o William Cotton, for my 'servant and kinswoman'.[12] In bad time particularly, the servant-keeping household of a wealthy relative could represent a haven of refuge for poor kindred, though the tie of blood in themselves might make for difficulties in the relationshij of master to servant. William Dawson, a draper and innkeeper, fo example, required of his widow that during her life she should 'fynde unto Henry Dawson' (clearly his own brother) 'and to hy: wife now beinge meate drinke and iij marks in money . . . in condicion the said Henry and his wif can be content to doo thei service trewly as trew servants'.[13] Younger relatives might be assisted in other ways too. William Pysford appears to have helped his younger brother Roger by setting him up with household goods Henry Marler's nephew John, occupied a house owned by his uncle in 1522, though whether the rent he paid was reduced it is impos sible to tell.[14] One alderman provided £2 a year for five years no only for his stepson, but also for his son-in-law, towards thei exhibitions at the university, while Richard Dodde took upon him self the responsibility of relieving the poor children of John a Herington, 'my kinsman'.[15]

If these were some of the functions of the extended family at thi. level of society, it is relevant to enquire into its size. Such figures a: may be deduced are of course imprecise because of difficulties ii tracing genealogical connections. However, it may be said tha these twenty four members of the magisterial elite were able t nominate an average of seven relatives or affines outside their ow households. 13 named fewer, but only four could name a mere one or two. On the other hand, six nominated over twelve relatives each and of these, Julian Nethermill and Thomas Banwell named 17, and Richard Marler roughly 21. The number of households concerned also varied from one to eleven, the average being three or four Approximate as they are, these figures bear a remarkable resem-blance to those quoted for the working class district of Bethna Green in modern times.[16]

[11] P.C.C. 22 Adeane.   [12] P.C.C. 51 Alen.   [13] P.C.C. 19 Jankyn
[14] P.C.C. 9 Ayloffe; C.R.O. A96, fo. 77v.   [15] P.C.C. 17 Ayloffe, 6 Alen
[16] Peter Townsend, *The Family Life of Old People* (Harmondsworth, 1963) p. 127.

To make comparisons with the lower levels of society in pre-Reformation Coventry, however, is more difficult. Below this homogeneous social stratum, testamentary provisions may not have reflected so closely the numbers of intimate kin for obvious reasons. Nevertheless, there are a number of factors which suggest that this urban elite was unrepresentative of those of ordinary, as opposed to 'honest', commoner status and of the poor.

Most significantly, these 24 aldermen comprised probably the most stable and longest-lived group in the community. Attention has already been drawn to their length of service in the councils of the city.[17] It may now be added that at least 14, perhaps 16, of the sample (two of whom were possibly bachelors) were old enough at death to be the parents of married children. Seven, possibly eleven, of these were grandfathers. At least three of the sample, moreover, had been married more than once. William Pysford, indeed, who was one of three widowers in the group, had had three wives. By contrast, the shorter life-expectancy of many ordinary craftsmen, and most journeymen, would have militated against the possibility of experiencing grand-parenthood.

A second factor, that has as much to do with the bias of the sample, as with a genuine social difference, is that at least some aldermen were probably eldest sons. This may help to explain the numbers of siblings and lateral kin still surviving at the death of each testator. Ten or perhaps twelve magistrates were survived by at least one sibling. Nine or possibly eleven, nominated further kin, usually first cousins. A minority of two fifths nominated neither siblings nor further kin. Lower down society where life expectancy was low, younger sons at least would hardly have been able to nominate many siblings on their death-beds.

A third consideration heavily underlines a further distinction between the upper and lower levels of society in this respect. Not only did more children survive, and hence in larger sibling groups, within the homes of the wealthiest (as both increasing mean sizes *and* the distributions of such groups in 1523 demonstrate),[18] but it seems most probable that such children stayed on longer at home than was usual. A listing of all males of twelve and over for Gosford ward in 1534, for example, shows that when junior namesakes were mentioned they were not infrequently residing in households where

---

[17] *Supra*, p. 124.   [18] *Infra*, tables 29 and 30.

there also appear to have been servants.[19] Reference has already been made to the Drapers' ordinance allowing fathers to apprentice their own sons at 14, and a similar situation is implied by a rule of the Dyers which forbade a master to keep potential apprentices in his household more than a month, except in the case of his 'son or sons'.[20] Not only were wealthy families larger on average, therefore, but the surviving children in them are likely to have been more closely spaced in terms of years and to have forged a stronger family bond than in those poorer families where so few children survived and from which they were sent out to service quite probably at an earlier age.

All three of these factors which distinguished the elite from the poorer end of society have suggested that the extended family at the lower level can never have been very large. There is one final observation, however, that should be made in this connection. The operational extended family of the elite was not geographically restricted to the city. The eldest son of William Pysford, for example, had been set up apparently as a farmer at Baginton, some miles to the south of the city. Moreover, although two of William's daughters first married Coventry men, both of them re-married outside the city – one into the Wigston family of Leicester and the other to a London mercer. Similarly John Bonde's daughter Dorothy married Roger Gyllot of Leicester, while one of Julian Nethermill's sons-in-law was an alderman and knight of London. At this level of society, therefore, not only were there usually extended family contacts within Coventry itself, but the need for frequent travel probably meant that such contacts were also sustained over longer distances in a manner very similar to the habits of the present day.[21] To this extent then, the incidence of extra-familial relationships amongst the elite was correspondingly abbreviated within the city itself.

Below the level of the elite, reliable direct evidence is difficult to find, but a very approximate and one-sided measure of the extent of residential proximity between putative relatives throughout the city is furnished by the 1523 census. An analysis of this sort has to be based on the incidence of like-surnames (all Smiths here being excluded) within each of the wards. Many families with the same surnames would not of course have been related, but there must

---

[19] *Infra*, p. 230.
[20] *Supra*, p. 83; Reader 4, fo. 116v.   [21] *Supra*, p. 139

have been other links across ward boundaries that this method fails to recapture, and which would partially compensate for exaggerations in the results.[22]

Given these provisos, it would appear that, over the city as a whole, 18.6 per cent of the 1,274 households involved were headed by people with similar surnames to at least one other household head in the same ward. In the vast majority of these cases only two, or less often three, households (rarely more) comprised a like-surname group in each ward. Overwhelmingly, such groups were composed of males. Out of the 109 cases (involving 237 households), only 33 concerned a male and a female of the same surname, and a mere six (possibly eight) comprised females only.

Rough as these figures are, a closer look at 19 less ambiguous groups (where families are recorded as no more than six households apart in each listing), prompts some tentative conclusions. Of these examples, only five involved a male and a female; and one, females only. In such cases where for instance, a widow, Margery Wardlow is found apparently living three doors away from John Wardlow, butcher; or Agnes Taylor, widow, is listed next to one Christopher Taylor; or when Margery Stele (marital status unspecified) is living next door to Alice Stele, widow; it is hard not to conclude that elderly mothers are residing close to their offspring. Similarly, in those groups of surnames involving men, where John and William Joyner are found listed one after the other, and both turn out to be butchers; or where Robert and William Aston are listed four households apart and both are known to be cappers; there is a strong presumption that fathers and sons were deliberately living in close proximity.

Although the evidence is ambiguous, there are then some grounds for inferring that patterns of residential propinquity between parents and adult male offspring (if not their precise incidence) were already established by this period. The number of surname-groups is probably sufficiently large, even when allowance is made for accident. Not only does this method inevitably ignore possible linkages between newly-married daughters and their parents, but the documentation itself disguises those cases where close topographical relationships between like surnames on opposite sides of the same street might be suggestive. Moreover, the evi-

---

[22] For a description of the evidence provided in the enumeration *v.* appendix I.

dence emanates from a time of severe depopulation and a probably substantial turnover of property which might be expected to have reduced the number of surname-groups to below what was normal.

In the contexts of both social stratification and the ramifications of kinship amongst the elite, therefore, certain observations seem permissible. First it would appear that the great majority of surname-groups each involved one or more members of the *commoner* 'class'. Except in two wards (Gosford and Earl), occupational labels, which imply membership of one or other type of Craft fellowship, may usually be attached to such people from the evidence of the 1522 assessment or the 1524 subsidy instalment.[23] The 'submerged' quarter of poorer households at this period, in fact, is very largely excluded. The commonalty, mainly by virtue of the Craft system, was the more permanent 'fixed interest' in the city, and was doubtless sustained over crisis years, at least in part, by mutual help between members of the extended family. The same could not be said of the more vulnerable and more fluid unskilled labour-force.

Secondly, although the commonalty in general may have had more permanent roots in city society than their social inferiors, even at the former level the extended family can have been neither as durable nor, in consequence, as extensive as that of the elite. A lower life-expectancy, in particular, surely meant that neighbourhood propinquity at least was to be experienced only at the beginning and at the very end of each domestic cycle. It is interesting to note that, as might be expected, for the entire membership of the Cappers' Craft in 1546–7, there were more surname-links *between* masters and journeymen than within either category alone. In that year, ten masters were matched by eleven journeymen with the same names, most of the latter being no doubt sons.[24] Few fathers apparently lived long enough to see their sons set-up by themselves in business. Similarly the evidence for family structure in the 1523 census itself, implies that only in a tiny minority of cases (invariably mothers) can elderly parents have survived long enough to become so enfeebled that they had to be taken into a filial home.[25]

Within the community proper, therefore, kinship had a part to play, though its significance decreased towards the lower levels of

[23] C.R.O. access. 18: 96; P.R.O. E179/192/125.
[24] Cappers' accs., fos. 67v., 68.   [25] *Infra*, p. 203, table 15.

society. Transitory it may have been, but the extended family performed a vital function in helping to sustain a society dominated by the self-employed. Above all, it seems to have lent some reality to the concept of neighbourhood at the street level, a subject which it is now necessary to examine in rather more detail.

14. *Informal groupings (iii) Social topography*

Apart from the household and perhaps the extended family, none of the formal groups nor the informal groupings so far discussed necessarily involved daily face-to-face contact. They may have defined both a man's different social positions and the role-relationships that flowed from those positions, but the reality of every-day life was rooted in the home and the neighbourhood. For the journeyman and those others who walked elsewhere to work, of course, two different neighbourhoods may have been involved. Moreover, in discussing neighbourhoods from an inevitably static point of view, it must not be forgotten that there is evidence for substantial internal movement within the city at least at times of crisis.[1] The spatial pattern of neighbourhood relationships was therefore frequently shifting.

The nearest we can get to the character of the street-neighbourhood in the documents is at the level of the ward. There were ten wards in all, but each usually contained a stretch of important main road plus a greater or lesser number of side-roads or lanes. In the larger wards therefore only a very generalised impression may be gained, but the broad character of all quarters of the city emerges quite plainly.

The ward as an institution, moreover, had a social identity of its own in a city where, unlike York, Norwich or even Leicester with their numerous churches, there were only two vast parishes. By contrast to all the formal groups in the community except the household, the ward existed in space as well as being an intangible part of the social structure. In it, all males of twelve and over were gathered into tithing, while its most 'honest' inhabitants served as constables (roughly six to a ward, though the number varied) under the supervision of an alderman.[2] The wards provided the units for tax collection, fire-fighting and probably furnished the watch, duty

---

[1] *Supra*, p. 65; *infra*, pp. 303–4.
[2] This is indicated by the probable 1534 tithing list of Gosford, *L.B.*, p. 692. The exact numbers of constables per ward clearly varied cf. *L.B.* pp. 421–2 and 649–50.

in which appears to have rotated on a topographical basis.[3] Where relevant, they contained conduit-keepers to oversee the water supply, while every ward had its own ale-tasters.[4] Above all the wards claimed an indirect popular voice in the oversight and disposition of the city's common lands. When major changes involving the letting of private closes (and economic matters too) were envisaged by the city government, it was broadly established that 'the good myndes of euery warde' be consulted, and viewers of the lands be chosen (by the municipality) from each of them.[5] Whether or not the wards also furnished the members of all the other juries that frequently assembled for various purposes in the city, we do not know, but it seems probable.[6] Despite its shifting membership, therefore, the ward does comprise a relevant unit of study when assessing how the social topography of the city inter-mixed those who made up both the various formal groups and the other informal groupings in the community. The ward, after all, was the basic unit of social control: not only was it 'policed' by its constables, but many of the lane-ends had chains hanging ready for use as barriers probably for riot control.[7]

Certain historical and geographical determinants had broadly dictated the distribution of the population amongst the different wards of the city. Above all, the historic division of Coventry into the Prior's and Earl's halves was still reflected in the economic biases of each. The former contained the ancient marketing centre of the city – the food-stuff markets for grain, meat, poultry and fish in the Cross Cheaping, and, further north, over the river, probably the livestock markets for horses and cattle.[8] To these areas were therefore always attracted the occupations mainly concerned; the most conspicuous, as in other towns, being the butchers, the most

[3] Taxation: *L.B., passim*; fires: *L.B.* p. 414; watch: *L.B.*, pp. 256, 738–9; gates: *L.B.* p. 254.

[4] *L.B.*, p. 517. *L.B.*, pp. 541, 677–8, 725, 726.

[5] *L.B.*, p. 630, and cf. pp. 730, 760–1. For the earlier relationship between the wards and the Forty-eight, *ibid.*, p. 42.

[6] The earliest known jury-list known to me is for 11 March 1577/8 amongst the clerk of the market records. It is not, however, arranged by wards.

[7] *L.B.*, pp. 257, 261 initiated in 1451 as part of a general overhaul of the city's defences at this time of national turmoil.

[8] Davis, *The Early History of Coventry*, p. 25. The quadrilateral site (later in-filled) – at the junction of Bishop Street and Silver/Cook Street – is still clearly visible on Speed's map.

tightly grouped occupation in the city.[9] Nearby, were a number of fishmongers and vintners.[10]

In the old Earl's half which had thus been historically excluded from the traditional marketing area,[11] the emphasis was more on the wool, textile and clothing industries. Not only did this area contain the site of the sheep-fair, just inside Gosford Gate (and so well placed to receive the sheep of N.E. Warwickshire and of Leicestershire), but it could also boast the Wool Hall and the Drapery, that vast covered cloth market that stretched for 20 bays through from Bailey Lane to Earl Street, and the Welsh Drapery.[12] In this section of the city, therefore, were scattered the relevant occupations: mercers in Bailey Lane, and drapers in Earl Street and Little Park Street; weavers in Earl and Much Park street wards; and shermen and tailors in Earl and Gosford street wards. These last, indeed, had their gild chapel of St George at Gosford Gate, and a lodge somewhere outside the city to the south-east.[13] Lastly, in this connection, the capping industry (after the butchers, the most concentrated occupational grouping) was largely centred on Jordanwell ward, though it overlapped into neighbouring areas and even as far afield as Spon Street ward. Connected rather more loosely were those crafts that serviced these industries, like the cardmakers and sheargrinders. In none of these cases, however, was any occupation so concentrated as were the butchers and cappers. Even so, there were

[9] For facilities near the Butcheries, *supra*, p. 77, n. 36. No fewer than 30 butchers (i.e. excluding graziers) may be identified in Cross Cheaping in 1522. C.R.O. access. 18: A96, fos. 20–21v., and 23v. to 24, comprise almost continuous lists of butchers, and undoubtedly relate to Great and Little Butcher Rows respectively. It was perhaps appropriate that this tightly knit sub-community (many of them mastiff-dog owners apparently, *L.B.*, p. 623) with its chapel in the adjacent church of Holy Trinity (Sharp, *Antiquities*, p. 84) called its Craft fellowship the 'Fraternity of S. Antony' (Reader 4, fo. 100). Nothing else is known about the religious side of this organisation except that it observed two obits annually (Sharp, *Antiquities*, p. 94).

[10] The following generalisations about the distribution of occupations are based on the 1522 assessment augmented by information from e.g. the 1524 subsidy return, P.R.O. E179/192/125, and C.R.O. A6.

[11] Before the south aisle of St Michael's church was built, however, stalls had been set up in Bailey Lane, *L.B.*, p. 461. There was also a mysterious Spon market (*L.B.*, p. 338), which may have been strategically situated just over the outer boundary of that ward.

[12] *L.B.*, p. 770; Templeman, *op.cit.*, pp. 115–16 – where 33 shops, five standings and a chamber are described in addition to the Welsh Drapery and the Wool Hall; C.R.O. A24, p. 29.

[13] Dormer Harris, *Dr Troughton's Sketches of Old Coventry*, p. 37; *L.B.*, p. 763.

some butchers in the old Earl's half; some textile craftsmen in the old Prior's half.

The explanation for this lies not only in the time that had elapsed since the two halves were amalgamated, but also in geographical factors. Most particularly, the need for access to water by certain industries meant that dyers or tanners or whittawers, for example, were to be found in all wards through or by which the river Sherbourne ran. Though the fullers present a difficult problem in that many of those that may be identified worked outside the city and even its liberties;[14] in the case of the leather industries, it seems likely that the secondary occupations in industrial terms – the corvisors and glovers, for instance – were sited in relation to the primary producers, the tanners and the whittawers. There was then a marked tendency for the leather or leather-working industries to be concentrated towards the western end of the city with easy access, not only to water, but also to the Butchery from where the hides were bought. The Tanners' ordinances, indeed, specifically divided the Craft into two sections for the purpose of taking turns in this last connection – between those in Well Street and those in Spon Street.[15] It is thus notable that both the Barker's butts and the Whittawer's pageant-house lay out along Hill Street to the west.[16]

So obnoxious were the processes connected with leather-curing that, as in other towns, the most smelly activities were banished outside the city walls.[17] In the case of those crafts connected with sheep, lamb and pig-skins, this may well have meant that the products concerned largely by-passed the centre of the city altogether. The main long-distance route from Chester and hence Ireland, from whence came quantities of lamb-skin destined for London,[18] ended at Spon Street, around which suburban quarter were concentrated numbers of whittawers; while the skinners (many of whom lived in Little Park Street or Dead Lane) had their drying houses and pools (and incidentally their archery butts) south of the city walls in the Park.[19] Along the eastern side of the park itself and thus outside the walls, lay the main road south to London.

Long-term historical factors also determined the way in which the

[14] *Supra*, p. 49.   [15] C.R.O. access. 241, orig. fo. 5.
[16] C.R.O. C184.   [17] *L.B.*, pp. 302, 312.
[18] *L. & P. Addenda I* (i), no. 385.
[19] *L.B.*, p. 705, C.R.O. A3(b), pp. 141, 148; *L.B.*, p. 513.

residences of the wealthy were related to the ancient ritual and administrative core of the city. More than one observer noted that the ecclesiastical centre of Coventry comprised a single churchyard, the contiguous burial grounds of both the parish churches.[20] The entire northern side of this area, moreover, was delimited by the great Benedictine and cathedral church, the south porch of which gave onto the city cemetery, and in which, during times of plague only, the corpses were stacked for a ceremony of 'assoylement' by the monks as opposed to the parish priests.[21] Crossing and circulating the churchyard centre were the 'procession ways' along which wended the congregations of the two parish churches with their banners and other accoutrements on the great feast days of the church like Palm Sunday and Whitsunday.[22] Adjacent to the parish churches were halls for priests; and of whom (the chantry priests apart), 19 seem to have been attached to St Michael's in 1522, and 12 to Holy Trinity.[23] At the north-east corner of the churchyard, and east of the cathedral and its monastic community, was situated the palace of the Bishop of Coventry and Lichfield.

It can have been no coincidence, therefore, that the more important civic and commercial buildings were situated along the southern edge of this sacred area. The most significant of these was St Mary's Hall, the original centre of the Merchant Gild for the old Earl's half, and out of which the combined fraternity of Holy Trinity, St Mary, St John the Baptist, and St Katherine had eventually evolved. Closely linked as it was with the mayor-making ceremony, which even in post-Reformation times was still divided between the hall and the civic church,[24] St Mary's Hall was sited immediately opposite St Michael's church on the south side of Bailey Lane. In it met the court leet and the electoral jury, and accommodated within it was the council house, the armoury and the city treasury. Close by, to the east, and also fronting onto Bailey Lane, were probably the halls of the two leading fellowships in the city, the Mercers and the Drapers. Near these in turn were the

[20] *Leland's Itinerary in England and Wales*, ed. L. Toulmin Smith, 5 vols. (London, 1964), ii, p. 107. *L. & P.*, xiii (2), 674.
[21] *L. & P.*, xiii (2), 674; cf. Bliss Burbidge, *Old Coventry and Lady Godiva*, p. 139 regarding the 'apparille of wax' that was to accompany each corpse, and which became the property of the cathedral.
[22] Phythian-Adams, 'Ceremony and the Citizen', *loc.cit.*, p. 76.
[23] Sharp, *Antiquities*, p. 118; C.R.O., A24, p. 33. C.R.O. access. 18: A96, fo. 97v.
[24] C.R.O. A34, fos. 269–269v.

'Framing yard', the Wool Hall and the Draperies.[25] At the south-western corner of the churchyard, finally, were the gaol and the chambers belonging to the gaoler and the Steward.[26] The whole area in fact was topographically distinct from the open-air marketing centre of Cross Cheaping, although the country-bakers at least were allowed to sell near the gaol.[27]

The factors making for the broad distribution of occupations and, no doubt, both the prestige and the convenience that went with residence near the ritual centre and its isolation from the main through-routes in the city, had together also helped to dictate the evolving general pattern of housing at Coventry over the later middle ages. This distribution of the housing stock indeed provides us with the most relevant indicator of established residence patterns in the city. For, most fortunately, it is *broadly* possible to recapture the essential contemporary distinction between occupied cottages and houses, and their relative densities in each ward in 1522–3.

To achieve this it is necessary to apply the totals of various categories of rent specified in the 1522 assessment to the numbers of households given in 1523, on the not unreasonable assumption that those *excluded* in 1522 were too poor for inclusion. In Much Park and Bishop Street wards, for example, 30 and 21 cottages for poor folk were mentioned in 1522, even though their household heads were neither named nor assessed.[28] The total number of households is not likely to have been all that different between 1522 and 1523 but, in view of continuing depopulation and the probable under-counting of some possibly poor households in 1523, the results if anything perhaps exaggerate the proportion of better housing in each ward to some degree.

The two cut-off points for the rental categories concerned in the histogram (figure 2) have determined themselves. First, the evidence of both Trinity Gild and Corpus Christi Gild rentals makes it plain that cottage rents were overwhelmingly at the 2s., 4s., 5s. and 6s. level.[29] A minority were higher, but there can be little doubt that the category here isolated at the level of 6s. or less represents the

---

[25] It is not wholly clear whether the Mercers used the so-called 'Mercers' chapel' in St Mary's Hall before 1589, Sharp, *Antiquities*, p. 213; *V.C.H. Warks.*, viii, p. 145; Templeman, *op.cit.*, pp. 50, 75.
[26] *Ibid.*, p. 95.   [27] *L.B.*, p. 717.
[28] C.R.O. access. 18: A96, fos. 5r., 7v., 69v., 74r., 74v.
[29] Templeman, *op.cit.*, pp. 48 *et passim*; C.R.O. A6, fos. 147v.–148v., 246v.–247.

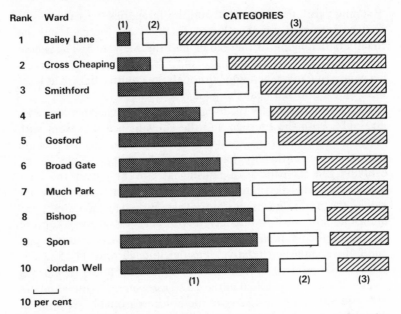

Figure 2   Ward-ranking by proportions of householders in each ward paying specific categories of rents in 1522–3

Numbers of inhabited houses categorised according to three broad rental valuations in 1522 and expressed as percentages of all households in 1523
(1) Houses valued at and under 6s. rent *p.a.*
(2) Houses valued at 6s. 8d. to 12s. rent *p.a.* inclusively
(3) Houses valued at *more* than 12s. rent *p.a.*
Notes: Freeholds have been apportioned proportionately between (2) and (3) only. For the numbers of households *vide* table 10

bulk of the working-class housing stock. The second cut-off point, at 12s. rent *per annum*, nevertheless acts as a cross-check on this, and it is noticeable that only in one instance, that of Broad Gate, is the ward ranking marginally changed thereby. Below this level, in fact, the distinction between a small house and a cottage was probably hard to sustain. Above this level, however, as later analysis will show (see table 29), roughly 50 per cent or more of the households concerned in each of the levels in an ascending scale of rental categories contained in-servants. Above the 12s. level, therefore, and arbitrary though it may be, we may be confident that it is the master craftsmen who are in question.

From the histogram, then, there emerges a broad but extremely

suggestive picture of the city's inhabited housing stock. The proportion of dwellings paying rents of over 12s. tends to corroborate
the usual image of the classic pre-industrial social pattern. The top
four wards, with over 50 per cent of their houses in this category
were all clustered together towards the centre of the city. Bailey
Lane ward contained the administrative and ritual centre (and
nineteenth-century sketches show part of it dominated by three
storied medieval houses);[30] Cross Cheaping, the major food-
market. Smithford ward was restricted to the important east/west
axial road, while Earl Street ward which contained, *inter alia*, the
residences of Messrs Marler and Nethermill, although similarly
biased, had a long tail of ever more modest housing out towards the
city wall. Once again local drawings show that the axial road
boasted many fine dwellings.[31] Topographically, only Broad Gate
ward appears to break this centralised pattern, but this is simply
because its main road housing was narrowly restricted by the ward
boundaries at this point (*v.* map 1). The bulk of its less substantial
dwellings clearly lay along the road towards Greyfriars Gate and
thence to Warwick. None of the top four wards gave onto an
important city gate: all the others did. (Cf. plates I and II)

Below this level the histogram reveals a remarkably consistent
proportionate spread throughout the wards of houses rented at
between 6s. 8d. and 12s. inclusively. Except in Bailey Lane, where,
significantly, they comprised only 10 per cent of the whole, and in
Broad Gate, where they represented some 30 per cent for the
reasons already suggested; in all other wards, the proportions
hovered around 20 per cent of each total.

The distribution of the 'working-class' housing, which constituted
an estimated forty per cent of all occupied dwellings by this stage in
the city's decline, thus furnishes an instructive contrast. Although
unevenly distributed, the percentages in each column show that all
the wards contained some. Even wealthy Earl embraced a sizeable
proportion at over 30 per cent. Not only Gosford on the eastern
edge of the city, but also Broad Gate, had about 40 per cent of their
properties in this category; while Spon, Bishop and Much Park all

---

[30] E.g. Dormer Harris, *Dr Troughton's Sketches of Old Coventry*, plate xxiv, the
Pepper Lane end.

[31] *Ibid.*, plates xxi, xxxi. Cf. Leland 'The strete that goithe from west up to este
southe est is the most principall of all the towne', Toulmin Smith (ed.), *op.cit.*, ii,
p. 107.

clustered near or over the 50 per cent mark. Jordan Well, at practically 60 per cent, finally emerges as containing the highest proportion of inhabited 'working-class' housing in the city.

While substantial housing was thus concentrated towards the centre of Coventry, there was no wholly consistent pattern with regard to the character of the housing at its periphery. If semi-suburban Gosford ranked as high as fifth, the other two semi-suburban wards – Bishop partly, and Spon, almost wholly – more nearly approximated to the traditional pattern of extra-mural poverty. It is evident, nonetheless, that the bulk of Bishop's housing was within the walls (see appendix 5), while the 'poorest' ward in the city, Jordan Well, was both adjacent to the wealthiest ward and entirely intra-mural.

Quite as marked as the social homogeneity of some wards whether rich or poor, therefore, was the considerable degree of inter-mixing: every single ward had housing at and above the 12s. level. In the folios of the 1523 census too, it is rare to come across as many as twenty households enumerated in a row that did not include at least one with in-servants.[32] That there were certain lanes containing poorer housing which are not specifically distinguished in the record is plain, but the overwhelming impression left by the evidence is that of residential intermingling between employers and employees with greater or lesser biases according to the ward concerned.

In a society where so much of life took place publicly in the street the mere fact of residence in a neighbourhood must thus have done something to dilute social segregation. At least one alderman's widow, Isabel Waide (a strong-minded but kindly busy-body, whose personality shines through the faded ink of her will), appears to have taken a personal interest in those living nearby to judge from her specific bequest 'to every of my pore Neyghbours wyfes betwene my house and the Hey Lane and betwene the lytle parke streat end and the Greyfreer lane' of 'a kercher and xijd. in monney'. A further reference to 'every of my other god-childerne beynge pore' suggests that she may even have acted as godmother to some of her poor neighbours' families; probably a quite common gesture at this level.[33]

---

[32] For the distributions of servant-keeping households in each ward v. table 17.
[33] P.C.C. 27 Alenger. Joan Banwell had god-children in three villages near which she had lived at the time of her first marriage, P.C.C. Alen 15.

Without in any way invoking an image of 'Merrie Englande', it is also fairly clear that street-parties were well-spaced but regular occurrences. Late sixteenth-century evidence demonstrates that, as elsewhere, May-poles for example were erected in the streets though we know nothing of their numbers.[34] Similarly, it would seem that the widespread custom of igniting bonfires on the road-ways at Midsummer was also observed, and if the usages of such contrasted communities as London, Warwick and Long Melford are any guide, this would also have been a time when the more prosper-ous provided food and drink for their poorer neighbours at trestle tables before their front doors.[35] Established neighbourhood arrangements of this kind, indeed, are further implied by the fact that when the Queen donated eight bucks to the city in 1474, six of them were then divided amongst the ten wards with gifts of money – no doubt for the purchase of drink.[36]

It is highly probable, that, despite their huge sizes, the two parishes into which the city was divided were also closely related to the ward system. Holy Trinity's two deacons, at least, were each responsible for a ward:[37] in this case Cross Cheaping and Bishop; and, in view of the greater number of priests attached to St Michael's, there cannot be much doubt that a similar arrangement existed in that case too. This subdivision of the parishes was very relevant to the nature of street-life and the neighbourhood, for contemporary religious practice was only partially an indoor affair involving large congregations, while even the provision of the holy-cake was organised by households on a street-by-street basis.[38] Above all the church came out to the people. The priest came to the house to escort the dead to church; he performed the marriage ceremony in the church porch; and, to judge from the fact that he had to bring the manuals back from his ward, he appears to have attended the newly-wed couple to their new home after the ser-vice.[39] Every Sunday, the deacons took holy water to each of their

[34] C.R.O. A14, p. 8.
[35] Phythian-Adams, 'Ceremony and the Citizen', *loc.cit.*, pp. 65–6; Charles Phythian-Adams, *Local History and Folklore: a New Framework* (London, 1975), p. 26. The street was also clearly an important venue for socialising at week-ends: cf. the ordinance of October 1588 against those who 'use any manner of plaie, or games in theire said houses, nor streets, no shall sit idle at their dores or on their bulks' during service times on the sabbath, C.R.O. A3(b), p. 3. For football in the streets, *ibid.*, pp. 13, 35.
[36] *L.B.*, p. 406.   [37] Sharp, *Antiquities*, pp. 122–4; *L.B.*, p. 110.
[38] *L.B.*, pp. 739, 669.   [39] Sharp, *Antiquities*, p. 123.

parishioners in their ward, and if too much holy cake had been provided probably distributed the surplus amongst the sick as well.[40] In ways such as these, the street-neighbourhood was physically related to the larger unit of the parish.

The parish church itself, moreover, was something of a social focus which openly involved its members from the different wards. The processions of the church-year around the churchyard centre have already been mentioned, and like so many other institutions in society periodic emphasis was laid on eating and drinking together. Whether or not, as was probably universally the case at this period, church ales were held for the sake of raising money for the upkeep of the church fabric, we do not know, but it seems likely.[41] Certainly the first deacon of Holy Trinity Church was required to 'help to sarve the parechshens, of bred & alle, and other thengs, at Mylborne's *derege*, and Meynley's, & other dereg's that byn made of the churche cost'.[42] In addition, the parishioners, or more probably some of them, had occasion to act together as a body. The churchwardens of St Michael's were apparently 'electyff yerely by the parisshons of the same chirche at their pleasir', and we can hardly doubt that this was done by a show of hands by those concerned.[43]

It is, of course, impossible to measure the extent of church attendance at this period, but it is likely to have been frequent for members of the community. That the poorer sort often drank elsewhere during divine service, and that importuning beggars were officially excluded are both matters beyond question.[44] But the Craft fellowships, particularly those that possessed chapels in one or other of the two parish churches, may well have attended *en bloc* as did the civic elite.[45] Indeed, so great does 'the presse of them' appear to have been, that when plague infected the city, many of the poorer citizens 'to avoyde all yll ayrs' resorted to St George's chapel

[40] *Ibid.*, p. 122.

[41] The second deacon of Holy Trinity was also 'to sarve at ev[er]y drenkyng, aftur ev[er]y derege done, at ye coste of ye churche', Sharp, *Antiquities*, p. 124. Cf. in 1521 'Item de potacionibus frequentatis in ecclesiis parochialibus' in *Bishop Geoffrey Blythe's Visitations c. 1515–1525*, ed. Peter Heath (Collections for a History of Staffordshire, 4th ser., vii, 1973), pp. 87, 86.

The evidence for parish gilds is very slight. For the quasi-Craft confraternity of Jesus at St Michael's *supra*, p. 118, n. 2, and a possible Holy Cross Gild at Holy Trinity, *V.C.H. Warks.*, viii, p. 324 though Sharp, (*Antiquities*, p. 88) describes the latter – probably rightly – as a chantry.

[42] Sharp, *Antiquities*, p. 123.   [43] *L.B.*, p. 460

[44] *Supra*, pp. 79, 66.   [45] *Supra*, pp. 137, 79.

instead; while others attended the two friary churches.[46] Within both of the unusually roomy parish churches themselves, however, and even without permanent pews, there was still a problem of space because the side aisles were taken up as separate chapels. It must have been the need to accommodate large congregations that determined the unusual position of the rood screen in Holy Trinity one bay deep *into* the chancel, thus leaving the crossing free (as well as the central nave aisle) for the audiences of sermons which were delivered from the great stone pulpit built into the south-*east* pier of the crossing. The influence of the Friars on the preaching mission in urban religion is here very evident.

Religious observances in fact crystallised different facets of the social structure in miniature. Men and women,[47] households and ward neighbourhoods, occupational fellowships and the elite: all were integrated in the religious dimension on Sundays, as were the great fraternities on other occasions. To those readers that have followed the intricacies of this analysis so far, it will therefore come as no surprise that even parochial office may well have inter-locked with the civic *cursus honorum*. The evidence is late, but there is no reason to suspect that the situation described was a recent innovation. In April 1609, St Michael's vestry ordered that the two men who had then been chosen wardens of the City, but had not yet 'been churchwardens of this parish, . . . shall pay for the use of the church 30s each, to be freed from that office'.[48]

Whatever the case, however, for the late medieval citizens of Coventry a practical facet of their sense of community lay in the inter-relationship of one Church and one people. Above all, a sense of the supernatural informed their view of that community. No discussion of social relationships and attitudes in the pre-Reformation period would be complete without at least attempting to probe, however clumsily, into this misty area of the contemporary mental world. Only in looking at this question of cultural attitudes will it be possible to draw together the threads of this analysis and so point the difference between the modern view of social structure presented in these pages and that held by those who were actually a part of it.

---

[46] Reader 4, fo. 140; *L. & P.*, xiii (2), 394; *L. & P.*, xiv (1), 34.
[47] For the probable separation of men and women in church, *supra*, p. 90.
[48] Reader 4, fo. 173v.

15. *Mirrors of a community*

For a modern anthropologist or the ethnographer, the study of a foreign culture is an objective process involving pre-conceptions and concepts that are imported from without. A vast literature abounds on the theory of social structure and, if nothing else is clear, it is certain that the analyst invariably imposes an external order onto real life that a member of the society concerned might well not recognise. For the historian of a society that existed nearly half a millennium ago and for which, even in a richly documented case, the information available is dauntingly incomplete, that probability is greater still. It is for this reason that the foregoing reconstruction of Coventry society has been restricted to what might correctly be described as simplistically ethnographic. In analysing a community as far as possible as a whole, it has been necessary to concentrate on what was 'normal', although the 'average man' never exists in real life. Moreover, some of what has been said has been derived from the 'norms' of behaviour as ideally expressed in, for instance, Craft ordinances as opposed to contemporary practice. In both these respects then, the Coventry that has been described represents an artificial construct. This is a crux of all social historical analysis about which the historian can do very little except be aware, and above all, admit to the interested reader.

But if this is a twentieth-century construct of a medieval communal structure, it is no less true that Coventry contemporaries too had their own image of the city which was quite as artificial. Its history was expressed in myth; the ideal of its contemporary structure in ritual. Both were detached from the actual realities of life; both were mediums of celebration; both were preserved or developed in all likelihood by the elite; both were lived rather than studied or articulated analytically. Together they served to identify and explain what made Coventry different from anywhere else.

A number of themes emerge from what little may be reconstructed of contemporary Coventry's view of its origins and past. First, unlike the foundation of Leicester by King Lear, and of London by Brutus of Troy, Coventry lacked an heroic male founder. On the contrary, great emphasis was placed on feminineness,

chasteness and saintliness. Was it not to the obscure village of
Coventry that the saint of Cologne

   . . . thither wisely brought that goodly Virgin-band

Th'eleven thousand maids, chaste *Ursula*'s Commaund;
and did not each virgin, when leaving, bequeath 'some special
virtue' to 'one of her own sex'?[1] The feast day of this remarkable
group of ladies was still specifically commemorated in the timing of
one of the fairs in the seventeenth century.[2] In like fashion, and
rather more accurately, tradition linked the beginnings of Coventry
with the foundation of a nunnery by the virgin St Osburg whose
skull was preserved as a precious relic in the cathedral (which itself
included the saint in its dedication), and whose day was still regularly observed by the Weavers' Craft in pre-Reformation times.[3]
Early attempts at interpreting the place name, Coventry, indeed,
sometimes (and mistakenly) emphasised 'convent' as the major
element in it.[4] Above all, it was not Earl Leofric, but Lady Godiva
who was most celebrated in the city's famous legend (the salacious
connotations of Peeping Tom being a later, seventeenth-century
addition),[5] though both were buried in the original abbey church
which together they had founded. Her memory was still marked in
the sixteenth century. Mass on 'Dame Goodyves daye' was annually
attended by the Cappers' Craft, and it was on this day too that
head-masters of the Weavers handed over the Craft goods to his
successor.[6] Her name moreover was corrupted significantly into
'Good Eve'.

With such emphasis on feminine responsibility for Coventry's
origins and development, a community immaculately conceived
and chastely nurtured as it were, the local pre-occupation with the
popular advocacy of the Virgin Mary may not have been uncon-
nected. Her's was the main dedication of the cathedral (as well as to

---

[1] J. W. Hebel (ed.), *Poly-Olbion by Michael Drayton* (Oxford, 1961), song xiii,
lines 259–60. Drayton noted that 'sufficient justification of making a Poem, may be
from tradition, which the Author here uses', *ibid.*, p. 287.   [2] L.M., fo. 37.

[3] Bliss Burbidge, *Old Coventry and Lady Godiva*, p. 120; C.R.O. access. 100:
Weavers 11, *passim*.

[4] Bliss Burbidge, *op.cit.*, p. 213; William Camden, *Britain or a Chorographical
Description*, transl. and enlarged by Philemon Holland (London, 1610), p. 567; cf.
William Dugdale, *The Antiquities of Warwickshire* (London, 1656), p. 85. Neither of
the latter could decide between this and the name of a local brook in this connection.

[5] Joan Lancaster and H. R. Davidson, *Godiva of Coventry* (Coventry, 1967),
pp. 52–5.

[6] E.g. Cappers' accs., fo. 34; C.R.O. access. 34: Weavers 2a, fo. 7v.

St Osburg) while St Mary's tower in the wall over-looking the way out of the city towards London, was passionately defended against criticism. One local priest who had criticised the advocacy of the Virgin and the daily saying of her Psalter as widely preached by a Franciscan Friar in the city was hissed and exluded from company as a result.[7] St Mary's Hall was where the mayoral inauguration took place on the Feast of the Purification, and was the meeting place of the combined gilds of the Holy Trinity, St Mary, St John the Baptist and St Katherine. As Miss Diane Bolton has pointed out, the seals of both the Mercers and the Shermen likewise show incidents in the life of the Virgin which may also have formed the subjects of their respective Corpus Christi plays.[8]

To the feminine creation myth was added another essential theme: that of patriotic Anglo-Saxon resistance against the Danish yoke. Whatever its sociological functions, the Hock Tuesday play annually commemorated the major contribution made by both the men and women of Coventry to the establishment of English freedom: 'the inhabitants of this Citye, with their neighbours utterly overthrew them [the Danes] in their last conflict with the Saxons'.[9]

Whether or not this nationalistic tradition was connected with what may have been a later legend which claimed Coventry as the birth and death place of the patron Saint of England, it is impossible to say.[10] The identification with St George, however, was considerable, though the fashion in his favour was a late medieval development, and spread too late for Coventry to create a leading civic gild in his name as in many other cities and towns like Norwich, Exeter and Leicester. Indeed the already existing gilds of Holy Trinity and Corpus Christi had fiercely resisted the establishment of such a fraternity, with its contemporary overtones of chivalry (Coventry

[7] Bliss Burbidge, *op.cit.*, pp. 141–2, and for the chroniclers' emphasis on Godiva's devotion to the virgin, *ibid.*, pp. 17–19, 25, 27–9. Amongst the relics in the cathedral were 'a piece of Our Lady's Tomb; and Our Lady's milk in silver gilt', *ibid.*, p. 120. On the exterior of St Mary's Chapel in the wall 'was a picture of the Blessed Virgin richly paynted', *ibid.*, p. 140.

[8] *V.C.H. Warks.*, viii, p. 213.

[9] Poole, *Coventry: its History and Antiquities*, p. 90 quoting the recorder's speech of welcome to Queen Elizabeth I in 1565.

[10] *V.C.H. Warks.*, viii, pp. 245–6. Mary Dormer Harris, it should be noted, made the brilliant point that the elephant on the city's seal and arms may also be connected with the slaying of the dragon, and is therefore to be associated directly with the St Michael bearing a shield charged with St George's cross as he kills the dragon on the reverse of the city's seal, *L.B.*, p. 857. St Michael was of course the dedication of the civic church.

had once belonged to the Black Prince himself), when the idea was first mooted by the relatively obscure Tailors and their journeymen in particular.[11] Nevertheless, St George's day was marked by a major civic procession, and the chapel of St George at Gosford Gate was probably its focus. At this gate also hung a giant bone of what was said to have been a fabulous boar slain by Guy of Warwick who, according to one tradition, was a son of St George.[12] Whatever else it may have represented, therefore, the cult of St George served to emphasise the identification of the city with the wider world of the nation although in a rather different way from the Hock Tuesday play. Xenophobia reinforced these sentiments: the 1452–3 ordinances of the Weavers, for instance, declare that 'no man of the Crafte take no prentys but that he be an Engelysch man borne & nother Frensche Skottysche ne Iryyssh And . . . [added relevantly but grotesquely] that he haue all his ryght lymes'.[13]

Historico-myth, furthermore, was used to validate freedom: it could be appealed-to as the ultimate customary precedent. The crucial beginnings of Coventry's commercial independence were traced back to Godiva's celebrated ride. Stained glass in Holy Trinity church, itself sited overlooking the medieval market area across which she was said to have ridden, portrayed both Leofric and Godiva with the words

>   I Luriche for the Love of thee
>   Doe make Coventre Tol-free.[14]

It was thus to this privilege that the protesting citizenry referred when they criticised the levying of an unprecedented toll on wool and cloth by the city government at the end of the fifteenth century:

>   Be it knowen & vnderstand
>   This Cite shuld be free & nowe is bonde.
>   Dame good Eve made it free;
>   & nowe the custome for woll & the draperie.[15]

What is also most marked about the citizens' apprehension of their past, and the authenticity that antiquity conferred on Coventry's urban status, was its emphasis on one city. The early middle ages had been dominated by incessant rivalry between the Prior's and the Earl's halves. Yet while tradition may have explained the

[11] C.R.O. B43.
[12] Phythian-Adams, 'Ceremony and the Citizen', *loc.cit.*, p. 77; *V.C.H. Warks.*, viii, p. 246, n. 70.   [13] C.R.O. access. 34: Weavers 2a, rule no. 13.
[14] Dugdale, *Antiquities of Warwickshire*, p. 86.   [15] *L.B.*, p. 567.

origin of this division (Dugdale for example probably reflected local thinking with regard to the origin of the Prior's half as an endowment of the original abbey by Leofric and Godiva), the years that intervened before 1345 were apparently not chronicled.[16] When the new craze for local history began about 1600, the mayoral annals, which must have been based on local tradition for the earlier years they describe, never seek to explain the period leading up to incorporation.[17] The late medieval sense of history thus seems to have been selective: relevance was restricted to origins and unity; to Coventry as an ancient undivided city. The welfare and the dignity, 'the welth & worship of the *hole* body', was the ideal.[18]

Even the crude form of sequential history represented in these later annals, however, marks a major step away from the cultural apprehension of the ordinary citizen in 1500. Such history purports to take objective note of singular events in particular: cultural involvement is by definition a subjective experience in which analytical observation at this period would have been to say the least, unlikely. Even the historico-myths just discussed were lived or celebrated in observance, ritual or protest. To complete this present analysis of an urban anatomy which perforce has concentrated on its bones, it is appropriate to turn now to this complex question of how myth, religion, superstition and customary practice informed the citizen's view of both his environment and the society in which he lived.

For the medieval townsman, the most obvious unthinking assumption is likely to have been the crucial distinction itself between town and country. For the intra-mural dweller (who represented the majority) in particular, the protective girdle of mighty stone walls (gradually joined over the period 1355–1534),[19] and nightly-closed gates, must have represented not only a physical, but also a psychological, frontier, while even suburbs were delimited by their 'bars'. Where not, there were crosses. It was surely no accident that locally, gallows appear to have been sited as far away from settlements as it was possible to be – on parish boundaries – themselves marked also by crosses, nor that executions took place outside the residential area. Lord Rivers and his son were beheaded on

[16] Dugdale, *Antiquities*, pp. 100–4.

[17] Bliss Burbidge, *op.cit.*, pp. 213–14, where in one version of the mayoral annals the story skips effortlessly from 'the days of King Edward the Confessor' to '288 years after this time'.   [18] L.M., p. 556; my italics.

[19] Gooder, *Coventry's Town Walls*, pp. 36–7.

Gosford Green to the east of the medieval suburb in 1469. Heretics were invariably burned in the Little Park, south of the walls.[20] Beyond the built-up area lay danger: not only the threat of siege at times of civil strife or the perils of the road, but also the menace of those less palpable forces which are commonly feared by all societies that live close to nature and whose working routines are dictated by the hours of daylight.

To deny the existence of such universal anxieties would be foolish, even though most of the detail of their local variation is unknown. It is no exaggeration to claim, however, that places which have long-standing superstitions or sacred connotations attached to them are treated with, at the least, respect by the society which perpetuates the superstition. Outside or on the strict topographical limits of Coventry, for example, lay the only three sources of water which appear to have been identified with sanctity, superstition or myth. St Osburg's pool lay on the other side of the river Sherbourne; further north was Swanswell pool (corrupted to Swineswell) which, it was said, had been excavated originally by the giant boar so stoutly slain by Guy of Warwick; and also on the very edge of the city was Hobb's Hole or Well, a site which the name implies was associated with the puckish Robin Goodfellow.[21] Beyond the walls, too, lay the cultivated land and the pastures, woodland and waste where the mysteries of growth were to be annually observed. Carvings of foliate 'masks' with boughs and leaves growing out of their distended mouths and which are to be found in both the vault of the entrance porch to the yard of St Mary's Hall, and more than once in wood within Holy Trinity church,[22] clearly reflect this contemporary sense of the magic, the forces, and even the menace, with which vegetation might be superstitiously viewed.

It is interesting to note, therefore, that it was only on specific 'sacred' occasions in the year that the concepts of town and country fused within the city and that living vegetation was brought into it

---

[20] *L.B.*, p. 346. L.M., fos. 15, 16.

[21] St Osburg's pool was artificially included within the circuit of the walls only at the request of the Prior, *L.B.*, p. 463. Dormer Harris, *Life in an Old English Town*, p. 13 n. 2. Bliss Burbidge, *op.cit.*, pp. 64–5. For the 'magical' ethos of the period generally *v.* the magisterial second chapter in Keith Thomas, *Religion and the Decline of Magic: Studies in Popular Beliefs in Sixteenth and Seventeenth Century England* (London, 1971), pp. 25–50.

[22] For the most recent discussion of these problematical representations *v.* Kathleen Basford, *The Green Man* (Ipswich, 1978), especially pp. 20–1.

for deliberate ritual purposes: at Christmas, when holly and ivy were brought into churches; Palm Sunday; May Day and the Midsummer and St Peter's celebrations. On these three last occasions not only did the citizens probably ransack the woods outside the city (the Prior's in particular), but the house-fronts were decked with the leafy boughs so collected. Only on the eves of Midsummer and St Peter's (five days later) was the prohibition against nocturnal activity suspended, and probable fears of the dark vanquished by communal acitivity, torch-lit processions, and street bonfires. Only at St Peter's, is it likely that the procession included rural participants.[23]

If the late medieval citizen, then, had barely severed himself from the outer environment of the countryside (and it should be recalled that many such pastured beasts or sowed crops on the city's common lands), it was no less true that what lay beyond the built-up area was quite distinct from it. The limits of this area were thus marked in certain respects as 'sacred' transitional points between the one zone and the other. Above all, the main exit points from the city were defined by chapels, churches, or crosses. To the east, and beyond St George's chapel at Gosford Gate itself, lay the chapel of St Margaret (another conqueror of the dragon which represented the embodiment of evil in both religious and popular superstitious mythology).[24] Within this area too, was the only anchorite's cell attached to the city, situated, as was often the case, extra-murally.[25] To the north, outside Bishop gate was the chapel of St Nicholas, a patron of travellers. To the west, at the limits of the city's suburbs before the great depopulation, were Hill Cross and Spon Cross. Between the two western exits through the walls was St John's Bablake, and further west still, beyond the Spon Bars was the chapel of Sts James and Christopher, the latter again representing a patron saint of travellers. Also in this extra-mural area, as was usual in the case of the unclean, lay the leper hospital.[26] At the gate towards Warwick were the Franciscans, and at the gate towards London, the Carmelites with the traveller's shrine of St Mary adjacent in the city wall. Appropriately outside the wall too in this direction was the home of the solitary order of Carthusians.

Passengers across the limits of the city might thus experience to

---

[23] Phythian-Adams, 'Ceremony and the Citizen', *loc.cit.*, pp. 72, 68, 78.
[24] *Ibid.*, p. 77, cf. *L.B.*, pp. 291–2.   [25] *L.B.*, pp. 118, 227.
[26] How many, if any, actual lepers it contained by this period is another matter.

an indefinable extent both a physical and a mental rite of passage from one situation to another. It was no accident that great efforts were made to impress visitors by building gateways on an imposing scale at the main exit points.[27] Nor is it surprising that the gates were the places where the heads and quartered remnants of the executed were displayed,[28] not only as a caution to the citizens, and as an illustration of local disgrace to the newcomer, but also because the mortal remains of these people had not received a consecrated burial and were thus outcast.

Within the city itself, finally, there was a similar distinction between zones. The unique concentration of religious activity in the ritual centre of the city has already been discussed. It is only worth reiterating that historico-myth and topography both met at this point: the connection between St Osburg and the priory; the Godiva legend with both the priory and the nearby market area to its south-west. The contrasts between this centre and both the commercial focus to the west and the administrative area to the south were thus well marked, as was the distinction between these two last and the residentially varied areas between them and the walls. Since the citizen had to live with the variegated functions performed in these physical zones, it can hardly be doubted that they helped to mould his assumptions about the nature of his urban and rural environment.

The ceremonial season,[29] which dominated the civic calendar between Christmas and Midsummer, involved ever-widening ritual movement from the centre outwards between these contrasted zones within the city walls. If the early period was dominated both by the mayoral inauguration at St Mary's Hall and St Michael's, and by parochial activity at the high feasts of the church, the focus of these occasions was the ritual centre. Only as the 'season' progressed, did ritual move outwards and involve the streets between the centre and the major gates: on St George's day, Corpus Christi, and Midsummer in particular.

---

[27] The gates are illustrated in Gooder, *Coventry's Town Wall, passim*. These positive barriers, not the edges of the suburbs, were regarded as the limits of the real city. In 1456 the Queen, and in 1474 Prince Edward, were welcomed at Bablake gate –*not* the Spon Bars. On the former occasion, a tree of Jesse was constructed over the gate; on the latter, it was here that the Prince was specifically welcomed to his 'chamber' (i.e. the city). *L.B.*, pp. 287, 391.

[28] Gooder, *op.cit.*, p. 37; *infra*, pp. 253–4.

[29] For what follows *v.* Phythian-Adams, *loc.cit.*, pp. 70–7.

All-male hierarchical events as they were, these processional idealisations of different group inter-relationships (especially Crafts, Gilds and civic government), were each enacted against a temporal back-cloth of major church observances commemorating the birth, life, death and resurrection of Christ, and, more dimly, pagan superstition. Such occasions brought together the community as contemporaries perceived it and at 'sacred' moments in time. At these moments, therefore, the secular working environment itself was temporarily transformed: the city as a whole became the unit of ritual. None of these activities appears to have taken place on waste ground outside the walls.

The converse of these exaggerated expressions of structure during the same six-month period was equally extreme. For, above all, this half of the year contained the only extended holiday times – at Christmas, Easter and Whitsuntide – throughout which formality might be relaxed. During this period, therefore, the obverse of high ceremony (much of it no doubt sanctimonious) was the ritualised distortion of the structure during short bursts of social licence: Misrule and the mayor at Christmas; Hocktide and the husbands after Easter; and the citizenry versus local landed proprietors in summertime. Much else has no doubt escaped the record: there are indications for example that Midsummer was an occasion for manslaughter and even riot in the early fifteenth century, while at Salisbury the cognate observance on St Osmund's eve (15 July) was known as 'the revel'.[30] The absence of Carnival in England is most marked, and there is a distinct possibility that the excesses so characteristic of that occasion in Europe, simply found outlets on other days in this country before the Reformation.

It is clear, nonetheless, that at Coventry during what I have ventured to describe elsewhere as 'the ritualistic' half of the year, the community dramatised its own image of itself: idealising, in public before crowds of spectators; distortively amongst themselves. Ritual was a living mirror of the city.

If contemporaries may not have sought for patterns in these traditionally time-bound activities, they cannot have been unaware of the heightened context in which they took place. In notable contrast, during the remaining six months of the year 'the secular

[30] L.B., pp. 35–6. Charles Haskins, The Ancient Trade Guilds and Companies of Salisbury (Salisbury, 1910), pp. 68–72. I am grateful to Dr Paul Slack for referring me to this volume.

half' and its undifferentiated sequence of Trinity Sundays, there was little in the shape of either extended holidays or high ceremonies to interrupt the weekly working routines. Localised ceremonies concerned particular groups within society – especially the election of the sheriffs for the city and county of Coventry, as well as the inaugurations of gild and craft officers; they did not seek to interrelate the structure as a whole. Moreover, if the ritualistic half was urban-focused, the secular period was both subject to the rural rhythms of sheep-shearing and harvest (with all that it meant for the supply of the city's textile industry and food), and also reflected a greater involvement of the citizenry in what took place outside the walls. The eve of St Peter's (29 June) has already been mentioned in this connection, while Lammas Day concerned a restricted party of citizens throwing open the private closes around the city to common use as pasture. For those that had Michaelmas lands the normal processes of the harvest were also necessary activities. Finally, it seems to have been during this half of the year that the triennial riding of the bounds of the county of Coventry took place too.[31]

Public ceremony in fact not only related men to each other, identified them with the community as a whole, and operated as a form of social control on otherwise unstructured holiday occasions; it also highlighted the extreme contrasts in the life-experience of the ordinary medieval citizen. It distinguished aspects of the environment, whether urban and rural or sacred and secular. It exaggerated the difference between the richness of pomp and the often impoverished reality of every-day life. It differentiated the daily and weekly context, with which this analysis began, from the overall cycle of the annual calendar. Ceremony and the attitudes that lay behind its observance, lay at the very heart of late medieval urban culture.

[31] Phythian-Adams, *loc.cit.*, pp. 77–8.

16. *Conclusion on social structure*

But if ritual was a mirror of the community, it is impossible for a modern historian to discover the precise degree to which contemporaries actually distinguished between ceremonial ideal and reality. The exercise of analysis alone tends to impose a neatness on past life: for contemporaries, what have here been presented as differentiated activities more probably fused into their total life experiences. Nevertheless one over-riding impression that might be left by this study would hopefully be the multi-faceted roles performed by all the formal groups and groupings in society. By not dealing with particular topics like the economy or religion as separate matters, insofar as that is possible, perhaps a little of this fusion of experience has been reconstructed.

Yet, however artificial may be the structure presented here (and it has been impossible for lack of evidence to deal with one of the most important social relationships to cut across its formality – the actual role of the entrepreneur in relation to masters in other occupations), there can be no denying the contemporary tightness of its communal organisation. This was a society that was bound together by oaths at each step in the citizen's life-cycle;[1] a society in which not only sexual and social roles, but also distinctive age-grades were precisely defined. (The identification of childhood, youth and old age, indeed, might well suggest a local view of the theoretical ages of man as falling into at least six twelve-year categories.) It was an hierarchical society. Yet in it, people from different backgrounds lived closely inter-mingled together, particularly in servant-keeping households or at the level of the street neighbourhood. It was a stratified society, yet in every formal and informal institution of the city, social eating and drinking together played a recognised part, and social advancement was at least possible. It was a society in which much of life, however private by our standards, was played out publicly in the streets and in the company of those who were not members of the family. It was a society where culture was essentially visual and musical,[2] but which

[1] Phythian-Adams, *loc.cit.*, pp. 59–61.
[2] Minstrelsy was provided not only at royal receptions (which included open-air organ-playing in 1474, *L.B.*, p. 393), but also at the great communal processions.

demanded not looking and listening, but personal participation by members of the community. Its mental world was permeated by an awareness of living forces on the one hand, and an abiding consciousness, bred of familiarity, with the facts of death on the other, with all that both these views implied for sustaining religious attitudes and superstitions. Above all, it was a society which saw itself as a community and which periodically celebrated its distinctiveness.

It was, however, also a community which, before the short-term crisis, excluded perhaps one in five of those resident in the city, and a society in which the details of every-day life, particularly for its poorest members, were thus minutely regulated. Even within the community, the structure was such as to ensure the maximum social control. Certain ideal elements in this structure were reflected imitatively at different levels: a Council House of twelve; ruling twelves, perhaps of the Trinity Gild, and certainly for the fellowships of masters and journeymen too. The citizenry were subdivided amongst themselves into tight groups of usually related occupations, and only the honest commoners belonged to organisations that brought together and inter-mixed large numbers of people on a formal basis. Likewise, only the honest commoners could afford to be 'love brethren' of Crafts practising occupations other than their own.[3] Moreover, the honest commoners alone, as constables, controlled the wards. In these circumstances of restrictive social organisation, practically every eventuality in terms of unrest was catered for.

It was thus no accident that in only two areas did trouble ever really threaten the *status quo*. The first could not have been anticipated, and was anyway nipped in the bud before it became serious in 1511. It involved a secret cell of 74 heretics, drawn from some 25 different trades and included a substantial quota of women. The majority came from Coventry itself, some from a cell at Birmingham, while others, who may well have been the carriers of these pernicious ideas, had travelled from town to town throughout Eng-

The city waits, indeed, not only played through different parts of the night according to the season (*supra* p. 74), but even accompanied enclosure rioters back to the city in 1469. Dormer-Harris, *Life in an Old English Town*, p. 211.

[3] 'Love brethren' appear in C.R.O. access. 100: Weavers 11, *passim*. It seems likely that such people were compounding with the fellowship in order to be able to practise some aspect of the weavers' business, as well as ensuring their future prayers.

land.[4] Their success, however, may have had more to do with the sympathy of some of the leaders of society than with social unrest. No common labourer was a member, but a powerful influence had clearly been exercised over a number of years previously by one Mistress Alice Rowley, who may have been the widow of an earlier mayor, Will Rowley; while there are also hints that two living magistrates were interested.[5] Heresy was well rooted in the city: several heretics had had to do penance at the behest of the Bishop in 1485–6; yet others, once again comprising a group from different occupations, and of whom seven were burned, were insisting on saying the Lord's Prayer, the Creed, and the Ten Commandments in English in 1520.[6] This latter group had certainly not been deterred by the execution of seven of the cell arraigned in 1511–12 when 'another did pennance one a pipe head, while the other were burning, holding a fagott one his shoulder'.[7]

Heresy, however, hardly posed a threat to the social order, provided numbers remained small, no radical programmes for social reform were included, and some control was exercised by reliable members of the honest commoner class. What did represent a potential danger, was the perpetual trouble which divided the city against the municipality, over the common lands. Mary Dormer Harris was undoubtedly correct in tracing the roots of this continuing conflict to a tension between the wards on the one hand, as the immemorial representatives of the popular voice and hence as the defenders of customary ownership, and on the other, the city government which, as an entity officially controlling the whole town, could not claim an authority reaching further back than the mid fourteenth century.[8] It was, for example, the wards that were each specifically represented as from 1495 by two or three hand-picked individuals in the chamberlains' annual procession every Lammas Day (1 August) to throw open the common lands to public use.[9]

When either private person, be he Prior or self-styled gentleman,[10] surcharged or encroached upon the commons; or ward-juries, chosen for their compliance by the city government, sought

[4] J. Fines, 'Heresy Trials in the Diocese of Coventry and Lichfield 1511–12', *Journal of Ecclesiastical History*, xiv (1963), pp. 161–4.

[5] L.M., fo. 15, and *infra*, p. 278, n. 9.

[6] *Ibid.*, fo. 16: for some background to this, *v. Bishop Geoffrey Blythe's Visitations c. 1515–1525*, ed. Heath, pp. 101–2.   [7] L.M., fo. 15.

[8] Dormer-Harris, *Life in an Old English Town*, p. 110, though cf. *supra*, p. 118, n. 1.   [9] L.B., p. 565.   [10] E.g. L.B., pp. 349–50.

to enclose on behalf of the city; trouble was likely to follow. Forcible entry or riot by the citizens had become traditional as in 1421, *c.* 1430, 1469, 1473, 1495 and 1509.[11] The details do not concern us, but in the context of social organisation and control some observations are relevant to what was to happen in 1525. These outbreaks had never involved anything more serious than a brief assertion of customary rights: once this was accomplished, life returned swiftly to normal. In none of these instances was the magistracy forced to call in outside assistance to quell the rioters: occasionally, some of the elite openly sympathised. Only if a leader emerged was anything more critical likely to be feared by the authorities. Such a man was Laurence Saunders in the 1480s and 1490s. A chamberlain of the city in 1480 and a paid-up member of the two Gilds by 1496 in which year he threatened, in almost as many words, to lead a riot against the magistracy (which never transpired); he eventually disappeared into the Fleet Prison as a result.[12] Only a substantial honest commoner on the edge of the city's elite was thus likely to command and articulate the opposition of the commonalty in such circumstances. Only a confusion of the situation with other issues could seriously endanger the social order. In 1525 that happened, as we shall see.[13]

The moral of this digression is important for an appreciation of the continuity of Coventry's social structure and the absence of attempts at social revolution at this time. The safety of the social order rested on the dependability of the honest commoner 'class', and they more than any other section of society probably felt most keenly the need for a sense of community. For these people were the lynch-pins on which the whole system depended: as servant-keeping householders; as craft and gild officers; as ward constables; jury-men; ale-tasters, searchers, church-wardens, and as civic officers. They may have had both the wealth that was necessary to achieve such positions, and such glory as there was to be derived from them, but most of these activities were unpaid, greedy of time, and above all inescapable. Such citizens could not look to paid public servants to act on society's behalf; they had to do these tasks themselves often under threat of fine if they refused.[14] If the

[11] The history of these is concisely and conveniently brought together in *V.C.H. Warks.*, viii, pp. 202–3.

[12] Dormer-Harris, *op.cit.*, pp. 219–22.

[13] *Infra*, pp. 254–7.   [14] *Supra*, pp. 47, 112.

accounts for which they were responsible did not balance, the sums owed were met out of their own pockets.[15] Privileged they may have been, and conscious of their monopoly of influence in directing the affairs of the city, but it would be simple romanticism to deny that they did not also live their lives under a heavy burden of social obligation.

Romanticism too has to be avoided in looking at a community holistically. In seeking for structure and its ceremonial expression it would be wrong to suggest that life in such a community was an enviable condition. As earlier sections have shown, late medieval urban society was being subjected to forces over which it had little or no control. Poverty and homelessness were becoming major problems, and the social system itself was beginning to betray those signs of distortion that were to lead eventually to its transformation. It is then to the process of depopulation, to its impact on the household as a part of the demographic and economic structure, and to the wider structural strains to which the community was now increasingly prone, that this study must now turn.

[15] E.g. Richard Smith's account for the Craft year 1534–5 (C.R.O. access. 100: Weavers 11) ends 'the expences ys more then the Reysetts ys be – xviijs ixd whych he hath gyffyn clere to the craft'.

Part IV

An anatomy deformed

'... Where as nother warre pestylens nor famyn hathe mynystryd cause to the desolatyon of cytes & townys, hyt must nedys appere that the dekay & ruyne therof spryngeth much of the penury of pepul & lak of inhabytantys, for of thys desolatyon other grete causys & other chefe groundys I fynd not many ...'

> (Thomas Starkey; *England in the Reign of King Henry the Eighth*, pt. i, ed. S. J. Herrtage, Early English Text Society, extra series, xxxii, 1878, p. lvii.)

'MERCHANTMAN: ... And albeit there be many things laid down now, which beforetimes were occasions of much expense – as stage plays, interludes, May games, wakes, revels, wagers at shooting, wrestling, running, and throwing the stone or bar, and besides that pardons, pilgrimages, offerings, and many such other things – yet I perceive we be never the wealthier but rather the poorer.'

> (Mary Dewar (ed.), *A Discourse of the Commonweal*, p. 18.)

II Modest houses inside Cook Street Gate, Bishop Street ward, as they survived into the nineteenth century (Troughton drawings: C.R.O.)

17. *Introductory*

In the first two thirds of this study, the analysis of decline, both economic and demographic, has been kept distinct from the reconstruction of Coventry's social structure. The story of decay was traced only so far as the period of short-term crisis between 1518 and 1525 and then only in outline. It is now necessary to look in more detail at both the inter-action between demographic and economic factors, and their impact on the fabric of society. In so doing, emphasis must be laid not only on the detailed evidence from the period of crisis, but also upon its implications for the longer-term distortion of the city's social anatomy.

The core of that evidence for both demographic and economic matters has to be the 1523 enumeration, the results of which have been correlated in a substantial number of unambiguous cases with the information on occupations, wealth and rents from the 1522 assessment. A census of this kind, however, furnishes only a static picture of a single moment in contemporary experience, and a picture that cannot be accepted at its face value. The enumeration comprises in practice ten *separate* listings each made by a different person for every one of the city's wards. This evidence has thus to be compared with the surviving *totals* for those same wards as calculated in the dearth census of 1520, and thoroughly tested for internal inconsistencies. The problems of analysis are thus formidable, and while much of the technical discussion which compares the results of 1520 and 1523 has been relegated to appendix 2, it is clearly quite impossible to dispose of the problems of internal interpretation in similar fashion and so retain only the conclusions in the text. Detailed as the analysis therefore has to be, and imperfect as it no doubt is, the wider significance of this unique documentation for an English medieval city can hardly be denied. It has thus seemed best to illustrate the results as generously as possible in tabular form both in the text and the appendices. No attempt has been made to superimpose a sophisticated statistical superstructure on the figures. Not only is the writer unqualified to effect this, but the evidence is demonstrably too fragile to bear such a weight.

Part IV is consequently divided into two halves which merge into each other. The first of these concentrates on population and the economy. It begins with an examination of depopulation between 1520 and 1523 and seeks to identify both the forces at work and the victims of them. The analysis then turns to the demographic and economic structures as viewed through the household unit and its constituent parts in the 1523 enumeration. The long-term situation revealed by the shortage of male-servants in that year is pursued chronologically in the context of the continuing decay of Coventry's economy into the mid sixteenth century. In similar fashion, the implications of the paucity of children in 1523, for the city's demographic decline thereafter, are then also followed through over the same time scale. In the cases of both these themes, therefore, while most of the analysis is concerned with the evidence for 1523 and the strains that it exposes, the subsequent ramifications of those pressures and the additional factors that accelerated the city's late medieval demise are also considered. In doing so, it is thus possible to provide the essential context within which social structural change has to be assessed.

The succeeding sections of part IV similarly focus to begin with on the period of short-term crisis and the stresses which then became so apparent. The manner in which the social anatomy of the city was being deformed is epitomised at this time in a number of ways: in the size and composition of the household; in the near breakdown of the civic-office-holding system; and in both conspiracy and riot. The programme for reform which originated in this period, but which only surfaced a decade later, has also to be considered in these circumstances. Moreover, just as economic and demographic decline of the city was accelerated by the 1518–25 crisis, so too did the traditional social structure show increasing signs of buckling thereafter. The shrinkage of the honest commoner class, the continuing burdens of the communal culture on the system of office-holding; and the institutional adjustments and changes that marked the close of the middle ages all require examination in this light. Part IV concludes with assessments both of the degree to which the customary mirrors of popular 'superstition' and ritual were shattered by the events of the Reformation and of the extent to which such ideals were any longer realistic. In doing so, it traces the manner in which the images and the realities of late medieval urban community finally contradicted each other.

(A) A penury of people

18. The depopulation of households 1520–3

In part II, the story of Coventry's economic and demographic decline was taken down to 1525, and it was argued that the pace of decay was accelerating particularly after 1510. Although the peak year of the short-term crisis may have been 1524–5, it is apparent that the worst damage was inflicted between 1520/21 and 1522/3. It is thus peculiarly fortunate that the documentation permits a close scrutiny of the local situation at this strategic point in the process of decline.

Although the crude figures are problematic, an analysis of the depopulation of Coventry during the crisis has to revolve around the raw findings of the two enumerations of 1520 and 1523. It is suggested in appendix 2 that the second count was deliberately designed to be comparable with the first for the purpose of measuring the scale of depopulation; and that the figures for vacant houses which were included in 1523 represented an attempt to estimate the numbers of *all* such houses in the city whether evacuated in the short or the long term. The most crucial information which may be derived from the two censuses is illustrated accordingly in table 10, where, as in succeeding tables, the wards are ranked according to the semi-independent measure discussed above (figure 2) – the distribution of the housing stock in each. It should be recalled throughout that the one ambiguous point in this ordering is with regard to the relative positions of Broad Gate and Much Park.

These figures exclude the inmates of the religious houses since both censuses were organised by the civic government. They are furthermore not exactly comparable in the sense that the 1520 totals have had to be accepted as counted by the enumerators. By contrast, the figures for 1523 are my own, except in the two cases where reliance has had to be placed on the original ward totals. It is worth emphasising that in not one ward where a check is possible do

Table 10. *Crude results by wards for populations and population changes 1520–3; and for households and vacant houses in 1523*

Wards as ranked	1520 Pops.	1523 Pops.	1520–3 changes %	Total hhs.	Total vac. hs.	Vac. hs. as % of hhs. + vac. hs. %
					1523	
Bailey Lane	459	397	− 13.5	81	16	16.5
Cross Cheaping	884	738	− 16.5	173	59	25.4
Smithford	406	322	− 20.7	77	38	33.0
Earl	707	595	− 15.8	135	38	22.0
Gosford	875	602	− 31.2	157	62	28.3
Broad Gate	552	388	− 29.7	127	25	16.4
Much Park	719	464	− 35.5	155	28	15.3
Bishop	1,018	'853'	− 16.2	(262)	131	(33.3)
Spon	627	'878'	+ 40.0	(274)	107	(28.1)
Jordan Well	354	462	+ 30.5	143	61	29.9
Whole city	6,601	5,699	− 13.7	1,584	565	26.3

Notes
Sources: The 1520 results are recorded in *L.B.*, pp. 674–5. For 1523 see appendix 1.
Pops. = populations   hhs. = households   vac. hs. = vacant houses
' ' = Original totals based on those provided by the enumerator. For both Bishop and Spon the surviving schedules are incomplete (*vide* appendix 3 table 36, footnote).
( ) = Numbers of households calculated by arbitrarily applying the uncorrected mean household sizes (calculated for those domestic groups covered in the surviving schedules) to the given contemporary ward totals (*vide* table 37).
N.B. The inmates of Ford's hospital (max. 12, plus a chantry priest) were not included under Broad Gate in 1523, nor those of St John's Bablake under Spon (max. 11, plus a priest).

my figures agree precisely with the contemporary totals. In the case of Spon indeed, the enumerator undercast his summarised subtotals by exactly 100 (*vide* appendix 3a). When this mistake is allowed for, the 1523 total for the whole city as computed by contemporaries should have come out at 5,707.

The table demonstrates what remains true even when allowances are made for under-counting only in 1523: that, in all but two wards, the poorest in the city, the populations fell disastrously during these three years. All but the wealthiest ward, lost 15 per cent or more of their 1520 populations and in three unambiguous cases (even after smoothing the 1523 results) the proportion was more like 25 per cent (compare table 34 in appendix 2). It is noticeable in fact that, for the leading *seven* wards, there was a clear distinction between the experiences of the top four and those of the three middling wards of Gosford, Broad Gate and Much Park where depopulation was dramatic. The problems arise when attention is turned to the junior three: Bishop, where the scale of depopulation is improbably more in line with that in the wealthiest wards in the city; and Spon and Jordan Well, where the figures suggest that the populations were growing.

Both the scale of depopulation where it was experienced, and the evidence to be drawn from a comparison between those recorded in the 1522 assessment and the 1523 census, indicate that in at least the top eight wards depopulation involved not only individuals, but also whole households. The numbers of dwellings lying vacant in 1523, therefore, had evidently been swollen over the preceding three years whatever may have been the empty housing situation in 1520. The crude estimates in the table of the proportions of houses vacant in each ward, however, indicate further contradictions in the evidence. In this case, the low proportion of empty houses in Bailey Lane is consistent with the evidence for depopulation, but the only other two wards with similarly low proportions were those amongst the worst hit by short-term depopulation, Broad Gate and Much Park. In these two cases it seems likely that the enumerator under-counted the empty houses. Rather more remarkable, however, is the fact that over half the *counted* vacant houses in the city were located in those very wards where either depopulation is repre-sented as uncharacteristically slight (Bishop) or populations are recorded as having risen. For these and other detailed reasons which are argued in appendix 2, the author would conclude that all three of the poorest wards in the city were seriously under-counted in 1520, and that it is more probable than not that every ward experienced depopulation. It is evident, moreover, that there was a substantial degree of movement and hence a rapid turn-over of property as between different wards in the city. But whether many of those dislodged from the middling to wealthy wards then removed themselves to those areas where cheaper housing was more readily available, as the figures seem to imply, is open to question. Such movement as there was towards the poorer outskirts of the city is at the very least exaggerated by the population totals, and indeed may well have been no more marked than inter-ward mobility elswhere in the city.

Although it is consequently difficult to measure or map precisely the impact of depopulation at the ward level, it is possible to characterise the households most likely to have been affected. Despite some difficulties of interpretation a first step is to isolate the names of those listed in the very full 1522 assessment but later omitted in the even more embracing enumeration of 1523, *after* account has been taken of such households as *re*-appear in the 1524 subsidy instalment (i.e. only 36 households out of the $8\frac{4}{5}$ wards that can be checked).[1] It is important to emphasise, however, that the figures so calculable are no more than pointers. First, it is sometimes very difficult to match names with total confidence where there are variant spellings; or when christian names or surnames only are given; or where, as in the schedules, two widows might be so specified, but not named. Secondly, the households thus identified represent those which were *dislodged* but not necessarily depopulated. The evidence for *inter*-ward movement simply cannot be quantified owing to obvious problems of identification. Despite all this, however, and even though the figures reflect only the tail-end of the process, a number of suggestive inferences may be drawn from them.

Table 11, for example, implies that, as was to be expected, occupation may have had a marked effect on physical mobility. Thus when all those with occupational labels only are combined, it may be seen that no less than 45 per cent of this total was comprised of persons in clothing (including 17 cappers) and textiles (including ten weavers). This proportion compares very closely with Professor Hoskins' pioneer study which yielded a figure of 47 per cent, but in

Table 11. *Occupations of 'dislodged' householders 1522–3*

Unknown	79	Leather	8
Females	50	Metals	8
Clothing	27 ⎱ 47	Distributive	6
Textiles	20 ⎰	Miscellaneous	6
Building	15	Wood	5
Victualling	12	Grand total	233 Householders

[1] P.R.O. E179/192/125.

this case no drapers at all (one of the leading occupations to inflate his categorisation) are represented under textiles.[2] The pressures on the city's two key industries were thus greater than this tiny sample might imply. Also noteworthy is the impact of crisis on the basic services provided by the builders (including nine labourers), and the victuallers (including six bakers but, significantly perhaps, no butchers). Finally, the figure for females (both single and widowed), 21.5 per cent of the *grand* total, although impressive, may well comprise a very representative sample of such persons. In 1523, 19.7 per cent of all households were to be so headed.

More positively, poverty was demonstrably an influential factor. This obvious point is strongly reinforced, despite the inexactitude of the figures, when it is remembered that the basic document upon which this analysis is founded, the 1522 assessment, in fact omitted over 20 per cent of all households remaining in the city. What is here being examined thus represents no more than the tip of the iceberg. Even so, a comparison of the two sources reveals that 84.1 per cent of those 'dislodged' possessed, for what this is worth, *less than* £2 in goods or officially nothing. Unfortunately this evidence cannot be accepted at its face value: there are far too many examples in the assessment of householders paying substantial rents but assessed at nothing in goods. Very much more precisely, then, 71.6 per cent of the householders 'dislodged' paid 12s. or less rent *per annum*, whereas only 50.05 per cent of all those assessed fell in this bracket. Even the tail-end of the movement under investigation, therefore, was overwhelmingly composed of the cottage-dwelling population and its immediate economic superiors.

From this information may be settled a crucial matter with regard to the character of the households affected. For, as will be discussed below, it is possible to calculate the mean sizes of households for these strata of society in 1523. Table 29 demonstrates not only that cottage households were very small and that even the 6s. 8d. to 12s. category was well below the average for the whole city, but that the low mean size in the 'not known' group (being almost certainly largely composed of cottagers) fully supports these findings. Taking all three categories together – a very large sample of the whole city – some 65.4 per cent of all households then *averaged* around 2.6 to 3.3 persons. The mean density of homes headed by females (table

[2] Hoskins, *Provincial England*, p. 80 and cf. p. 79.

31) at a mere 1.8, is yet further corroboration. It can thus hardly be doubted that the depopulated households themselves fell mostly within this range of sizes, though as will be seen, some allowance must needs be made for under-counting at this level.

If the households most vulnerable to the impact of crisis were on the whole poor and small, the susceptibility of each ward to depopulation may be partially estimated from the proportion of poorer housing it contained when this is also set against two more circumstantial factors – the local availability of bread-corn in 1520 and the topography of the clothing and textile industries. Both are measured in table 12.

In 1520 the bakers' stated weekly requirements of wheat alone represented an average consumption of 0.16 bushels per person counted – probably a maximal figure since no adjustments for possible under-enumeration in that year have here been attempted. But even on this basis, it may be seen that when (or if) all possible bread-corn supplies available were pooled in each ward, Gosford,

Table 12. *Measures of vulnerability*

	Bread-corn per person ratios (bushels) 1520	Clothing and textile craftsman as a percentage of known occupations % 1522
Bailey Lane	0.55	25.5
Cross Cheaping	0.18	10.9
Smithford	0.54	28.6
Earl	0.61	52.5
Gosford	0.16	71.4
Broad Gate	0.07	29.6
Much Park	0.24	58.5
Bishop	0.21	26.5
Spon	0.05	39.5
Jordan Well	0.07	73.7

Col. 1: Bread-corn comprised rye, maslin, and to a lesser extent wheat, oats and peas. (Source: *L.B.*, pp. 674–5.)
Col. 2: 'Known occupations' refer only to those assessed at £2 or more in goods in 1522, augmented by information from the 1524 subsidy return where this is possible. Below this line, the coverage of the wards is too uneven for comparative analysis. In this case the drapers *have* been included.

Broad Gate, Spon and Jordan Well had stock for only a week or less on October 10. In the cases of the other two junior wards, neither of which had as much as two weeks' supply on this reckoning, it is fair to add that Much Park's ratio may be artificially inflated by the presence of a number of millers; and Bishop's, as is discussed in appendix 2, by the probable under-enumeration of its population. In marked contrast, the leading four wards seem to have been safely buttressed against starvation; for even though Cross Cheaping's ratio is very low, this ward was, in all other respects, the victualling centre for the city. It contained not only the major food markets, but also the Butcheries.

The pattern with regard to the clothing and textile industries is also very suggestive. 63 per cent of it was concentrated in the eastern part of the city: in Earl, Jordan Well, Much Park and Gosford, where the occupational structure of what was clearly the employing class was thus heavily weighted. Of these, however, wealthy Earl contained a number of prosperous drapers who would probably have been able to tide over the bad times. Jordan Well was the centre of the capping industry, the numbers of masters in which trade did not slump during the crisis, though their employees were certainly affected.[3] Gosford and Much Park by contrast, contained the more traditional crafts of the industry like those of the shermen and weavers. Spon, on the western side of Coventry, finally, had the next greatest proportion of both textile and clothing craftsmen in the city.

It is, of course, important to recall that dislodgement was by no means restricted to craftsmen in these staple industries; but even such crude measures as those discussed would seem to imply that every one of the five junior wards was exceedingly vulnerable to varying degrees. Between 40 and 60 per cent of the housing in all of them was at the very poorest level in 1522; Much Park alone had just more than $1\frac{1}{2}$ weeks' supply of bread-corn in 1520; and only Broad Gate and Bishop were not heavily dependent on textiles or clothing. Above this line, Gosford contained proportionately as many poorer dwellings as Broad Gate; was dangerously low on bread-corn; and was highly susceptible to the fortunes of the cloth trade.

The picture which thus emerges would seem to confirm that even the four most affluent wards were affected by both long-term

[3] *Infra*, p. 212.

decline and short-term depopulation despite possible omissions from Smithford (*vide* appendix 2). The marked contrast provided by Gosford (even after some allowance has been made for the possible under-counting of a number of small households in 1523), Much Park and Broad Gate, fully bears out the circumstantial evidence, which has already been advanced, with regard to the greater vulnerability of these wards. The impact of crisis on Broad Gate in particular, which was more insulated than either of the other two from the fluctuations of the cloth trade, suggests that here poverty and famine were the chief factors at work.[4] While Bishop, therefore, could claim a similar occupational immunity, inflation of its 1520 population would correspondingly reduce its estimated bread-corn supplies drastically; and suggest that its proportion depopulated was at the least in excess of that experienced by the top four wards. The argument with regard to bread-corn is immeasurably strengthened in respect of Spon and Jordan Well where, to all intents and purposes, supplies of bread must have been practically non-existent in 1520. In these cases, moreover, the occupational structures were also more vulnerable to the effects of trade depression than either Broad Gate or Bishop. Depopulation of the two most junior wards in the city could thus well have exceeded that experienced by Broad Gate.

The scale of depopulation

Although an assessment of the short-term population fall for Coventry as a whole is very difficult to make, the preceding discussion has narrowed the range of possibilities considerably. For such an estimate, if restricted to the top eight wards, is hardly likely to exaggerate the process over the entire city, particularly when the 1520 totals (including Bishop's, the under-enumeration of which is scarcely going to out-weigh the possible omission in 1523 of a scattering of a few small households in Smithford or Gosford and conceivably, Broad Gate and Much Park) are allowed to stand unaltered; and the upwardly adjusted 1523 figures are used against

---

[4] Annual payments to 'mendifaunts in money' by the Corpus Christi Gild (cf. p. 135, n. 29 *supra*) support the view that the harvest crisis was the most critical factor: 1515 – 30s.; 1516 – 35s.; 1517 – 43s.4d.; 1518 – 45s.; 1519 – 43s.6d.; 1520 – 63s.8d.; 1521 – 48s.4d.; 1522 – 55s.8d.; 1523 – 44s.6d.; 1524 – 39s.; 1525 – 35s.10d.; 1526 – 33s.4d. C.R.O. A6, fos. 212v. *et passim*.

them. The result demonstrates that even with this heavy bias towards the wealthiest wards, the drop was as great as 20 per cent. In round terms, therefore, this would suggest that the total population of Coventry fell from about 7,500 in 1520 to a possible maximum of 6,000 (i.e. comprehending the probable over-inflation of Spon's adjusted population and allowing for other unverifiable omissions) in only three years: a process involving the depopulation of whole households and of individuals from others; and probably a substantial increase in mortality amongst the young, weak and aged. So a great decrease, indeed, would appear to have been at least equivalent to the total decline over the preceding 20 years, since a population of something between 8,500 and 9,000 seems to represent a reasonable estimate for 1500.[5]

The quantity of housing left vacant over the long term, moreover, bleakly illustrates the physical impact of this decline; and, by lending credence to those assessments of empty dwellings made by contemporaries elswhere, helps to put the generally underestimated scale of late medieval urban decay into a more realistic perspective. It also suggests that Coventry's inclusion in the 1540 statute for re-edifying urban buildings, was by then a matter of

---

[5] Cf. fig. 1. On the basis of a minimal estimated total of 1,584 households (*v.* table 34) plus a minimum of 565 vacant houses in 1523; and using a multiplier of four (*infra*, pp. 244–5); a conservative estimate of 8,596 persons may be calculated for a time when all dwellings were inhabited. Although some houses were vacant in 1500, a number may have collapsed since that date, while the 1523 total is suspiciously low (*infra*, pp. 300–2). In addition, it is conceivable that higher proportions of children and male servants in the population might indicate that the multiplier should also be inflated (though cf. *infra*, p. 247). Finally, it should be borne in mind that these rough and ready figures refer only to the secular population. The 1522 assessment (C.R.O. access. 18: A96, fo. 97v.) indicates the presence of some 48 clergy (including chantry priests) at St Michaels, Holy Trinity and St John's Bablake, only a tiny minority of whom may be identified with confidence in the census. Most probably lived in halls for priests which were not itemised by the enumerators (*supra*, p. 162). A further three priests were attached to St John's Hospital (W. G. Fretton, 'Hospital of St John Baptist, Coventry', *Birmingham and Midland Institute, Archaeological Section, Transactions*, xiii (1886), pp. 41–2. Moreover, at Dissolution, at least, the Priory contained thirteen monks, the two friaries, twenty-five or more friars altogether; and the Charterhouse, eight inmates, *V.C.H. Warks.*, ii, pp. 58, 104–5, 85. How far such figures represented normality fifteen or more years earlier, however, is difficult to ascertain. The Benedictine priory in 1518, for example, then contained seventeen monks and six novices, Heath (ed.), *Bishop Geoffrey Blythe's Visitations*, pp. 15–17. In 1496, there had been fifteen monks and two novices, *ibid.*, p. 169. It is perhaps too easily forgotten that religious houses were quite as subject to the general demographic contraction as the secular population. A total of roughly 100 clerics in the city, however, seems reasonable.

overwhelming urgency.[6] Even though vacant houses were probably under-counted in Broad Gate and Much Park, the total of 565 such houses in the city in 1523 together exceeded all the inhabited dwellings in its two largest wards. In broader terms still, this was equivalent to the obliteration of at least 20 to-be-deserted villages; or of five simple market towns; or even of the whole county town itself: as late as 1563, Warwick could only claim a total of 410 families.[7] Such then was the damage that long-term decline, plague, famine and mass unemployment between them might inflict on a major medieval English city.

[6] *Statutes of the Realm*, 32, Henry VIII, cap. 8.

[7] Beresford and Hurst, *Deserted Medieval Villages*, p. 26 – assuming a generous estimate of 20 families for an average doomed village. Few Warwickshire market 'towns' exceeded 110 households even when the population recovery was under way by 1563. B.L. Harl. MSS. 594, fos. 165v.–167v. and 595, fos. 211v.–212v. *Ibid.*, 595 fo. 212r.

19. *The distribution of the people*

If the rapid and disastrous depopulation of whole households was a critical feature of the short-term crisis, it is hardly surprising that within the household unit, both its productive and reproductive functions were similarly depleted with all that that portended for the future of the city. Even at the risk of pursuing the anatomical metaphor too far, it is no exaggeration to compare the condition of Coventry at this time with a state of haemorrhage. For the sake of analytical clarity, indeed, it is useful to distinguish between on the one hand, the structure of communal positions as the social skeleton, and on the other, the personnel who occupied those positions as the blood supply of the social system. Before turning to the rather more protracted manner in which the framework of positions was deformed, therefore, it is necessary to concentrate on the processes whereby its incumbents were so diminished in number that this in itself contributed to the disfiguration of the social order.

The most fundamental characteristic of any population is the proportion of males and females. So far as medieval cities were concerned, the sex ratio (M per 100 F) most characteristically favoured the females. Thus Professor J. C. Russell has calculated for some European cities in the fifteenth century that the ratio stood at approximately 93 for Basle and 85 for Fribourg, Nuremberg and Ypres, though it should be added that Herlihy's figure for Pistoia's adult population is higher at 103 – a ratio which drops with advancing years.[1] Coventry, however, seems to have been no exception to the more general rule although the nature of the evidence makes precise comparison impossible with either the European evidence or Mr Laslett's results for his largely rural early modern communities.[2] One point, however, does seem clear: the distortion so evident at Coventry as reflected in the imbalance between males and females is too consistent to be dismissed purely on the grounds

[1] J. C. Russell, 'Late Medieval Population Patterns', *Speculum*, xx (1945), p. 163; David Herlihy, *Medieval and Renaissance Pistoia* (Yale, 1967), pp. 81, 83–4.

[2] Peter Laslett, 'Mean Household Size in England Since the Sixteenth Century' in Peter Laslett and Richard Wall (eds.), *Household and Family in Past Time* (Cambridge, 1972), p. 145, table 4.7: overall sex ratio calculated for 70 communities; p. 152, table 4.13: the mean of means for the sex ratios of servants in 62 communities; p. 148, table 4.10, the overall sex ratio of children in 61 communities. No

Table 13. *Sex ratios (M per 100 F)*

	Coventry	100 later communities (Laslett)
Adults	82.3 ⎫	— ⎫
	⎬ 72.0	⎬ 91.3
Servants	55.0 ⎭	106.6 ⎭
Children (Broad Gate only)	128.9	91.4

Notes on Coventry data
'Adults' include all householders, couples, and single status
pairs, mothers and one sister.
'Servants' include six 'sons'.

of under-counting (though two wards do display suspiciously low
results with regard to servants). More generally, the serious shortage of males in the two upper age levels is most marked. At the
adult level, taking unmarried household heads alone, the men were
outnumbered by 257 to 61. It would thus appear that for the
operation of 'successive polygamy' to work – that is the re-marriage
of widowers, which Hajnal adduces as the solution to a surplus of
women[3] – impossible feats of survival would have been necessary
for the male population of the city. At the servant level, there was a
disastrous lack of male employees, the implications of which for the
future of the city's economy will be critically discussed in the next
section.

In this connection it is worth re-emphasising an important point
well made by Mr Laslett: that in a male-dominated society it would
be more reasonable to expect females to be under-counted than vice
versa.[4] Some reinforcement for this suggestion comes from the only
evidence which survives for the sex ratio of children. The
enumerator of Broad Gate undoubtedly under-counted the children in his ward, yet either he, or the householders he questioned,
mentioned the presence of far more boys (who were invariably
written down first) than girls – 58 as opposed to 45. Exactly the

indication as to the chronological, geographical or urban/rural weightings of these
overlapping samples is provided. The figures therefore furnish only a blanket comparison over some 250 years. For the sake of convenience I have retained Mr
Laslett's general description of '100 communities' here and in what follows.

[3] Hajnal, 'European Marriage Patterns in Perspective', *loc.cit.*, p. 128, using a
phrase coined by Süssmilch.   [4] Laslett, *loc.cit.*, p. 146.

same phenomenon has been observed at Pistoia, where the sex ratio is likewise distorted as a result, but at the lower rate of 125.[5]

It may nevertheless be unwise to dismiss out of hand the Broad Gate evidence despite its short-comings. Even though the ratio is doubtless inflated in favour of boys, it still looks very much as though during childhood there was, as would be expected, a much more equitable balance between the sexes than was to be the case later in life. What determined the swing towards females is more difficult to establish. Even if Dr Hatcher is correct in his revival of the view that male children may have been more susceptible to plague than girls,[6] the most recent epidemic at Coventry, that of 1519, does not appear to have been a catastrophic visitation.[7] Even if the records deceive us on this, it is still difficult to account for the reversal of the balance in favour of girls only at the level of the servant age group on these grounds. In the light of the discussion which follows, it seems more likely that a two-way process was in operation at this later age level. If rural immigration to the city for the sake of jobs in service was perhaps normally biased towards adolescent females, it is no less likely in the shorter term that Coventry fathers were reluctant to place their sons in apprenticeships within the city.

The major division of the population may have been that between the sexes, but the unit in which each was distributed was the household. Before turning in more detail to the problems just outlined, it is therefore essential to place that analysis in the context of household composition. Even with respect to household heads, however, the schedules themselves are far from unambiguous. While only the householders themselves are named, their marital statuses are not always clear. Comparison between the 1522 assessment and the 1523 census has revealed a number of cases where single women are described in the other document as widows and vice versa. Either way, the use of the term 'widow' has been preferred and adopted here. In some wards – Bishop, Earl, and Jordan Well – a suspiciously low total of widows may be contrasted with a high proportion of unspecified females whose status may thus be guessed, but not exactly determined (appendix 3 table 36). 'Single' men are even worse categorised: only two widowers are mentioned, 14 'single-

---

[5] *V.* table 23; Herlihy, *op.cit.*, p. 80; children of 15 or less.

[6] John Hatcher, *Plague, Population and the English Economy 1348–1530* (London and Basingstoke, 1977), pp. 58–62.   [7] *Supra*, pp. 53–4.

Table 14. *Proportions of householders by marital status*

Marital status	Coventry %	100 communities (means) %
Couples (including 5 wives)	75.6	70.4
Widows	12.1	12.9
Single women and unspecified females	7.6	3.4
Single men, widowers and unspecified males	4.7	12.3

men' (some of whom have children), and a further 46 males are unspecified.

These points must needs be borne in mind, therefore, on turning to the proportions of households when these are characterised by the marital status of their heads. It is consequently reassuring to find that Coventry's 1,302 analysable households compare reasonably closely with the means of proportions of Mr Laslett's 100 best community listings from the later period.[8]

Clearly, Coventry's proportion of widows should be higher for the reasons already stated, and the percentage of other females correspondingly lower. The most marked difference is the smaller proportion of male-headed households, a matter to which this survey will have to revert later. More generally, and unlike Mr Laslett's communities,[9] the overall proportion of households headed by single or widowed persons did *not* exceed a quarter of the total, although, as will be discussed below, there were significant variations as between wards when these are examined by rank.

On this basis, then, it is possible to survey broadly the various elements of the household as revealed in the enumeration before turning to these component parts in more detail. The figures are presented accordingly in the accompanying table 15.

When this table is examined in rather wider terms, a number of contrasts emerge. With respect to the proportions of servant-keeping households, for example, there is a close similarity, as should be expected, between homes headed by couples at 42.7 per cent of their total, and male headed households at 41 per cent. More households headed by widows contained servants than those by

[8] Laslett, *loc.cit.*, p. 147, table 4.9 – comprising 70 out of 100 listings, 1574–1821. For the sake of comparisons here, I have had to amalgamate some of Mr Laslett's means of proportions.   [9] Laslett, *loc.cit.*, p. 147.

Table 15. *Household composition by marital statuses of heads*

	% Couples	% Widows	% Males	% Females
Offspring/relatives	0.3[a]	—	—	—
Relatives/servants	0.4[b]	—	—	—
Offspring/servants	28.8[c]	9.5	21.3	5.05
Offspring only	30.3[d]	11.4	14.75	16.2
Relatives only	0.3[e]	1.3[f]	—	1.0[g]
Servants only	13.5	21.5	19.7	15.15
In pairs only	0.1[h]	5.7	—	6.1
'Alone'	26.3[i]	50.6	44.3	56.6
Numbers of households	984	158	61	99

Notes:
[a] 3 households each containing a mother.
[b] 1 household containing a mother, and 3 each a 'son'.
[c] 1 of these couples is represented by the wife only.
[d] 2 of these couples are represented by the wife only.
[e] 1 household containing 1 mother, and 2 each a 'son'.
[f] 1 household containing 1 mother, and one a 'son'.
[g] 1 household containing a sister.
[h] Apparently 2 couples in 1 household.
[i] 1 of these couples is represented by the wife only.

other females, the ratio being 31 per cent to 20.2 per cent. Children too provide instructive comparisons. Nearly 60 per cent of all families headed by couples contained them, but it is notable that the *male* headed households constitute the next highest proportion at 36.05 per cent – clearly many of these unspecified men were widowers. By contrast, homes with children and headed by widows or other females, comprised markedly lower percentages at 20.9 and 21.25 per cent respectively.

Of those living 'alone', either married or single, the most significant proportion is that for couples, over a quarter of whom have no recorded children or servants. It will be at this area, therefore, that suspicions of under-representation will need to be directed in later discussion. There were fewer solitary male householders (44.3 per cent), than either widows (50.6 per cent), or other females (56.6 per cent). In numerical terms, indeed, these men were totally outnumbered when all sole women are counted together; males merely mustering a meagre 27 against 136 females. It is also noticeable that only women lived in pairs, and even then in a tiny minority of cases (about 6 per cent in each category).

20. Servants and the economy

Living-in servants comprised almost a quarter of the recorded population of Coventry (24.8 per cent), a very similar situation to that discovered for two parishes at Rheims in 1422,[1] where the proportion hovered between 21.6 per cent and 23.8 per cent; and significantly *dis*-similar to the findings of Mr Laslett.[2] In his later English communities (1574–1821) – most of which were rural – the overall percentage was as low as 13.4 per cent, while the mean of proportions was 14.6 per cent. Discussion of this matter, however, must be postponed to a later stage. But even taking into account the restricted nature of the Rheims sample, it is again interesting to note that the *distribution* of domestics was more widespread in the two cities than in Mr Laslett's communities. 39.4 per cent of Coventry's analysable 1,302 households contained servants, the mean of proportions for the ten wards being 41.6 per cent. At Rheims where there may have been a slight bias towards the wealthier sector of the population, the distribution affected 46 per cent and 49 per cent of the households in the two parishes respectively.[3] By contrast, in the much larger English sample, which is heavily weighted to the period 1695–1705, only 28.5 per cent of all households contained servants, though this percentage rises to 32.9 per cent when the mean of proportions is calculated.[4]

The overall distribution of in-servants according to the households concerned at Coventry resemble the Rheims figures to a much lesser extent. In the French city, 56 to 57 per cent of all servant-keeping households contained but one servant, while 9.0 to 9.5 per

[1] Pierre Desportes, 'La Population de Reims au XVe siècle d'après un dénombrement de 1422', *Le Moyen Age*, lxxii (1966), p. 491. When comparisons are made with Rheims, both here and below, it is necessary to remember that the enumeration of the French city was far less complete than that at Coventry.

[2] Laslett, *loc.cit.*, p. 152, table 4.13, based on 63 listings: urban or rural provenances unknown.

[3] Desportes, *loc.cit.*, p. 489, n. 84. Depopulation has obviously inflated the Coventry figures. In 1377, at York 'some third of the tax payers had servants', *V.C.H. York: the City of York*, p. 110. At Hull, the proportion was under one sixth, with 53 per cent of such households containing only one servant over 14, *V.C.H. York: East Riding*, i, p. 81. In both cases, of course, the proportions are distorted by the omission of exempted households (presumably without servants) from the calculations.

[4] Laslett, *loc.cit.*, pp. 130–1, table 4.1; p. 152, table 4.13 (66 communities).

Table 16. *Percentages of servant-keeping households with 1 or 4+ servants*

Households containing	No. of hhs.	1 servant only %	4 or more servants %
Servants of either sex	513	45.5	19.5
Female servants	441	55.8	8.2
Male servants	242	55.4	6.2

cent contained four or more.[5] The Coventry evidence is set out in table 16. The obvious contrast here is that, taking servants as a whole, there were proportionately twice as many large servant groups as at Rheims. Indeed, from the servants' viewpoint, 60.7 per cent of them lived in groupings of *over* two – 31 per cent comprising pockets of three or four; though, as at Rheims, the mean size of all servant groups in the city was only 2.3. At the higher end of the scale, there were three households with ten servants, and one each with 12, 14 and 16 respectively. Not unexpectedly, these belonged to the outstanding figures in the city – Julian Nethermill, Richard Marler, and Thomas Warren. Equally unsurprising is the fact that when servants are reshuffled according to their respective sexes, a more pronounced proportion of households containing only one such servant is apparent in each case.

The possession of an in-servant was a palpable expression of a householder's status. In looking at this subject in rather more detail, therefore, it is essential first to test the recorded results against the suggested ward ranking for the possibility of under-counting (table 17).

On this basis then, the ranking of the leading five wards is broadly corroborated by the distributions of servant-keeping households, which range from just below the city's overall average, in the case of Gosford (37.6 per cent), to as high as 67.9 per cent of all households in Bailey Lane. In these cases, furthermore, between 50 and 68 per cent of all *servant-keeping* households contained more than one servant. As a corollary, with one exception, the mean sizes of servant groups extended from 2.45 to 2.7. The case of Cross Cheaping, where the density is as low as 2.1, however, does serve as a

[5] Desportes, *loc.cit.*, p. 489.

Table 17. *Servants according to ward ranking*

	% of all hhs. containing servants	% of servant-keeping hhs. with more than 1 servant	Mean sizes of servant groups	Sex ratios of servants M per 100 F
1. Bailey Lane	67.9	67.3	2.5	55.2
2. Cross Cheaping	56.1	50.5	2.1	65.9
3. Smithford	54.8	55.0	2.5	61.3
4. Earl	54.8	66.2	2.7	53.4
5. Gosford	37.6	64.4	2.7	48.5
6. Broad Gate	24.4	41.9	2.1	39.1
7. Much Park	26.5	48.8	2.4	56.5
8. Bishop*	24.9	40.4	2.0	31.6
9. Spon*	36.7	50.0	1.6	45.0
10. Jordan Well	32.2	47.8	2.1	67.2

* It should be recalled that the schedules for neither of these wards is complete, though this is less serious in the case of Bishop where 209 households may be analysed, than for Spon where there are only 49.

reminder that a wide distribution does not necessarily betoken an equivalently high density and vice versa. (While in this case, the possibility of under-counting cannot be ruled out, this would appear to be contradicted by what is, in Coventry terms, a strong servant sex ratio and a comprehensive enumeration of children.)[6] Conversely, therefore, it is worth noting that Gosford's equal highest density of 2.7 is far from matched by the relatively low distribution of servant-keeping households in the ward. Again, of course, it is not impossible that a number of servants – in this instance solitaries – may have been omitted, the recovery of whom might inflate the overall distribution and shrink the mean density. In both Earl and Gosford, however, it is necessary to remember that each contained a marked nucleus of wealthy households and, at the other extreme, a sizeable proportion of cottage homes as well.[7]

With regard to the junior five wards, the distribution of servant-keeping households also *broadly* reflects the ward-ranking – this time at the appropriately lower range of between 24 and 37 per cent of all households in each. Again, the distributions of *servant-keeping* households containing more than one servant are also

[6] *Infra*, table 23.   [7] *Supra*, figure 2.

suitably restricted as between 40 and 50 per cent of the households concerned. As a result, the mean sizes of servant groups are correspondingly low, ranging from 1.6 to 2.4.

A closer inspection, however, reveals a number of discrepancies, where the ranking does not appear to be echoed in the population figures. Most conspicuously Broad Gate, which is already suspect on other grounds, should be more on a par with Much Park's results. Not only is the distribution of servant-keeping households somewhat low, but so too is the mean density of servant groups, while the sex ratio (which as will be shown is closely connected with occupation) is quite out of proportion in a ward with a bias towards leather-working.[8] In this instance, therefore, not only may servants have been wholly omitted from some households which contained them, but under-counting may also have affected those households which did admit their presence. If the Much Park overall distribution may be accepted, however, then Bishop's corresponding figure might also be. In the latter case, however, the combination of the lowest percentage of households containing *more than one* servant, with the weakest servant sex ratio in the city, is distinctly suspicious, and is not wholly explicable in terms of the occupational tendencies of the ward. Indeed some under-counting of male servants within recognised servant-keeping households here seems very probable. While Spon's inflated overall distribution, finally, may be a product of the smallness of its sample, it is nevertheless interesting to compare it with the Jordan Well results. For these together may comprise an indirect confirmation of the suggestion made in appendix 2 with regard to the cumulative scale of long- and short-term depopulation in these very wards – a process which may have artificially inflated the *proportion* of servant-keeping households by 1523. Indeed, if this be so *and* the Bishop results are reasonably accurate, then the scale of short-term depopulation in the former two wards may conceivably have been even greater than was allowed in the general result previously estimated.[9]

The very weak servant sex ratio has already received notice in general terms, but the dependence of the city's domestic economy on female labour is more strongly emphasised by analysis of the wards (table 17). In only two of them, Cross Cheaping and Jordan Well, does the ratio begin to approach 70 men for every 100

[8] *Infra*, table 19.   [9] *Supra*, p. 196.

women. In four cases, indeed, even allowing for some under-
counting, the ratio does not reach fifty. On the broad view, of all
domestic servants practically two thirds (64.8 per cent) were
females, while a mere 18.6 per cent of all households in the city
actually contained male servants. What then were the implications
of this in economic terms?

To see the problem in perspective, it will be easiest to begin by
examining servants as a whole by occupational categories (for the
exact composition of which, reference must be made to appendix
3c), and on a trans-city basis.

From this it emerges that the occupational categories (to which
have been added comparable results for female-headed households
and for the unclassifiable remainder of the city) break down into
four fairly well-defined groups. The merchant category, which
includes *inter alia* the Mercers' and Drapers' companies – the two
wealthiest in the city – of course stands pre-eminent, combining, as
it does, an almost maximal distribution of servant-keeping households with a sizeable servant-group density of 4.0. Second come the
victualling to metal crafts inclusively, whose distributions of
servant-keeping households range from 72 to 54 per cent and which
exhibit mean densities of between 2.0 and 2.9. Next is a small

Table 18. *Servants by occupational categories*

Groups Category		Distributions of servant-keeping hhs. %	Mean sizes of servant groups	Distributions of hhs. containing male servants %	Mean sizes of male servant groups
1.	Merchants	90.0	4.0	56.7	2.3
2.	Victuallers	71.8	2.4	32.9	1.5
	Officials	61.9	2.5	33.3	1.0
	Textiles	60.8	2.9	37.1	2.0
	Leather	56.7	2.4	40.0	2.0
	Clothing	56.3	2.6	35.6	1.9
	Metal	54.5	2.0	30.9	1.2
3.	Wood	47.8	1.5	17.4	1.0
	Professional	47.8	1.3	8.7	1.0
	Others	47.4	1.4	16.7	1.25
4.	Female-headed hhs.	26.8	1.7	5.1	1.6
	Building	23.7	1.2	7.9	1.3
	Rest of city	21.8	1.8	8.3	1.4

cluster of three, somewhat miscellaneous, categories (from 'wood' to 'others'), which display consistent distributions of between 47 and 48 per cent and rather low mean sizes – of between 1.3 and 1.5 for their servant groups. The remaining categories show a markedly thinner spread of servant-keeping households – at between 21 and 27 per cent, although only the lowly building trades have the diminutive mean size of 1.2 servants which is consonant with this. The higher averages for female-headed households and the 'rest' reflect small concentrations of wealthier homes headed by widows or those males who have escaped an occupational label. In this last case, it is worth noting that the low distribution of 21.8 per cent may perhaps be taken as a reassuring sign that the sample which has been successfully categorised is probably not too unrepresentative of the whole.

The manifestly thin spread of households containing *male* servants and the mean sizes of these groups, however, demonstrate the scale of the city's economic problems. In this instance, even the merchants could boast no higher a distribution than 57 per cent despite a reasonable average of 2.3 male servants for each household concerned. The next grade – from victualling to metal crafts inclusively – betrays some appreciable alterations in the ranking just established with regard to the distributions, which are variously restricted to between 30 and 40 per cent of the households in each category. Of these, furthermore, only leather, textiles and clothing display a mean servant group size of about 2.0. For the rest, wood and 'others' alone can show distributions of even 16 to 18 per cent, while the densities range between a mere 1.0 and 1.4, although a tiny proportion of female-headed households does push this up to 1.6.

Revealing as these findings are, it is necessary nonetheless to look more closely at the implications of this evidence. Table 19 thus concentrates on two relevant and strategic ratios which betray even more accurately the situation within not only the occupational categories already indicated, but also certain specific trades. The latter are particularly interesting in that although the sample of each is hardly large, the bias is clearly towards the middling to wealthier households in the trades concerned (because these have been identified from the 1522 tax assessment, with its in-built tendency to give occupational labels *systematically* only at the £2-worth-in-goods level and above). The spread of households containing *male* servants in each of these trades is therefore significant. Only in the case of the bakers did some three quarters of the households contain men-servants, though for the mercers the proportion was two thirds. Below this level the proportions were a little over a half for the dyers; and somewhat under a half for the drapers, tailors and corvisors. Just over one third of the shermen's households contained male servants, while both the butchers and the weavers had proportions that fell short even of that. Not surprisingly, only one labouring household contained a male in-servant.

Of all occupational *categories* in this table, only leather could

Table 19. *Servants: sex and replacement ratios by occupational categories and some specific trades within them*

Categories/ Trades	No. of hhs.	Sex ratios, M per 100 F		Maximal replacement ratios	
Merchants	60	56.1		1.3	
Drapers	28		46.8		1.0
Mercers	28		64.6		1.5
Victuallers	85	42.1		0.5	
Bakers	18		72.0		1.0
Butchers	37		45.9		0.5
Officials	21	26.9		0.3	
Textiles	97	72.7		0.7	
Dyers	26		82.9		1.3
Shermen	34		66.7		0.7
Weavers	23		75.0		0.4
Leather	60	137.1		0.8	
Corvisors	30		258.3		1.0
Clothing	87	92.3		0.7	
Cappers	49		113.5		0.9
Tailors	20		108.3		0.7
Metal	55	50.0		0.4	
Wood	23	30.8		0.2	
Professional	23	16.7		0.1	
Others	19	62.5		0.2	
Female-headed households	257	22.1		0.1	
Building	38	57.1		0.1	
Labourers	23		25.0		0.04
Rest	477	41.5		0.1	

boast a healthy excess of male over female servants – a proportion which was clearly inflated by the staggering ratio of 258.3 male servants to every 100 of their female counterparts amongst the corvisors. If no other category could exhibit a stronger sex ratio than those for clothing and textiles – at 92.3 and 72.7 respectively – nevertheless a scrutiny of some specific trades does help to redress the balance. The clothing ratio for example was well buttressed by scores of over 100 for both the cappers and the tailors, while, with regard to textiles, both dyers and weavers had ratios in excess of the category as a whole. Especially notable, finally, in the wake of a subsistence crisis was the healthy position of the Bakers by contrast with the Butchers.

Clearly a low servant sex ratio, however, need only mean that the more prosperous citizens could afford a strong domestic work force of female labour *in addition to* an irreducible nucleus of males. In other words, the full implications of a male servant shortage may only be measured meaningfully in terms of occupational replacement rates. This operation is extraordinarily difficult to accomplish on the basis of the existing evidence, but enough may be deduced with which to expose the weak and strong sectors of the economy beyond much reasonable doubt.

Thus the column in table 19 depicting a crude replacement ratio for each category and certain specific trades lists maximal figures which need interpreting with some latitude. The ratio is achieved by dividing *all* male servants by the number of known households in each category or specific trade. Both quantities are distorted to an unknown extent, however, for it is impossible not only to recover the exact relative proportions of masters to journeymen (which were undoubtedly variable from craft to craft), but also to distinguish between in-servants who were either journeymen or apprentices or merely unskilled menial servants. Moreover, far from all the male servants recorded could possibly have afforded to set up as either masters or journeymen, quite apart from the imponderable extent of the drop-out factor, through desertions, emigration to other towns, mortality and the sack. This crude ratio thus merely states that there was an inflated number of males available, at this one moment in time, to replace a minimal number of householders: it does *not* reveal the proportion of apprentices to masters.

Inexact as these figures nevertheless have to be, comparison with craft records does help to indicate the level below which the future of an occupation might be in danger. Most specifically, fairly accurate figures for the then thriving Cappers' company do demarcate some sort of standard. This craft had steadily increased in numbers, with few fluctuations, from a membership of 35 to 40 masters between 1500 and 1506, to a reasonably constant total which hovered between 60 and 71 from 1523 to the late 1540s. Yearly membership after 1523, when it was 60, indeed usually exceeded 64 with (in view of the fellowship's seven-year apprenticeship rule) the significant temporary exception of four to seven years later, when the crisis years seem to have been echoed in a drop to well below 60, and even to 54 in the craft year beginning in 1530.[10] It may well be, therefore, that a ratio of between 0.8 and 0.9 on the table roughly represents the danger level. Any score below this almost certainly reflects the decline of the occupation or category in question.

The perilously low replacement ratio of 0.4 recorded for the Weavers, for instance, undoubtedly betrays grim realities in this sector of the economy, despite a relatively strong servant sex ratio. Calculations made from quarterage payments during the 1520s and 1530s unambiguously corroborate the continuing decline of the company's membership in these decades.[11] From the seven years of the 1530s for which such information survives, it appears that the average number of master weavers per year had dropped to about 29. Sure confirmation of this decline was the difficulty experienced by the fellowship in maintaining its Corpus Christi pageant. In 1529 indeed, the play, props and wagon were temporarily conveyed lock, stock and barrel to the wealthy Cappers' fellowship, the Weavers being left responsible only for an annual subvention of 6s. 8d.[12] Two years later, however, even if the play was then back in the hands of the Craft, its performance was now being subsidised by contributions from two other fellowships.[13] Not only, as has been seen, was this a time when the occupation was feeling increasingly vulnerable to rural competition, but, in 1544, it was being complained that many weavers even lacked big enough looms with which to meet national standards of broad cloth manufacture.[14] As a direct result, the city's clothiers were now officially freed from their obligation to

[10] Cappers' accs., *passim* (no account survives for 1529–30); for the growth of the Craft *v. supra*, p. 44.
[11] C.R.O. access. 100 Weavers 11. Cf. *supra*, p. 49, n. 47.
[12] *L.B.*, p. 697.   [13] *L.B.*, p. 710.
[14] *Supra*, p. 48; *L.B.*, pp. 776–7.

respect the Craft's monopoly, being now permitted to weave their own cloths for themselves.[15] By the later 1540s, if the annual payment of journeymen's groats is any guide, the skilled workforce of the occupation had dwindled to a couple of dozen men at the most.[16]

Two other replacement ratios are similarly revealing in the context of the textile and clothing trades. It is noticeable that both the shermen and the tailors, with ratios of only 0.7, scored distinctly below the suggested standard. Unfortunately, it is impossible to substantiate this finding further in the absence of supporting documentation.

The dyers, with the second highest replacement rate in the city, however, present an interesting contrast. In this heavily male-labour intensive trade which involved the handling not only of wool but also of substantial weights of damp cloth, it may well be that not all the male servants in question were necessarily skilled. The earlier decline of the Craft has already been indicated,[17] and they were soon to be dominated in practice by their wealthier rivals, the drapers. Not only was the fellowship of journeymen dyers (perhaps temporarily) disbanded in 1528, but in the following year the occupation as a whole was thrown open to anyone who wished to practice it, provided they did not entice away the journeymen or apprentices of already established dyers.[18] The reason for this was said to be the 'makyng disceavable Coloures in Cloith' as recently introduced by a Frenchman.[19] Whatever the truth of the matter, there can be no doubting the alacrity with which at least two senior drapers in the years immediately following overcame the resistance of the Dyers' Craft by muscling in on the trade.[20] By 1540 indeed, the Drapers were in a position to agree to boycott any dyer or sherman who took cloth – even remnants – from a foreigner or a townsman that was not a member of their fellowship.[21]

In the case of the Drapers themselves, there is consequently no reason to doubt that their replacement score of 1.0 at the least represented a degree of stability in the short term. The Craft accounts, however, reveal that this must have been sustained at a

---

[15] *L.B.*, p. 777.

[16] C.R.O. access. 100: Weavers 11. The highest income to come from this source appears to have been 6s. 6d. in '1546'.

[17] *Supra*, pp. 41–2.   [18] *L.B.*, pp. 694, 697–8.

[19] *L.B.*, p. 698.   [20] *L.B.*, pp. 704, 714.

[21] C.R.O. access. 154: Drapers 1c, Daffern transcript, p. 19.

very modest level of numbers. For the years when the evidence survives (never less than six years in any one decade), the average intake of new brethren was only 1.8 masters per year in the 1530s – when the fellowship only totalled some 35 members – and fluctuated slightly between a mere 2.0 and 2.4 for the following three decades up to 1570.[22] For one of the wealthiest companies in the city, these low figures surely echo the continuously stagnant state of the textile industry over this period.

Three further sectors of the economy exhibited alarming tendencies on the basis of these replacement ratios. The diffuse metals category in table 19, for example, with its low score of 0.4 (the same as that of the weavers), hardly evinced those signs of resilience which might have armed the city against the gradual emergence of Birmingham in this field during the coming century. In view of the run-down in the textile industry, indeed, it is significant that, by 1531, card-making must have been on the verge of collapse. Not only had it long been associated with the Craft of Saddlers, but by then even the combined fellowship was said to be 'now but a fewe persones in nomber'.[23] The Crafts devoted to wood-work of various kinds make an even poorer showing, while the building industry (the sample of which is admittedly weighted by the number of labourers and households from Bishop Street ward) nevertheless unambiguously betrays the general decline of the city. In particular, the steep drop in the membership of the Carpenters' Craft during the crisis fully supports this evidence, while the collapse in the numbers of their apprentices represents the nearest corroboration of the inferences drawn from these rates that it is possible to find. In this Craft, a five-year apprenticeship was compulsory, so successive quinquennial totals of apprentices indentured are the most revealing.[24] It was thus no accident that by the middle of the sixteenth century the total number of masters had been practically halved since the beginning of the crisis. Nor is it surprising that down even to the late eighteenth and early nineteenth centuries, Coventry was to remain to all intents and purposes, a timber-framed city of the later middle ages.[25] From a building point of view, the city was fossilised for hundreds of years in a mould that had been largely set in the fifteenth century.

[22] *Ibid., passim.*   [23] *L.B.*, pp. 707–8.
[24] C.R.O. access. 3: A5, fo. 1; *ibid.*, fos. 34 *et passim.*
[25] Dormer Harris, *Dr Troughton's Sketches, passim.*

Table 20. *Quinquennial totals of apprentices in-dentured to the Carpenters' Craft*

	Nos. of apprentices
1504/5–1509/10	12 (?13)
1510/11–1514/15	17
1515/16–1519/20	15 (?16)
1520/1–1524/5	5
1525/6–1529/30 (4 years only)	0

If there can be no doubt of the continuing decay of the city's textile industry, the weakness of its metal industries and the demise of its great building tradition, it may be asked what brought the city through the years of decline at the now reduced level of the economy? Once again the replacement rates on table 19 serve to identify the trades in question. The only contradiction is with regard to the victuallers. If many bakers had successfully come through the subsistence crisis and now boasted a high replacement rate so far as the survivors were concerned, it does need to be recalled that at least six were 'dislodged' during the crisis, while one baker is actually written-off in the 1522 assessment as *'fugit villum'*.[26] No butchers, however, were identified as 'dislodged' during that time, and the size of the sample in this case is very reassuring (cf. table 11 *supra*). Their score of 0.5, however, is well below the arbitrary safety level which has been suggested, and is surprising in view of the fact that the majority resided in Cross Cheaping where male servants seem to have been more efficiently counted than in any other ward except Jordan Well (*vide* appendix 3c and table 17). It is possible that the prosperous future of the occupation was to be due essentially to its rural roots; but perhaps more probably in this male-labour intensive trade which necessitated much heavy lifting work, the explanation lies in the fact that sons may have stayed on longer at home or may have been more often apprenticed to their own fathers than was customary elsewhere.[27] It will be shown below that the distribution of households containing children in this Craft

[26] *Supra*, p. 193; C.R.O. access. 18: A96, fo. 60r.
[27] I am particularly grateful to Mrs Wendy Warren for this eminently practical suggestion.

was exceptionally high by the standards of the city as a whole (table 24).

A related area of the economy was that devoted to leather-work. Here unfortunately, it has been impossible to identify a sufficient number of craftsmen in the most crucial trades, those of the Tanners and the Whittawers. In the former case, at least, this failure may be more than accidental. The Craft entered the sixteenth century in a much depleted state. A lost act of Leet preserved amongst the early Tanners' ordinances, and probably pursuant to the general principles laid down in 1494, recognised that 'the Tanners are not of Substance as they haue bin in tymes past', and made the Butchers therefore contributory to their pageant, as were the Corvisors in 1507.[28] The latter Craft in fact was beginning to take on a new importance at this time. By 1524, it looks as though they had only recently acquired their own priest, for which reason they were released from their subvention to the Tanners' pageant.[29] The buoyant replacement rate for the shoemakers in table 19 (quite a reasonable sample of whom is comprised) is therefore significant, and the wide cross-section of other occupations devoted to leather in the category as a whole still produces a rate even in excess of the Cappers.

It was the meat and leather trades in particular which were to help Coventry to survive at its reduced level of importance. It is notable that over the critical period, 1520–59, approximately one quarter of all the sheriffs belonged to these two categories.[30] As between the two halves of the sixteenth century, the numbers of butchers or graziers who became mayors doubled from three to six; while those involved in leather trades trebled from two to six. Insofar as comparability is possible, an analysis of freemen receiving annual loans from the later sixteenth century onwards, seems to indicate that the proportion of craftsmen concerned with leather manufacturing may even have doubled since 1522 when it was only 11 per cent. Most of those involved in this growth were shoemakers.[31]

[28] *L.B.*, p. 556; C.R.O. access. 241, orig. fo. 5. For reduced admission fines, *supra*, p. 46. *L.B.*, p. 607.   [29] *L.B.*, p. 687.

[30] Calculated from the names and occupations that may be derived from *L.B.* *passim* and L.M. *passim*. Some occupations have been derived from C.R.O. A6.

[31] The proportion of those involved in leather has been derived from C.R.O. A12(a) and 12(b), *passim* (for regular earlier entries regarding alms money from White's loan *v.* C.R.O. A14(a), *passim* and particularly pp. 50–90 for an alphabetical list of those concerned). Allowing for the odd duplication and omitted occupational

Two other fellowships, finally, boasted healthy replacement rates in 1523, the Cappers and the Mercers. The former has already been discussed in terms of both numbers and the stability of its membership through to the mid century. It seems clear, however, that the *prosperity* of the occupation was short-lived. Some fifteen years after the taking of the 1523 census, John Leland was commenting unequivocally that 'the towne rose by makynge of clothe and capps, that now decayenge, the glory of the city decayethe'.[32] That this was due to a contemporary change of fashion from knitted woollen head-gear to felted hats is not to be doubted: cries of woe were to be heard on all sides from urban manufacturers at this time: from Bristol, Chester, Gloucester and Lichfield.[33] Coventry capping may have persisted a little longer than in some other centres, but by the mid sixteenth century its fate as the major compensatory factor for the demise of the traditional textile industry was also sealed.[34]

It has already been suggested that the mercers were largely responsible for handling the wholesale and export trade of the city's caps. Even if their replacement rate in 1523 was the highest in the city, it is therefore not wholly surprising that the prosperity of this leading occupation was similarly short-lived. Mercers and grocers certainly continued, in company with the drapers, to dominate the upper echelons of the city throughout the century, but with the extinction or emigration of the great families who made their last public appearances for posterity in the subsidy rolls of the 1520s – the Pysfords, the Marlers and the Doddes – their days of national significance were numbered: their later pre-eminence was relative.

labels, the result – for what it is worth – is based on some 439 recipients (twelve per year), who thus profited between 1583 and 1623.

[32] Toulmin Smith (ed.), *Leland's Itinerary*, ii, p. 108. Cf. Humfrey Reynold's comment, *infra*, p. 219.

[33] Leadam (ed.), *Select Cases before the King's Council*, ii, pp. 268–9; R. H. Morris, *Chester in the Plantagenet and Tudor Reigns* (Chester, n.d.), pp. 318, n. 4; 435; Peter Clark, 'The Ramoth-Gilead of the Good: Urban Change and Political Radicalism in Gloucester 1540–1640', in P. Clark, A. G. R. Smith and N. Tyacke (eds.), *The English Commonwealth 1547–1640: Essays in Politics and Society Presented to Joel Hurstfield* (Leicester, 1979). I am extremely grateful to Peter Clark for letting me see his typescript of this important article. For later cooperation between the Cappers of Coventry and Lichfield, *v.* Cappers' accs. fos. 103v., 105v., 114v., 127.

[34] The membership of the fellowship held up well into the middle of Elizabeth's reign, the lowest period in the Craft's fortunes being delayed until *c.* 1614 – *c.* 1640. The essential transition to felt-making (presumably for the manufacture of hats) was not made until 1640, Cappers accs., fo. 172v.

The measure of their delayed decline may be deduced from the opening pages of their surviving account book, where a short-lived attempt to divide up the component parts of the trade amongst the membership is recorded. Leaving aside the later additions made to each category, a mere 26 names are entered for the year 1566.[35] Under the heading, 'Hats, caps & trimmings thereof', there is only one. The reason for this effort at rationalisation was then unambiguously defined. 'The burden & charge' of the occupation, it was said 'hathe been so greate that Fewe or none can Furnyshe the trade By reason wherof, Occupyeng is of Late greatelie dekaied. And wares at no man's handes to be had thoroelie to [re]sorte the Traders to the Cittie.'[36]

The year 1566 represented no more than the culminating period of a longer-term process which is undocumented. It seems likely however that over the fifty years prior to 1570, merchandising had moved away from being an export/import service for the city; *via* a stage that was largely to do with imports; to a point where it was largely concerned with regional retailing. It is significant that the castigations of urban economies made by the author of *A Discourse of the Commonweal*,[37] were anticipated long before at Coventry by an intelligent local observer in 1533, who claimed that 'ther was few thynges to be worne or occupied, but lightelie it was maid w[i]t[h]in yo[u]r seid Citie, & now ther is little maid ware or none but suche as com[m]eth frome beyonde the See'.[38] If the city was so deluged with imports in the 1530s, by 1566 over half the Mercers' company was now specifically restricted to retailing within it.[39]

If Coventry's role as a major distributional centre for scarce products was thus reduced, that process was undoubtedly hastened by the events of the Reformation. Those that had visited it as pilgrims, as supplicants in its ecclesiastical courts, as dependents on the priory's far-flung manors, as spectators of the city's ceremonies and as brothers of its gilds, no longer had to do so. Such inter-dependence as there had been with regard to the supply of wool by established monastic economies to the city's textile industry was decisively snapped. No doubt as a direct reflection of its reduced

[35] C.R.O. access. 15: A99, fo. 8v. [36] *Ibid.*, fo. 8r.
[37] Dewar (ed.), *A Discourse of the Commonweal*, pp. 33, 62–9.
[38] P.R.O. SP 1/141, fo. 54v. Cf. *supra*, p. 41, n. 6. For typical imports through Lynn, some of which probably found their way to Coventry, *infra*, p. 286, n. 11.
[39] C.R.O. access. 15: A99, fo. 8v.

status, the city even ceased to be the undisputed head of its shared diocese. Demolition of the cathedral may well have already begun in July 1539; and the bishop's palace was later sold.[40] There can be no gainsaying the sudden dislocation of Coventry's already weakened economy as a result of the Dissolution, the city's diocesan demotion and the later abolition of its gilds. It is significant that in 1542 the city was itself unable to raise the huge sum of £1,378 necessary for the essential purpose of purchasing many of the priory's lands within and around the town.[41] Only the massive generosity of Sir Thomas White's loan, made because of its great ruin and decay, saved Coventry from what could have been a difficult situation had this property fallen into the hands of a powerful outsider.[42] How the Corporation raised the further £1,315 it had to find for the purchase of the properties of the two gilds in 1553, we do not know.[43]

The state of the city even before Dissolution was forcefully described by the eye-witness, some of whose observations to the king have already been invoked in this study. Writing as early as 1533, Humfrey Reynolds was remarking on 'a great decay in this Citie, for that handie Craftemen be not sett on' work as they have been' in tymes past, for the Citizens wer wont to liff by the Craftes of Clothemakyng, Cappyng, hatmakyng w[i]t[h] other occupacions'. The effect of overseas imports, he claimed, was such 'that if yo[u]r Co[m]ens wold work, they cane not sell that they make. Wherfore wee haue meny poore folkes & vacabundes moo then the riche be able to meynteyn'.[44] The increase in unlawful games – dicing, cards, and bowls – 'maketh men to sitt at the ale howse when the[y] have goten a peny to spende it. And ther, they havyng litle or nothyng to leese, care not what Invencions they Imagyne.'[45]

The familiar scene of unemployment, poverty and compensatory drinking that Reynolds conjures up may be substantiated from other sources. An unprecedented spate of bye-laws on drinking is especially to be remarked. Reference has already been made to the banning of ale-house visits during divine service in 1539.[46] Five years later, it was being claimed that so many inhabitants were

[40] *L. & P.*, xiv (1), no. 1350.   [41] *L. & P.*, xvii, no. 556 (21).
[42] Poole, *Coventry: its History and Antiquities*, pp. 302–3; *V.C.H. Warks.*, viii, pp. 403–4.
[43] C.R.O. B75.   [44] P.R.O. SP 1/141, fos. 54r.–54 v.
[45] *Ibid.*, fos. 56r.–56v.   [46] *Supra*, p. 79.

becoming brewers and tipplers, and so forsaking their previous occupations that decay, 'vice, Idelness & other innumerable myscheves[were] norisshed and encreased'.[47] In 1547, many alehouses, inns and other suspect houses were suppressed, specifically because they were being patronised by the poorest sort during working hours.[48] Despite this, alewives and tipplers were again on the increase by 1552.[49] The following year, unemployed labourers and others were being commanded to assemble in the early morning each day for possible employment so 'that non of them be found idell at whome or in any alehouse, vpon peyne of Impresonment'.[50]

By the middle years of the sixteenth century, in fact, Coventry's traditional economy had not only lost its *raison d'être*; the city was sunk in the depths of a long-term depression. By 1547, the authorities were taking yet another census (the results of which have unfortunately not survived), but this time to discover 'whethere there be moo people in this Citye of the pooreste sorte that muste be sette on worke then othere that be able to sette theym on worke'.[51] In the light of what has already been discussed, the answer cannot have been much in doubt. It was this very year that seems to have witnessed the first attempts to distribute parochial poor relief, collected every Sunday, amongst

such as for age, impotencye, or sickness, cannot get ther lyvyng w[i]t[h] ther handes; or such as by reason of multitude of children, cannot w[i]t[h] ther honest labour get somoche as will fynde themselfs & ther children, an honest poore livyng, and in nowise uppon such as be wilfully poore, that is, that will not labour for ther lyvyng, or be drunkerds, whoremongers, dysers, carders, contempners of goddes worde, or such like lewde p[er]sones.[52]

In view of their undoubted numbers, this roll-call of the unfortunate represents a fitting epitaph on Coventry's economic decline from medieval greatness.

[47] *L.B.*, p. 771.   [48] *L.B.*, pp. 785–6.
[49] *L.B.*, p. 801.   [50] *L.B.*, p. 807.   [51] *L.B.*, p. 783.
[52] Sharp, *Antiquities*, p. 126. Cf. C.R.O. A9, fo. 38 (Corporation accounts), where, in 1 Edward VI, 52s. 1½d. was paid 'to poore people more thene was gethered in the wards'.

21. Children and the future

Just as the short-term crisis of 1518–25 exacerbated pre-existing weaknesses in the economy and thus accelerated Coventry's decay, so too did it distort still further the demographic structure of the city with all that that meant for the future of the city's population. To trace the implications of this situation, it is necessary to revert to the problems of the 1523 census.

Establishing the proportion of 'children' in medieval populations is one of the most searching problems to vex demographic historians. Such evidence as survives from 'pre-industrial' enumerations, however, does appear to provide an approximate yardstick – no more – from which to begin. It seems probable that, broadly

Table 21. *Percentages of 'children' and servants in populations: select European and English communities*[1]

	Children	Servants	Totals
Rheims 1422			
St Pierre	24.3	23.8	48.1
St Hilaire	28.4	21.6	50.0
Fribourg 1447–8	41.3	9.5	50.8
Nuremberg 1449	35.1	18.6	53.7
Ypres 1506			
Poorterie	43.0	10.0	53.0
Coventry 1523	26.8	24.8	51.6
100 English Communities			
1574–1821	42.6	13.4	56.0

[1] For the general rule that over 50 per cent of early populations were unmarried, *v.* Roger Mols, *Introduction à la Démographie Historique des Villes d'Europe du XIVe au XVIIIe Siècle*, 3 vols. (Louvain, 1955), ii, p. 199. The table is derived from Desportes, *loc.cit.*, p. 491 and n. 88; H. Pirenne, 'Les Dénombrements de la Population d'Ypres au XVe Siècle (1412–1506) (Contribution à la Statistique Sociale du Moyen Age)', *Vierteljahrschrift für Social- und Wirtschaftsgeschichte*, i (1903), p. 15; and Laslett, *loc.cit.*, p. 148, table 4.10 (66 listings) and p. 152, table 4.13 (63 listings). In this last instance again, the figures given (representing *overall* proportions) can only furnish a very rough guide. The means of means are given as 41.5 per cent and 14.6 per cent respectively.

speaking, in any such population, the total of 'children' *and* servants combined should at least comprise about half the numbers recorded, since, again very generally, those in question should comprehend practically all those aged under twenty-five (although obviously *some* people may have married earlier, while others – female domestics in particular – may have toiled through to old age as in-servants). Certainly, such relevant comparisons as may be made, seem to support this suggestion. Clearly there are some fundamental variations here which are best explained by taking into account not only differences in terminology (and, as between each ward, Coventry was probably no exception to this), but also the demographic fortunes of the communities concerned. Thus, all but the parish of St Pierre at Rheims reach a combined total of, or in excess of, 50 per cent of each population as a whole. Only in the two most rapidly declining and crisis-stricken populations – those of Rheims and of Coventry – however, does the proportion of 'children' drop below, and well below, 30–35 per cent.

The Coventry distribution represents an overall view: closer inspection on the same lines betrays some significant variations as between wards. Once again, revealing differences between the senior and junior five wards become apparent. The combined totals

Table 22. *'Children' and servants as percentages of each ward's population*

Ward	'Children' %	Servants %	Totals %
Bailey Lane	29.7	34.0	63.7
Cross Cheaping	31.3	27.6*	58.9
Smithford	26.2	32.3*	58.5
Earl	25.9	33.8	59.7
Gosford	25.3	26.3	51.6
Broad Gate	26.6	16.5	43.1
Much Park	20.0	20.9	40.9
Bishop† (209 households)	30.9	15.3	46.2
Spon‡ (49 households)	22.8	20.0	42.8
Jordan Well	22.9	22.1*	45.0

* Including 'sons'.
† In the *whole* ward, the enumerator counted 252 'children' or 28.4 per cent of the population.
‡ In the *whole* ward, the enumerator counted 244 'children' or 27.8 per cent of the population.

for the senior wards are well above the line – according to the rule of thumb just propounded – ranging from 51.6 to 63.7 per cent. The junior five, however, fall markedly below the 50 per cent level, as between 40.9 and 46.2 per cent of the totals. The detailed distributions are equally illuminating: the proportions of servants amongst the senior wards ranges from 34.0 to 26.3 per cent, and among the juniors at the much lower level of from 22.1 to 15.3 per cent. Likewise, the percentages of children amount to between 25.3 and 31.3 per cent in the senior wards, but fluctuate more violently amongst the junior, notably at the 20.0 to 22.9 per cent mark, though Broad Gate, Spon as originally counted, and Bishop are rather higher.

It is evidently on the lower five wards that critical attention must first be focused. Indeed, it has already been shown that Broad Gate's servants are almost certainly under-counted, while suspicions with regard to male-servants in Bishop have also been aired.[2] All this, in fact, fits neatly with the artificially low percentages of servants recorded in both these wards, the only ones thus to register below 20 per cent of their populations in the whole city. It has also been suggested that Broad Gate's girl children were palpably under-counted,[3] so by inflating the *actual* totals for both servants and 'children' in this ward, a total *proportion* of much nearer 50 per cent than the present 43 per cent could be achieved without violation of the evidence. In the case of Bishop, on the other hand, while compensation for under-counted male servants would similarly raise the combined proportion to nearer the desired level, it would nevertheless correspondingly reduce the anyway slightly exaggerated proportion of children recorded in the surviving schedules for this ward. Even so, comparison of the percentages of children for both these wards (while keeping the above provisos in mind) with the senior five wards does spotlight what is either serious under-enumeration or the demographic results of famine or both in Jordan Well, the Spon sample and above all Much Park.

A yet closer examination helps to clarify the position a little further. The distributions of families containing children, of course, corroborate the previous table. In the top five wards the spread of such households ranges from a maximum of 69.1 per cent in Bailey Lane to 55.6 per cent in Earl. In the junior wards, by contrast, the

---

[2] *Supra*, p. 207.   [3] *Supra*, p. 200.

Table 23. *'Children': factors affecting distributions and sizes of groups*

Ward	% of hhs. with 'children'	% of hhs. headed by single people	% of solitary hhs.	% of couples without 'children'	'only' children as % of all children	Mean sizes of 'sibling' groups*
Bailey Lane	69.1	22.2	6.2	22.2	17.8	2.1
Cross Cheaping	63.0	24.9	11.0	25.4	19.1	2.1
Smithford	61.6	19.2	11.0	30.5	*29.3*	*1.8*
Earl	55.6	22.2	12.6	31.4	20.1	2.05
Gosford	*56.7*	15.9	8.3	*37.1*	29.6	*1.7*
Broad Gate	*42.5*	27.6	14.2	*52.2*	*24.3*	*1.9*
Much Park	*31.0*	26.5	14.8	*63.2*	*19.4*	*1.9*
Bishop	55.0	28.7	11.5	37.6	23.7	1.8
Spon	*42.9*	30.6	18.4	*50.0*	*36.4*	*1.6*
Jordan Well	*33.6*	25.9	19.6	*55.7*	*11.3*	2.2

(Suspect results are italicised)

* Relationships are not specified in the enumerations, and 'only' children have been included in the calculation of what are described, purely for convenience, as 'sibling' groups.

distributions were lower – as between 31 per cent for Much Park and 42.9 per cent in Spon. Bishop's results despite their probable bias, however, restore some of the balance by exhibiting a spread which is almost on a par with Earl.

Nevertheless, it would seem that certain broad factors were at work which varied markedly between the more affluent and the poorer wards. From the marital statuses of the householders (which, despite ambiguities, is still probably about the most reliable evidence surviving for each schedule), it may be seen that proportionately far fewer households in the wealthier wards were headed by 'single' people (between 15.9 per cent and 24.9 per cent), and contained correspondingly less solitaries (6.2 per cent to 12.6 per cent), than their poorer neighbours. In the latter, between 25.9 per cent and 30.6 per cent of all households were headed by 'single' people, and from 11.5 per cent to 19.62 per cent consisted of solitaries, a revealing indication of the familial implications of poverty at times of crisis in particular. Influential as such factors may have been on the distribution of families containing children, however, it is important not to exaggerate their impact. For the Bishop *sample*, although not boasting a very remarkable percentage of solitaries, did contain the second highest proportion of households headed by single people in the city.

The crux of the matter, indeed, is evidently the omission of many children from households headed by couples. Once more the first five wards exhibit a relatively smooth and reasonably acceptable upward progression in this regard, though Gosford's 37.1 per cent looks suspiciously high. Proportions of over 50 per cent of all couples without children in the more junior wards, however, cannot be accepted as normal when Bishop's (despite its bias) was as low as 37.6 per cent. It is thus particularly fortunate that the children were so well counted in this ward.

Inspection of results for the 'children' themselves, however, unfortunately serves to increase the areas under criticism. To the aspersions already cast, have to be added the facts that in the cases of both the Spon *sample* and Jordan Well, such extreme proportions are recorded for solitary children (36.4 per cent on the one hand and only 11.3 per cent on the other), that the mean sizes of sibling groups in both wards must clearly be wildly distorted – in opposite directions. While chance may have resulted in a not wholly unrepresentative sample of Much Park's children, despite the probability of some under-counting, the same cannot be said of either Smithford or Gosford. In both these senior wards the inflated proportions of solitary children, which so obviously disrupt an otherwise descending sequence of mean sizes of 'sibling' groups for the first five wards, arouse the strongest suspicions.

If these remarks be broadly acceptable, then, only four of the city's wards remain above reasonable criticism. Even so, with the exception of Smithford, children seem to have been under-represented in the schedules for precisely those wards which appear to have been most vulnerable to the shortage of bread-corn supplies in 1520, and to the continuing upheavals in the textile and clothing industries.[4] Especially notable, consequently, is the small mean size of the 'sibling' group even in the wealthiest wards: in none does it exceed 2.1 – only 0.3 greater than Bishop's average; while only four households are recorded as containing more than five children (the highest number, twice registered, being seven) in the entire city. To dismiss this as purely a product of under-counting would be stretching scepticism to extremes though the Spon *sample* is clearly

[4] *Supra*, pp. 195–6.

distorted. Inefficient enumeration there almost certainly was (as the contradictory results for some means and distributions show); but the classic demographic symptoms of crisis simply cannot be ignored. If the diminutive mean of densities exhibited by the more *affluent* wards are at all representative of normality in a declining population – and they may well exaggerate the position; then among the less fortunate wards, perinatal, infant, and child mortality in that large number of poorer homes, which can only have contained, or have been expecting, one child in say 1520, would partially help to explain the considerable total of childless couples three years later. Moreover, not only may those who had married since 1520 have postponed starting a family; but those other couples who might have delayed their weddings until 1523 would also appear as childless in the schedules. It is therefore possible that the three affluent wards reflect more normal times; and that Bishop, with its sizable sample of poor households, most accurately mirrors the vulnerability of the lower end of society. Indeed, the bias of its sample may well minimise the seriousness of the situation. In the remaining poor wards, which seem to have been even more susceptible to the impact of crisis, the figures may thus be distorted as much by its effects as by under-counting.

Small densities for the wards, however, do disguise some marked variations as between occupational categories and some specific trades, when this evidence, with all its drawbacks, is re-assembled on a trans-city basis. But it is worth stressing that since, by and large, this more detailed picture is heavily biased towards the upper end of society where 'sibling' groups were larger on average, and more resistant to crisis, such groups were more probably included by the enumerators. While in some cases, therefore, the distributions amongst households may be questionable, the averages need not necessarily be too badly warped. The smallness of the samples among the specific trades, however, must always be borne in mind.

Particularly notable here is the distinctly lower level of Coventry's results when compared with Professor Thrupp's figures for London between 1401 and 1500. Widowed *merchant* families in the capital could boast an average of 2.6 opposed to Coventry's 2.5 (although the Mercers achieve the London level), while 'other citizen' families had mean sized 'sibling' groups of 2.35 as compared with Coventry's 2.05 (if this category is taken to include all those

Table 24. *Percentage distributions and mean sizes of 'sibling' groups by occupational categories and some specific trades*

Categories and trades	% of households containing children	Mean sizes of 'sibling' groups
Merchants	75	2.5
Mercers	85.7	2.6
Drapers	67.9	2.5
Victuallers	75.3	2.3
Bakers	66.7	2.2
Butchers	80.0	2.1
Officials	71.4	1.9
Textiles	55.7	1.9
Dyers	42.3	2.0
Shearmen	52.9	1.7
Weavers	60.9	2.1
Leather	60.0	2.2
Corvisors	66.7	2.2
Clothing	57.5	2.0
Cappers	61.2	1.9
Tailors	55.0	2.3
Metals	65.5	1.9
Wood	65.2	2.0
Professional	52.2	2.0
Others	73.7	2.1
Female-headed households	21.0	1.4
Building	57.9	1.7
Labourers	43.5	1.7
Rest of city	50.9	1.8

other households with occupational labels, and thus to exclude female-headed households and the rest of the city).[5]

At this provincial level also, therefore, the merchant category was unrivalled both with regard to mean size and to distribution. Only the victuallers, significantly enough in the wake of a dearth, could aspire to anything approaching these results; and the high distribu-

[5] Thrupp, *The Merchant Class of Medieval London*, p. 206, n. 22.

tion of households containing children amongst the butchers is especially conspicuous in this respect – a point which supports the possibility that male children in this occupation remained longer at home.[6] Interestingly, too, the general buoyancy of the leather trades seems to be underlined by this evidence; the figures for the category as a whole being convincingly upheld by the results for the corvisors.

A significant contrast is provided by the textile and clothing categories, however. The distributions in both are at much the same low level (although the bias of the sample towards those textile wards which have already been criticised must be remembered in this context). The mean sizes of 'sibling' groups, however, were only 1.9 and 2.0 respectively – figures which are less easily dismissed on sampling grounds. Even the cappers have a low score. When all these results are compared with those for both the metal and wood categories, therefore, it is impossible to avoid the strong impression that the rolling impact of national and local trade depression in the wake of famine is being directly reflected by these figures.

Poverty in general, whether the product of short-term or long-established causes, must clearly be regarded as primarily responsible for other low means and distributions. Good examples are the building category as a whole, the labourers in particular; and, even more obviously, the female-headed households. As with the servants, finally, the very thin spread for the rest of the city combined with the low mean size of its 'sibling' group would seem to increase confidence that the best results have in fact been invoked for the foregoing survey.

In addition to such matters, however, it is necessary to remember that these children were future adults – potential citizens. Extrapolating forward from the basis of this demonstrably fragile evidence, where ages are not even specified, is clearly a hazardous proceeding, but if the germs of Coventry's continuing decline are to be even approximately diagnosed such an operation must at least be attempted. To do so it is essential, first, to establish broadly who were actually comprehended in the term 'children'. They were clearly not 'houseling people' (as servants were usually described at the heads of the schedules),[7] but since the age of confirmation before the Reformation (let alone the age of first communion) is

[6] *Supra*, p. 215.   [7] *Infra*, appendix 1.

still very much a question of doubt and probably varied from diocese to diocese, this only implies that children were of any age under say 14 or 16 years old down to about seven when an 'infant' became 'of perfect age'.[8] By the same token neither were 'children' servants, although a degree of overlap in terms of age would have been very probable. At what age, then, did the transition from the one state to the other usually occur? Contemporary comment put it early. An Italian observer remarked that English parents, having kept their children 'at home till they arrive at the age of seven or nine years at the utmost, they put them out, both males and females, to hard service in the houses of other people'.[9] On the basis of somewhat later evidence, however, Mr Laslett has stated that 'A boy, or a girl, born in a cottage, would leave home for service at any time after the age of ten', and that '12 may have been the most common' age.[10]

Oblique local evidence serves to confirm that at Coventry the upper age limit of childhood was indeed probably about twelve. On 21 May 1534, a listing – very probably of tithing men – was taken to discover 'the names off men and theyr seruants with their chyderen off ye Gossford Strett ward ffrom xij yers off age and oldyr'.[11] While there are ambiguities (noted here in brackets) as to what exactly are households and in allowing for erasures and queries a comparison with the 1523 results is still illuminating. Despite problems of interpretation, these figures are so close as to be very suggestive. Examination of surnames, furthermore, reveals that only nine households definitely contained sons (or rather namesakes) in 1534, though with the addition of two erasures and two queries, this

[8] The phrase 'of perfect age' (*i.e.* completed infancy) is to be found in the preliminary rubrics of the 1549 Prayer Book (*ex. inf.* the late Rev. Anthony Hardcastle). Some concrete evidence is noted by Dr D. M. Palliser, to whom I am grateful for permission to consult his thesis 'Some Aspects of the Social and Economic History of York in the Sixteenth Century' (University of Oxford D.Phil. thesis, 1968), pp. 77–8.

[9] *A Relation, or rather a True Account of the Island of England . . . about the Year 1500*, ed. C. A. Sneyd (Camden Soc., xxxvii, 1847), p. 14.

[10] Peter Laslett, *The World We Have Lost*, 2nd edn (London, 1971), pp. 15, 264. Cf. Alan Macfarlane, *The Family Life of Ralph Josselin* (Cambridge, 1970), pp. 93, 205–10. For the age of apprenticeship, which may not necessarily have been the same as that for entering service, *v. supra*, pp. 83–4, and in London, Thrupp, *op.cit.*, pp. 11, 193.

[11] C.R.O. uncatalogued MS. (16.3 inches × 11.8 inches unfolded with a crown watermark – and entitled 'Thys byn the names off men . . . *etc*' under the heading 'Jh[e]sus'. This valuable document was disinterred and kindly brought to my attention by the late Mr Norris of the C.R.O. during an inter-regnum between archivists.

Table 25. *Numbers of 'adult' males in Gosford Street ward 1523–34*

	1523	1534
'Households' headed by males (husbands & single men in 1523)	135	133 (128)
Total males	190	194 (190)
Total male 'servants' (including namesakes 1534)	55	60 (61)

Note: 'Householders' in 1534 may have included male servants in houses headed by unattached females.

total rises to a maximum of 13. In 1523 the Gosford enumerator did not distinguish sons like his Jordan Well colleague, so it is impossible to tell whether he counted them under children or servants; but on this later evidence, the son who stayed at home after twelve would certainly seem to have been the exception, not the rule. Even as late as 1605, indeed, by implication twelve seems to have remained the approximate customary age for entering service, for an act of Leet in that year penalised masters or parents 'if any Servant or servants or children of any the Inhabitants . . . and that they be of the age of twelve yeares or above' played ball in the streets on the sabbath.[12]

In attempting to establish some sort of meaningful reproduction ratio (children:adults), the other crucial item of information is the adult expectation of life. Again what little evidence there is comes from the Cappers' accounts where, unlike the Carpenters, there is less possibility that the figures are being dislocated by short-term crisis and the depopulation of small masters. Even at this stratum of society, and including the craft officers as well (the majority of whom were moderately wealthy and long-lived), the figures demonstrate that for masters, at least, the expected working life (which seems to have coincided pretty closely with actual adult life) was alarmingly short. Of 39 'New Brethren' joining the Craft between 1497 and 1517 (i.e. before the crisis), 61.5 per cent (24) lasted only up to and including 20 years. The median duration of working life was 12 to 16 years and the mean 16.8. When to these are added 23 others, whose first appearance in the accounts is not marked by the

[12] C.R.O. A3(b), p. 35.

payment of an admission fee, and whose possibly delayed appearance may consequently exaggerate *vita brevis*, the previous results are broadly confirmed. For this new total of 62 masters, the median length drops, as expected, to 12 to 13 years and the mean to 14.7.[13] Now there is, of course, no evidence from which to judge the age at which a man became a master. Mid-century evidence from the same Craft shows, as we have seen, that a number of masters had, not unsurprisingly, served for an unknown duration as journeymen before setting-up; but again the age at which apprenticeship was completed (varying as it anyway did from Craft to Craft), is unknown.[14] Even on this very rough and ready basis, it may be claimed that the average length of working life from *about* 25 (i.e. allowing for an apprenticeship of seven years from around 14, and up to four years as journeyman) was unlikely to have been more than 20 years for *masters*, and there is no reason at all to believe that the poorer sectors of the populace lived longer than this.

On such a basis, therefore, a *very* approximate standard with which to assess the ratios of 'children' to 'adults' may be established. For to replace each adult of 25 and over with an average life expectancy of 15 years, in a *stable* population, there would need to be present at any one moment 0.8 children of up to 12 years of age (i.e. $1/15 \times 12$). If the expectancy was somewhat longer – at 20 years – the ratio would fall to 0.6. In neither case, however, is provision made for mortality or emigration between 12 and 25. A meaningful 'reproduction' ratio, in fact, would need to be well in excess of these minima. For the sake of argument in the following discussion, nevertheless, the lower ratio of 0.6 has been adopted as a premise and arbitrarily inflated to 0.7. The ratio calculated, finally, *minimises* the numbers of 'adults' who had to be replaced, since only married or single householders or inmates *other* than servants have been incuded under this head. It seems very probable that, in a late-marrying population, there would have been more in-servants of 25 and over, than householders under that age. An unknown total of 'adults' has thus been excluded.

Even on this ultra-cautious basis, it is abundantly clear from table 26 that only the two wealthiest wards in the city could have been reproducing themselves. It must be borne in mind, however, that no allowance can be made for the very real probability that in wealthier

[13] Cappers' accs., *passim.*   [14] *Supra*, pp. 144, 84 n. 23.

Table 26. *'Reproduction' ratios by wards*

Ward	Children per 'adult'	Children per household
Bailey Lane	0.82	1.5
Cross Cheaping	0.76	1.3
Smithford	*0.63*	*1.1*
Earl	0.64	1.1
Gosford	*0.52*	*0.97*
Broad Gate	*0.47*	*0.8*
Much Park	*0.34*	*0.6*
Bishop (209 households)	0.57	1.0
Spon (49 households)	*0.40*	*0.7*
Jordan Well	*0.42*	*0.7*

(Suspect results are italicised.)

households children stayed on longer at home than was otherwise customary, and that therefore an unknown proportion of children in the calculations may well have been over twelve – a factor which may have been balanced by greater longevity. So these wards, too, could have been perilously near the danger line. By the same standard, not only Bishop – with its probably exaggerated result – but also Earl (ranked fourth in the city) were simply not reproducing enough children for the future. It can hardly be doubted, consequently, that those wards where children were conspicuously under-represented, all but one of which were less affluent than Earl, were similarly sub-fertile – or over-affected by mortality. In Broad Gate, for example, where it is possible that all, or very nearly all, *boys* were counted, the masculine reproduction ratio for one *male* adult was only 0.58.

The ratios for children per household seem to confirm these findings. Bailey Lane and Cross Cheaping, with the provisos just suggested, may have been just holding their own, since somewhat less than a quarter of the households in both wards were headed by single persons (see table 23). When allowances are made, however, for the fact that Earl's proportion of single-headed households was the same as Bailey Lane's, the much lower ratio of just over one child for each household in this case is most marked, as is Bishop's probably inflated ratio of exactly one.

This crucial point – the existing paucity of children at Coventry –

Table 27. *Percentages of households containing numbers of children: Rheims and Coventry*

| | | Children | |
Population	% 1–2	% 3	% 4+
Rheims 1422			
St Pierre	77.1	15.3	7.5
St Hilaire	76.3	12.2	11.5
Coventry 1523	75.8	15.5	8.8

may be vividly illustrated, finally, in a temporal perspective. For
when Coventry's figures are taken together with respect to all those
660 *households* that contained children (thus evading the problem
of *overall* distribution), the results are uncannily similar to those
found for Rheims a century earlier.[15] Even allowing for some distortion in the Coventry figures – a distortion which may anyway be
partially smoothed by grouping together children in their ones and
twos – the resemblance is too striking to be ignored. In both cities
the populations were rapidly declining.

The comparison which may therefore be made between the distribution of *children* at Coventry with Mr Laslett's later 100 communities is peculiarly significant.[16] In this instance, the local evidence, having been firstly restricted to those wards which are

Table 28. *Percentages of children in groups:
Coventry and 100 English communities*

| | | Groups of children | |
Populations	% 1–2	% 3	% 4+
Coventry Bailey Lane	48.3	30.5	21.2
Cross Cheaping	43.3	28.6	28.1
Earl	46.1	35.1	18.8
Bishop	67.3	15.6	17.1
'Whole' city	55.9	23.6	20.2
100 later English communities	29.6	23.1	46.4

[15] Desportes, *loc.cit.*, p. 488, table iv.
[16] Laslett, *loc.cit.*, p. 148, table 4.11 (66 listings).

immune from obvious criticisms of under-representation, thus over-emphasises the pattern to be found in the wealthier wards – those also most resistant to the 'normal' demographic effects of subsistence crisis. This in fact buttresses the argument, for the later English sample is clearly heavily weighted by *whole* populations which were, at the very least, reproducing themselves, and, more probably, growing.

This table exhibits the varying distributions behind the descending order of mean sizes for Coventry's 'sibling' groups. Particularly remarkable is the evident contrast provided by Bishop's concentration of children living singly or in pairs – as much as 20 per cent in excess of the other, more affluent, wards. Quite as significant, however, is the difference between the earlier and later periods with regard to this very point; for even omitting Bishop for the moment, the wealthiest wards in the city themselves exhibit a glaring contrast with Mr Laslett's overall proportions. Indeed, the massive increase in large families, during the ensuing century and thereafter, was such as to reverse the proportional distribution absolutely: whereas, at Coventry, between 43.3 and 48.7 per cent of all children in these *affluent* wards resided in groups of only one or two; by the later period 46.4 per cent of the *total* populations comprehended, were in groups of four or more. If, in addition, the probably exaggerated Bishop results are taken as representative of Coventry's poorer wards, this contrast is immeasurably increased. Well over 50 per cent, perhaps 60 per cent of all children in the 'whole' city must have lived in only ones *or twos*, particularly when the circumstances of crisis and hence the artificially inflated numbers of childless couples are allowed for (cf. table 29). In 1523, 34 per cent of all children resided in groups of two over the 'whole' city (the proportion in Bishop being 43.6 per cent), as opposed to 18.4 per cent in post-medieval England generally. On this evidence, then, it might well be that the Coventry proportion of children in clusters of three is unrepresentative of 'normality'. But even so, it would seem difficult to explain away the subsequent radical change in family size on the grounds that either the crisis has wholly distorted the results, or a slightly lower age group than later was comprised at Coventry. The real expansion was to be in the percentage of children in the much larger groupings of four or more. The mean size of 'sibling' groups was then to rise from 1.94, as represented at Coventry (the average for the wealthiest ward being no more than 2.1 children), to 2.76 by the later period.[17] Though the increase may be exaggerated, yet it cannot be gainsaid.

On any view, therefore, it would seem incontrovertible that what remained of Coventry's population in 1523 was already beginning to breed itself out of existence. Even if allowances are made for a marked upswing of conceptions following the subsistence crisis which, by usual historical demographic standards, should already have borne fruit in an increase of births by 1523, it is difficult to see how a palpably ageing population, which also exhibited a serious imbalance between the sexes, could possibly have reversed the downward trend. Only massive immigration would have compensated; yet in the circumstances of depopulation, the prolongation of the crisis after 1523, and the reluctance of stranger craftsmen to settle for even a year in the city,[18] this was out of the question. If, consequently, the more affluent wards reflect anything like normality with regard to their children, then this evidence vividly demonstrates just how critical a protracted period of intense crisis could be for the future of an already shrinking urban population.

The atrophied total of Coventry's inhabitants in the mid sixteenth century was thus, to some extent, already determined a generation earlier. Not only did economic circumstances continue to militate against the immigration of new blood from the countryside, but in addition to the plague visitation of 1525 and subsequent harvest failures, other pressures were soon to be at work to diminish the survivors of the short-term crisis even further. In the meantime, although the last three years recorded on the histogram (figure 1) show a reduction in the amount of rent lost by the Corpus Christi Gild since the peak of the crisis, there is little reason to suppose that the slight recovery continued. Indeed, during the year or two after the histogram ends, the fraternity must have sold or written-off large amounts of unlettable property, for by 1528–9 its theoretical maximum income from rents had been reduced from £78.7s.0d. to £55.12s.8d., a total which had fallen to nearer £50 by 1532–3.[19] Similarly, the city chamberlains' fixed income from murage – an annual tax on property within the walls, which was based on rentable values – dropped suddenly and sharply in 1528–9, from the

[17] *Ibid.*, p. 148, table 4.10 (66 listings).
[18] *Supra*, pp. 65–6.
[19] C.R.O. A6, fos. 281r., 305v. There are no figures for 1527–8.

usual £51.7s.10½d. to £35.12s.9d.[20] The 1534 listing of all males of twelve and over in Gosford (table 25), moreover, seems to indicate that there had been no recovery in the numbers of households there since 1523. It is thus relevant to note that an outsider, writing prior to the dissolution of the greater monasteries, when proposing a still-born 'Court of Centeners', wished to site that body at Coventry, not only because of the city's convenient position at the heart of the kingdom, but 'also for the relyef and socour of the sayd cytee whyche now ys yn gret ruyne and decay'.[21]

The Dissolution itself was thus the last nail in Coventry's medieval coffin. With unconscious irony, even a Protestant genera-tion attributed to it the sad fate of the city. Sir William Dugdale's version bears repeating:

for to so low an ebbe did their trading soon after grow, for want of such concourse of people that numerously resorted thither before that fatal dissolution, that many thousands of the Inhabitants to seek better livelyhoods, were constraind to forsake the City: inso-much, as in 3 E.6 it was represented unto the D. of Somerset . . . by John Hales . . . that there were not at that time above 3000 Inhabitants, whereas within memory there had been 15000.[22]

No doubt the latter figure was exaggerated, though the estimate of 10,000 plus in the earlier part of the fifteenth century suggested above is probably a conservative estimate.[23] No doubt, Dugdale was unaware of the depopulation of the city that had occurred over the thirty years preceding Dissolution. But the figure of 3,000 souls in 1550 needs to be taken seriously. John Hales as a Coventry prop-erty owner and founder of the Free School in 1545, was well placed to know the facts.[24] He could hardly have been ignorant of the findings of the unemployment census taken in 1547,[25] however

[20] *L.B.*, pp. 545, 596; C.R.O. A7(a), p. 98; this reduced figure excludes £6 allowed to the chamberlains for profits from the Little Park.

[21] Laurence Stone, 'The Political Programme of Thomas Cromwell', *Bulletin of the Institute of Historical Research*, xxiv (1951), pp. 16–17.

[22] Dugdale, *The Antiquities of Warwickshire*, p. 96, and cf. C.R.O. A35 (unfol.).

[23] *Supra*, p. 35. The figure of 'xj or xij thowsand howseling people' sometimes quoted from *Acts of the Privy Council, 1547–1550* (6 May 1548), p. 193, must surely represent special pleading, and refers most likely to the estimate quoted by Dugdale for more prosperous anterior times.

[24] *L. & P.*, xx (1), nos. 1335 (38), (39).

[25] *Supra*, p. 220. There is also good reason to suspect that 1546–7 was a year of epidemic. Mortuary figures (for burials as opposed to masses where these may be distinguished) from Cappers' accs., *passim*, suggest the following patterns of mortali-ty: 1540–1, 13 deaths; 1541–2, 13 or 14; 1542–3, 11; 1543–4, 11; 1544–5, 9;

inefficiently that may have been achieved. The 1563 return of families to the Privy Council, indeed, although incomplete for the city, suggests a dramatic fall in population since 1523. For St Michael's parish, which covered nearly two thirds of the city, seems to have contained in the region of 1,100 households in the earlier year, but only 503 families exactly forty years later.[26] While the drop is clearly exaggerated by unknown factors to do with the manner in which the 1563 estimate was made, and no doubt by the impact of epidemics, it remains extraordinarily difficult to inflate the total population of Coventry in that year to more than four to five thousand at most. Since the beginning of the sixteenth century, in fact, the city's population may have practically halved.[27]

1545–6, 16; 1546–7, 33; 1547–8, 8; 1548–9, 8; 1549–50, ?12. The 1546–7 figures are significantly inflated by suspiciously unusual numbers of deaths within the same families (*ibid.*, fo. 68v.).

[26] B.L. Harl. MS. 594, fo. 165v. Holy Trinity appears on the same folio under the heading 'Churches or chapelles havinge cure without institution or Inductions', and is credited with only 49 families. Many of the other places mentioned under this head were within the county of Coventry, and it may be suspected that this figure therefore refers only to a scattering of families within the rural parts of the parish and therefore outside the city.

[27] *Supra*, p. 167. It is worth noting that another dearth census in 1586–7 (L.M., fo. 27v.) then counted 6,502 persons. The only parish register to survive is that for Holy Trinity which begins in 1561 (and for the loan of a microfilm of which to the Bodleian, I am grateful to the Warwickshire County Record Office). From this it is clear that – as elsewhere – only part of the demographic recovery since the mid century can be ascribed to natural increase. Between March 1561 and March 1590, the surplus of baptisms over burials amounted to 304. If we estimate St Michael's parish to have contained twice as many people, the increase for the whole city may have been of the order of some 900 persons over that period. To these should be added the swarms of migrant poor, if other towns of the period are any guide. In 1588, the Leet was already complaining that 'diverse and sundrie persons, poore, loose of life, or ill behaviour, or not conformable to good order, (being no freemen of this citie) do daily, more and more resort to this Citie . . . whereby this Citie and liberties thereof is greatly annoyed pestered and burthened with such persons', C.R.O. A3(b), p. 2. The problem became worse thereafter, *infra*, p. 271, n. 9.

22. Coventry and the size of the late medieval urban household

The paucity of people surviving at Coventry in 1523 has now been discussed in both economic and demographic terms, and the logic of the situation pursued in each case down to the middle of the sixteenth century. Before transferring attention to the changing structure of the community as a whole, it remains to be seen how the basic unit in that structure, the household, was itself affected. Not only will it be necessary to look at household size and structure at different levels of Coventry society in 1523; it will also be essential to place the problem of overall size in a wider chronological and comparative perspective.

Controversy has surrounded the size of the English medieval household, but not until recently has even passing attention been paid to variations in density, which might reasonably be expected to have accompanied the waxing and waning demographic fortunes of the community concerned.[1] However imperfect the Coventry evidence may be, therefore, it is to be hoped that, at the very least, it may contribute some factual fuel to an argument that has, of necessity, been conducted hitherto on largely hypothetical lines.

This particular discussion has so far been concerned with a critical examination of the component elements of the average household; it is consequently not before time to judge these in the context of what was clearly the single most important determinant of composition and hence size – wealth. This may be accomplished in two ways: from the evidence both of rents and of wealth assessed in goods. In each case detailed analysis is only possible on a trans-city basis; but as the results demonstrate, such an exercise does most convincingly smooth imperfections in the ward enumerations, and thus also helps to assuage doubts about *very* serious under-counting. Since, moreover, the best evidence on wealth comes from those thought to be at least potential candidates for taxation, it is very probable that

---

[1] A brief, but useful survey of the literature may be found in T. H. Hollingsworth, *Historical Demography* (London and Southampton, 1969), pp. 118–20, to which may be added Desportes, *loc.cit.*, pp. 493–5 and P. Deprez, 'The Demographic Development of Flanders in the Eighteenth Century', in Glass and Eversley (eds.), *Population in History*, p. 619.

in this upper stratum (as is so often the case, when censuses are taken), more accurate returns were made to the enumerators than lower down. The figures for the former elements in the population, which were also most resistant to depopulation, may well be more representative of normality *at that level*, than those for the less fortunate.

The evidence for rents, however, does allow of a deeper penetration of society than that based on assessed goods, for it isolates unambiguously the cottagers (those paying rent of 6s. *p.a.* or less) and their immediate economic superiors. It therefore constitutes an appropriate starting point.

Insofar as rents should reflect, to some degree, the actual sizes of houses inhabited, these results convincingly demonstrate an uninterrupted upward sequence of household densities: from the diminutive, and probably under-represented, size of 2.6 for the very poorest, the cottagers; through a small band of moderate freeholders (category 8), occupying a suitably middling position; to the substantial households of over nine persons. Broadly speaking, however, the beginning of this sequence – categories (1) to (4) and (9) (the last of which, 'the rest of the city', is clearly biased towards the less wealthy also) – is due more to increasing *distributions* of servants and children, than to dramatic differences in the mean *sizes* of these component groups. If the average densities of both ele-

Table 29. *Sizes and composition of households by rental categories etc.*

Categories	No. of house-holds	% of all house-holds	Mean sizes of house-holds	% of house-holds with servants	Mean sizes of servant groups	% of house-holds with children	Mean sizes of 'sib-ling' groups
1. 1–6s.	149	11.4	2.6	13.4	1.35	37.6	1.7
2. 6s. 8d.–12s.	174	13.4	3.3	28.2	1.5	50.0	1.9
3. 13–18s.	105	8.1	3.9	49.5	1.6	66.7	1.86
4. 20–29s.	157	12.05	4.64	72.0	2.0	65.6	2.0
5. 30–49s.	90	6.9	6.04	85.6	2.9	71.1	2.25
6. 50–69s.	37	2.8	7.30	91.9	3.6	86.5	2.5
7. 70s. +	20	1.5	9.2	90.0	6.3	85.0	2.2
8. Freeholders	45	3.45	5.4	77.8	3.1	53.3	2.3
9. Rest of city	525	40.3	2.75	21.9	1.8	39.4	1.8

Note: For distributions of rental and other categories by wards see appendix 3e, table 40.

ments here range between 1.35 and 2.0, the distributions jump markedly at different points. Although, interestingly enough, servants were to be found even at the cottager level, the rapid rise in the proportion of households containing servants, from 13.4 per cent to 72.2 per cent by the 20–29s. category, is very noticeable; the most obvious breakthrough point, with respect both to means and spread, being delayed until this last category itself. In the case of children, the distributions increase most emphatically between the first two categories, and between the second and third. But only at and above the fifth category, comprising the 30s. to 49s. group, are distributions of over 70 per cent of all households concerned, combined with 'sibling' groups of 2.2 or more. When the freeholders are also included, from about this level too, *both* the distributions *and* the mean sizes of servant groups overtake those for children, the only part-exception being the remarkable jump between categories (3) and (4), where the proportions of households containing small servant groups on average increase by 23 per cent.

But if rents help to differentiate some of the gradations at the poorer end of society, the broad assessments taken of goods do the opposite. While both approaches agree as to the tiny size of the average household at the bottom end of urban society, table 30 thus masks the intermediate stage between the lowest level and those assessed as possessing goods worth taxing. The gap, however, does serve to underline strongly the understandable, but erroneous tendency of some historians to lump together those assessed at £2 worth of goods or less with the poor.[2] This new evidence shows that, on the contrary, people in this category headed households *above* the overall mean size in the community, with nearly half of them containing servants, and over 60 per cent an average of about 2 children.

In table 30, the distributions and means for servants overtake those for children as low as the £3–5 level; an indication that this assessed group also was further from the poverty line than is usually assumed.[3] Categories (4) and (5), however, comprise something of a plateau despite quite wide ranging differences in wealth from £6 to £16. But as from the £20 grade upwards, the mean household densities increase rapidly again: from 6.6 to 11.8 persons in the very

[2] Thus, MacCaffrey, *Exeter, 1540–1646*, p. 249.
[3] J. F. Pound, 'The Social and Trade Structure of Norwich 1525–1575', *Past and Present*, xxxiv (1966), p. 50.

Table 30. *Sizes and composition of households by categories of goods*

Categories	No. of house-holds	% of all house-holds	Mean sizes of house-holds	% of house-holds with servants	Mean sizes of servant groups	% of house-holds with children	Mean sizes of 'sib-ling' groups
1. Nil assess-ments	268	20.6	2.8	17.2	1.3	42.9	1.8
2. £0–2	218	16.7	3.9	45.4	1.5	61.5	2.06
3. £3–5	120	9.2	4.8	73.3	2.1	66.7	2.0
4. £6–10	72	5.5	5.4	86.1	2.4	70.8	2.0
5. £11–16	32	2.5	5.7	87.5	2.6	71.9	2.2
6. £20–49	65	5.0	6.6	92.3	3.4	67.7	2.3
7. £50–99	25	1.9	7.3	100.0	4.0	76.0	1.95
8. £100 +	14	1.1	11.8	100.0	7.6	78.6	2.8
9. Rest of city	488	37.5	2.6	18.4	1.8	37.5	1.7

Note: For distributions of categories of goods by wards see appendix 3f, table 41.

wealthiest homes of the city. At such levels, as might be expected, the presence of servants, and in considerable numbers, was universal or practically so. The only major anomaly in the sequences is the low mean size recorded for sibling groups in category (7) – probably a sampling freak since the distribution is increasing proportionately. Particularly interesting, therefore, in this respect, is the fact that the wealthiest households of all could boast an unrivalled mean density of 2.8 for their sibling groups, and a distribution of practically 80 per cent. This provides an instructive contrast with the previous table, where the highest category (of rents worth 70s. *p.a.* and over) had children in 85 per cent of its households, but equivalent densities of only 2.2. Reshuffling households headed by much the same people into slightly different categories, thus helps to highlight the very considerable household densities which might be attained at the top of urban society.

On this evidence, then, the correlation between wealth and household size is undeniable. It has of course, therefore, much to do with the variation as between occupational categories. Since these too are weighted towards the wealthier end of society (although not all the constituent households were assessed on goods), the following table indicates the extent of possible tax 'evasion' (col. 2). It then ranks the categories by the proportions of their households *assessed* on more than £5 worth of goods, for the general bias of the sample is well over the usual household mean. Specific internal differences – with regard to servants and children – have already been discussed. Here the general correlation between household size and wealth seems to hold with two exceptions: 'clothing' whose wealth ranking (according to the last column) is quite out of sequence, which might well partly be a temporary reflection of the trade depression; and 'wood'. In both, however, the omission of 30 per cent of the category from those assessed has clearly distorted the ranking. Obviously the rankings for the 'rest of the city' and for 'female-headed households' are also virtually meaningless because the categories are so huge, and the number of those assessed minute. From this it would seem that the average enfranchised citizen's household comprised four to five persons. Only the victuallers at 5.4, and the merchants at 7.4 could exceed this. Significant exceptions, however, were the so-called 'professionals' – who comprehended a much humbler group of people than the modern connotation of their occupational label might imply, and the 'building' category. Both fell well below the mean for the whole city. Both also serve as healthy reminders that, despite the evidence for under-representation, which is probably most reflected at this level,

Table 31. *Sizes of households by wealth of occupational categories*

Categories	1 Mean sizes of households	2 Per cent of category assessed on goods which were valued	3 Households as- sessed on over £5 worth of goods as a per cent of households as- sessed on goods
Merchants	7.4	96.7	91.4
Victuallers	5.4	94.1	52.5
Officials	4.9	85.7	50.0
Textiles	4.8	82.5	33.8
Leather	4.6	73.3	31.8
Clothing	4.6	69.0	18.3
Others	4.3	89.5	29.4
Metals	4.2	74.5	26.8
Wood	4.0	69.6	31.3
Professionals	3.4	52.2	16.7
Rest of city	3.3	14.7	14.3
Building	3.2	34.2	7.7
Female-headed households	1.8	14.0	44.4

the majority of the households had densities smaller than 3.5. The 'rest of the city' and 'female-headed households' categories between them comprised 56.3 per cent of all households, and only a few really wealthy homes were to be found amongst them. A mean of 3.3 for the former, which embraced 36.6 per cent of the whole, therefore, demonstrates how representative of this more humble half of society were the 'professional' and 'building' categories. The smallest households on average, however, were of course those headed by females, where the mean was well under two persons per house. It is necessary to remember, in this context, of course, that the subtraction of female-headed households from the rest has obviously inflated the mean sizes in the other categories correspondingly: the occupations of deceased husbands cannot be recovered.

In these circumstances, an examination of the only households in the city to be classed as 'pauper' by the enumerators is most suggestive. 19 such domestic groups in Spon were headed by eleven widows, one widower and seven couples. 31.6 per cent of these households (only three of them headed by couples), contained a mean size for their 'sibling' groups of 1.33, no group comprising more than two children. The average household density for this sample thus works out at even less than that calculated for cottagers in general: i.e. at 1.8 as opposed to 2.6 persons (table 29): the same, in fact, as for all female-headed households in the city put together.[4]

It is thus possible to establish some very credible results for much of society with regard to the range of mean household sizes; but to reach a conclusion on an overall domestic density for the whole city, it is clear that some adjustments to the ward figures need to be made. Such an exercise (as attempted in appendix 4a to provide no more than a rough measure) adds a further 171 children and 18 servants to those already recorded. The result is to alter the relative proportions of these to 29.2 per cent and 24.2 per cent respectively – the former figure suggestively matching quite neatly with Professor Russell's proposed 33 per cent for under-fourteens.[5] Adjustment of the population counted *in the surviving schedules*, thus

---

[4] Cf. Paul Slack, 'Poverty and Politics in Salisbury 1597–1666', in Clark and Slack (eds.), p. 177.

[5] Russell, *British Medieval Population*, pp. 24, 143 – but cf. p. 146 where he takes 50 per cent as the proportion of under-fourteen.

raises the grand total to 4,986 persons (including the nine people entered without grouping by households under Smithford, but who have here been taken to comprise four such units). This operation, however, still only inflates the mean household density for most of the city from 3.68 (the mean of means for the ten wards being 3.72, *vide* appendix 3b, table 37) to 3.82 persons in 1523 (the revised mean of means rising accordingly to 3.86). Furthermore such a result, although conservative, implicitly assumes that all those 'missing' were under-enumerated, even though it has been suggested that in the most vulnerable wards an unknown proportion of those in question, whether children or male servants, may in fact be accounted for as a result of the crisis. More important still, it has to be remembered that the total number of households analysable in the schedules exclude a further 278 households or so from two of the poorest wards in the city (quite apart from those possibly omitted in Smithford, Gosford and even perhaps Broad Gate and Much Park) the addition of which would be more likely to reduce this adjusted mean than otherwise. In time of crisis, therefore, it can reasonably be claimed that the average did not much exceed 3.8 persons per household, and may even have been lower.

Is it then possible to calculate a household mean which reflects more 'normal' times for this declining population, i.e. prior to the crisis? What would seem to represent a realistic maximum may indeed be estimated. Because the major reason for the low ward averages is clearly the lack of children, some *over*-compensation may be made for this. Nearly 70 per cent of the households in Bailey Lane (which appears to have been very competently counted in 1523) contained between them a mean sized 'sibling' group of 2.1 children, and boasted a reproduction ratio of 0.82 (*vide* tables 23 and 26). It would be absurd to argue, even bearing in mind the circumstances of crisis, that this, the wealthiest ward, was really representative of the whole city at other times: it quite clearly exaggerated 'normality'. But even if this ratio is applied to all adults in the city, the proportion of children is inflated accordingly by 610 to 35 per cent of the adjusted population. And yet, despite this substantial addition, the mean household size rises only to 4.14. It is true, of course, that no allowance has here been made for the conspicuous absence of many male in-servants, but a number of factors, quite apart from the exaggerated proportion of children thus estimated, can be invoked to balance this. Concern over the shortage of apprentices ante-dated the crisis itself, while the presence in 1523 of a considerable female labour-force hints strongly at some compensatory longer-term immigration. It must also be recalled again that this inflated average is based on evidence that omits about one fifth of the households in 1523, most of which were concentrated in two of the city's poorest wards. Finally, and surely decisively, the depopulation of many small households during the crisis has also to be taken into consideration. In particular, prior to 1518, the presence of proportionately many more single male-headed households of below average density seems entirely likely. In all these circumstances, what may well have been a *maximum* urban mean household size of only four persons during a period of more protracted decline appears far from improbable.

Comparative distributions of households by size, indeed, serve to emphasise the overwhelming evidence, which is now accumulating, to demonstrate the fundamental differences that distinguished declining from static or expanding populations in medieval and post-medieval Europe. In placing the Coventry evidence alongside the results surviving for certain very similar urban demographic structures in Europe, it is nonetheless important to remember that this English example is in fact the only city here represented by a practically complete enumeration. The other cases, although involving much larger places, are illustrated by particular parishes or quarters.

Even so, the unanimity both with regard to mean domestic densities (3.6 to 3.8), and to the general pattern of household distribution by size is most striking. The range of households containing one to three persons fell between 50.6 per cent and 57.3 per cent of the totals, with Coventry comprising the highest proportion. In the four to five size bracket – 24.3 per cent to 32.3 per cent of the totals – by contrast, Coventry had the lowest proportion. Particularly impressive is the close bunching of the proportions of households containing six and more people, at between 15.5 per cent and 19.9 per cent of the respective totals. Here Coventry seems very representative at 18.4 per cent. In general, the city's results are thus closest to those recorded for Dresden.

Equally remarkable, therefore, is the contrast between this early English evidence and Mr Laslett's later results (excluding London), in which he claims, perhaps somewhat prematurely, there is little discernible difference between town and country that might other-

Table 32. *Comparative distributions of households by numbers of persons in medieval Europe and 'pre-industrial' England*[6]

Household sizes	% 1–3	% 4–5	% 6+	Mean sizes
Rheims 1422				
St Pierre	56.5	26.9	16.6	3.6
St Hilaire	50.6	32.3	17.0	3.8
Ypres 1437				
Ghemeene Neringhe	53.2	27.9	18.9	3.6
Fribourg 1444				
Spitalpanner	52.7	27.7	19.3	3.8
Aupanner	55.2	29.8	15.5	3.7
Dresden 1453				
1 quarter	55.1	25.0	19.9	3.6
Coventry 1523				
Most of the city (unadjusted)	57.4	24.3	18.4	3.7
100 later English communities 1564–1821	36.3	30.5	33.2	4.75

Note: For the detailed ward distributions at Coventry, *vide* appendix 3b.

[6] Desportes, *loc.cit.*, p. 494, table VII; Pirenne, *loc.cit.*, p. 12; Mols, *op.cit.*, ii, p. 138; Laslett, *loc.cit.*, p. 136, table 4.3. In the latter case, it is not apparent how many or which listings are comprehended. Moreover, the figures are slightly different from those in Peter Laslett, 'Size and Structure of the Household in England over Three Centuries', *Population Studies*, xxiii (1969), p. 212, table 4, where it is made clear that the results relate to 91 communities (largely rural) and therefore omit nine London parishes. Again in the original article, a mean household size of 4.722 (excluding London) was provided to match the distributions in question (*ibid.*, p. 210, table 3). In *Household and Family* (p. 138, table 4.4), however, not only is there a choice with regard to this figure for the period 1564–1821 – as between 4.768 and 4.470 persons per domestic group (cf. *ibid.*, p. 133, table 4.2), but whether or not this refers to all 100 communities is not revealed. In the face of this, I have therefore arbitrarily adopted Mr Laslett's own 'standard' of 4.75 (*ibid.*, p. 139), although this figure does not appear on his table 4.2. For the purposes of this broad discussion, it does not look as though such a figure would be markedly altered by taking account of Richard Wall's penetrating study in the same volume, 'Mean Household Size in England from Printed Sources', and especially p. 192, table 5.2. It need hardly be added that, for reasons already explained, I am not seeking to engage in a pointless duel over statistical *minutiae*. Rough and ready as the medieval figures admittedly are, they indubitably point a profound contrast with later times. The problems surrounding the comparisons in question revolve rather around the possible differences between town and country in the same periods, and whether or not the populations concerned were expanding or declining.

With regard to the continental examples, Fribourg (Switzerland) seems to have stagnated after 1444, Karl F. Helleiner, 'The Population of Europe from the Black Death to the Eve of the Vital Revolution', in E. E. Rich and C. H. Wilson (eds.), *The*

wise have obscured the issue.[7] Thus, if Coventry is at all representative of declining English urban communities, then, even when the evidence is taken at its face value, there were 20 per cent more small households of one to three persons in the early sixteenth century, containing between them some 32.8 per cent of the population; as opposed to a mere 17.5 per cent of all households in the later period. The major new development, in fact, was to be the sizable increase in households containing six or more people. Whereas at Coventry in 1523, only 38 per cent of the population were so housed, by the later period this proportion had risen dramatically to 53.0 per cent.[8] Nor can this inflation in household size be dismissed on the grounds of either under-counting or the demographic impact of crisis at Coventry by 1523. For it is hardly necessary to recall yet again that, first, under-representation and/or inefficient enumeration seems to be most obviously associated with households headed by couples, and apparently living without children or servants; and that, secondly, depopulation had probably *decreased* the percentage of tiny households. Thus, if anything, the Coventry evidence probably under-estimates the 'normal' number of households containing up to three persons, and possibly the proportion of those with four or five members; and so exaggerates the percentage boasting six or more. The proportional increase in large domestic units, to which Mr Laslett's figures bear witness (and thereby apparently inflating the mean household size to 4.75), therefore, may have been even greater than these results imply, since the most substantial households at Coventry do seem to have been thoroughly recorded. No fewer than 208 households comprised six to nine persons, while a further 31 homes contained ten or

Cambridge Economic History of Europe, iv (1967), p. 16. I have not been able to consult D. O. Richter, 'Zur Bevölkerungs- und Vermögensstatistik Dresdens im 15. Jahrhundert', *Neues Archiv für Sächsische Geschichte und Altertümskunde*, ii/iv (1881), pp. 277–89. Moreover, for the sake of contrast, I have deliberately excluded the cases of Carpentras (R.-H. Bautier, 'Feux, Population et Structure Sociale au milieu du XVe Siècle. L'Exemple de Carpentras', *Annales E.S.C.* (1959), pp. 255–68); and Rheims in 1594 (though here the absence of any households containing only one person is extremely suspicious, Desportes, *loc.cit.*, p. 494). Both in their own ways, however, seem to underline the relevance of demographic growth for household size which Mr Laslett appears to deny for later centuries, Laslett, 'Mean Household Size', *loc.cit.*, pp. 136–7. With regard to the later English evidence, finally, we badly need sets of figures which distinguish between town and country.

[7] Laslett, *loc.cit.*, p. 145: 'the surprisingly slight contrasts between rural and urban communities – always excepting central London'.

[8] Laslett, *loc.cit.*, p. 136 and table 4.3.

248 AN ANATOMY DEFORMED

more members. The largest, composed of 20 persons in all, was appropriately under the regimen of Mr Richard Marler.

It can hardly be doubted that this fundamental increase in mean household size – roughly equivalent, it would seem, to a 21 per cent addition per domestic unit – ought to be associated with the demographic recovery which marked the ensuing century and thereafter. It was, then, no accident that, as has already been demonstrated, the greatest *numerical* change in household composition – between the earlier and later period – was to be with respect to the inflated size of the 'sibling' group. When viewed from the demographic stagnation of the Later Middle Ages, indeed, the so-called 'Vital Revolution' itself would only be possible basically on the longer-term foundations of renewed fertility, and the increased chances of survival. In England at least, the real revolution which, by totally reversing an existing trend, more properly merits that description, was to be the most far-reaching achievement of the Tudor period.

Whatever the truth of these matters, however, one thing is sure. The diminutive size of the household at Coventry in 1523 epitomised not only the decline of the city in both economic and demographic terms, but also the profound strains to which its social anatomy was being increasingly subjected. It is, then, to the wider structural ramifications of this 'penury of people' that we must now return.

(B) The distortion of the social structure

23. Violence and structural stress 1520-5

Introductory

It seems certain that the short-term crisis of 1518–25 constituted a major watershed in the decline of Coventry not only as an industrial unit, but also as a late medieval city community. The extreme disjunction between the *ideal* of this community structure before 1520, which part III of this analysis sought to reconstruct, and the *reality* of life for the survivors thereafter is most marked. Above all, the paucity of people, particularly appropriate people, meant that increasingly the system of social positions could not be fully manned. It also seems likely that a number of those with a long-established and influential interest in the preservation of the old way of life, both experienced a failure of nerve and themselves failed to conform to the old ideals. If then an internal (and essentially impractical) programme for reform inevitably foundered against the resistance of these vested interests, there can be little doubt that when institutional change did eventually come the citizens of Coventry were already pre-disposed by their experience to accept it – even perhaps with relief.

To trace the changes experienced in the wider social structure of the city during the last decades of the medieval period, while yet retaining the flavour of chronological development, an approach which recognises both the enduring qualities of the social structure and the unfolding pressures which led to its alteration, is surely appropriate. In the following analysis, therefore, the short-term crisis of 1518–25 will again be taken to epitomise the stresses imposed upon the social system at this key period, before turning to the consequences of these circumstances. The campaign for reform

249

which emerged out of the crisis years thus acts as a logical link with the nature of the situation in the 1530s, and serves to identify many of the continuing themes of structural distortion that became so conspicuous in that decade. The study concludes with a survey of the institutional changes which resulted both then, and, where relevant, thereafter; and as a corollary seeks to sketch the attendant disruption of the cultural assumptions on which the ideal of civic community was based. Throughout this approach to the erosion of social norms and institutions, neither ideals nor realities will any longer be kept analytically separate. It was the gulf between them in real life that marked the end of the medieval tradition.

Structural stress

When the problems of Coventry's *long*-term decline were examined, attention was drawn to the reluctance of wealthier honest commoners to accept the obligations of civic office-holding. The subsequent multiplications of such refusals during the short-term crisis are therefore hardly surprising. Because their effects were thus felt even at the very highest levels of the city, indeed, the ramifications of the crisis for the rich comprise a penetrating gauge of its profundity. Only in following the situation back through the civic office-holding system, however, does the seriousness of these refusals for the future of the traditional social structure become apparent.

It is best to begin with the shrievalty which, it will be recalled, represented the *entrée* to the civic elite of the city. In 1520, not only did a weaver, John Mors, successfully gain exemption from ever serving as sheriff,[1] but one of two persons actually elected to that office created a public scandal by refusing to serve. Thomas Harvey's reluctance in the face of a quite arbitrary election was understandable, since not merely had he recently settled in the city, but he had never even served the customary stint as a junior civic officer. Indeed his sole qualification would appear to have been his marriage to the widow of a lately deceased alderman – a revealing admission of the lengths to which the Council House had been forced to go by the shortage of potential officers.[2] Being fined £200 for his defiance, however, Harvey appealed in desperation to the

---

[1] *L.B.*, pp. 667–8.   [2] L.M., fo. 16a r.

king and Council. Albeit, the most he could extract from Henry and Wolsey was a letter sparing him the office for one year. As the city annals succinctly put it: 'then the said Harvey went out of the Citty', though he does re-appear in the records three years later.[3]

For those elected thenceforward, however, office was immediately made compulsory, a scale of expensive penalties for refusing any gild or civic office being laid down in 1521.[4] Even so, the following year saw yet more trouble, for the new sheriffs had then to be relieved of their customary obligation to pay the Recorder's fee 'in condicion that the seyd scheryffes newe electe take ther office on them lovyngly withowt contradiccion'.[5]

Such resentful stirrings amongst the more inferior officers, however, were but symptomatic of the back-stage contortions of their seniors. Since the precedent set in 1507, when a number of ex-mayors had permanently evaded a second term – a practice which was also given legislative backing in 1521, the reservoir of potential mayors had been seriously depleted.[6] Once the hiatus created by the office-holding crisis of 1509 had been settled, with one exception, the established rate of promotion between 1511 and 1519 was the elevation of the senior ex-Master of the Corpus Christi Gild to the mayoralty after a gap of at least two years.[7] According to this sequence, then, the Gild's Master of 1517, Thomas Smythe, should have become Mayor in 1520. But since his successor as Master, John Bonde, took on the office instead, it would seem that Smythe probably secured a postponement, an action he may have attempted to repeat the following year when a special election had to be held 'secundum antiquam Consuetudinem Ciuitatis'.[8] The outcome of this evasion, however, was to reduce the gap between being Master of the Gild and Mayor to one year – an added disincentive to service.

Inevitably, 'ancient custom' had to be reinvoked in January 1524,

---

[3] *L.B.*, pp. 668–9; L.M., fo. 16a r.; C.R.O. A6, fo. 258.
[4] *L.B.*, pp. 676–7.   [5] *L.B.*, p. 681.
[6] *Supra*, p. 47; *L.B.*, p. 677.
[7] For the relationship between the mastership of the Gild and the mayoralty, cf. C.R.O. A6, fos. 149 *et seq.* and *L.B.*, pp. 631 *et seq.* Thomas Grove (Mayor in 1514) served only one year after evacuating his Gild office, presumably because John Clark, who had been master in 1508–9, postponed taking up the mayoralty until 1515.
[8] C.R.O. A6, fos. 220, 225; *L.B.*, p. 667; *L.B.*, p. 676 cf. p. 620: 'a newe eleccion . . . accordyng to the olde custome'.

at the height of the crisis, when Smythe must yet again have successfully refused, although he remained on the governing body for many
years after.[9] The one alternative candidate was thus the only available ex-Master of the Gild (from 1522), Henry Wall, who himself
seems to have obtained a postponement until 1526.[10] The aldermen
consequently had to look elsewhere, and they lighted on a capper,
Nicholas Heynes, who had held the most senior position of precedence in the city after the Master of the Corpus Christi Gild since
1515. Heynes had served as sheriff as long before as 1506, and by
rights should have been Master of the Gild in about 1518, by when
his two shrieval predecessors had filled the post.[11] It seems very
possible indeed that Heynes had refused to serve in that office, since
the aldermen now turned on him with singular ferocity and elected
him Mayor on pain of £200 – *double* the penalty laid down in
1521.[12] Despite this, however, Heynes still managed to secure a
postponement of office for a further year, although he was obliged
to act as deputy alderman for the Spon Street ward in the meantime.[13] As a last resort the Council elected to the mayoralty the
retiring Master of the Gild, Thomas Banwell, who consequently
proceeded from the one office to the other within the space of three
months.[14] In such circumstances, therefore, it was perhaps to be
expected that in 1525 the very governance of the city itself was to be
put at risk as a direct result.

Violence

Nor does it come as any surprise that these were years of seething
unrest in general. Fear of what Bacon was later to call 'rebellions of
the belly', in particular, must have been uppermost in the minds of
the city's governors throughout the dearth.[15] Indeed a hint of the
disorder usually to be anticipated at times of shortage may be
gleaned from an ordinance of 1520 for shutting the city gates

[9] *L.B.*, p. 686, n. 3.   [10] C.R.O. A6, fo. 254; *L.B.*, p. 692.
[11] *L.B.*, pp. 643 *et seq.* – the Master was not always present. *L.B.*, p. 606 (the entry
for the Michaelmas Leet, when the sheriffs were elected is missing for this year);
ibid., p. 604, n. 2; C.R.O. A6, fos. 206, 220.
[12] B.L. Harl. MS. 7571, fo. 34v.; *L.B.*, p. 677.
[13] *L.B.*, p. 689; B.L. Harl. MS. 7571, fo. 31r.
[14] C.R.O. A6, fo. 258; *L.B.*, p. 686.
[15] *The Works of Francis Bacon – I Essays*, The World's Classics edn (London,
1902), p. 38.

between 8 p.m. and 5 a.m. 'and thus to contynue as long as hit is thought necessarie therfore for the preseruacion of good rulee etc.'[16] Yet it is most noticeable that both actual manifestations of local discontent at this time neither reflected the desperation of the very poorest sectors of society nor coincided with the worst moments of the crisis. They occurred, by contrast, during the 'lull' of 1523, and the first year of marginal recovery, 1525.

It was not until December 1523 that a conspiracy of menacing, if impractical, proportions was unearthed and reported by the draper William Umpton.[17] The intrigue seems to have fused the plans of certain undistinguished hotheads at court led by one Francis Philips, 'scholemaster to the kynges Henxemen', with local dissidence crystallised under the leadership of two citizens, Pratt and Slouth, the second of whom was probably a scrivener.[18] Taking the local and central evidence together it seems that the plot included firstly the assassination of the mayor and aldermen, and subsequent to this, the robbing of St Mary's Hall where lay arms and armour, the city chest, the common box containing other moneys, and where, significantly in view of the massive loan so recently extorted from the city, was due to lie in all probability 'the kynges treasure of his subsidie as the collectors of the same came towards London'. The second stage of this mad-cap scheme was to raise men – presumably from the disaffected at Coventry – and to seize and hold Kenilworth castle against the king. Well before the event, all the leading culprits were hied to London for trial, after which Pratt and Slouth were returned to Coventry for execution, and the subsequent exhibition of their eviscerated and quartered corpses as a grisly public warning

[16] *L.B.*, p. 669.
[17] B.M. Harl. MS. 7571, fo. 34r.; *L. & P.*, v (1), no. 105. The Wanley version of the City annals (B.L. Harl. MS. 6388, fo. 29v.) has been responsible for some confusion over this plot. The writer, in paraphrasing Edward Hall's chronicle (Charles Whibley (ed.), *Henry VIII* (London, 1904), p. 318), incorrectly added the court end of the story, dated by Hall to December (1523) in the *regnal* year, 7 April 1523–4, to the annals under the *mayoral* year, 2 February 1523–4 (*old* style), as though it must therefore relate to 1524. The local aspect (best represented in the very reliable and earlier L.M. version of the annals, fo. 16a v.) and the central politics thus became divided, and so uncharacteristically ensnared Mary Dormer Harris, *The Story of Coventry* (London, 1911), p. 161, into mistaking one for two plots in successive years.
[18] C.R.O. A6, fo. 217v. Thomas, son of Nicholas Slought, wheelwright, seems the most likely candidate, for his father survived the year in question (C.R.O. A5, fos. 92v. *et seq.*), and there do not appear to have been any other city families with this surname at the time.

at the four principal gates of the city.[19] It is not impossible, even so, that the extent of local misery so evident in these desperate intentions may have helped to persuade the central government to moderate Warwickshire's contribution to the Amicable Grant two years later.[20]

Far more serious than this affair, however, were the events of 1525, the gravity of which has received scant attention from national historians. The immediate background to the emergency was provided by the Leet ordinance of 1522 according to which at least half of those common lands of the city that had recently been enclosed were to be ploughed and sown.[21] Thus instead of keeping the land available for common pasturage during the six months from 1 August, the traditional date at which enclosed grounds were thrown open, some of these were now effectively closed to communal use until the harvest was over. But jealous of their customary rights as the enfranchised citizens undoubtedly always had been, there is good reason, nonetheless, to suspect that deeper issues were also at stake. Contemporaries writing after the event emphasised that not only had discontent within the city been kept in check by the powerful recorder Ralph Swillington, who unfortunately died in the spring or early summer of 1525, but that also there was in existence at this time a confederacy of citizens with unconventional (and unspecified) plans for local constitutional reform.[22]

So it was that although in 1524 the citizens appear to have contented themselves with merely throwing down the enclosures on Whitley common to the south of the city;[23] in the following year, a similar situation deteriorated into an ugly insurrectionary riot. The occasion, so typical of other 'pre-industrial' riots, was the annual ceremonial ride of the chamberlains on Lammas day to open up the city's lands for common use. In this year the formal party (composed since 1474 of hand-picked upholders of the *status quo*), seems to have been followed by a group of commoners who tore down gates, hedges and one particularly obnoxious ditch which had not been breached by the chamberlains.[24] Meanwhile an angry crowd had gathered within the city presumably to await the ceremonial re-entry of the chamberlains through the New Gate.

---

[19] L.M., fo. 16a v.   [20] *Supra*, p. 63.   [21] *L.B.*, pp. 679–80.
[22] P.R.O. SP1/141, fo. 56v; SP1/74, fo. 16.
[23] B.L. Harl. MS. 6388, fo. 29v.
[24] *L.B.*, pp. 843, 566; L.M., fo. 16a v.; C.R.O. A79, i, p. 60.

'Almost smothered in the thronge', was the Mayor, Nicholas Heynes, who having had little personal reason to support the policies of the city government now 'held with the Commons'. No doubt emboldened by this backing, one part of the crowd shut the New Gate against the chamberlains' procession – an audacious act of defiance towards officials of the city, while another group with even greater temerity actually broke into the city treasury in St Mary's Hall and seized the Common box which contained the rents for the closes.[25]

Law and order in one of the leading cities of the realm had disintegrated. The box was successfully retained for four days, while the ring-leaders remained at large until 12 August.[26] Even as late as 6 August, when the king issued commissions to suppress riot, it was 'as yet unknowen whether the said enormytes be repressed or not'.[27] The emergency indeed was evidently far more serious than had been originally suspected. The sympathy of the mayor for the opponents of earlier Leet action in particular was clearly a complicating and exacerbatory factor which the authorities were still trying to unravel in the third week of August.[28] The Marquis of Dorset, who was made responsible for restoring order, moreover, undoubtedly under-estimated the gravity of the situation from his distant residence at Bradgate in Leicestershire. When he arranged, in a somewhat leisurely fashion not to meet up with Sir Henry Willoughby and others until Friday 11 August, he also confidently predicted that if he brought 30 or 50 bowmen and the latter notable 20 or 30, that would 'be sufficient for this time'.[29] Within three days, however, it seems that Willoughby's retinue had swollen to 140, while the Marquis, when reporting on 13 August, claimed to have by then the sizable force of 'two Thousand p[er]sonnes in aredynesse and shall make redy in all haste possible a grete nombre to come unto me if nede bee'.[30] Either the city was still in turmoil at

[25] L.M., fo. 16a v.; for the 'circuits' *v.* Poole, *Coventry: its History and Antiquities*, p. 357; B.L. Harl. MS. 7571, fo. 32r.
[26] Reader 5, fo. 218v.; B.L. Bibl. Cotton Titus B.1, fo. 81r.
[27] H.M.C. *Middleton*, p. 141.
[28] C.R.O. A79, i, p. 59c.
[29] H.M.C. *Middleton*, p. 514.
[30] *Ibid.*, p. 378; B.L. Bibl. Cotton Titus B.1, fo. 81v. How tense the situation was may be inferred from Dorset's concern at only having £100 available – a sum which 'wolbe spent in a daye. For me to Rayse so grete a nombre and haue not money to mayntene theym, I fere me lest they wolbe the furst whiche shall put me in daungier.' He had already spent 100 marks.

this stage or it was feared that it might be necessary to over-awe the citizens with a military demonstration of this magnitude.

Tactically and tactfully stationing himself to begin with at Astley, just to the north of Coventry's county boundary, Dorset, supported by Willoughby and Sir Edward Ferrys, summoned the mayor and his brethren to him on 11 August. He then requested the surrender of the four principal agitators behind the riot (whose names have regrettably not survived), and, on pain of confiscating the city's liberties, moreover, demanded of the aldermen 'whether they could or wold undertake to rule and ordre the said Citie'.[31] Not until the following day, however, did the Mayor and his brethren return with the four ring-leaders and a revealing admission that only with the help of the Marquis and 'thassistence of the c[ou]ntrey aboutes theym they durste well and wold undertake to rule and ordre the said Citie'.[32]

Dorset now acted briskly. Having declared a riot he moved past the city to Kenilworth, from where he held a special session of the Peace somewhere in the liberties on 14 August.[33] Then, or at least by 19 August, Heynes was deprived of his mayoral office; sent to London for interrogation by the Council; and replaced by the senior *quondam* mayor who was intimidatingly styled 'governor'.[34] 37 rioters were committed to Warwick and Kenilworth castles, and seven to London at the Marshalsea, from where after 18 weeks imprisonment five were released only to have their ears nailed to the pillory.[35] Those that were still in custody and banished the city were however eventually released on the occasion of the Pope's Jubilee.[36] Heynes, however, seems to have vindicated himself before the Council for apparently he was warmly greeted back in Coventry by his own Craft, the Cappers, with 'ij galons of wyne, a pownd of marmeret and a cowple of Cakes', probably before the end of August. He was certainly regularly attending craft meetings thereafter, though never again did he sit with the city Leet.[37] Having mingled severity and clemency, the king bade for the continuing loyalty of his subjects with typical Tudor touch, by sending Princess Mary to visit the city in 1526.[38]

---

[31] *Ibid.*, fo. 81r.   [32] *Ibid.*, fo. 81.
[33] *Ibid.*, fo. 81v.; H.M.C. *Middleton*, p. 378.
[34] C.R.O. A79, i, p. 59c.; *ibid.*, p. 60.
[35] Reader 5, fo. 218v.   [36] C.R.O. A79, i, fo. 27.
[37] Cappers' accs., fos. 36r. *et seq.*; *L.B.*, pp. 691 *et seq.*
[38] *L.M.*, fo. 17.

For the outcome of this riot hardly strengthened the position of the city government. The king himself insisted that 'the title of the Comens' should be 'indifferently ordred accordyng to the lawe', and it is significant that a special meeting of the Forty-eight in fact justified the actions of the rioters.[39] On October 10 it was enacted 'that all such comen grounds as haue bene latelie inclosed about this Citie shall fromehensfurth bee Comen as they haue bene vsed in auncient tyme & no more to be enclosed.'[40] It was soon plain, moreover, that the more profound problems which had lain in the background of this unrest would not remain dormant. The city government, from whose bunglings Heynes had dissociated himself, remained a target for attack. Even as soon as the first week of November, a royal proclamation was necessarily issued against those evilly disposed persons who 'haue not oonely of late eftsoones priuely renewed thair seid combynacions and unlaufull confederacons but also they haue caused sedicious billes and writinges to be made ayenst certen well disposed Aldremenne and Burgesses'.[41] There can be little doubt, indeed, that all these activities represented the first stirrings of a vociferous local 'commonwealth group' which was only to find a mouthpiece in the next decade. Small wonder, therefore, that in 1533 the current Recorder, in an obvious reference to the events of 1525, was commenting bitterly on the trouble so caused 'which is not yet recou[er]ed ner like to be in many yeares to com[m]e'.[42]

[39] C.R.O. A79, i, p. 60.   [40] *L.B.*, p. 692.
[41] C.R.O. A79, i, p. 28; C.R.O. B62.   [42] P.R.O. SP1/74, fo. 16.

24. *Matters for reform: the 1530s*

By 1533, indeed, a secret group of citizens from the very edge of the magisterial elite had already compiled a sweeping programme of reform which, if executed, would have seriously undermined the independence of the city government. The membership of this group was unknown even to the authorities, but the 'vaunt parlar and chefe chapteyn' was Humfrey Reynolds, ably abetted 'by oon Foster, A Sergeaunt of the Cite & a veray besy felowe'.[1]

Reynolds was a younger son of an honest commoner who had been a sheriff of Coventry in 1499–1500, and, like his father, had started out as a fuller.[2] A member of the Corpus Christi Gild since 1502–3, when his father had paid for him probably as a minor; by 1521, he was, like Foster later on, one of the city sergeants, having, it would seem, abandoned his business to supervise his lands.[3] Very probably married to the daughter of an ex-sheriff, the wealthy draper, Hugh Dawes, Reynolds is to be found living in 1523, with his wife and child, in a substantial household containing four servants, apparently next door to none other than Richard Marler in wealthy Earl Street ward.[4]

Even by this stage in his career, Reynolds must have been expecting the call to undertake junior civic office, but as he himself explained to the king ten years later, he dreaded the financial risks involved.[5] Like many similarly placed,

> I, with other which come of the yonger brether hauyng no Fee ne wages of no man ne no occupacion; but that I haue commeth by my wiff & my frendes; & if my wiff dies I shuld leese part of my landes & then shuld be takyn into office of the Citie; shuld within ij or iij yeir spend all that my frendes have goten for me so that in my age I shuld have nothyng lefte.[6]

---

[1] The recorder, Roger Wigston, reported to Cromwell that the group contained no more than five or six persons 'or there aboute', P.R.O. SP 1/74, fo. 16.

[2] *L.B.*, p. 599, n. 2.

[3] C.R.O. A6, fos. 131 *et seq.*; *ibid.*, fo. 249v. In 1522 (C.R.O. A96, fo. 44v.) he is to be found paying a rent of 5 marks (to, of all people, the Prior of Coventry) but with no assessment. In fact, he was taxed on £4 in goods in 1524, P.R.O. E 179/192/125, fo. 8. No occupation is given in either year, but, given his pretensions, it is noteworthy that a considerable quantity of arms was in his possession in the former.

[4] P.C.C. 29 Maynwaryng; C.R.O. access. 263, fo. 8.

[5] *Supra*, p. 48.   [6] P.R.O. SP 1/141, fo. 58v.

It was for this reason that recently he had deliberately and success-fully sought the help of Sir Francis Bryan, a trusted diplomat of Henry VIII and a cousin of Anne Boleyn, in procuring him admission as a 'yoman of your Crowne' – an established escape route for those that wished to evade office in the city.[7]

There is little need, as subsequent events showed, to accept Reynolds' pleas of potential poverty wholly at their face value, although part of his forecast did come true. He represented, nonetheless, a vulnerable group of people in contemporary society whose standing was far from secure. Reading between the lines of his lengthy supplication to the king, it seems very probable that for him, as for others with developing pretensions to gentility, the avenues for landed advancement traditionally open to 'the yonger brether' had been financially blocked. On the one hand, according to him, yeomen could be, and easily were, outbid in the payment of monstrous entry fines for leases of monastic lands by gentlemen and wealthy merchants. On the other, they were similarly out-priced in the exorbitant auctions held for profitable monastic stewardships. In the case of Coventry priory, 'I know they have an hundred li. for the seall of tene li. Fee.'[8]

Although Reynolds' vision was wider than the frankly admitted bias of his personal standpoint, it was nevertheless the bitterness engendered by his own experiences which dictated the two objects of his critique of the situation at Coventry, the priory and the city government. 'Religiouse men' and 'speciallie of blake monkes' were the main target.[9] Despite their great wealth (and the Coventry house, he claimed, could dispend little less than £1,000 *per annum*, even though the bishop had £300 worth of their best lands), such monasteries were in debt; were not up to numbers in terms of their inmates; while 'few or none of theme do liff after this profeccion'.[10] Even their various benefices 'as hospitalles, Chauntries & other like ... be contrarie vsed to the willes of the founders'.[11] Above all, one suspects, it was because 'ther is no good household kept & very fewe men' menteyned & ther houses goo downe' that Reynolds was most troubled;[12] and it was certainly true that there were very few superior servants of the Priory resident in the city at this time.[13]

---

[7] J. J. Scarisbrick, *Henry VIII* (London, 1976), pp. 161, 266–7, 290–2, 295. P.R.O. SP 141/1, fo. 35v.　　[8] *Ibid.*, fo. 47v.　　[9] *Ibid.*, fos. 36v.–37.
[10] *Ibid.*, fo. 37.　　[11] *Ibid.*, fo. 48v.　　[12] *Ibid.*, fo. 38v.
[13] Between 1515 and 1524 inclusively, for example, only eight such men – four of

The other target was the government of Coventry. In particular, the 'due mynystracion of Justice for this Citie is in great decay'.[14] Instead of enforcing the law, those in authority were concerned only to see through their spells of office without incurring trouble and in a manner which simply courted popularity: 'the meir is but for one yeir. He dryveth out his tyme as other have doon' before so that the verey affecte of the comens care not what they doo, for they know they shall not be punnysshed.'[15] Acts made to reform the decay of manufactures were not enforced, while instead of other acts to punish vagabonds, 'it were expedient to fynde a meanes how they myght be sett on' worke'.[16] Unemployment was leading to potential trouble fomented in the city's ale-houses. There was, claimed Reynolds, only one respected magistrate left since the days of the 1525 insurrection, 'in whome standeth the hole welthe of the Citie, who is boith loved and dred for his humanitie'.[17] When he died – and there can be no doubting that the man in question was Julian Nethermill – anarchy was to be feared: 'they wold nother sett by meire nor Recordyr nor one by another'.[18]

Neither for this reason, nor for the policies which Reynolds proposed, were the Recorder and the current magistrates of the city likely to look kindly on this submission to the king. For Reynolds now propounded a solution which might be applied not only to the ills of Coventry, but also to no less than all the monasteries and towns of England in which they were situated. His suggestions, which later bore partial fruit as a policy of the Commonwealth group in London,[19] were cunningly calculated to appeal to Henry's conservatism in religion, his cupidity and his lust for power. Reynolds' idea was that all urban monasteries, like that at Coventry, should still retain a minimum number of inmates – an abbot or prior, sub-prior and 20 ordained monks 'to serue god & to teche & preiche the true gospell without dissimulacion', and each of which was to have his 'scoler founde in the ambre'.[20] Bed and board,

them designated Master – appear in C.R.O. A6 as members of the Corpus Christi Gild. Some attended only once, the best represented year being 1520 when six are recorded, *ibid.*, fos. 241, 243. The *Valor*, p. 52 names eight bailiffs.
[14] P.R.O. SP 1/141, fo. 49r.   [15] *Ibid.*, fo. 50v.   [16] *Ibid.*, fo. 54v.
[17] *Supra*, p. 143; P.R.O. SP 1/141, fos. 56v.–57r.   [18] *Ibid.*, fo. 57r.
[19] 'I wold speke for the reformacion of oon' house, And also of the Citie of Couentre. And if it be lefull to refo[u]rme that, to refo[u]rme all other in like case', *ibid.*, fo. 38v; cf. fos. 62v–63r. *Infra*, p. 277.
[20] P.R.O. SP 1/141, fo. 40v. Reynolds' ideal number of monks should be compared with that in the year 1518 when, it was said, 'Numerus confratum est completus',

parchment and services (a barber and a launderer), would be all found. The surplus funds thus made available out of monastic incomes, and the accommodation left free in these houses, would be used to support and house a royal military establishment in each urban monastery. This would comprise a head captain (who would also be a J.P.), a petty captain, an attorney and controller of each house, a receiver, a physician and fifteen fully-armed and horsed gentlemen, with equivalent numbers of yeomen, grooms and pages. Wives would be housed elsewhere in the city.[21]

There is no need to recite the detailed financial provisions made for these people (in terms of liveries and monastic fees), and their suggested back-up force of surgeons, armourers, physicians and victuallers, plus a small army of 28 servants to attend on the needs of the leading officers. What matters is that Reynolds' proposal, had it been implemented, would have struck at the very roots of the hard-won chartered liberties of England's towns. For these provisions would not only have furnished the monarch with a fully equipped army 'in a redyness' (in addition, tenants of monastic lands were now to 'fynde men with horse & harness for a monethe or ij after ther abilities' rather than pay entry fines);[22] they were also deliberately designed to provide for the close supervision of urban governments.

It was the head captain in each town, and in his capacity as a Justice of the Peace, who would 'set all such actes as be maid for your lawes to be truelie executed'. Thereby, the lack of learned men in England's towns would be met: 'wherfor lett your Justice with your councell ther sitt in iugement, or his depute, in all Courtes, Cessiones & letes & Inquisiciones by the clerke of your markettes next the meir, so that ther may no man take no wronge'.[23] Even Reynolds in his enthusiasm, glimpsed the dangers here: 'some men' wold thynk that this shalbe ageynst ther liberties. It is not so, for these men shalbe citizens & townesmen & to do that they may for the Citie & the good inhabitaunce of the same, & not to be aboute to hurt ther liberties, but to meynteyn them to the best of their powers'.[24] Each military Justice was to go in general processions only 'next the meir with the recorder'; and ideally, they were not 'to

supra, p. 197, n. 5, and Heath (ed.), *Bishop Geoffrey Blythe's Visitations*, pp. xxxv, 15.　　　[21] P.R.O. SP 1/141, fos. 42–43, 52v.
[22] *Ibid.*, fos. 44v.–45v.; 63r.–64r.; 60.
[23] *Ibid.*, fos. 49r.–50v.　　　[24] *Ibid.*, fo. 51r.

come into the councell house with the meir & his brethern except they be called'.[25] No one in contemporary local government was going to believe this sort of fantasy.

Probably even before Reynolds had submitted his supplication to the king, the Recorder was writing post-haste to Cromwell; begging him not to believe a word of it; asking for Reynolds and Foster to be forced to reveal the names of their sympathisers in the city; and forecasting that if these people were to find 'eny favour or comfort in theyr said malicious myndes & ententes, yt is to be drad that right shortlye they wold bryng it [Coventry] to A more & deper daunger then it was at before' in 1525.[26] There can thus be no doubting the degree to which the city authorities feared the continuing ground-swell of popular dissatisfaction with the state of the city.

Yet in three major respects, Reynolds' submission accurately reflected what may be deduced from the records of the municipality itself. In the first case, he himself was a prime example of the lengths to which a citizen might be forced to go if he were to escape the expense of civic office-holding. The even wider ramifications of this situation for society at large, a recurring theme in this study, now require further exploration.

The most obvious disincentives, and, given the processual struc-ture of senior civic office-holding, also the most serious, were the annual payments of the £50 fee farm and the Recorder's salary of 20 marks, both of which had to be met by the sheriffs. Reference has already been made to the situation regarding the arrears of fee farm in the fifteenth century.[27] By 1522, moreover, the sheriffs were being released from the payment of the Recorder's fee for the ensuing three years, obviously because of refusals to accept the shrieval office.[28] A dozen years later, in 1534, they were even unable to afford sufficient liveries for their serjeants in view of 'ther great charges'.[29] It must have been about this time, or early in the following decade, that a penalty of £500 was being threatened on the sheriffs if they did not appear forthwith at the Exchequer with £200 (four years' worth of fee-farm payments) and failed to account for this state of arrears.[30] By the reign of Edward VI, it was being claimed that one or two persons were being annually ruined by the fee-farm payments.[31] It was undoubtedly because of the truth of this

---

[25] *Ibid.*, fos. 53r., 51r.   [26] P.R.O. SP 1/74, fo. 16.
[27] *Supra*, p. 35.   [28] *L.B.*, p. 681.
[29] *L.B.*, pp. 718–19.   [30] C.R.O. B70.   [31] C.R.O. A79, fo. 63.

statement that in 1549 the sheriffs were released from paying the fee farm though they were now to meet the Recorder's fees so long as this situation lasted.[32] Coventry would have furnished a compelling example to central government of the need for this burden to be lifted from many towns at this time.[33]

But if external renders, municipal fees and the provision of liveries made men reluctant to enter the magistracy of the city, there were also internal traditional expenses at all levels of society which, in its reduced economic state, the citizens could no longer afford. So well established were the social conventions concerned, however, that by 1539 it was necessary for the then mayor to write, under popular pressure, to Thomas Cromwell about 'such thynges as partelie be thoccasion of the decay & pouertie of the said citie'.[34] His revealing critique falls under several heads. First,

the chargeable offices of meire & shireffes be a great occasion of ... decay ... And therin it is thought' by the comeners here that many priuate charges now accustamed in the said offices myght' be right well spared & dymynysshed. For on candlemas day, the newe Meire is sworne & taketh vpon' hyme the office, which day he feasteth such number of Citizens & Straungers that with th'expenses then more then convenyentlie nedeth, he myght well keipp' his house half a yeire after.

The tradition of hospitality by a newly-elected superior lay at the heart of the late medieval social system as it was described in part III of this study. It is thus notable that, despite the mayor's representations, so deep rooted was this custom that it was not even eradicated when the mayoral election day was altered in 1555. Even then, it was said, 'the new maior makes a great feast in St Mary Hall, & bids abundance of people to make merry with him there, further as he shall like either in towne or country or in both, either riche or poore or both'.[35]

A second point made by the mayor in 1539 was that 'likewise at Corpus Christi tide, the poore comeners be at suche charges with ther playes & pagyontes, that they fare the worse all the yeire after'.[36] Repeated reference has been made throughout this study to

[32] *L.B.*, p. 793.
[33] E.g. *Statutes of the Realm*, 1 & 2 Mary, cap. 7: Fee-farms were temporarily diverted to finance local schemes of public works in 1548–9, 2 & 3 Edward VI, cap. 5; 3 & 4 Edward VI, cap. 18.   [34] P.R.O. SP 1/142, fo. 66.
[35] L.M., fo. 20r.   [36] P.R.O. SP 1/142, fo. 66.

the amalgamation of Crafts for the purpose of financing these pageants when the fellowship originally responsible became too poor to act alone. It only needs to be added that the periods when this factor was most marked were the early 1490s (1493–5) before the *fin-de-siècle* recovery; and between 1526 and 1533, in the wake of the short-term crisis.[37] In these circumstances, the tenacity of the citizenry in holding on to these customary practices is conspicuous. In 1495, for example, it was the Fellowship of Carpenters, Tilers and Pinners itself which actually petitioned the Leet that a number of craftsmen in related wood-working occupations might be compelled to join the Wrights' fellowship for the purpose of subsidising their pageant; while similar initiatives were then taken for the same reason by the Cardmakers, and very probably the Girdlers.[38] Even during the crisis, the normal processional demonstrations of the social structure continued unabated; even in the early 1530s the plays were being re-written and more professionally presented.[39]

A final observation made in 1539, was that 'on' midsommer even & on seynt peters even the maisters & kepers of craftes use suche excesse in expenses in drynkyng, that some suche as be not worthe v.li. in goodes shalbe then at xls. charges to ther undoyng'.[40] Once again it was a matter of obligatory hospitality (and in addition to any contribution made by a newly-elected Craft officer to the cost of his inaugural feast).[41] This in fact is the clearest evidence we have for the financing of these customary drinkings for Craft members; though whether, as has been suggested elsewhere, the civic officers on such occasions furnished the wherewithal for the masters, and the craft officers invariably entertained the journeymen, is not certain.[42] Whatever the case, it is relevant to note that the costs

[37] *L.B.*, pp. 547, 553, 555–6, 558–9, 564–5; 693, 697, 699, 701–2, 707–10, 712–13, 716.

[38] Levi Fox, 'Some New Evidence of Leet Activity in Coventry 1540–41', *English Historical Review*, lxi (1946), p. 235, n. 4; *L.B.*, pp. 564–5.

[39] E.g. Cappers' accs., fos. 22v., 24r., 26v., 31r., 32v., 34r., 36r. Craig (ed.), *Two Coventry Corpus Christi Plays*, pp. 31, 70 – both re-written in 1534. For the activities of Robert Crowe, *supra*, p. 144, n. 8.

[40] P.R.O. SP 1/142, fo. 66. It should be emphasised that although the Leet ordinance of 1494 – amongst others – referred to the costs of '*pagantes* & such other' (my italics, *L.B.*, p. 556), the Carpenters' petitions to the Leet on this matter refer specifically also to 'kepyng *watches* with od[e]r charges' (my italics: C.R.O., Carpenters 9a & b.: late F10).

[41] Phythian-Adams, 'Ceremony and the Citizen', *loc.cit.*, pp. 61–2.

[42] *Ibid.*, pp. 64–5. For over-spending by the Smiths at Midsummer and St Peter's eves, brought under control in 1472, *v.* Sharp, *Mysteries*, p. 183.

borne respectively by the mayor at midsummer and the sheriffs at St Peter's may well have been curtailed by the attenuation of these observances in 1545 when these drinkings were to be held *before* the Watch, and not after it.[43] Four years later the St Peter's Watch was scrapped altogether.[44]

In these widely-experienced burdens then probably lies a major clue to what was discouraging apprentices from setting-up in the city; strangers from staying; and really wealthy men from continued residence. Quite simply, the medieval social structure was too elaborate a framework to be supported as before by a community reduced in numbers and circumstances. Diminished numbers of members in both Crafts and Gilds thus took on an increasing strain in financing the communal structure. Admission to the Trinity Gild probably cost £5, while brethren of the Corpus Christi fraternity usually paid out 3s. 4d. at each of the banquets which were held thrice-yearly before 1520, but significantly only twice-yearly thereafter.[45] The earliest account of the Weavers' fellowship moreover reveals the social cost of these splendid traditions all too clearly. Of a total of £7.9s.1½d. spent in 1523, a mere £1.9s.8d. went on paying the clerk and summoner and on providing alms-bread. All the rest went on socialising activities: £3.7s.5d. on services, elections, meetings (which would, of course, have involved business), and especially dinners; and a further £2.12s.0½d. on the Corpus Christi and Midsummer celebrations.[46] This is not to mention the unknown cost to officers of purchasing a livery, or working-time lost for the sake of official duties. How much less expensive would it have been to follow an 'urban' occupation in the countryside.

If Humfrey Reynolds' strictures on the cost of urban office-holding have to be taken seriously, so too do his remarks on the decline in the numbers of highly respected and substantial men. By 1533, Julian Nethermill was the last of the three great men who, between them, had paid over a quarter of the city's tax in the early 1520s. He must also have been the only survivor of the four 'substanciall men' whom Reynolds mentioned, but did not name, in connection with the quelling of the 1525 insurrection; and of which four 'one is dead & ij of theme be goon' out of the Citie'.[47] By early

[43] *L.B.*, p. 779.   [44] *L.B.*, p. 791.

[45] Templeman (ed.), *The Records of the Guild of the Holy Trinity*, p. 178; C.R.O. A6, *passim; ibid.*, fos. 239 *et seq.*   [46] C.R.O. access. 100: Weavers 11.

[47] P.R.O. SP 1/141, fo. 56v.: presumably referring to Richard Marler (died 1527, P.C.C. 20 Porch); and perhaps Thomas White (*supra*, p. 140, n. 14) who disappears

1540, Nethermill too was dead.[48] In 1537 yet another mayor was writing to Thomas Cromwell in view of the fact that 'oure eleccion of substancyall men' ys not nowe in this Cytte as yt hath byn' in tyme paste', and begging him to block the suit of the man secretly chosen as the next mayor by the Council House, in his attempts to be exonerated from that office. The alternative candidates were either heady and wilful, and likely to trouble the city, or not of sufficient substance.[49]

It was irony or poetic justice that, in the context of this shortage and despite the unpopularity which he had incurred, Humfrey Reynolds himself eventually found himself enmeshed in office, and, as he himself had forecast, following the death of his wife in 1536.[50] By the late 1530s, however, he had not only acquired leases of lands that had belonged to the priory at Stoneleigh to the south of the city's county boundary; he had also received the grant for life of the office of bailiff and collector of all the rents and farms of that monastery.[51] Presumably he was no longer immune as a yeoman of the Crown, for at this time he is also to be found as a member of the Drapers' fellowship, of which organisation he became senior officer in 1546–7.[52] A year later in 1548–9, and, without ever serving as a junior civic officer, he was elected sheriff.[53]

The most intangible aspect of his criticisms of the city in the early 1530s to substantiate is that which relates to its misgovernance. That the difficulties over, and even the causes of, the 1525 insurrection reflected deep divisions within the governing body, is not to be doubted. The ambivalent role played by Heynes, the reluctant mayor, has already been indicated, and others may also have been similarly involved: Reynolds specifically refers in the plural to 'a litle supportacion of some of the hedes of the Citie' in this connec-

from the record after 1526 (*L.B.*, pp. 692–3) – probably to Bristol (*infra*, p. 276); and John Bonde who seems to have left Coventry in 1532 (*L.B.*, p. 711), but died as a gentleman of Lancashire in 1537/8 (P.C.C. F19 Dyngeley).
[48] P.C.C. 6 Alenger. [49] P.R.O. SP 1/114, fo. 156.
[50] Cappers' accs., fo. 49; C.R.O. access. 100: Weavers 11, *sub* '1536' burials.
[51] *L. & P.*, xiii (1), nos. 1520, 887; *Abstract of the Bailiffs' Accounts of Monastic and Other Estates in the County of Warwick*, translated by W. B. Bickley with an introduction by W. F. Carter (Dugdale Society, ii, 1923), pp. 3, 4, 9, 10 and 46–7 (the latter entry being misdated to 39 Henry VIII (*sic*)).
[52] C.R.O. access. 154: Drapers 1c, pp. 14, 21, 28: he never seems to have done a term as junior Craft officer.
[53] *L.B.*, p. 788; the only year for which the names of the city wardens are not known is 1542.

tion.[54] The social background of Reynolds' own Commonwealth programme may also imply that dissenting views were circulating at the edge of the elitist group. What cannot be denied, however, is the inertia of many of those that survived in power over this period and despite popular agitation for reform. Revealing light is thrown on this matter by William Cotton, the reformist mayor who wrote to Cromwell in 1539 about the traditional costs incurred by the citizens:[55]

> and moche exclamacion is maid to me beyng meire by the comeners for reformacion therein; and I, without th'assent of my bretherne cannot help it. And meny of my said bretherne beynge past all such offices & charges do litle regarde theme that be to come, nor do not [sic] esteme the undoyng of half a dosen honest comeners to be so ill a deid, as is the omyttyng & lesyng of on accustumed drynkyng.

Without the specific directives which he asked of Cromwell, the mayor admitted that he was powerless to act.

With regard to the half-hearted enforcement of the law during this period, the documents shed but a single shaft of illumination. The only surviving records of the court Leet at work in its judicial capacity survive for 1540–1.[56] In them, the petty offences against which the Leet in its legislative capacity was accustomed to enact, like forestalling, false weights and measures, blocking ditches, unlawful games and so on; all came up for judgement. Out of 80 cases between October and June, at least six concerned ex-sheriffs or ex-mayors for various offences like 'selling salt herryngs for excessyue lucre'[57] or buying and engrossing great quantities of rye. A further six were committed by past or present junior civic officers, like Henry Godsone 'beyng Chambeleyn for receivyng money of commoners and soefferyng their cattell vpon the commons contrarie to his othe'.[58] If such men could certainly be brought to book, their carelessness of detection implies nevertheless that the penalties were too trivial (rarely more than 3s. 4d. for most offences) to

[54] P.R.O. SP 1/141, fo. 56v. Reynolds implies at this point that he himself was not involved in the 'insurreccion'.

[55] P.R.O. SP 1/142, fo. 66.

[56] Fox, 'Some New Evidence of Leet Activity', *loc.cit.*, pp. 235–43.

[57] *Ibid.*, p. 242.

[58] *Ibid.*, p. 241: my figures in this paragraph include identifications of civic officers in addition to those made by Dr Fox. A further two men involved were to become junior civic officers within the next three years.

ensure the observance of those very laws they were themselves sworn to enforce.[59] By the 1540s at the latest, therefore, the rich were setting a disgraceful and blatant example to their poorer neighbours over whom they were expected incorruptibly to govern.

[59] By this period, of course, inflation was fast reducing the deterrent value of the traditional level of fines. It would be interesting to know whether the incidence of petty offences elsewhere could be correlated with the tempo of inflation.

25. Institutional and social change

During the three decades following the short-term crisis there can be little doubt that most formal institutions in the city experienced a contraction of membership and a distortion of function, while some were abolished altogether. Most critical of all was the rapid shrinkage of the honest commoner class because of its implications for both employment in the economy and the membership of traditional institutions in society.

In 1534, the last, and hence possibly a rather special, banquet was held by the Corpus Christi Gild.[1] It was certainly patronised to an unusual extent by practically and the aldermanic elite of the city. The Master of the Trinity Gild, Hugh Lawton (or at least his son); the Mayor; the Recorder (and his relation, Mr William Wigston of Leicester); the aldermen, present and past sheriffs; even Nicholas Heynes (amidst the ruck of the commonalty) – they were all there, though Humfrey Reynolds conspicuously was not. It was perhaps almost a family affair. Even the visitors were largely the regulars from the surrounding parts of Warwickshire, including in company with the Prior of Coventry, the heads of the houses of Combe, Kenilworth, Stoneleigh, Merevale and Maxstoke. There were no visitors from monasteries further afield, and no delegations from other large towns.

It was a meeting that symbolised the end of an era. Not only were the monastic representatives making practically their last public appearances, but Coventry membership of the Gild had halved since the eve of the crisis. Even counting the aldermen, this last banquet was attended by no more than some 140 lay brethren from the city, most of whom paid half the normal subscription of 3s. 4d. A year later, and appropriately, only by a majority vote of 20 to four, the Leet 'agreed that Corpus Christi gilde shal-be annexed & vnyte vnto the Trinitie gilde & maid boith on'.[2] At a single stroke, the

---

[1] C.R.O. A6, fos. 306v.–310. *Ibid.*, fos. 312v.–314 (1535) do not seem to list those attending a dinner.

[2] *L.B.*, p. 772: for the drop in the Gild's income from rents, *supra*, p. 235. Although the decline in membership is undeniable, it is nevertheless a matter for curious remark that the continuous registration of membership in other Warwickshire gilds also ceased at precisely this time. Cf. *The Register of the Gild of Knowle*, ed. W. B. Bickley (place n.g., 1894); *The Register of the Gild of the Holy Cross, the*

social age-compartmentalisation at the upper end of society and the traditional sequence of senior civic office-holding were swept away. The amalgamated fraternity itself, of course, barely survived a further decade. With the abolition of the gilds and chantries, the medieval social superstructure of society was no more. The great processional occasions of St George's day, Ascension, Whit Sunday and Corpus Christi, all disappeared as a result from the civic calendar.

With the regard to the Craft fellowships, release from the burdens of pageantry was rather more delayed. If the marching watch and its attendant drinkings at St Peter's were abolished in 1549; the Midsummer Watch just survived the first five years of Elizabeth's reign. The Corpus Christi pageants, indeed, were last performed in 1579.[3] Within the Crafts like the Weavers and the Carpenters, there are signs that by this stage, the office-holding system was becoming less fluid than it had been before: fewer people, and often from the same families, were beginning to repeat spells as senior officer more frequently than hitherto.[4] To that extent, the upward direction of social mobility was consequently slowed.

Moreover, for at least a spell, and quite possibly even permanently, all the journeymen organisations were dissolved in 1549. Whether or not this was done in exaggerated pursuance of the terms of the statute passed by Parliament in that year is not clear.[5] It looks very much as though the Cappers at least had already subsumed their journeymen under the mantle of the masters' fellowship two years before this date.[6] Even in this case, however, the lists of

Blessed Mary and St. John the Baptist, of Stratford-Upon-Avon, ed. J. Harvey Bloom (place n.g., 1907). I owe these references to the kindness of Miss Susan Wright.

[3] Phythian-Adams, 'Ceremony and the Citizen', *loc.cit.*, p. 79.

[4] Cf. *supra*, p. 145. These tendencies were becoming noticeable in the 1540s and 1550s, but a log-jam did not build up until the last two decades of the century, when in twelve or thirteen years out of twenty (1580–99), senior office was repeated by *ex*-senior office-holders in the fellowships of Mercers, Drapers, Weavers and Carpenters. In the case of the Cappers, senior office was held for the first time in only four of those twenty years. An ex-senior officer, John Roe, by contrast held the senior post four times during that period. The domination of certain families was most marked in the Carpenters' Craft, where – to judge from namesakes – of the 133 official posts that are known to have been filled between 1533 and 1617 inclusively, thirty-four (27 per cent) were occupied by the two families of Packwood and Pickering. All these figures are derived from the annual accounts of the fellowships concerned.

[5] *L.B.*, p. 792; *Statutes of the Realm*, 2 & 3 Edward VI, *c.* 15 – aimed mainly at victuallers. [6] Cappers' accs., fo. 68.

journeymen's names stop abruptly at the year in question, as do the regular subscriptions made by the journeymen weavers. Insofar as it is possible to tell from the accounts of the Mercers, Drapers, Cappers, Weavers and Carpenters, there is little to suggest that journeymen organisations ever existed independently after this.[7]

The mid sixteenth century in fact marked a watershed in the development of this urban society. Most fundamentally perhaps, the traditional mechanisms whereby institutional status had been publicly and ceremonially transformed into social standing within the community as a whole were largely obliterated. Craft attendances at weddings and funerals certainly survived into the seventeenth century, as did most conspicuously the inaugural ceremonies of both the fellowships and the municipality.[8] But both those institutions which had defined a citizen's place in society and the manner in which that was regularly displayed on the great ceremonial occasions, had largely disappeared. With them vanished a number of occasions for commensality in which social divisions had been temporarily blurred.

The reign of Elizabeth, in fact, was characterised above all by a polarisation of society that was widely experienced in English towns. As the population of Coventry recovered, the growing problem of poverty became as much to do with immigrant paupers as it was with the indigenous poor.[9] The concept of the freeman as essentially a master gained ground.[10] The governments of both

[7] C.R.O. access. 100: Weavers 11, *sub* '1550'. There are only occasional references to the journeymen thereafter, e.g. in 1582, 1599 and 1613, though they sometimes appear to have been given money at 'The Choyce day' (fos. lllv., 119).

[8] Even a new company like that of the Worsted Weavers and Silk-weavers insisted on attendance at 'Weddings and Buryings' in 1650, C.R.O. access. 117. It was symptomatic of change, however, that a reissue of the Weavers' ordinances in 1639 (C.R.O. 100/4: Weavers 2b) included a new clause (no. 47) to deal with refusals to help carry corpses to the church, and also appears to have excused those of the degree of sheriff and above from such obligations.

[9] *Supra*, p. 237, n. 27. It is clear that this became a major problem: C.R.O. A3(b), pp. 5–6, 21–2, 30, 50, 83; *L.B.*, pp. 837–8, 839; C.R.O. A3(b), pp. 117, 143.

[10] *Supra*, p. 99, n. 6. It is difficult to be precise about the definition of a freeman at this period, so casually were admissions and fines recorded. It is only possible to recover some ninety-seven *individual* entries for the period 1563–1600 from a collation of C.R.O. A14(a), pp. 830–45 with C.R.O. A17, pp. 32–8, 62. Some of these were strangers, other were 'of this city', and one was admitted as 'a free woman'. The fines varied from 13s. 4d., to 20s. (the most usual) to 26s. 8d., 30s., 40s., £3 and £5. By an ordinance of 1600, sons of freemen had to be also apprenticed in the city, C.R.O. A3(b) p. 24. Another bye-law (*ibid.*, p. 22) speaks of 'freemen being householders of this Citie' (cf. *ibid.*, p. 17), while the re-issued ordinances of

Craft and city became more inbred and more oligarchical.[11] In the latter case, indeed, it is relevant to add that the last *recorded* mention of the Common Council was in 1534: by 1605, it had been so long in abeyance that its pre-existence could only be claimed from what 'appereth in ancient records'.[12] By then undiluted power had long lain with the Council House. Only on Sundays was the ordering of society as a whole now publicly symbolised in the hierarchical seating arrangements within the two parish churches: civic officers and aldermen towards the east end and the pulpit; in the body of the church, the Craft fellowships with their 'ancients' to the fore, and the younger men behind; those of the poorer sort who attended,[13] to the west. More preached against than practising, a society (and a culture) had congealed into sober Protestant rows.

The eventual demise of the late medieval social structure and the assumptions on which it was based, was undoubtedly a protracted affair, but this study would be incomplete without a brief mention of three further matters. All of these may be documented only from the last decade of the sixteenth century, but they involved such deeply embedded social norms that the subtle pressures making for their alteration must have been present long before. Each was rooted in the household.

It was probably not until the period of demographic recovery, the 1560s onwards, that the composition of the household was expanded not only by more children, but also, at the earliest stage in the domestic cycle, by the temporary doubling-up of newly created families with the parental or even sibling survivors of one or other spouse's family of origin. By the 1590s at the latest, whichever

the Weavers (C.R.O. access. 100: Weavers 2b, regulation no. 43) make it quite clear that journeymen were not comprehended. The Mercers, however, who in view of their wealth may well have been atypical, recorded a minute in 1608 which spoke of 'Anye person . . . made a freeman of our Company . . . whether he do occupye our trade, or do serve as a Jorneman for wages', C.R.O. access. 15: A100, fo. 36. Efforts made in 1593, 1594 and 1602 to swear in the memberships of particular fellowships *en bloc*, by contrast, seem to indicate that the masters alone were concerned, C.R.O. A14(a), pp. 842–4, 849, 851–6.

[11] For the Crafts, *supra*, n. 4. In only ten out of fifty-two years (1508–60) does the mayoralty appear to have been held by putative relatives (namesakes). Between 1561 and 1613 this proportion doubled.

[12] *L.B.*, p. 720; C.R.O. A3(b), fo. 37.

[13] L.M., fo. 36; C.R.O. access. 14: 98 (unfol.), 'For comynge to the Churche' (Cordwainers), Poole, *Coventry: its History and Antiquities*, p. 157. Women clearly still sat separately, cf. Cappers' accs., fos. 126v., 139v.

family in such cases was dominant (in the sense that its head – whether father, mother or adult married son, was the accepted householder), there is no mistaking the sociologically significant emergence of the temporarily resident mother-in-law.[14]

In the 1590s, and from then to the civil war period, moreover, there is also no doubting an enhancement of the woman's position generally in the economy, in religious and in socialising activities, even though sexual roles were to a decreasing extent still demarcated.[15] During this period, the wives of Craft officers were admitted to Craft dinners, free-women appear for the first time, and even weavers' widows were now permitted to take on apprentices.[16]

A final social norm to be challenged at this time was that to do with the gerontocratic ideal and social-age categorisation. Between 1590 and 1620 in particular, there were confrontations or conflicts between 'young' and 'old' at all the structural levels of society: within the household, between masters and apprentices (from the 1560s, the Drapers' apprentices at least were not even taking up

[14] For the probable increase in the size of the sibling group by this period, *v.* p. 234, *supra*. These generalised observations on family composition are based on a detailed analysis of two rate-books for St Michael's parish (which covered practically two thirds of the city). Both list what appear to have been communicant members in each household (C.R.O. Rates of St Michael's Church 9a (1594) and 9b (1595). The proportion of 'extended' family units (both lineal and lateral) had by then risen to about 8.75 per cent. Cf. *supra*, pp. 94–5.

[15] For the excommunication of a schoolmaster's wife for teaching, C.R.O. A14(a) p. 215. For Ann Sewell (died 1609), 'an humble follower of her Saviour Christ and a worthy stirror up of others to all holy vertues', Poole, *op.cit.*, facsimile between pp. 138 and 139; for separatist single women in the civil war, Reader 8, p. 111. The most extreme and therefore significant illustrations of role demarcation come from the civil war period when squads of women, organised by women, filled in the quarries south of the city, *ibid.*, fo. 89v. On another occasion a troop of women, mustered by the Mayor's wife, ran after and captured the baggage-train of a local royalist, T. A. Blyth, *The History of Stoke* (London, 1817), p. 66. It may well be significant that sexual nuances were freshly imported into the Godiva legend by the creation of Peeping Tom at this period, when social roles between the sexes were becoming more blurred than before. For the contemporary literary background to the early feminist movement at this time, *v.* Louis B. Wright, *Middle Class Culture in Elizabethan England* (London, 1958), ch. xiii.

[16] C.R.O. access. 18: A99, fos. 18v., 62v., (Mercers); C.R.O. access. 241, orig. fo. 11v., Cappers' accs., fo. 185; C.R.O. access. 100: Weavers 9, *sub* 1603; C.R.O. access. 100: Weavers 11, last page; C.R.O. Fullers' Ordinances, fo. 17; C.R.O. A44 (Carpenters) *sub* 1665 and 1667. C.R.O. A14(a), p. 835. C.R.O. access. 100/4: Weavers 2b, a few fos. on after the revised ordinances. It is noteworthy that references to apprenticeship with a master weaver 'and his wife' begin to occur as from 1600, C.R.O. Weavers 5 (unfol.).

their indentures until they were eighteen);[17] within the craft companies, between 'young men' and ancients;[18] and between junior and senior civic officers.[19] That this was largely due to increased life-expectancy by this time, and in the latter two cases to a frustrating log-jam in the system of senior official positions, seems probable. It appears also to have led gradually to an extension of the definition of 'young man' to include all those who had not achieved senior office regardless of their age.[20] As such, and like so many other changing features of post-medieval society that have been outlined here, it represented a distinct move towards a definition by class, whereby 'young' was coming to mean no more than 'junior' or 'inferior'.

Whether this change, as in the case of both family structure and the position of women, should be traced back to the mid sixteenth century it is impossible to say. What is clear, is that the essence of medieval community was already being rapidly displaced at that earlier date by a version of urban society which, although markedly less institutionalised in a formal sense, was distinctly more stratified than theretofore.

[17] C.R.O., A3(b) p. 24 and cf. C.R.O. Weavers 5, *passim*, for the period 1550–1650, during which the only recorded cases of running away, abuse and misdemeanour by apprentices occurred between 1590 and 1616 (10 per cent of the 216 apprentices indentured). C.R.O. access. 154: Drapers 1c, p. 64.

[18] C.R.O. A3(b), pp. 6–7, 44. E.g., C.R.O. access. 15: A99, fos. 16, 15v., 57, 72v., 95v.; C.R.O. access. 241, orig. fo. 11.

[19] L.M., fo. 29v.; C.R.O. A3(b), pp. 23, 37–8 – the outcome in 1605 being the resurrection of the Common Council, which was largely dominated by past, present and future sheriffs, Reader 8, fo. 74v.

[20] Separate arrangements for drinkings and meals for 'the young men' make their appearance in the earlier seventeenth century: e.g. C.R.O. access. 15: A99, fo. 187v.; C.R.O. access. 100/17/1: Weavers 11, fos. 110v., 111v., 113v.; C.R.O., Weavers' second account book, fo. 9v.; C.R.O. A41, fos. 7, 7v. Some of these mentions may still refer to apprentices, but references to 'young men' or 'younger men' in Craft ordinances are fairly clear in suggesting that such terms covered all but the ancients, e.g. C.R.O. access. 14: A98, unfol., under the rubric 'That no straunger be made free, without consente.'

26. Medieval mirrors shattered

If the Reformation represented a line drawn under the long and evolving tradition of medieval urban community, it also signalised a final disruption of cultural assumptions. There is no need to labour the complete collapse of the ceremonial system as an ideal mirror of that community, nor is it necessary to detail the gradual eradication of many 'superstitions' that had under-pinned these rituals. Most markedly, the physical expressions of the cultural environment lost their symbolic quality as boundary crosses ceased to have any meaning; as the religious houses on the periphery of the city; and near the gates, the chapels of St John's, Bablake, St Nicholas, St George and St Mary's in the tower; all fell into disuse.[1] As outdoor ceremonies vanished, and the cathedral was demolished, so too did the ritual centre of the city lose its significance. It was apposite that by the seventeenth century the Mayor's Parlour, which was situated not in the old ritual centre but in Cross Cheaping, the commercial focus of the city, had taken on a greater importance than it had ever had before.[2]

For many citizens such changes must have been bewildering; for others, the ideal of the corporate community had been long replaced by an acceptance of a wider pluralistic society. The former concept has necessarily been the over-riding theme of this consequently introspective study. It is appropriate to conclude, therefore, by returning to some of the wider topics only touched upon elsewhere, but this time to view them through the eyes of contemporaries.

For medieval merchants, with their personal and business connections in other towns, their rural estates[3] and even rural manufac-

[1] Phythian-Adams, 'Ceremony and the Citizen', *loc.cit.*, pp. 79–80. *V.C.H. Warks.*, viii, pp. 330–1, 332.

[2] The parlour was said to have been built in 1573–4 and elaborated in 1582–3 (L.M., fos. 25v., 26v.), but this must have represented an extension of the parlour apparently situated next to the Peacock Inn still earlier, C.R.O., A6, fos. 148, 247; C.R.O. A24, p. 53. Cf. *V.C.H. Warks.*, viii, p. 144.

[3] Coventry citizens were members, *inter alia*, of gilds at Stratford-upon-Avon (*The Register of the gild of the Holy Cross . . . of Stratford-upon-Avon*, ed. Bloom), Knowle (*The Register of the Gild of Knowle*, ed. Bickley), Ludlow (W. C. Sparrow, 'A Register of the Palmers' Guild at Ludlow in the Reign of Henry VIII', *Transactions of the Shropshire Archaeological Society*, 1st ser., vii (1884), pp. 102–3: I owe this

turing workers, their contacts with London and overseas; a declining city like Coventry was more relevantly a power-base than otherwise. Many of the ceremonies instituted even in the late fourteenth or fifteenth centuries,[4] one suspects, were incidentally contrivances by the elite to enhance their position and so to preserve the social order on which their influence rested. Such men, unlike most of the commonalty, although wishing to preserve the political independence of their urban community, were more realistically citizens of a wider world.

It is here that the ideas which Humfrey Reynolds, and presumably his friends, had in common with the later Commonwealth group, are *à propos*. For leaving aside the inherent contradiction in his supplication – whereby gentlemen would have been imported into the city – he shared with subsequent writers a deeply troubled feeling about the growing complexity of contemporary society and the desire to return to a simpler order. Yet, given the existing inter-penetration of town and country both economically and socially, it was simply anachronistic for such as Reynolds to hope for great lords to abandon farming and trade and to live only on their lands; for priests to remain on their benefices; for merchants to reside only in towns; and so let the poor husbandman live uninterrupted by his husbandry.[5] It is perhaps significant that there is no evidence for popular opposition at least to the Dissolution of the monasteries at Coventry.

Symptomatic as early Commonwealth thinkers were, so far as the

reference to the kindness of Mr William Champion) and Nottingham (*The Account Books of the Gilds of St. George and of St. Mary in the Church of St. Peter, Nottingham*, ed. R. F. B. Hodgkinson and L. V. D. Owen, (Thoroton Society Record Ser., extra ser. vii, 1939, p. 86)). For an obvious personal connection between gilds at Coventry and Chesterfield, *v.* C.R.O. C201. The geographical spread of property-holding by such people is well brought out not only by the numbers of wills that had to be proved at the Prerogative Court of Canterbury (e.g. *supra*, p. 148, n. 3), but also by implication in royal pardons (e.g. *L. & P.*, i(1), no. 438 for Thomas White of Coventry, London, Bristol and Hull in his varying roles as fishmonger, mercer or merchant; or *ibid.*, no. 1266 for Robert Raulyns, alias Cowper of Coventry, chapman or draper, alias of London, chapman, alias of Boston, clothier, alias of Lynn, draper).

[4] Phythian-Adams, *loc.cit.*, p. 69.

[5] P.R.O. SP 1/141, fos. 61r.–62v. At least three members of the Council house appear to have possessed arable farms in the vicinity of Coventry, probably in 1555–6, C.R.O. A94. Equally conservative was Reynolds' proposed policy of civic supervision (*supra*, p. 261), which in some respects simply reflected a detailed provincial application of the traditional view of 'good counsel' in government, Arthur B. Ferguson, *The Articulate Citizen and the English Renaissance* (Durham, N.C., 1965), ch. iii.

identification of problems was concerned, their solutions were more than a little tinged with a retrogressive view of an idealised past. Reynolds' own proposals involved both a revised form of feudalism and a revival of the monastic *raison d'être*. Thomas Gibson, the London grocer, who appears to have absorbed Reynolds' ideas into his own programme, clearly took much the same view. In one draft bill, he was concerned to restrict craftsmen and traders to towns.[6] In another, of 1536–7, all the surviving inmates of religious houses were to remain, now wholly incarcerated from the world; with their revenues administered by secular governors who had the power to apply the incomes to the relief of the poor, and who were to be responsible to a military court of Centeners sited at Coventry. Though now centralised, and ruled by a 'lord admyrall', who was to be placed at the head of a national hierarchy of captains, petty captains and soldiery stationed in 'the townes castelz or forteresses with yn thys realme'; Gibson's abortive plan obviously represented no more than a logical extension of Reynolds' original proposals. As such, the relationship between the views of these two men incidentally represents a very interesting indication of the way in which ideas from the provinces were filtering through to the edges of court circles, and even to Thomas Cromwell, in the 1530s.[7]

It is perhaps the ultimate irony in the drawn-out saga of Coventry's decline that the ideal of community which it sought to sustain at such cost was, in a sense, already irrelevant. Insofar as it represented a move away from the medieval tradition into the early modern period, the future lay not with outmoded conventions; not even with the radical policies of a Reynolds; but with the openness of the magisterial elite to new ideas, for all their governmental conservatism. The signs were already there: unprecedented classical touches in civic receptions for royalty; the Reformation details of Nethermill's tomb;[8] the desire for quantitative evidence evinced

[6] G. R. Elton, 'Parliamentary Drafts 1529–1540', *Bulletin of the Institute of Historical Research*, xxv (1952), pp. 122–3.

[7] Stone, 'The Political Programme of Thomas Cromwell', *Bulletin of the Institute of Historical Research*, xxiv (1951), pp. 13–17; Elton, *loc.cit.*, pp. 126–30. All this was in profound contrast to the almost contemporary *radical* programme actually pursued at Canterbury, Peter Clark, *English Provincial Society from the Reformation to the Revolution: Religion, Politics and Society in Kent 1500–1640* (Hassocks, 1977), pp. 38–44.

[8] *L.B.*, p. 590. Nethermill's tomb, with its non-committal imagery (a crucifix), its emphasis on the prayers of the individual, and the absence of weepers, is discussed in Mercer, *English Art 1553–1625*, pp. 221–2.

in the taking of censuses; and more than a little curiosity about new religious attitudes. Even William Pysford had several beautiful books of an heretical (probably Lollard) nature in 1511–12;[9] two probably close relatives of the elite were conspicuous amongst those charged with heresy in 1543.[10]

In the new age that was dawning under Elizabeth, as both rural and urban populations revived, the future lay in an increasingly pluralistic society where town and country industries could at the least co-exist; where the mobility of people, of commodities and of ideas was on the increase; and where choice, even in religion, was more varied. It was to be a society in which culture was no longer a public, visual affair concerning all those who participated or cared to watch; but a private matter for the individual citizen in the furnishing or decoration of his house, his reading matter and his worship. Still imbued with many medieval traditions, not the least of which was the survival of the Craft fellowships; disfigured by desperate poverty problems; and to some extent blighted by its lost greatness; the new society which was emerging at Coventry as elsewhere by the seventeenth century, may have lost many of the advantages of medieval community life in the process of change, but it had also cast off its shackles.

[9] Fines, 'Heresy Trials in the Diocese of Coventry and Lichfield 1511–12', *Journal of Ecclesiastical History*, xiv (1963), p. 162. There are a number of hints that the local predeliction for heresy may have partly grown out of an earlier conservative move for ecclesiastical reform. John Wigston (to whom may have belonged similar heretical books, *ibid.*) had not only striven against the Mariolatry cult at the White Friars' tower in 1491–2 though with no permanent success (cf. renewed criticisms in 1511, *ibid.*, p. 166, n. 6), but either he, or his successor William Rowley, had suspended the Mass of Jesus in St Michael's church (*supra*, p. 118, n. 2; Bliss Burbidge, *op. cit.*, p. 223). The latter mayor may well have also initiated both the ordinance of 1492, which tightened up the moral conduct of the elite (*supra*, p. 138), and the regulation that Craft priests were to observe both work-days and holy days 'in encreasyng of dyuyn seruice dayly to be songon in the parish Chirches of this Cite' (*L.B.*, p. 544–5).

[10] *L. & P.*, xvii, no. 537. For Henry Over (sheriff 1537–8), a 'lively politic man' who acted locally as Dr London's trusted assistant at the Suppression, *L. & P.*, xiv, (1), nos. 83, 150.

Part V

Coventry and the urban crisis of the late middle ages

'And then were the coste men and marchauntes nor husbondmen nor grasiers, but trusted onlye to ther trades of marchaundice, and other handyecraftes, suche was the wisedome and pollycye of our auncestours to devorse the marchauntes and handycraftes men from the husbondes and Tylthe men, that none of them sholde savour on thothers gayne, And by this meanes the good Townes were buylded, inhabyted and maynetened, whiche nowe are decayed and depopulated, the markettes plentyfull, with all kinde of provicions and victualls, whiche nowe are unfurnisshed and the countrye replenysshed with gentlemen and husbondes, whiche now are inhabyted with marchauntes and men of occupacion, so that no man is contented with his owne estate, which hathe brought all thynges to such extremytie, as they have not bene of many yeres before.'

(William Humberston, 1559. Quoted by D. M. Palliser, 'The Boroughs of Medieval Staffordshire', *The North Staffordshire Journal of Field Studies*, xii, 1972, p. 71.)

The desolation of one of the great provincial cities of medieval England, which has been chronicled here, was dramatic. In round terms, if the various estimates proposed in this study are broadly correct, Coventry's population appears to have shrunk from over 10,000 in c. 1440, to between 8,500 and 9,000 in 1500. Thereafter it collapsed with appalling rapidity: to perhaps 7,500 in 1520, to about 6,000 in 1523, with the downward spiral reaching its nadir of something in the region of 4,000–5,000, by the mid sixteenth century.

Contrary to what might have been expected according to the theory of late medieval economic growth, the process did not lead to a healthy redistribution of wealth.[1] In fact the numbers of poor increased markedly and the numbers of the very rich decreased. By involving all levels of urban society, the process of decay fed on itself. The signs were already there, even before the disastrous crisis of 1518–25 exacerbated the situation still further, and starkly revealed the serious nature of both the long- and short-term problems of the city: a paucity of citizens wealthy enough to hold office, and, by implication, to initiate economic ventures involving widespread employment especially in the city's staple industry; a desperate shortage of trained man-power with a consequent over-dependence on female labour, except in a few resilient sectors of the economy; an ageing population that was clearly not only unable to reproduce itself, but which was not being replenished by male immigration; and above all a vulnerability to massive depopulation. Where the evidence has allowed, the manner in which most of these themes were played through over the succeeding twenty-five years has been traced in some detail. Indeed not until the 1570s were there to be recognisable signs of economic and demographic recovery,[2] though the city never recaptured the glories of its medieval past during the succeeding 'pre-industrial' period.

[1] Bridbury, *Economic Growth*, p. 82.

[2] *Supra*, p. 237, n. 27 for population. To judge from accumulating numbers of new brethren in both the Drapers' and the Weavers' fellowships by 1600, textiles staged a remarkable recovery. The decennial numbers of weavers' *apprentices* grew (without fluctuation after 1590) from 33 or 34 between 1550 and 1559 to 188 between 1640 and 1649. C.R.O. Weavers 5.

Whatever the longer-term origins of the decline of Coventry, it is clear that well before the end of the middle ages, the traditional framework within which the urban community operated was already buckling. The crux of this situation lay with the social stratum through which this framework was held together, the main employers of labour and the people who ran the social system as office-holders; in other words the honest commoner class. Any explanation of urban decay at this period has thus to account for the evident shrinkage of this essential layer of contemporary society. The main solution proposed here is that, internally, there were expensive disincentives to urban residence; and, externally for some, attractions and opportunities to settle in the countryside. If it has thus been possible to identify the manner in which the urban social system was itself further distorted as a result; with regard to the wider regional picture, the social historian of a single community has inevitably to depend on the work of others. In this case, as in most other regions of England, that work has simply not been done for the period in question.

All that may be claimed in the case of Coventry's regional sphere of influence is that residence in towns does not seem to have attracted those settled in the area of the Birmingham plateau to the west. There, a dispersed but very considerable population could practice 'urban' occupations as bye-employments – whether metal-working or textiles – and conveniently shop in one or other of the sturdy market towns that characterised that locality. Towns of this kind had neither the expensive social overheads nor the elaborate economic structures of cities like Coventry. Their modest populations could subsist comfortably enough on periodic marketing functions; and in their ability to provide quite rare products or services, such places could even draw away potential customers from larger centres. In this area, true urbanisation – the 'balling' of surplus populations into recognisably urban locations – would only take place over the succeeding century. For the meantime, residence in a city like Coventry, which was rapidly losing its manufacturing raison d'être, held little attraction for those who could find similar work in these rural areas.

In fact, early-sixteenth-century society generally, was experiencing strains which could no longer be adapted to the old medieval world order. If the towns themselves, Commonwealth writers, and the drafters of Parliamentary statutes alike expressed concern at, and sought to stem, the widespread drift away from urban centres, from market towns as well as cities;[3] those who dwelt in the countryside themselves, and those in central government, were equally worried by the problems of the husbandmen. To contemporaries, in fact, even the fundamental distinction between town and country was at stake when merchants and 'men of occupacion' began taking over the land and simultaneously planted their business concerns in the countryside.

No doubt they exaggerated (though a great deal more local research needs to be done into the difficult documentation of this period), but the thought itself was symptomatic of a serious situation. It is generally accepted that there was a major collapse of population in the later middle ages (whatever its exact order of magnitude, and from whenever the slow rate of recovery may be dated); that villages were gradually shrunk or deserted by the hundred; and that rural markets lost their commercial functions by the score. A good deal less attention has been paid to the state of the towns in these circumstances.

Yet the case of Coventry, extreme though it may have been, did not stand alone. I have argued elsewhere that a parallel process of demographic and economic attrition worked its way up the urban system, so that by the opening years of the sixteenth century, not only had a major geographical alteration to the urban network taken place, but many of the leading cities in the hierarchy were at last in trouble.[4] Even before the fire that destroyed 718 houses in the early sixteenth century, Norwich was complaining of how 'many houses, habitacions and dwellynges stode onlaten and grue to ruyn'.[5] In the light of Coventry's count of vacant houses, both this complaint and that of Bristol in 1518 from where it was claimed that there were 'about viij^c howsholdes . . . desolate vacante and decayed',[6] have to be taken seriously. At York, Dr Palliser has

[3] E.g. *Statutes of the Realm*, 3 Henry VIII, cap. 22; 6 Henry VIII, cap. 5; 7 Henry VIII, cap. 9.

[4] Phythian-Adams, 'Urban Decay in Late Medieval England', *loc.cit.*, pp. 159–85. Cf. R. B. Dobson, 'Urban Decline in Late Medieval England', *Transactions of the Royal Historical Society*, 5th ser., xxv, 1977, pp. 1–22. For the probable depopulation of Lincoln, *supra*, pp. 14–16, n. 14.

[5] Francis Blomefield, *An Essay towards a Topographical History of the County of Norfolk*, 11 vols. (1805–10), iii (1806), pp. 182–3; *The Records of the City of Norwich*, ed. W. Hudson and J. C. Tingey, 2 vols. (Norwich and London, 1910), ii, pp. 105, 122.

[6] *Select Cases Before the King's Council in the Star Chamber*, ed. I. S. Leadam, (Selden Soc. xxv, 1910), p. 146. Cf. P.R.O. SP 1/236.

estimated that the population fell from 'perhaps over 12,000 in the early fifteenth century to 8,000 in the mid-sixteenth'.[7] Between 1377 and 1563, the city of Lincoln may have shrunk by as much as two thirds of its earlier population. By the latter date, Southampton and Salisbury and probably Hereford were in the doldrums.

If a number of major centres were already becoming vulnerable by the opening years of Henry VIII's reign, it is relevant to enquire whether Coventry's experiences during the short-term crisis of 1518–25 were unique. In this connection, it is worth noting that had it not been for the fortunate survival of not one, but two census returns from this period, the gravity of that crisis would probably have remained unsuspected. The absence of such evidence elsewhere (and in what is anyway an under-researched period), therefore, does not rule out the very real possibility that, while Coventry may have suffered unusually badly, other urban centres were affected to a lesser degree. The crisis in the textile industry in the early 1520s, for example, as reflected in the slump in national cloth exports, clearly must have impinged on the economies of Bristol, Southampton and Hull (and even London, Ipswich and Exeter), all of whose cloth exports were adversely affected at this time. Evidence of urban unrest comes not only from East Anglia – from Lavenham, Bury St Edmunds, Norwich and Great Yarmouth – but also from York as well as Coventry. All this surely represents the essential groundswell of local experience, against which Henry and Wolsey were framing and modifying their grandiose policies; and from which a plausible explanation may be proffered for the sudden spate of legislation on re-edifying town housing in the succeeding decade.

Thereafter, and perhaps until about the first decade of Elizabeth's reign, there is so little to suggest an improvement in the condition of English towns, that this period as a whole may be regarded quite relevantly as one of urban crisis generally. The word 'crisis' is an over-worked one, and in the context of much that this book has had to say about the short term, the author is well aware of the danger in extending its use over a longer time-scale. But since the word is difficult to better, and this is not an essay in semantics, it seems best to retain it as the most expressive of the contemporary situation. For although Coventry's experiences between c. 1520

[7] Palliser, 'The Trade Gilds of Tudor York', in Clark and Slack (eds.), *Crisis and Order*, p. 87.

and c. 1570 may have been extreme, the fact remains that practically every major theme on which this study has dwelt in some detail is to be found reflected in the records both of other provincial towns and of central government and society. Indeed it could be claimed somewhat boldly, but with justice and afore-thought nevertheless, that at no other period in national history since the coming of the Danes have English towns in general been so weak. The middle decades of the sixteenth century in fact marked a major turning point in the development of urban populations, economies and societies. To that extent, the use of the term 'crisis' is justifiable.

By the mid sixteenth century, not only were there fewer places with a claim to urban status than in the high medieval period, but those centres above the level of the established market town that had survived were for the most part much smaller in size, industrially debilitated, commercially vulnerable, and increasingly prone to structural strains within their societies. The smaller size of nearly all provincial towns is hardly a matter of question, but the implications of this for urban economies, based as they were on the domestic system of production, have not been followed through. Insofar as it is possible to assess the situation in the earlier sixteenth century from occupational structures, it seems likely that few towns had sufficient numbers of employers involved in industrial activities to manufacture for export. Even major regional centres, it would seem, must have been producing largely for internal and regional consumption. Of those significant towns for which the information is at present available, only the economies of Coventry and Norwich appear to have been biased towards some sort of export effort in textiles and caps, if it is even permissible to make such evaluations from the numbers concerned.[8] The state of the former at this time has already been described; in the case of Norwich, it need only be added that it was, of course, also a centre for a cloth-manufacturing region which extended as far as King's Lynn and Great Yarmouth.[9] For the majority of urban economies, the emphasis lay on clothing, shoe-making and victualling, the latter being most marked in the form of service trades at ports like Bristol, King's Lynn and Hull.

The implications of this situation were serious indeed. First, country-based merchants and, did we but know it, perhaps some of

[8] Phythian-Adams, 'The Economic and Social Structure' in *The Fabric of the Traditional Community*, pp. 16–20.
[9] *Statutes of the Realm*, 14 and 15 Henry VIII, cap. 3.

their urban colleagues too, were in a position to by-pass their local inland town in the handling of country-woven cloth, and to deal directly with the capital or another major port for the purposes of export. Secondly, by the mid sixteenth century, there are signs that urban economies were then importing many of the products from abroad which they traditionally should have been manufacturing for themselves. Humfrey Reynolds was not alone in singling this out and so implying a local balance of payments problem. The same theme was expressly identified by Clement Armstrong – himself an ex-grocer – William Lane[10] and Sir Thomas Smyth:

> Of the which sort I mean glasses as well looking as drinking as' to glass windows, dials, tables, cards, balls, puppets, penhorns, inkhorns, toothpicks, gloves, knives, daggers, owches, brooches, aglets, buttons of silk and silver, earthen pots, pins, points, hawks' bells, paper both white and brown, and a thousand like things that might either be clean spared or else made within the realm sufficient for us.[11]

A third factor so far as town economies were concerned, was the breakdown of urban controls over manufacturing and retailing. Dr Whitney Jones has counted over 40 statutes 'wholly or partly concerned with maintenance of standards' between 1509 and 1559 alone.[12] Other legislation sought to protect the urban manufacturing monopolies of Worcester and its satellites; Bridport; Bridgwater; and even Norwich.[13] Similarly aimed at the inroads made by rural competition was the Act of 1554–5 which sought to restrict retailing within towns.[14] Urban centres as different as Leicester and Norwich had been deleteriously affected by the profit-making of rural retailers who contributed nothing to either the economies or the charges of the towns concerned.

[10] Tawney and Power (eds.), *Tudor Economic Documents*, iii, p. 104–12; 116–18; ii, p. 184.

[11] Dewar (ed.), *A Discourse of the Commonweal*, pp. 63–4; and cf. *Statutes of the Realm*, 5 Elizabeth, cap. 7. *V*. Thirsk, *Economic Policy and Projects* pp. 15–17. Cf. the shift in imports recorded for Lynn in 1503–4 to 'an almost infinite number of lesser consumer goods like feather beds and feather-bed ticks, lamps, copper kettles, drinking glasses, tankards, pepper grinders, knives and scissors, playing tables and counters' etc. Carus-Wilson, 'The Medieval Trade of the Ports of the Wash', *Medieval Archaeology*, vi–vii (1962–3), p. 201. For the imports of one Worcester merchant, *v*. Dyer, *The City of Worcester*, p. 107.

[12] Whitney R. D. Jones, *The Tudor Commonwealth 1529–1559* (London, 1970), pp. 176–82.

[13] *Statutes of the Realm*, 25 Henry VIII, cap. 18; 21 Henry VIII, cap. 12; 2 & 3 Philip and Mary, cap. 12.   [14] *Ibid.*, 1 & 2 Philip and Mary, cap. 7.

Above all, the shortage of 'good able persons' in towns during this period was recognised both locally and nationally. Centrally this was so largely because of difficulties over the fee-farm payments owed by bailiffs or sheriffs: as was admitted in for example such statutes as those of 1511–12 and 1554–5, to name but two.[15] The former was particularly sweeping in its application since it publicly recognised the reduced numbers of merchants and drapers on whom medieval economies had depended, and of necessity permitted the election of victuallers to senior civic offices in their stead.

Within towns, and as at Coventry, the burden of urban charges placed on the shoulders of small masters and officers alike was widely recognised. The cost of sustaining Corpus Christi pageants was admitted at Chester; the expense of popular ceremonies and the excesses of dinners were complained of even at Norwich; the extravagance incurred by civic officers in customary diversions, drinkings or liveries were either criticised or ended at Bristol, Leicester and probably Salisbury. At all of these places the heavy cost of ceremonialising the traditional social structure was widely experienced. For towns such as these, the cancelling of obligatory membership of civic gilds when these were abolished; the decline of the Corpus Christi plays, and the ending of the summer marchings of the watch, would have hardly been unwelcome. At declining Canterbury, the watch was suspended as early as the 1530s.[16]

If the leading citizens in many substantial towns were increasingly discouraged by traditional financial obligations, there can be no doubting either the new seriousness of the poverty problem. In the context of the widely experienced 1519–21 dearth, the national trade depression and of the massive loans and taxes taken thereafter, the timing of the administrative measures now taken at the local level once again suggests that Coventry's experiences were not unique. Only London and York anticipated the years of short-term crisis, but, even including them, it was between 1514 and 1534 in particular that procedures for licensing beggars, who were then often counted, and the appointment of special officers to control them were now approved for the first time in these centres and at Shrewsbury, Bristol, Norwich and Southampton. Matters scarcely improved thereafter: inflation; difficulties for the textile industry in the 1540s; and especially depression in the following decade; two

[15] *Ibid.*, 3 Henry VIII, cap. 8; 1 & 2 Philip and Mary, cap. 7.
[16] Clark, *op.cit.*, p. 39.

successive years of dearth in 1555 and 1556, and serious epidemics. If Norwich and Great Yarmouth were then setting up permanent grain-stores, the number of those on poor relief even at Worcester rose from 700 to 1,000 in the one year 1556–7.[17]

The poverty problem, of course, would continue to increase in severity even when the towns began to recover. But, with regard to the period of 'urban crisis', what made matters critical for the towns at this time appears to have been the *conjunction* of so many underlying factors to do with their weakened economic roles as centres of industry and commerce; with the increasingly an-achronistic nature of their social structures; and with the reduced sizes of their work-forces. While poverty and short-term crisis would continue to affect towns and while some towns would even continue to decline, nevertheless the period of recovery – broadly between 1570 and 1640 – would see those underlying problems largely remedied in most centres.[18]

With respect to the earlier period, however, there is still much that is unknown about the inter-relationship between town and country and the wider implications of that inter-play. In particular, the evolving debate on demographic movements at this time might usefully profit from the need to distinguish between urban and rural fortunes. Practically all authorities agree that a recovery was already in progress by the time of parish registration; most, indeed, placing this resurgence far back in the fifteenth century.[19] Yet such

[17] Dyer, *The City of Worcester*, pp. 109, 166–7.

[18] For a brief discussion which links up with this later period *v.* Charles Phythian-Adams 'Urban Crisis or Urban Change?' in *The Traditional Community Under Stress* (The Open University, course A, 322 unit 9, 1977), part A, pp. 19–25; and Paul Slack, 'A Brief Comment', *ibid.*, part B, pp. 27–9. Aspects of the recovery are pursued more particularly in A. M. Everitt, 'Urban Growth 1570–1770', *Local Historian*, viii (1968), pp. 118–25; Thirsk, *Economic Policies and Projects*, ch. iii, and Peter Borsay, 'The English Urban Renaissance: The Development of Provincial Urban Culture c. 1680 – c. 1760', *Social History*, v (1977), pp. 581–603.

[19] Russell, *British Medieval Population*, pp. 220–81; M. M. Postan, 'Some Economic Evidence of Declining Population in the Later Middle Ages', *Econ.H.R.*, 2nd ser., ii (1950), p. 245; Hollingsworth, *Historical Demography*, pp. 375–87; E. A. Wrigley, *Population and History* (London, 1969), p. 78; Julian Cornwall, 'English Population in the Early Sixteenth Century', *Econ.H.R.*, 2nd ser., xxiii (1970), p. 46; Hatcher, *Plague, Population and the English Economy 1348–1530*, pp. 68–71. The only seriously dissenting voice would seem to be that of Ian Blanchard, 'Population Change, Enclosure, and the Early Tudor Economy', *Econ.H.R.*, 2nd ser., xxiii (1970), pp. 427–9, 435, 439. His case, however, depends heavily on the delayed upswing of rents in the Midlands, and seems to ignore the possible influence of contemporaneous price inflation on landlords.

evidence as there is suggests that for many *urban* centres above the level of the superior market town, populations were probably still falling between 1524 and 1563, or, at the most, remaining stable at their existing low level.[20] As might be expected, in fact, the initial expansion of population was primarily a *rural* phenomenon – itself, perhaps, partly stimulated by the flight of urban capital and expertise to the countryside in those areas where there was no alternative, compensatory, urban expansion nearby.

It is then tempting to enquire, finally, whether this probable demographic disparity between town and country may not have been an important *contributory* factor in the take-off for the Tudor price inflation which has now been securely pinned to the period 1520–30.[21] At present, price indices compare 'industrial' products with food, both of which were largely rural in origin. But could it be that an accelerating rural demand for specifically urban commodities – like hats, shoes or finished metal products, for example – was beginning to exceed the dwindling capacities of some towns to meet it from their own manufacturing resources; the inevitable results being that scarce local commodities would thus have fetched increased prices and expensive imports were sucked in from abroad? In a domestic system of production, where seven-year apprenticeships were already quite normal, there would necessarily be a continuing time-lag between increasing demand and the ability of the skilled work-force, when measured by number, to meet it.

Whatever the answers to these large and highly tentative propositions, however, a radical and locally detailed re-assessment of this entire period is surely long overdue. If, or when, that is accomplished, it can only be hoped that closer consideration will be given to the impact of urban decay, and the gravity of short-term crises in that context, than has been the case hitherto. For although Coventry's decline may well have been even more serious than that experienced elsewhere at this time, the city's deposition as a leading provincial centre would necessarily have had implications too for those other towns with which its interests interlocked. Indeed, the erosion of its unique standing as the nodal point in the provincial network of English towns thus marked the final stage in the geo-

[20] Phythian-Adams, 'Urban Decay in Late Medieval England', *loc.cit.*, pp. 172–3.
[21] R. B. Outhwaite, *Inflation in Tudor and Early Stuart England* (London, 1969), pp. 11, 13.

graphical re-alignment of the traditional urban system before 1550. More generally still, the fate of Coventry effectively symbolised the end of an era: economically, socially and culturally, these truly were the last days of medieval urban community.

Appendix 1 *The 1523 enumeration*

The recovery of the original schedules was due in the first place to a passing reference to, and brief extracts from, an undated sixteenth century 'census' covering Gosford, Much Park and Jordan Well wards in one of a number of notebooks deposited by Dr Levi Fox at the City Record Office. Despite an unsuccessful search instigated by the author in 1964–5, it was not until later in the latter year that the then newly-appointed archivist, Mr A. A. Dibben, having kindly remained constantly alert to their existence, came across these returns amongst a bundle of miscellanea. They have now been given the temporary call number W.1405. Not until December 1967, however, were the schedules for the other seven wards brought to light by Mr David Smith, then assistant archivist, from amongst a number of uncatalogued accessions received in 1957 from Dr Romana Bartelot of Trowbridge. These are now referenced as Accession 263. That all ten returns had been together at Coventry until at least the last century, may be inferred from the fact that the schedules for both Jordan Well and Spon had then had their populations totalled in pencil by the same contemporary hand.

The date, format, and information required, prove that all were the products of the same original enumeration. Accession 263 is prefaced by a loose leaf with a contemporary dating 'in Jun' 1523', and internal evidence from the other schedules (W.1405) supports this. In the Gosford document appears 'Mr Shreyff', and written above this entry in smaller writing, the name 'Wydr' (*sic*), which clearly refers to Richard Wether (spelt 'Wyther' in 1519 when he became chamberlain; *L.B.*, p. 665), who took office as sheriff at Michaelmas 1522 (*ibid*., p. 682), and who appears under Gosford in the 1522 assessment. His colleague for the year 1522–3, (William) Tyllet, appears under Much Park, without mention of his office, but with the designation 'Master', which could only be acquired on becoming sheriff. These schedules also post-dated some point between 4 October and 18 December 1522, when the will of Mr Hugh Dawes (of the 1522 assessment) was drawn up and later proved (P.C.C., 29 Maynwaryng, no. 2 calendar); since his wife, Mistress Dawes, appears without her husband under Much Park in the census. Also noted in the same ward, was the presence of Thomas Kewette without a wife, the mortuary payment for whose burial is the last to appear under this head in the Weavers' first account book for the craft year July 1522–3. The overall acceptability of a June dating for the census, finally, is reinforced by the absence of any ordinance instructing its execution in the Leet record for 21 April 1523 (*L.B.*, pp. 684–6); and a similar lack of reference to either initiation or results in the earliest surviving council minute – that for 3 July 1523 (B.L., Harl. MS. 7571 fo. 32 r.) and thereafter. A date between these two extremes therefore seems entirely probable.

The format of the documents fully supports the contemporaneity of the schedules. With the exceptions of Spon and Gosford, the returns were all made on sheets of paper measuring 12–12½ inches by 17–17½ inches after these had been folded lengthways. The water-marks are the commonly found glove and flower. The Gosford schedule has slight variations with regard to the same type of water-mark, and is about ¾ inch shorter in length than the others; while what remains of the Spon return – apparently the last folded sheet of the schedule (though it contains no names on the recto of the first fold), has no water-mark and is only 13 inches in length.

'The vewe of ye wardes', as it was described on the title page of Accession 263 (the 1520 count was also called 'a veu', *L.B.*, p. 674), underlines the secular provenance of the enumeration, which was thus not taken by parishes, and excluded all religious institutions. It was also centrally inspired and issued. Both the wording and hand-writing of the *headings*, the second of which is different from that of the individual enumerators concerned in the body of each document (to judge from a temporary change of hands, only Much Park had more than one enumerator), are the same for Bailey Lane, Cross Cheaping, Earl, Broad Gate, Much Park and Jordan Well; while the headings for Smithford and Bishop, though written by the ward enumerators, also have the same wording (without sub-headings) thus:

(x) ward

The names of men' & wyfes

hosowlyng people & child[re]n'

The men' & their wyfes   hosowlyng people   child[re]n'

The names of each householder are then tabulated under the first sub-heading, and are usually followed on the same line be 'et ux[or]' and either numerical or short-hand notations for servants and children where any of these were relevant or present. The Spon heading does not survive, but that for Gosford, as written by the enumerator himself, reads:

The nowambyr of ye gosfordstret ward

& ye Names of every howskepper

though, as with the other wards, the inmates of the households are also enumerated. The totals of people at the end of the enumerations are subdivided into the numbers of men, women and children (as is implied for the 1520 count) in the cases of Bailey Lane, Bishop and Spon; houseling people and children under Smithford; with more detailed breakdowns to include servants by sex (and also widows under Jordan Well) in all other cases, except Broad Gate and Much Park, where only the grand totals are reckoned. In every single instance, finally, the total of vacant houses is given with the population summary in each return; though in Bishop, every street is also separately totalled (thus showing that the contemporary grand total of 127 was under-cast by four).

While with respect to Smithford, Gosford, Bishop and conceivably Spon, it is possible that the schedules represent fair copies, there can be little doubt that the enumeration was 'actual' for the day in question, as opposed to 'ideal'. Not only is there a reasonably close correlation (varying from ward to ward) between the orders of names or groups of names in both the census and the 1522 assessment, so that even in the cases of Bishop and Spon, where the returns are incomplete, many adjacent households may be categorised by wealth etc.; but there are also a few but significantly obvious omissions. In four wards, four wives and one 'goodwife' of named husbands, who were evidently absent at the time of the count, are specifically so described. Two examples from Jordan Well, finally, suggest that the enumerators in some cases may have had to depend on the testimony of neighbours, for not only are the surnames not recorded, as happens elsewhere in the city, but in these instances the householders are described respectively as 'strengar' and 'Thomas Strengar'.

Appendix 2 *The ward listings of 1520 and 1523: the problems of analysis*

The most fundamental problem is that of comparability: in examining the two enumerations, is like being contrasted to like? The 1520 count, after all, could have been inflated in two ways which did not apply in 1523. There is, first, the possibility of a temporary migration to the city of neighbouring rural poor, seeking succour from the dearth and perhaps lodging with relatives. No evidence survives for this either way, but a numbering of all the citizens (as opposed to the poor alone) when food was short, accompanied by a search of households for grain, would presumably have sorted out the extra mouths which did not belong to the city as at Nuremberg, Strasbourg and elsewhere on the continent (Roger Mols, *Introduction à la Démographie Historique des Villes d'Europe du XIVe au XVIIIe Siècle*, 3 vols. (Louvain, 1955), ii, pp. 340–1). In England itself, a century later, a Salisbury census of the poor certainly isolated the urban from the rural needy (Paul Slack, 'Poverty and Politics in Salisbury 1597–1660', in Clark and Slack, *op.cit.*, pp. 166–9, 173, 175–6. Cf. the Coventry ordinance for the banishment of 'bygge beggars' in 1518, *L.B.*, p. 658). In the second place, it is just possible that homeless beggars were included in 1520 but not in 1523. Since it was not until 1521 that the city recognised some responsibility towards these unfortunates, this would also seem unlikely. Again, a clear distinction was successfully made at Rheims when a similar count was taken (J. N. Biraben, 'La population de Reims et son arrondissement et la verification statistique des recensements numeriques anciens', *Population*, xvi, 1961 p. 723). However inefficient they may have been as enumerators of detail, 'pre-industrial' census-takers, with all their knowledge, were probably not easily gulled in emergency situations. Unless, then, the city government recognised that the 1520 count was misleadingly unrepresentative of the real state of affairs and therefore needed to be taken again (in which case it is hard to see why *its* findings, and not those of 1523, were formally recorded in the Leet Book), it is worth emphasising that the taking of a second census within three years, must itself be the clinching factor in this context. By also including a count of vacant houses on this occasion, it seems fairly evident that the population had diminished substantially; was seen to have diminished; and that the decrease was being deliberately measured accordingly. Whether this was done for the sake of local economic planning, or to provide ammunition with which to wring either trading or tax concessions from the Crown, it is impossible to say. What does seem clear is that the city authorities themselves were aiming at comparability between the two counts. As such it represents a remarkably early attempt at measuring demographic trends in this country.

This said, a far more difficult problem presents itself, for could it be that the 1520 count was simply more efficiently taken than its 1523 successor?

The more glaring defects in the latter are all too apparent from an examination of the schedules themselves, but the absence of these for 1520 should not necessarily pre-dispose us in the latter's favour. Is there then a reasonably neutral yardstick by which to compare the two counts?

The ranking of wards by housing in 1522–3 set out in figure 2, while clearly closer in its applicability to the 1523 results than to those of 1520, does indeed permit a rough and ready comparison of the two censuses on the basis of housing : people ratios. For since that more affluent section of the population, which occupied houses worth *over* 12s. *p.a.*, seems to have been the most stable; and because the *numbers* of these houses inhabited in each ward are known for 1522, i.e. at a date *between* the two enumerations; it should be possible to test for some consistency in the relationship between such housing and population in both years. To this end, therefore, ratios of persons counted in each ward both in 1520 and in 1523 (the latter before and after adjustment) to every house, whether freehold or valued at an annual rent of over 12s. in 1522, have been computed and plotted on the accompanying figure 3. Because this level of housing displayed household densities well above the overall mean for the city in 1523 (*vide* table 29), only the first point on this index will even approximate to the mean of the wealthiest ward. In broad terms, the less affluent the ward, the greater should be the ratio. Furthermore, since the population fall was most closely associated with those occupying the poorer housing, the results for both years might be expected to show trends that are within reasonable limits, proportionate to the ward ranking and hence consistent with each other. It must be emphasised, of course, that equi-distant spacing on the horizontal axis is for the sake of clarity only, and has no significance in itself.

The results of this exercise are instructive. Confirmation of the accuracy of the proposition with regard to the general upward trend of the ratios is to be found in both the traces for 1523, the closer of the two years to the ranking of 1522. The only exception is Much Park (the ranking position of which *vis-à-vis* Broad Gate is anyway somewhat ambivalent (cf. figure 2), but after adjustment this is convincingly smoothed. It is therefore most encouraging to note that the 1520 trace also exhibits a consistent trend as far as Bishop. At this particular point, however, the tendency of the 1520 trace to diverge, even from its adjusted 1523 counterpart, is noticeably reversed. This in itself raises grounds for disquiet; but in the cases of Spon and Jordan Well, the trend collapses completely (although, suggestively enough, the ranking relationship between the two remains the same in each year). In these instances, therefore, either the ward rankings have radically changed due to shifts in the population, or these wards were badly under-enumerated in 1520. Both alternatives need to be borne in mind on turning to the actual figures for population themselves.

On this basis, despite allowing every one of the 1520 totals to stand unaltered, and raising most of the results for 1523, depopulation would seem to have been substantial in all but two wards. Even the wealthiest four wards lost from 13.5 per cent to 18.5 per cent of their 1520 totals, while Gosford and Much Park shrank by over a quarter of their populations.

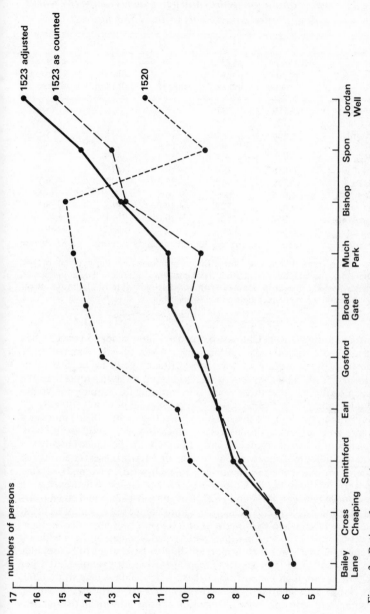

Figure 3   Ratios of persons by wards, in 1520 and 1523, to every inhabited house, whether freehold or valued at *over* 12s. rent *p.a.* in 1522

For the ward ranking *vide* figure 2, and for population adjustments in 1523 – appendix 4

Table 33. *Crude population figures and percentage changes by wards 1520-3 (before and after adjustments to the 1523 figures)*

Ward	1520 popu- lations	1523 popu- lations	% change	1523 popu- lations adjusted	% adjusted change
Bailey Lane	459	397	−13.5	—	—
Cross Cheaping	884	738	−16.5	—	—
Smithford	406	322	−20.7	331	−18.5
Earl	707	595	−15.8	—	—
Gosford	875	602	−31.2	625	−28.6
Broad Gate	552	388	−29.7	418	−24.3
Much Park	719	464	−35.5	527	−26.7
Bishop	1,018	'853'	−16.2	867	−14.8
Spon	627	'878'	+40.0	963	+53.6
Jordan Well	354	462	+30.5	501	+41.5
Whole city	6,601	5,699	−13.7	5,962	− 9.7

Note: The original 1523 totals for Bishop and Spon are those given by the enumerators, the schedules for neither having survived complete. For adjustments, which may include an over-inflation of Spon, *vide* appendix 4. In 1523, the inmates of Ford's hospital were not included under Broad Gate.

Adjustment brings Broad Gate's loss down to a little under 25 per cent, but most markedly Bishop's population appears only to have dropped by a proportion commensurate with the most affluent wards in the city. Spon and Jordan Well, finally, seemingly increased their totals to a quite remarkable degree during these three years, thus reducing the drop for the whole city to less than 10 per cent of its 1520 population after adjustment.

Unfortunately, by themselves, these results reveal little of the processes at work. To test their credibility further, therefore, it is necessary to look more closely at the situation in terms of households. For undoubtedly the population fall comprised two elements, the first of which was the shrinkage in size of an unknown and (according to each ward concerned) varying proportion of households. Compared with Mr Laslett's figures for 91 communities between 1574 and 1821, Coventry in 1523 could claim overall proportionately twice as many households composed of solitaries (12.6 per cent) as later, when there were to be 6.02 per cent (appendix 3b, table 37). At Coventry the vast majority were females, many of them widows. Moreover, not only was there a markedly higher percentage of households headed by couples (75.6 per cent) than in Mr Laslett's sample (70.4 per cent), but a very high proportion of these were childless (*supra*, pp. 203, 225). Hence, as enumerated, no less than 39 per cent of all households in the city comprised only one or two persons, as contrasted with an overall proportion of 20.77 per cent in the later period (appendix 3b, table 37). In addition to the significant paucity of solitary males, there was also a glaring shortage of male servants in practically all areas of the economy. Not only may such in-servants have been laid off during the crisis, but would-be apprentices were very probably not indentured at the normal rate (*supra*, pp. 45, 212, 215). The impact of crisis on an unverifiable proportion of surviving household sizes can thus hardly be doubted.

The second element in the population fall was clearly the depopulation of whole households even in the most affluent wards. The figures themselves immediately contradict any suggestion that household shrinkage could possibly have been wholly responsible for this decrease. For if it be assumed that the number of households remained stable over these three years, then for every household present in 1523 there would have had to be present in 1520, 0.8 more persons in Bailey Lane, Cross Cheaping and Earl, and one in Smithford. Since, as is to be seen from the distributions in appendix 3b, all these wards in the later year had between 64 and 73 per cent of their populations living in what may reasonably be supposed to have been wealthy and hence more stable households containing five or more persons: by far the greater part of this shrinkage must be ascribed to households below this level. Even here uniformity cannot be assumed, so it is not difficult to conclude that groups of one, two, or three persons comprising whole households would have been so affected. This point is sufficiently obvious not to require labouring with regard to the next three more junior wards where the ratio in all cases exceeds one person, even before allowances are made for the presence of proportionately fewer 'stable' large households. In the case of Bishop, however, the ratio is again surprisingly lower (0.6) than even the top four wards; while the junior two wards will be discussed below.

Since the depopulation of whole households was a factor in the population decrease, some sort of estimate of household turn-over must be a crucial step in the analysis. Only in so doing will it be possible to probe more deeply for inaccuracies through an examination of the inconsistencies between all four unverifiable quantities given for each of the ten wards: in 1520 the numbers of people, in 1523 the populations and the totals of both households and vacant houses. To achieve this, however, a fifth unknown quantity has to be imported into the analysis of each ward: that of changing mean household size.

This problem of varying household density is complicated by a number of factors. First, there is no way of differentiating between the impact of long-term decline (and immediately prior to 1520, of 'plague', famine and unemployment), and the results of short-term crisis between 1520 and 1523. Secondly, as is to be expected, the variability of levels of wealth within any one ward does not result in a neat correlation between household size and ward ranking: in a small ward the movement away of even five outsized families would be enough to distort the household average completely. Finally, and above all, there is no means of weighing the depopulation of whole households against the shrinkage of the remainder. All that may be guessed (since there is no knowing for certain whether larger or smaller families were the most usually depopulated – though the latter seems more likely) is that in those wards where there would appear to have been a consistently high 'stable' population of large households; a slight reduction in the average size of the surviving remainder, and a minimal depopulation of whole households; the overall mean density may have stayed stable or might even have risen. Where the population decrease was highest, however, and usually in those wards with a lower proportion of 'stable' large households, a very vulnerable layer of survivors, and a greater degree of total depopulation; the odds would seem to be on the overall average falling between 1520 and 1523.

Because of these imponderables, the ensuing discussion must be restricted to balancing probabilities with a view to reaching some conclusion with regard to the population decrease over the whole city; greater precision would seem to be quite impossible. To this end, therefore, *some* compensation for the likelihood of a diminution in household density in most cases may be claimed through the application of the household means for 1523, after upward adjustment, to the unadjusted totals given for 1520. It would be credulous in the extreme to assume that the earlier count was 100 per cent efficient.

Even using this, the only available measure, some estimate of the accuracy of the given quantities may be achieved. Thus table 34 demonstrates that the possibly exaggerated number of households 'depopulated' in Bailey Lane, Cross Cheaping and Earl is still consistent with the evidence on vacant housing. In each of these senior wards, dwellings must already have been standing empty in *1520* – an indication that the object of this part of the enumeration was to total *all* such houses in the city.

Problems, however, now rapidly emerge. Although Smithford too must have contained vacant houses in 1520, nevertheless it appears not only to have experienced an inexplicably bigger population drop than its affluent compeers, but also to have ended up with the second highest proportion of empty dwellings in the city. Gosford, on the other hand, would seem to have been fully occupied in 1520 on these calculations, and, although immune to long-term demographic erosion, was so badly smitten after 1520 as to emerge with its population and inhabited housing reduced by nearly 30 per cent. In each case the simplest explanation might be that an unknown number of households was inadvertently omitted by the enumerators in 1523. Table 37 in appendix 3b would seem to imply that in Smithford the percentage of households containing four persons is suspiciously low in the context of the ranking sequence; while Gosford's percentage of solitary householders is conspicuously out of line. Such a solution would reduce the population drop and the proportion of houses vacant for both wards in 1523. It would also deflate the ward household averages for 1523 (most markedly in the case of Gosford), so increasing the probability that the 1520 means were correspondingly bigger; and would hence reduce the numbers of households estimated for the earlier year. In both instances, the assumption remains (somewhat shakily in the case of Gosford) that the figures for empty dwellings are reasonably accurate.

Table 34. *Estimated turnover of households between 1520 and 1523 compared with the evidence for vacant housing*

Ward	1523 Mean household size	1520 Estimated number of households	1523 Total households	1520–3 Crude change	1520–3 % change	1523 Number of vacant houses	1523 Vacant houses as % of all 'houses'
Bailey Lane	4.90	94	81	− 13	−13.8	16	16.5
Cross Cheaping	4.26	208	173	− 35	−16.8	59	25.4
Smithford	4.30	94	77	− 17	−18.1	38	33.0
Earl	4.41	160	135	− 25	−15.6	38	22.0
Gosford	3.98	220	157	− 63	−28.6	62	28.3
Broad Gate	3.29	168	127	− 41	−24.4	25	16.4
Much Park	3.40	211	155	− 56	−26.5	28	15.3
Bishop	3.32	307	(262)	− 45	−14.7	131	(33.3)
Spon	3.24	194	(274)	+ 80	+41.2	107	(28.1)
Jordan Well	3.50	101	143	+ 42	+41.6	61	29.9
Whole city:		1,757	1,584	−173	− 9.8	565	26.3

Notes: Adjusted means are italicised and are calculated from the 'corrections' estimated in appendix 4. For 1523, the numbers of households in Bishop and Spon have been calculated by applying the uncorrected household means to the given contemporary ward totals. For Smithford, *vide* p. 244. In the last column all 'houses' have been taken to comprise all households counted in 1523 plus all vacant houses. While there may have been some sharing in this year, the evidence of rents in 1522 does not suggest it.

With the next two wards, Broad Gate and Much Park, however, massive population falls amounting to between 24 and 27 per cent of the 1520 household totals are accompanied by diminutive numbers of houses vacant; in both cases the proportions of these latter are less even than Bailey Lane's. Any compensation for the possible omission of numerous small households in 1523 would here reduce the proportion of vacancies even further. It would also deflate the 1523 means; inflate the numbers of households hence calculable for 1520; and thereby exaggerate still further the improbability already implicit in these results, that within these two wards alone substantial numbers of houses had been shared in 1520, although there were empty dwellings available all over the rest of the city. Furthermore, considerable upward internal adjustments have already been made to the 1523 ward totals, so the absolute population fall from the unadjusted 1520 totals should not be much exaggerated. Hence, the sizes of the household means must have shrunk substantially during the three years. The estimated totals of households in 1520 are therefore too high.

If this reasoning is correct, could the vacant houses totals then represent a count of dwellings deserted only since 1520? Such a solution would imply household means of 3.9 and 3.6 for Much Park and Broad Gate respectively in 1520 which, if not exactly convincing when regard is paid to the ward ranking, is not wholly incompatible with the evidence. It is tempting, nonetheless, to suspect that the totals given for vacancies are in fact still too low even to account for depopulated households in these wards. Unfortunately, to accept that the empty housing figures cannot be used as a control in the argument, is but to admit that a number of householders may also have been omitted in 1523 after all!

When Bishop's results are included with the other estimates, table 34 suggests that, if the figures are taken at their face value, the city experienced a maximum net loss of 173 households. Yet because of population *increases* in the two poorest wards, a further 122 dislodged households would seem to have been re-settled. To ascribe this increase to a sudden swarm of *rural* squatters scarcely seems realistic in view of a still under-populated countryside; the harsh discriminatory Leet legislation on rural and urban poor in 1518 and 1521; the thoroughly uninviting state of Coventry's crippled economy; and, in the last two circumstances, both of which were currently exercising the city government, the practically conclusive facts that the 1523 census neither (a) included an investigation into such people; nor (b) exposed an outstanding proportion of solitary male householders (*vide* pp. 203, 224), the presence of whom (as Dr Paul Slack kindly informs me) is a marked symptom of vagrant migration. Indeed, a mere two out of the 49 households in Spon were headed by single men (both widowers), while only seven out of 143 households in Jordan Well were headed by 'unattached' males. The only possible candidates, indeed, are the nine men, women and children who were not categorised by households in the Irish Lane (Smithford): a 'street' name which is otherwise unrecorded, and may therefore conceivably refer to the native origins of its 'temporary' inhabitants. It is worth recalling finally, that Jordan Well at least was wholly intra-mural.

Immigrant cottagers would there have found themselves liable conse-quently to murage payments – hardly an inducement to settle.

Even if the increase involved only urban dwellers, however, on these calculations the areas most affected by long-term depopulation in *1520* would appear to have been Bishop, with around 86 empty houses; Spon with up to 187; and finally Jordan Well with perhaps 103. On this view, consequently, the more prolonged demographic decline of the city was chiefly reflected topographically in widely separated concentrations of decaying houses, most of them away from the more affluent centre of the city which, as the figures demonstrate, was itself not wholly immune. Into this vacuum would appear to have poured some of the refugees from elsewhere in the city. For not only do the populations of Spon and Jordan Well increase, but Bishop's inhabitants merely decrease by a proportion which is more consonant with the wealthier wards in the city than its immediate seniors in rank.

However attractive this hypothesis of a directed flight to the poorer outskirts of the city may be, it does not withstand close scrutiny. First, it has to be recognised that the notional increase of about 122 households must represent a net estimate, not gross. If all the other wards in the city suffered some depopulation, then the poorer inhabitants of the two most junior in 1520 can hardly have remained staunchly invulnerable. In the latter cases, therefore, any in-migration would have had to be vastly in excess of that estimated to 'over-spill' the areas evacuated in the short term. Not merely is it clear, secondly, that there was working-class housing in practically every ward, but it is also apparent that any movement to cheaper dwellings would have been possible only for those who were already living *above* the lowest level. In other words, re-housing could only have been afforded by a proportion of those dislodged. It is thus relevant to note that the mobility of this minority was widespread, and was not confined to the very poorest wards.

Table 35 accordingly compares the *totals* for the assessment of 1522 with those for the 1523 enumeration in those wards where the figures, with all

Table 35. *Turnover of households in four wards 1522–3*

Ward	1522 total	1523 total	1522–3 hhs. dis-lodged	1520–3: estimated households depopulated (see table 34)
Bailey Lane	82	81	11	13
Cross Cheaping	164	173	7	35
Smithford	75	77	15	17
Broad Gate	118	127	32	41

their faults, are closest. In two cases – Bailey Lane and Smithford – the totals are very close, while in both, the numbers 'dislodged' (i.e. those not re-appearing in 1523) substantially exceed the changes in totals between these two successive years. Even if some allowance is made for the omission of a few households in 1523 from these wards – the smallest in the city – it would seem clear that emigration was being to some extent counterbalanced by immigration. Similarly, although there is a difference of nine between each of the two totals for Cross Cheaping and Broad Gate in 1522 and 1523, it seems probable that a similar compensatory factor was at work in both cases. Thus even where the numbers 'dislodged' approach the estimated totals depopulated (which represent maximal results), it is evident that a proportion of the former were being replaced. In-migration in fact was not restricted to Bishop, Spon and Jordan Well. Indeed, a highly complex degree of internal mobility and a rapid turnover of property throughout the city seems very probable.

It is therefore significant that in Bishop, where depopulation is disproportionately low for its ranking, what may be a maximal estimated number of depopulated households for the *whole* ward (45) is actually exceeded by the maximal total 'dislodged' (48) in only 4/5ths of it. In other words, if the schedules had survived complete, the numbers 'dislodged' between 1522 and 1523 would have been probably in excess of the numbers depopulated between *1520* and 1523. In a ward which theoretically should have been absorbing some of the refugees from elsewhere, therefore, the rate of emigration on this evidence, inflated though it may be, is extraordinarily high.

Even more suspicious are the results for Jordan Well where, despite an estimated increase of 42 households between 1520 and 1523, no fewer than 31 households appear to have been 'dislodged' between *1522* and 1523. Unfortunately Spon cannot be tested in this way, but it is interesting to observe that, if the estimated 1520 totals are even approximately correct, this ward should have contained about 100 fewer households than Bishop in that year. By 1522, however, it is surprising to find that they had already an almost identical number of households assessed – i.e. 185 and 186 respectively.

Finally, if the hypothesis of a considerable migration of households to the poorest quarters only of the city be correct, then the ranking of the two most junior wards must have changed markedly between 1520 and 1523. The *combined* evidence of vacant housing and the ratios graphed in figure 3 would suggest that, if this was the case, in 1520 both Spon and Jordan Well would have contained groups of wealthy households, boasting mean household sizes respectively perhaps in excess of Smithford's and Gosford's set, in most unlikely fashion, amidst that unmitigated decay and squalor which was the outcome of long-term depopulation. On this calculation, Spon would then have dropped from third to ninth place in three years, and Jordan Well from sixth to tenth. Examination of the 1522 assessment, however, suggests that if this was indeed the case, then it occurred with baffling rapidity, particularly when regard is paid to the numbers still being 'dislodged' from Jordan Well, at least, in the year following. A comparison of those assessed in 1522 as worth £10 and over in goods, in fact reveals that 22.8 per cent of those comprehended under Smithford were at this level, and only 8.1 per cent in Spon; while Gosford's complement amounted to 18.3 per cent as against Jordan Well's 9.7 per cent. While the penetration of the assessment varied from ward to ward, the discrepancies here are still too great to be accounted for in this way. But even if they could be, the implications are worth exhausting. For if the 1523 household means for Smithford and Gosford respectively are invoked (in the full understanding that figure 3 can only be a very rough indicator in this respect); Spon's households would fall to 146 and its vacant houses would rise to no less than 246 in 1520; while Jordan Well's occupied houses would drop to a mere 89 and its empty dwellings would be increased to 115. Acceptance of this, which also implies a *net* increase of 172 householders altogether in three years (as against the 122 previously estimated), is but to exchange controlled speculation for pure fantasy. On the measures available, therefore, the populations of both wards cannot have risen. Could then the total number of households in each have remained stable? Again, the 1520 totals demonstrate that this is most improbable, because the mean sizes of households in that year would have had to be implausibly low: at 2.3 for Spon and 2.5 for Jordan Well.

Thus, as figure 3 suggests, the only alternative is to accept that the 1520 results for these two wards are completely unreliable. Was but one of Spon's two extra-mural streets counted; and were merely the members of one or other of the two parishes included under Jordan Well (for the boundary bisected the ward); did the enumerators simply total up the heads of households and their servants in both cases; or were these 'working-class' districts semi-deserted by the men-folk, who worked elsewhere in the city during daytime? It is impossible to tell. What may be claimed, however, is that these two wards and Bishop were very probably losing their inhabitants like all the others, a view which is reinforced by the presence in them of over half the counted vacant houses in the whole city by 1523.

Appendix 3 *Various overall distributions of persons and households by wards in 1523*

(a) Table 36. *Distributions of persons by household status, and proportions contributed to every category by each ward*

Wards	BL		XC		SM		E		G	
Status		%		%		%		%		%
Husbands	63	6.4	130	13.3	57	5.8	104	10.6	131	13.4
Wives	63	6.4	130	13.2	59	6.0	105	10.7	132	13.4
Widowers	—	—	—	—	—	—	—	—	—	—
Widows	6	3.6	30	17.8	8	4.7	6	3.6	19	11.2
Single men	—	—	9	64.3	—	—	—	—	—	—
Single women	1	11.1	2	22.2	—	—	—	—	1	11.1
Unspec. males	10	21.7	2	4.3	1*	2.2	7	15.2	4	8.7
Unspec. females	1	1.0	—	—	5*	5.2	18	18.8	2	2.1
Mothers	—	—	—	—	—	—	—	—	3	50.0
Sister	—	—	—	—	1	16.7	—	—	—	—
Sons	—	—	—	—			—	—	—	—
Children	118	9.2	231	18.0	82*	6.4	154	12.0	152	11.8
Menservants	48	15.1	81	25.6	37	11.7	70	22.1	—	—
Apprentices	—	—	—	—	—	—	—	—	—	—
Lads	—	—	—	—	1	1.8	—	—	55	98.2
Journeymen	—	—	—	—	—	—	—	—	—	—
Women servants	87	17.6	123	24.8	15	3.0	131	26.5	—	—
Maids	—	—	—	—	47	17.0	—	—	103	37.3
Totals	397		738		313*		595		602	
		8.3		15.4		6.5		12.4		12.6
Contemporary totals	395		735		319		618		604	

Notes: * Seven unspecified males and females and two children, who were not counted by households, should be added to the Smithford totals.

( ) These totals, of course, exclude persons lost in the missing sheets for these two wards.

† The Spon enumerator undercast his sub-totals of 245 men, 389 women and 244 children by exactly 100.

G	MP		BP		SP		JW			Wards
%		%		%		%		%	Totals	Status
9.4	113	11.5	149	15.2	34	3.5	107	10.9	980	Husbands
9.3	114	11.6	149	15.1	34	3.5	107	10.9	985	Wives
—	—	—	—	—	2	100.0	—	—	2	Widowers
14.2	29	17.2	30	17.8	13	7.7	4	2.3	169	Widows
28.6	—	—	—	—	—	—	1	7.1	14	Single men
33.3	1	11.1	—	—	—	—	1	11.1	9	Single women
6.5	8	17.4	5	10.9	—	—	6	13.0	46	Unspec. males
3.1	7	7.3	33	34.4	—	—	27	28.1	96	Unspec. females
—	1	16.7	1	16.7	—	—	1	16.7	6	Mothers
—	1	100.0	—	—	—	—	—	—	1	Sister
—	—	—	—	—	—	—	5	83.3	6	Sons
8.0	93	7.2	211	16.4	33	2.6	106	8.3	1,283	Children
5.7	4	1.3	25	7.9	9	2.8	25	7.9	317	Menservants
—	22	61.1	—	—	—	—	14	38.9	36	Apprentices
—	—	—	—	—	—	—	—	—	56	Lads
—	9	100.0	—	—	—	—	—	—	9	Journeymen
8.1	—	—	79	16.0	20	4.0	—	—	496	Women servants
2.2	62	22.5	—	—	—	—	58	21.0	276	Maids
	464		(682)		(145)		462		4,786	Totals
8.1		9.7		14.2		3.0		9.7	*(+9=4,795)	
	466		853		778† 878†		448		5,607+100	Contemporary totals

Appendix 3b

Table 37. *Distributions of households and persons according to household size: (Coventry and 91 later communities)*

Wards	BL				XC				SM				E			
hh. size	hh.	%	Pers	%	hh.	%	Pers	%	hh.	%	Pers	%	hh.	%	Pers	%
1	5	6.17	5	1.25	19	10.98	19	2.57	8	10.95	8	2.55	17	12.59	17	2.85
2	10	12.34	20	5.03	28	16.18	56	7.58	11	15.06	22	7.02	26	19.25	52	8.73
3	11	13.58	33	8.31	30	17.34	90	12.19	16	21.91	48	15.33	20	14.81	60	10.08
4	14	17.28	56	14.10	24	13.87	96	13.00	7	9.58	28	8.95	21	15.55	84	14.11
5	16	19.75	80	20.15	21	12.13	105	14.22	11	15.06	55	17.57	14	10.37	70	11.76
6	5	6.17	30	7.55	24	13.87	144	19.51	7	9.58	42	13.41	13	9.62	78	13.10
7	6	7.40	42	10.57	12	6.93	84	11.38	4	5.47	28	8.94	7	5.18	49	8.23
8	5	6.17	40	10.07	4	2.31	32	4.33	5	6.84	40	12.77	5	3.70	40	6.72
9	4	4.93	36	9.06	5	2.89	45	6.09	1	1.36	9	2.87	3	2.22	27	4.53
10	2	2.46	20	5.03	3	1.73	30	4.06	1	1.36	10	3.19	2	1.48	20	3.36
11	2	2.46	22	5.54	1	0.57	11	1.49	1	1.36	11	3.51	3	3.22	33	5.54
12	—	—	—	—	1	0.57	12	1.62	1	1.36	12	3.83	—	—	—	—
13+	1	1.23	13	3.27	1	0.57	14	1.89	—	—	—	—	4*	2.96	65*	10.91
Totals	81		397		173		738		73		313		135		595	
Means	4.90				4.27				4.29				4.41			

* Households with 13, 15, 17 and 20 persons respectively.

Table 37—*continued*

Wards	G				BG				MP				BP			
hh. size	hh.	%	Pers	%	hh.	%	Pers	%	hh.	%	Pers	%	hh.	%	Pers	%
1	13	8.28	13	2.15	18	14.17	18	4.63	23	14.83	23	4.95	24	11.48	24	3.51
2	32	20.38	64	10.63	46	36.22	92	23.71	67	43.22	134	28.87	64	30.62	128	18.76
3	44	28.02	132	21.92	23	18.11	69	17.78	21	13.54	63	13.57	46	22.00	138	20.23
4	27	17.19	108	17.94	13	10.23	52	13.40	18	11.61	72	15.51	36	17.22	144	21.11
5	12	7.64	60	9.96	13	10.23	65	16.75	7	4.51	35	7.54	22	10.52	110	16.12
6	9	5.73	54	8.97	8	6.29	48	12.37	7	4.51	42	9.05	5	2.39	30	4.39
7	10	6.36	70	11.62	4	3.14	28	7.21	5	3.22	35	7.54	4	1.91	28	4.10
8	—	—	—	—	2	1.57	16	4.12	5	3.22	40	8.62	3	1.43	24	3.51
9	7	4.45	63	10.46	—	—	—	—	—	—	—	—	3	1.43	27	3.95
10	—	—	—	—	—	—	—	—	2	1.29	20	4.31	1	0.47	10	1.46
11	1	0.63	11	1.82	—	—	—	—	—	—	—	—	—	—	—	—
12	1	0.63	12	1.99	—	—	—	—	—	—	—	—	—	—	—	—
13+	1	0.63	15	2.49	—	—	—	—	—	—	—	—	1	0.47	19	2.78
Totals	157		602		127		388		155		464		209		682	
Means	3.83				3.05				2.99				3.26			

Table 37—continued

Wards	SP				JW				Totals				91 later communities[1]	
hh. size	hh.	%	Pers	%	hh.	%	Pers	%	hh.	%	Pers	%	hh. size	% of hhs.
1	9	18.36	9	6.20	28	19.58	28	6.06	164	12.59	164	3.42	1	6.02
2	14	28.57	28	19.31	46	32.16	92	19.91	344	26.42	688	14.37	2	14.75
3	11	22.44	33	22.75	17	11.88	51	11.03	239	18.35	717	14.98	3	16.72
4	6	12.24	24	16.55	18	12.58	72	15.58	184	14.13	736	15.37	4	15.69
5	4	8.16	20	13.79	12	8.39	60	12.98	132	10.13	660	13.79	5	14.62
6	4	8.16	24	16.55	9	6.29	54	11.68	91	6.98	546	11.40	6	11.69
7	1	2.04	7	4.82	9	6.29	63	13.63	62	4.76	434	9.06	7	7.91
8	—	—	—	—	1	0.69	8	1.73	30	2.30	240	5.01	8	5.32
9	—	—	—	—	2	1.39	18	3.89	25	1.92	225	4.70	9	2.91
10	—	—	—	—	—	—	—	—	11	0.84	110	2.29	10	1.74
11	—	—	—	—	—	—	—	—	8	0.61	88	1.83	11	0.94
12	—	—	—	—	—	—	—	—	3	0.23	36	0.75	12	0.60
13+	—	—	—	—	1	0.69	16	3.46	9	0.65	142	2.93	13+	1.08
Totals	49		145		143		462		1,302		4,786			
Means	2.96				3.23				3.676					
							Mean of means =		3.72					

[1] Peter Laslett, 'Size and Structure of the Household in England Over Three Centuries' pt. I, *Population Studies*, xxiii, no. 2, 1969, p. 212, table 4.

Appendix 3c *Occupations of householders in the enumeration*

Table 38. *Distribution of occupational categories and specific trades by wards, from conflation with the 1522 assessment, the 1524 subsidy return, and only in unambiguous cases, from the Register of the Corpus Christi Gild. (A few occupations are mentioned in the census.)*

Wards	BL	%	XC	%	SM	%	E	%	G	%	BG	%	MP	%	BP	%	SP	%	JW	%	Totals	%
Categories and trades																						
Merchants																						
Clothier	—		1		—		—		—		—		—		—		—		—		1	
Drapers	2		—		3		11		3		1		4		—		1		3		28	
Grocers	1		—		—		—		1		1		—		—		—		—		2	
Mercers	15		5		—		4		1		3		—		—		—		—		28	
Merchant	—		—		—		—		—		1		—		—		—		—		1	
Totals	18		6		3		15		4		6		4		—		1		3		60	
		30.0		10.0		5.0		25.0		6.7		10.0		6.7		—		1.7		5.0		100.1
Victuallers																						
Bakers	—		2		3		2		5		—		4		1		1		—		18	
Bitter (Water carrier)	—		—		—		—		—		—		—		1		—		—		1	
Brewer	—		—		—		—		—		—		—		1		—		—		1	
Butchers	1		31		—		1		—		—		—		4		—		—		37	
Cooks	—		1		—		—		—		2		—		—		—		1		4	
Fishmongers	—		9		—		—		—		—		—		—		—		1		10	
Graziers	1		2		—		—		—		—		—		1		—		—		4	
Innholders	—		—		3		—		—		—		—		—		—		—		3	
Millers	—		—		—		—		—		—		1		—		—		1		2	
Vintners	—		4		1		—		—		—		—		—		—		—		5	
Totals	2		49		7		3		5		2		5		8		1		3		85	
		2.4		57.7		8.2		3.5		5.9		2.4		5.9		9.4		1.2		3.5		100.1

Table 38—continued

Wards	BL	%	XC	%	SM	%	E	%	G	%	BG	%	MP	%	BP	%	SP	%	JW	%	Totals	%
Textile crafts																						
Bedders	—		2		—		—		—		1		—		—		—		—		3	
'Brotherer' (Embroiderer?)	1		—		—		1		—		—		—		—		—		—		1	
Dyers	1		6		1		1		5		1		—		3		3		6		26	
Fustian-maker	—		—		—		—		—		1		—		—		—		—		1	
Shermen	2		—		2		10		9		—		7		—		1		3		34	
Walkers	—		—		—		1		3		1		1		1		1		1		9	
Weavers	—		1		—		1		5		4		3		7		—		2		23	
Totals	3	3.1	9	9.3	3	3.1	13	13.4	22	22.7	8	8.3	11	11.3	11	11.3	5	5.2	12	12.4	97	100.1
Clothing crafts																						
Cappers	9		1		1		2		6		2		7		4		1		16		49	
Hatmakers	—		—		—		—		1		—		2		—		1		5		9	
Hosiers	1		—		—		1		—		2		2		—		1		1		8	
Point-maker	—		—		—		—		—		—		—		—		—		1		1	
Tailors	3		4		—		3		1		5		2		1		—		1		20	
Totals	13	14.9	5	5.8	1	1.2	6	6.9	8	9.2	9	10.3	13	14.9	5	5.8	3	3.5	24	27.6	87	100.1

Table 38—continued

Ward / Categories and trades	BL	%	XC	%	SM	%	E	%	G	%	BG	%	MP	%	BP	%	SP	%	JW	%	Totals	%
Leather crafts																						
Cobblers	—		—		1		—		1		—		—		1		—		—		3	
Corvisors	—		10		1		—		2		9		4		2		1		1		30	
Curriers	—		—		1		—		—		2		—		—		—		—		3	
Glovers (pursers)	—		—		1		—		1		3		—		1		—		—		6	
Pouchmakers	1		—		—		—		—		1		—		—		—		—		2	
Saddlers	—		—		1		1		—		—		1		—		—		—		3	
Skinners	1		—		—		5		—		2		1		2		—		1		9	
Tanners	—		—		—		—		—		—		—		2		—		—		2	
Whittawers	—		—		—		—		1		—		—		—		—		1		2	
Totals	2	3.3	10	16.7	5	8.3	6	10.0	5	8.3	17	28.3	6	10.0	6	10.0	1	1.7	2	3.3	60	99.9
Metal crafts																						
Bladesmith	—		—		—		—		—		1		—		—		—		—		1	
Bucklemakers	2		—		—		—		—		—		—		—		—		1		3	
Cardmakers	—		2		—		2		—		—		—		—		—		—		4	
Cutlers	1		3		—		—		—		—		—		—		—		—		4	
Girdlers	4		—		—		2		—		—		1		—		—		2		9	
Goldsmith	—		1		—		—		—		1		—		—		—		2		4	
Locksmith	—		—		—		—		—		1		—		—		—		—		1	
Pewterers	—		—		—		—		—		1		—		2		—		—		3	
Pinners	2		—		—		—		—		—		—		—		—		—		2	
Plumbers	2		—		—		—		—		—		—		—		—		—		2	
Sheargrinder	—		—		—		—		1		—		—		—		—		—		1	
Smiths	—		1		2		—		1		2		3		2		—		1		12	
Spurriers	—		—		—		—		1		1		1		—		—		—		3	
Wiredrawers	1		1		—		—		1		—		2		—		—		1		6	
Totals	12	21.8	8	14.6	2	3.6	4	7.3	3	5.5	7	12.7	7	12.7	4	7.3	0	—	8	14.6	55	100.0

Table 38—continued

Categories and trades	BL	%	XC	%	SM	%	E	%	G	%	BG	%	MP	%	BP	%	SP	%	JW	%	Totals	%
Building crafts																						
Carpenters	—		1		—		—		—		2		—		2		—		—		5	
Glazier	—		—		—		—		—		—		—		1		—		—		1	
Labourers	—		1		—		1		—		4		7		4		—		6		23	
Masons	—		1		—		—		1		—		1		—		—		—		3	
Tilers	—		2		—		—		—		2		—		2		—		—		6	
Totals	0	—	5	13.2	0	—	1	2.6	1	2.6	8	21.1	8	21.1	9	23.7	0	—	6	15.8	38	100.1
Wood crafts																						
Bowyer	1		—		—		—		—		—		—		—		—		—		1	
Carvers	—		1		—		—		—		—		2		1		1		—		5	
Coopers	—		1		2		1		—		—		—		—		1		—		5	
Fletchers	—		1		1		—		—		—		—		—		—		2		4	
Sawyer	—		—		—		—		—		1		—		—		—		—		1	
Wrights	—		1		—		—		—		—		1		3		—		2		7	
Totals	1	4.4	4	17.4	3	13.0	1	4.4	0	—	1	4.4	3	13.0	4	17.4	2	8.7	4	17.4	23	100.1
Officials																						
Sealer (of cloth)	—		1		—		—		—		—		—		—		—		—		1	
Sergeants	—		1		—		—		—		1		—		1		—		—		3	
Summoner	—		1		—		—		—		—		—		—		—		—		1	
Superior servants	1		4		—		1		1		—		—		4		—		—		11	
Sword Bearer	—		—		1		—		—		—		—		—		—		—		1	
Yeomen	—		1		—		1		—		—		2		—		—		—		4	
Totals	1	4.8	8	38.1	1	4.8	2	9.5	1	4.8	1	4.8	2	9.5	5	23.8	0	—	0	—	21	100.1

Table 38—continued

Wards Categories and trades	BL	%	XC	%	SM	%	E	%	G	%	BG	%	MP	%	BP	%	SP	%	JW	%	Totals	%
Professionals																						
Apothecary	1		—		—		—		—		—		—		—		—		—		1	
Clerks	—		—		—		1		—		—		—		1		—		1		3	
'Luter' (Lutenist?)	—		—		—		—		—		—		—		—		—		1		1	
Minstrels	—		—		3		—		—		—		—		—		—		—		3	
Organ-player	1		—		—		—		—		—		—		—		—		—		1	
Painters	—		1		—		—		2		—		—		—		—		—		3	
Physicians	—		—		—		—		—		—		1		1		—		—		2	
Priests	—		—		—		—		—		2		1		—		—		—		3	
Schoolmaster	—		—		—		—		—		—		—		—		—		1		1	
Scribe	1		1		—		—		—		—		—		—		—		—		2	
Surgeons	—		—		1		—		—		—		—		—		—		—		1	
Waits	—		2		—		—		—		—		—		—		—		—		2	
Totals	3	13.0	4	17.4	4	17.4	1	4.4	2	8.7	2	8.7	2	8.7	2	8.7	0	—	3	13.0	23	100.0
Others																						
Barbers	—		3		—		2		—		1		1		1		1		—		9	
Chandlers	—		1		—		1		1		—		1		1		—		—		5	
Gentleman	—		1		—		—		—		—		—		—		—		—		1	
Herdsman	—		—		—		—		1		—		—		—		—		—		1	
Hosteler	—		—		—		—		—		—		—		—		—		1		1	
Slaughtermen	—		1		—		—		—		—		—		1		1		—		2	
Totals	0	—	6	31.6	0	—	3	15.8	2	10.5	1	5.3	2	10.5	3	15.8	1	5.3	1	5.3	19	100.1
Grand totals	55	9.7	114	20.1	29	5.1	55	9.7	53	9.3	62	10.9	63	11.1	57	10.0	14	2.5	66	11.6	568	100.0

Appendix 3d

Table 39. *Overall occupational structure by householders successfully labelled*

Merchants	10.6%
Victuallers	15.0%
Textiles	17.1%
Clothing	15.3%
Leather	10.6%
Metals	9.7%
Building	6.7%
Wood	4.0%
Officials	3.7%
Professionals	4.0%
Others	3.4%

Appendix 3e

Table 40. *Distributions of rental categories etc. by wards from conflation with the 1522 assessment*

Wards	BL		XC		SM		E		G	
Categories		%		%		%		%		%
1. 1–6s.	—	—	14	9.4	15	10.1	11	7.4	13	8.7
2. 6s. 8d.–12s.	5	2.9	32	18.4	10	5.8	7	4.0	22	12.6
3. 13–18s.	14	13.3	16	15.2	14	13.3	9	8.6	14	13.3
4. 20–29s.	19	12.1	37	23.6	5	3.2	19	12.1	21	13.4
5. 30–49s.	9	10.0	30	33.3	5	5.6	13	14.4	8	8.9
6. 50–69s.	8	21.6	13	35.1	2	5.4	8	21.6	1	2.7
7. 70s. +	4	20.0	8	40.0	1	5.0	4	20.0	—	—
8. Freeholders	2	4.4	7	15.6	6	13.3	4	8.9	6	13.3
9. Others	20	3.8	16	3.1	15	2.9	60	11.4	72	13.7
Total households	81	6.2	173	13.3	73	5.6	135	10.4	157	12.1

No freehold was valued at more than 80s. *p.a.* or less than 7s. *p.a.* Of the total, the main clusters

Note to Appendix 3d

For reasons of classification, this table is not strictly comparable with that in Hoskins, *Provincial England*, p. 80, the 'Merchant' category in particular having been segregated from 'Textiles' and 'Clothing'. In this case too, labourers have been included, and deliberately classified under 'Building' (cf. the ordinance ordering the members of the fellowship of rough-masons and dawbers to revert to the status of common labourers 'as they were afore' in 1517, *L.B.*, p. 653). Nevertheless, the similarities between the two systems of classification remain striking with one notable exception. While difficulties with regard to correlation between the documents must have had some effect (although 85 different occupations have been successfully included here as compared with Professor Hoskins' 90), the shrinkage of all the groups devoted to textiles and clothing combined is most suggestive. In 1522 the proportion was 47 per cent: in 1523 the percentage may only be raised to 43.0 per cent by including *all* those here categorised under 'Merchants'. This fits too well with the evidence for the impact of the deepening national trade depression to be lightly dismissed. It remains true, of course, that the evidence available for both dates is distorted to an unknown extent by the uneven coverage of the wards with respect to the occupations of those deemed too poor to be potential candidates for taxation.

BG	%	MP	%	BP	%	SP	%	JW	%	Totals	Total percentage of each category
25	16.8	14	9.4	30	30.1	2	1.3	25	16.8	149	100.0
26	14.9	19	10.9	31	17.8	4	2.3	18	10.3	174	99.9
9	8.6	10	9.5	14	13.3	2	1.9	3	2.9	105	99.9
8	5.1	19	12.1	15	9.6	5	3.2	9	5.7	157	100.1
8	8.9	6	6.7	2	2.2	3	3.3	6	6.7	90	100.0
2	5.4	2	5.4	1	2.7	—	—	—	—	37	99.9
1	5.0	1	5.0	1	5.0	—	—	—	—	20	100.0
3	6.7	4	8.9	4	8.9	2	4.4	7	15.6	45	100.1
45	8.6	80	15.2	111	21.1	31	5.9	75	14.3	525	100.0
127	9.8	155	11.9	209	16.1	49	3.8	143	10.9	1,302	100.1

were: six at 14s., ten at 20s., nine at 27s., and seven at 40s.

Appendix 3f

Table 41. *Distributions of goods categories by wards from conflation with the 1522 assessment and the 1524 subsidy return*

Wards	BL		XC		SM		E		G	
Categories		%		%		%		%		%
1. Nil assessments	6		35		18		15		33	
		3.2		13.1		6.7		5.6		12.3
2. £0–2	21		48		15		23		14	
		9.6		22.0		6.9		10.6		6.4
3. £3–5	15		19		13		8		20	
		12.5		15.8		10.8		6.7		16.7
4. £6–10	4		25		5		6		9	
		5.6		34.7		6.9		8.3		12.5
5. £12–16	2		8		2		9		7	
		6.3		25.0		6.3		28.1		21.8
6. £20–49	12		15		2		10		7	
		18.4		23.1		3.1		15.4		10.8
7. £50–99	3		6		5		5		—	
		12.0		24.0		20.0		20.0		—
8. £100+	—		3		1		4		3	
		—		21.4		7.1		28.6		21.4
9. Others	18		14		12		55		64	
		3.7		2.9		2.5		11.3		13.1
Total householders	81		173		73		135		157	

BG	%	MP	%	BP	%	SP	%	JW	%	Totals	Total percentage of each category
47	17.5	38	14.2	41	15.3	4	1.5	31	11.6	268	100.0
20	9.2	13	6.0	33	15.1	7	3.2	24	11.0	218	100.0
8	6.7	13	10.8	14	11.7	3	2.5	7	5.8	120	100.0
6	8.3	3	4.2	8	11.1	4	5.6	2	2.8	72	100.0
—	—	2	6.3	—	—	—	—	2	6.3	32	100.1
2	3.1	7	10.8	6	9.2	—	—	4	6.2	65	100.1
1	4.0	1	4.0	1	4.0	1	4.0	2	8.0	25	100.0
2	14.3	—	—	1	7.1	—	—	—	—	14	99.9
41	8.4	78	16.0	105	21.5	30	6.1	71	14.6	488	100.1
127		155		209		49		143		1,302	

Appendix 4 *Suggested adjustments and estimated revisions*

(a) *Suggested adjustments to the surviving 1523 schedules*

Any adjustment to given figures from the past has to be arbitrary, but in view of the criticisms formulated in part IV(A) chapters 20 and 21 some conservative 'corrections' do seem necessary and possible. A definitive solution, however, is clearly impossible.

The under-representation of children has been compensated by applying what seem to be fair 'reproduction ratios' to the numbers of adults counted in those wards where this seems appropriate. Using table 26 as a yardstick, therefore, Smithford's ratio has been inflated to 0.7 (i.e. lower than Cross Cheaping's 0.76), and Gosford's to 0.6 (i.e. between Earl's 0.64 and Bishop's 0.57). In the cases of the four more junior wards, however, it has seemed best to apply the Bishop ratio in blanket fashion since the results are too erratic to permit a form of crude scaling.

With respect to servants, the sex ratios (cf. table 17) have had to be invoked. Bishop's ratio has thus been raised to be in line with Spon's 45.0; while in the case of Broad Gate, with its marked occupational bias towards leather-working, a ratio of 55.0 has seemed more appropriate and could well be too low.

An approximate cross-check of the plausibility of these estimates may be attempted by weighing the relative proportions of children and servants in the revised populations as *per* table 22. The results would seem to be well within the bounds of reasonable probability.

Table 42. *Proportions of children and servants as a cross-check on suggested population adjustments*

Ward	Children No.	%	Servants No.	%	Combined proportions	Revised ward totals in the schedules
Smithford	91	28.3	100	31.1	59.4	322*
Gosford	175	28.0	158	25.3	53.3	625
Broad Gate	126	30.1	71	17.0	47.1	418
Much Park	156	29.6	97	18.4	48.0	527
Bishop	211	30.5	115	16.6	47.1	693
Spon	47	29.6	29	18.2	47.8	159
Jordan Well	145	28.9	97	19.4	48.3	501

* Omitting the nine adults and children in the Irish Lane.

(b) *Estimated revisions of the contemporary ward totals for Bishop and Spon*

Bishop: On the basis of the foregoing adjustment, the 'error' in the surviving schedules is only 1.6 per cent. When this is applied to the difference between those described and the given contemporary total, the total population of the ward is thereby raised to 867. This low adjustment is justifiable when it is remembered that the proportion of children calculable from the surviving schedules exaggerates the position in the ward as a whole.

Spon: In this case, the sample already discussed – a mere 145 out of the '878' which may be calculated from the enumerator's sub-totals, is very small. The percentage 'error' of 9.66 per cent, therefore, might well be unrepresentative of the rest of the ward. The enumerator, for example, counted 244 children in the *whole* ward: an unadjusted proportion of 27.8 per cent (cf. table 22, *supra*). It is worth recalling, nevertheless, that not only is the 'error' calculable for Much Park practically 12 per cent of the revised total, but that Spon itself seems to have been badly counted in 1520 and carelessly totalled in 1523. The possibility that the estimated population of 963 may thus be inflated, however, is kept before the reader in appendix 2, where this is relevant. Whatever the truth of the matter, the ward total is most unlikely to have been less than 920, a result which is reached by arbitrarily halving the estimated 'error'.

Appendix 5 *A note on the topography of late medieval Coventry as shown on map 1*

Despite cartographical distortions and the incorrect attribution of a few street names, John Speed's map of Coventry (*c*.1610) remains the earliest source for reconstructing the built-up areas of the late medieval city. His *general* accuracy is supported by other documentation – the Drapery for example, which stretched, bay by bay, through from Bailey Lane to Earl Street (cf. C.R.O. A24) is clearly shown; while the extent of standing housing roughly represents the area covered in late medieval times particularly without the walls. Well Street extended extra-murally in 1410–11 (*V.C.H. Warks.*, viii, p. 38); the New Rents first appeared in documents in 1518 (*ibid.*, p. 29 *sub* King Street); Bishop had buildings without the gate (Templeman, *op.cit.*, pp. 84, 91, 112, 133); as did both Gosford (*V.C.H. Warks.*, viii, pp. 27–8), some 38 per cent of the counted households in which were extra-mural in 1534; and Much Park (Templeman, *op.cit.*, pp. 82, 100, 127). Hill Street may well have been originally a wholly extra-mural street name: the connection between Fleet Street and the Hill Gate was very probably known as Essex Lane in medieval times (cf. the consistent positioning of this name in the surviving Trinity Gild rental, *ibid.*, pp. 59, 73, 89, 107, 131; and *V.C.H. Warks.*, viii, p. 24 *sub* Abbott's Lane, and p. 29 *sub* Hill Street). The medieval existence of the suburb outside Grey Friars Gate is alone unsupported by contemporary documents examined by the author, but only an intensive search of surviving deeds could clarify this matter.

The evidence for ward boundaries has had to be taken from Samuel Bradford's plan of 1748–9. Continuity here is nevertheless very probable. In particular, the extra-mural boundaries of Bishop and Spon clearly illustrate the fossilisation of the medieval system, despite the fact that what had once been a densely housed area had become relatively deserted by the eighteenth century. The case of Bishop, at least, may be proved against the evidence of C.R.O. Accession 263, for it is almost certain that this ward's schedules (fos. 14–16), as *now* foliated, are continuous only to the end of fo. 15v., at the foot of which Cook Street's vacant houses are totalled. Apart from Well Street, which appears to have been counted quite logically as a whole, however, the other suburbs, e.g. the New Rents and Dog Lane (cf. Templeman, *op.cit.*, pp. 66, 75, 80), are obviously those lost on the missing folio. The last 14 households of one or other of these would seem to be carried over onto what is now fo. 16r., a quarter of the way down which appears the heading, 'Sent Nycollas strete'. Allowing for the estimated 53 households lost on the missing folio, therefore, the housing densities for each street may be tabulated (see table). Thus, when due allowance is made

Streets	Households	Vacant houses	Total 'houses'
Bishop St	46	15*	61
Well St	54	22	76
Cook St	49	46	95
? New Rents *etc.* +	14 + ?53 ⎫	48 ⎫	?161
St Nicholas St	46 ⎭	⎭	
	209 + ?53	131	?393

* Between the St John's bridges.

for the suburban part of Well Street, between one third and one half of the ward was wholly extra-mural.

It is important to note, finally, that Spon Street was fringed by housing which extended over the western boundary of the ward (the Bars), and even beyond Spon bridge (off map to W.), where was sited the chapel of St James (Templeman, *op.cit.*, pp. 109, 132; *V.C.H. Warks.*, viii, pp. 332–3). The apparent inflation of Spon's population by 1523 might thus also be explained by the possibility that the enumerator then included households outside the ward boundary, whereas his 1520 predecessor had not.

Bibliography of sources cited

Only over the last decade or so have major efforts been made to systematise the cataloguing of Coventry's archives. There are now three partially overlapping systems: (a) that instigated idiosyncratically by J. C. Jeaffreson (ed.), *Coventry Charters and Manuscripts* (Coventry, 1896) and partially perpetuated in the *Supplementary Catalogue* (1931); (b) a classified but inconsistently arranged card-catalogue that partly overlapped (a) and which operated continuously between 1948 and 1960 – although I was not made aware of its existence for some years; and (c) a more recent attempt, initiated by Messrs. David Smith and Alan Dibben, to embrace most of the collection (including accessions acquired since 1960) within an orderly system of accession numbers. That gigantic task is still in progress, and in the continuing absence of a complete up-to-date classified catalogue, and because of the impossibility of keeping abreast with a changing system of references, I have had to employ call numbers here that apply to any one or two of these systems. Consistency in fact has been quite impossible, while even folio numbers have now been added to some documents since I first consulted them.

The situation is further complicated by both the destruction of Thomas Sharp's collection of Coventry manuscripts in the fire at the Birmingham Reference Library in 1879, and the fact that a number of other documents recorded by him or his fellow antiquaries cannot now be traced. It has thus been necessary to search for relevant extracts from these as transcribed in the nineteenth century. The most valuable sources in this connection have been William Reader's large volumes of somewhat chaotic transcripts that are now housed in the Bodleian. Others include various transcripts by Thomas Daffern and by George Eld, which are now deposited at the C.R.O.

In these circumstances it has seemed appropriate to adopt an unconventional approach in the presentation of this bibliography, which is consequently arranged in three parts:

(1) All primary material relating to Coventry, whether documentary, transcribed or printed in whole or part, and whether deposited in local or national repositories;

(2) Other printed primary authorities cited;

(3) Secondary authorities.

1 PRIMARY SOURCES

(Unless otherwise stated, MS. references are to those in the C.R.O.)

(a) *General*

Transcripts by William Reader Bodleian MSS. Top. Warwickshire c. 4–8.
George Eld, 'Coventry Free School: Catalogue of Library 1830' A166.

Thomas Sharp *Illustrative Papers on the History and Antiquities of the City of Coventry . . . from Original and Mostly Unpublished Documents,* reprinted with corrections, additions and a brief memoir of the author by W. G. Fretton (Birmingham, 1871).
Mayoral annals Bodleian MS. Top. Warwickshire d.4.
    B.L.Harl.MS. 6388.
    Bliss Burbidge, *Old Coventry*, pp. 208–67 (a sometimes misleading collation of various versions).
Survey of Corporation Lands (23 Elizabeth)   A24
Burton's Book (10 Charles I)   A34
Book of Matters Touching Ship-money   A35

(b) *Corporation business*
(i) *The Coventry Leet Book or Mayor's Register Containing the Records of the City Leet or View of Frankpledge A.D. 1420–1555 with Divers Other Matters,* transcribed and edited by Mary Dormer Harris (Early English Text Society, cxxxiv, cxxxv, cxxxviii, cxlvi, 1907–13).
    Petitions to the Leet: Carpenters 9a & 9b: late F.10
    Judicial: Levi Fox 'Some New Evidence of Leet Activity', *English Historical Review*, lxi (1946), pp. 235–43.
    Second Leet Book   A3(b)
(ii) Council Minutes (1523–5)   B.L.Harl.MS. 7571, fos. 31–4.
    Council Book (1557–1635)   A14(a)
(iii) Chamberlains' accounts (14 Henry VII to 16 Elizabeth)   A7(a)
      (17 Elizabeth to 11 Charles I)   A7(b)
    Corporation accounts (1542–61)   A9
    Books of Loans and Allowances (1551–1704)   A12(a)
    (19 Elizabeth – 1625)   A12(b)
    Book of Receipts (1561–1653)   A17
(iv) Statute Merchant Rolls: membranes for, 12, 13, 14, 25, 26, 27, 34, 37, 38 Henry VIII; '1551'; 6 Edward VI; 1 Mary; Philip and Mary 1 & 2, 2 & 3, 3 &4, 4 &5; 1, 2, 3, 4, 5 Elizabeth   E6
    Deeds etc. (various)   class C (Jeaffreson)
    A Census of grain of Knightlow Hundred (?1555–6)   A94

(c) *Gilds*
The Register of the Guild of the Holy Trinity, St Mary, St John the Baptist and St Katherine of Coventry, ed. Mary Dormer Harris (Dugdale Society, xiii, 1935).
The Records of the Guild of the Holy Trinity, St Mary, St John the Baptist and St Katherine of Coventry, ed. G. Templeman (Dugdale Society, xix, 1944).
An otherwise lost account and ordinance of the Trinity Gild, Poole, *Coventry*, pp. 210–11.
Register of the Corpus Christi Gild (3 Henry VII to 1 Mary)   A6
St George's Gild   B43, 46 (63, 76)

(d) *Craft fellowships* (apart from references in *L.B.*, and small lost items in the Reader MSS. and Sharp, *Antiquities*)

(i) Thomas Sharp, *A Dissertation on the Pageants or Dramatic Mysteries Anciently Performed at Coventry, by the Trading Companies of that City; Chiefly with Reference to the Vehicles, Characters and Dresses of the Actors* (Coventry, 1825).

Hardin Craig (ed.), *Two Coventry Corpus Christi Plays*, 2nd edn, (Early English Text Society, extra ser. lxxxvii, 1957). (A definitive new edition of these plays is currently being prepared by Professor R. W. Ingram).

(ii) Bakers: ordinances (up to 1623)   access. 8: A110

Cappers: accounts MS. in possession of the Company of Cappers and Feltmakers

Carpenters: ordinances and second account book (1478–1652)
     access. 3: A5

Cordwainers: ordinances (1577 and after)   access. 14: A98
     accounts (1653–1760)   A41

Drapers: accounts (Daffern transcript)   access. 154: Drapers 1c
     ordinances   Reader 4, fo. 92.

Dyers: ordinances (sixteenth century)   Reader 4, fos. 116–118.

Fullers: ordinances (sixteenth century)   Reader 4, fos. 112v–114v.
     ordinances   C.R.O. uncatalogued

Mercers: ordinances (from *c*. 1550) and accounts from 1579
     access. 15: A99

Minute Book (1602–1702)   access. 15: A100

Silk-weavers and worsted-weavers: ordinances (1650)   access. 117

Smiths: Records and accounts 1684–1822 (Daffern transcript) includes sixteenth-century ordinances.

Tanners: 'Transcription of the Ancient Minute Book of the Fellow-ship of Tanners' (includes material reaching back to 10 Henry VII)
     access. 241

Tilers: ordinances (fifteenth century)   B.L.Harl.MS. 6466
(transcribed, Reader 4, fos. 217–18).

Weavers: Craft ordinances (1453)   access. 34: Weavers 2a
     Journeymen's ordinances (sixteenth century)
     access. 100: Weavers 2a
     Misc. draft recensions of Craft ordinances (sixteenth century)
     access. 100: Weavers 2c
     Craft ordinances (1639)   access. 100/4: Weavers 2b
     First account book (1523–1635)   access. 100/17/1: Weavers 11
     Second account book (from 1636)   access. 34/2: Weavers 2a
     Rent-gatherers accounts (from 1523) vols. i & ii
     access. 100: Weavers 8 & 9
     Register of apprentices (from 4 Edward VI)   Weavers 5

(e) *Fiscal, demographic and testamentary sources*

'Certificate of Musters' (1522 assessment)   access. 18: A96

1523 enumeration   W.1405; access. 263
Loans and anticipations   B58, 59, 60
1524 Instalment of the Lay Subsidy   P.R.O. E 179/192/125
1525 Instalment of the Lay Subsidy   P.R.O. E 179/192/130
'Tithing' list of Gosford Ward (1534)
                              Uncatalogued (vide *supra*, p. 229 n. 11)
P.C.C. will registers (now P.R.O.) Adeane, Alen, Alenger, Ayloffe, Bod-
    felde, Dyngeley, Hogen, Holder, Jankyn, Maynwaryng, Mellershe,
    Porch, Spert, Thower, Wrastley
Parish register of Holy Trinity (from 1561)
                                Micro-film at Warwick Record Office
Returns of families to the Privy Council
                              B.L. Harl. MSS., 594, 595, 618
Ratebooks for St Michael's parish (1594 and 1595)
                        Rates of St Michael's Church 9(a) & 9(b)

(f) *Political* etc. (Letters, comments, petitions, disputes etc.)
Bristow dispute   F. 3, 4
Letter Book   A79, vol. i
State Papers   P.R.O. SP 1/74; 1/114; 1/141;
                                         1/142; 1/232; 1/236
Misc.   B.L. Bibl. Cotton Titus B1;
                                      B.L. Harl. MS. 6388;
                                               B 70, 75

2 OTHER PRINTED SOURCES

*A Discourse of the Commonweal of this Realm of England – Attributed to
    Sir Thomas Smith*, ed. Mary Dewar (Folger Shakespeare Library,
    1969).
A History of Newcastle and Gateshead, ed. R. Welford, 3 vols. (London,
    n.d. – 1887).
'A Register of the Palmers' Guild at Ludlow in the Reign of Henry VIII',
    Trans. of the Shropshire Archaeol. Soc., 1st ser., vii (1884).
*A Relation, or rather a True Account of the Island of England . . . about the
    Year 1500*, ed. C. A. Sneyd (Camden Soc., xxxvii, 1847).
*Abstract of the Bailiff's Accounts of Monastic and Other Estates in the
    County of Warwick*, transl. by W. B. Bickley with an introduction by
    W. F. Carter (Dugdale Society, ii, 1923).
Acts of the Privy Council of England, New Series, ii, A.D. 1547–1550, ed. J.
    Roche Dasent (H.M.S.O., 1890).
Bishop Geoffrey Blythe's Visitations c. 1515–1525, ed. Peter Heath (Col-
    lections for a History of Staffordshire, 4th ser., vii, 1973).
*Calendar of the Charter Rolls Preserved in the Public Record Office, v, 15
    Edward III – 5 Henry V, A.D. 1341–1417*, prepared under the
    superintendence of the Deputy Keeper of the Records (H.M.S.O.,
    London, 1916).

Calendar of Entries in the Papal Registers Relating to Great Britain and Ireland: Papal Letters, xii, A.D. 1458–1471, ed. J. A. Tremlow (H.M.S.O., London, 1933).

Calendar(s) of the Patent Rolls Preserved in the Public Record Office, prepared under the superintendence of the Deputy Keeper of the Records (H.M.S.O., London): *Richard II, v, 1391–6* (1905); *Henry IV, iv, 1408–13* (1909); *Henry VI, viii, 1436–41* (1907); *Henry VI, iv, 1441–6* (1908); *Henry VI, v, 1446–52* (1909); *Edward IV, 1461–7* (1897); *Edward IV, Henry VI, 1467–77* (1900); *Henry VII, ii, 1494–1509* (1916).

Calendar of the Records of the Corporation of Gloucester, ed. W. H. Stevenson (Gloucester, 1893).

Chester in the Plantagenet and Tudor Reigns, ed. R. H. Morris (Chester, n.d.).

Documents Illustrating the Activities of the General and Provincial Chapters of the English Black Monks 1215–1540, iii, ed. W. A. Pantin, 3 vols. (Camden Society, 3rd ser., liv, 1937).

England in the Reign of King Henry the Eighth, ed. S. J. Herrtage (Early English Text Society, extra ser., xxxii, 1878).

Henry VIII, ed. Charles Whibley (London, 1904).

Leland's Itinerary in England and Wales, ed. Lucy Toulmin Smith, 5 vols. (London, 1964), ii.

Letters and Papers Foreign and Domestic of the Reign of King Henry VIII preserved in the Public Record Office, arranged and catalogued by J. S. Brewer, James Gairdner and R. H. Brodie (H.M.S.O., London): *i(1), 1509–13* (2nd edn 1920); *iii(2), 1521–3* (1867); *iv(1) 1524–6* (1870); *iv(3), 1529–30* (1876); *xiii(1), Jan.–July, 1538* (1892); *xiii(2), Aug.–Dec. 1538* (1893); *xiv(1), 1539* (1894); *xvii, 1542* (1900); *xx(1), Aug.–Dec. 1545* (1907); *Addenda i(1), 1509–1537* (1929).

Minutes and Accounts of the Corporation of Stratford-upon-Avon and Other Records 1553–1620 (Dugdale Society, i, 1921–3).

Poly-Olbion by Michael Drayton, ed. W. Hebel (Oxford, 1961).

Report on the Manuscripts of Lord Middleton Preserved at Wollaton Hall, Nottinghamshire, ed. W. H. Stevenson (Historical Manuscripts Commission, Cd. 5567, H.M.S.O., London, 1911).

Rotuli Parliamentorum: ut et Petitiones, Placita in Parliamento, ed. J. Strachey, 6 vols. (London, 1767–77) ii.

Select Cases before the King's Council in the Star Chamber commonly called the Court of Star Chamber, ed. I. S. Leadam, 2 vols., ii, *1509–1544* (Selden Society, xxv, 1910).

Suffolk in 1524: Subsidy Returns, ed. S.H.A.H. (Suffolk Green Books, x, 1910).

The Brokage Book of Southampton 1443–1444, ed. Olive Coleman, 2 vols. (Southampton Records Series, iv (1960), vi (1961)).

The Domesday of Inclosures, ed. I. S. Leadam, 2 vols. (Royal Historical Society, 1897).

The Gilds of St. George and of St. Mary in the Church of St. Peter, Nottingham, ed. R. F. B. Hodgkinson with an introduction by L. V. D. Owen (Thoroton Society Record Ser., extra ser., vii (1939).

The Maire of Bristow is Kalendar, ed. L. Toulmin Smith (Camden Society, new ser., v, 1872).

The Records of the City of Norwich, ed. W. Hudson and J. C. Tingey, 2 vols. (London and Norwich, 1910), ii.

The Register of the Guild of Knowle, ed. W. B. Bickley (place of pub. n.g., 1894).

The Register of the Guild of the Holy Cross, the Blessed Mary and St. John the Baptist, of Stratford-upon-Avon, ed. J. Harvey Bloom (n.g., 1907).

The Statutes of the Realm, 11 vols. (Record Commission, London, 1810–28), ii (1816), iii (1817), iv(1) (1819).

The Works of Francis Bacon, i, Essays (London, 1902).

Tudor Economic Documents, ed. R. H. Tawney and Eileen Power, 3 vols. (London, 1924).

Valor Ecclesiasticus Temp. Henr. VIII Auctoritate Regia Institutus, 6 vols., ed. J. Caley and J. Hunter (Record Commission, 1810–34), iii (1817).

Visitations in the Diocese of Lincoln 1517–31, ed. A. Hamilton Thompson (Lincolnshire Record Society, xxxiii, 1940).

York Civic Records, iii, ed. Angelo Raine (Yorkshire Archaeological Society Record Ser., cvi, 1942).

3 SECONDARY AUTHORITIES

Allison, K. J., 'Medieval Hull', in K. J. Allison (ed.), *V.C.H. York: East Riding, i. The City of Kingston-upon-Hull* (Oxford, 1969).

Ariès, Philippe *Centuries of Childhood*, transl. by R. Baldrick (London, 1962).

Baker, A. R. H. and Butlin, R. A. (eds.) *Studies of Field Systems in the British Isles* (Cambridge, 1973).

Basford, Kathleen *The Green Man* (Ipswich, 1978).

Bautier, R–H 'Feux, Population et Structure Sociale au Milieu du XVe Siècle, L'Exemple de Carpentras', *Annales E.S.C.* (1959).

Bean, J. N. W., 'Plague, Population and Economic Decline in the Later Middle Ages', *Econ. H.R.*, 2nd. ser. xv (1962–3).

Beresford, M. W., *The Lost Villages of England* (London, 1954).

'A Review of Historical Research (to 1968)', in Maurice Beresford and John Hurst (eds.), *Deserted Medieval Villages* (London, 1971).

Biraben, J. N., 'La Population de Reims et son arrondissement et la verification statistique des récensements numeriques anciens', *Population*, xvi (1961).

Blanchard, Ian 'Population Change, Enclosure, and the Early Tudor Economy', *Econ. H.R.*, 2nd ser. xxiii (1970).

Bliss Burbidge, F., *Old Coventry and Lady Godiva: Being Some Flowers of Coventry History* (Birmingham, n.d.).

Blomefield, Francis *An Essay towards a Topographical History of the County of Norfolk*, 11 vols. (1805–10), iii (1806).

Blyth, T. A., *The History of Stoke* (London, 1897).

Borsay, Peter 'The English Urban Renaissance: The Development of Provincial Urban Culture c. 1680–c. 1760', *Social History*, v (1977).

Bott, Elisabeth *Family and Social Network* (London, 1957).

Bowden, Peter *The Wool Trade in Tudor and Stuart England* (London, 1962).

   'Agricultural Prices, Farm Profits and Rents' in Joan Thirsk (ed.), *The Agrarian History of England and Wales, iv, 1500–1640* (Cambridge, 1967).

Braudel, M. F., 'Les Emprunts de Charles-Quint sur la place d'Anvers' in *Charles-Quint et son Temps* (Paris, 1961).

Bridbury, A. R., *Economic Growth: England in the Later Middle Ages*, 2nd edn (London, 1975).

Butcher, A., 'The Decline of Canterbury 1300–1500', unpublished paper submitted to the Urban History Conference, 1971.

Camden, William *Britain or a Chorographical Description of the Most Flourishing Kingdom; England, Scotland, Ireland and Ilands* (sic) *adionyng, out of the depth of Antiquitie*, transl. and enlarged by Philemon Holland (London, 1610).

Carus-Wilson, E. M., 'The Medieval Trade of the Ports of the Wash', *Medieval Archaeology*, vi–vii (1962–3).

   Medieval Merchant Venturers (London, 1967).

Carus-Wilson, E. M. and Coleman, O., *England's Export Trade, 1275–1547* (Oxford, 1963).

Chatwin, Philip, B., 'The Medieval Patterned Tiles of Warwickshire', *B.A.S.T.*, lx (1936).

Clark, Peter, and Slack, Paul (eds.) *Crisis and Order in English Towns 1500–1700: Essays in Urban History* (London, 1972).

   'Introduction', in Clark and Slack (ed.) *op.cit. English Towns in Transition 1500–1700* (Oxford, 1976).

Clark, Peter *English Provincial Society from the Reformation to the Revolution: Religion, Politics and Society in Kent 1500–1640* (Hassocks, 1977).

   ' "The Ramoth-Gilead of the Good": Urban Change and Political Radicalism in Gloucester 1540–1640', in P. Clark, A. G. R. Smith and N. Tyacke (eds.), *The English Commonwealth 1547–1640: Essays in Politics and Society Presented to Joel Hurstfield* (Leicester, 1979).

Coleman, Olive 'Trade and Prosperity in the Fifteenth Century: Some Aspects of the Trade of Southampton', *Econ. H.R.*, 2nd ser., xvi (1963–4).

Cornwall, Julian 'English Population in the Early Sixteenth Century', *Econ. H.R.*, 2nd ser. xxiii (1970).

Coss, P. R., 'Coventry before Incorporation: a Re-interpretation', *Midland History*, ii (1974).

Davis, R. H. C., *The Early History of Coventry*, Dugdale Society Occasional Papers, xxiv (Oxford, 1976).

Deprez, P., 'The Demographic Development of Flanders in the Eighteenth Century' in Glass and Eversley (eds.), *Population in History*.

Desportes, Pierre 'La Population du Reims an XVe Siècle d'après un Dénombrement de 1422', *Le Moyen Age*, lxxii (1966).

Dibben, Alan *Coventry City Charters*, The Coventry Papers, ii (1969).

Dietz, F. C., *English Public Finance, 1485–1641*, 2nd edn, 2 vols. (London, 1964), i.

Dobson, R. B., 'Urban Decline in Late Medieval England', *Trans. of the Royal Historical Soc.*, 5th ser. xxv (1977).

Dormer Harris, Mary *Life in an Old English Town: a History of Coventry from the Earliest Times compiled from Official Records* (London, 1898).

   The Story of Coventry (London, 1911).

   Dr Troughton's Sketches of Old Coventry (Coventry and London, n.d.).

Dugdale, William *The Antiquities of Warwickshire* (London, 1656).

Dyer, Alan D., *The City of Worcester in the Sixteenth Century* (Leicester, 1973).

Elton, G. R., 'Parliamentary Drafts 1529–1540', *Bull. of the Institute of Historical Research*, xxv (1952).

   'An Early Tudor Poor Law', *Econ. H.R.*, 2nd ser. vi (1953).

Everitt, A. M., 'Urban Growth 1570–1770', *Local Historian*, viii (1968).

Fines, J., 'Heresy Trials in the Diocese of Coventry and Lichfield 1511–12', *Jnl. of Ecclesiastical History*, xiv (1963).

Fox, Levi 'The Coventry Gilds and Trading Companies with Special Reference to the Position of Women', *B.A.S.T.*, lxxviii (1962).

Fretton, W. G., 'Hospital of St. John Baptist, Coventry', *Birmingham and Midland Institute, Archaeological Section, Transactions*, xiii (1886).

Glass, D. V. and Eversley, D.E.C. (eds.) *Population in History* (London, 1965).

Glasscock, R. E., 'England *circa* 1334', in H. C. Darby (ed.), *A New Historical Geography of England* (Cambridge, 1973)

Godber, J., *History of Bedfordshire* (Luton, 1969).

Goodacre, J. D., 'Lutterworth in the Sixteenth and Seventeenth Centuries: a Market Town and its Area' (University of Leicester Ph.D. thesis, 1977).

Gooder, E. and A., 'Coventry at the Black Death and Afterwards' (unpublished paper to the Dugdale Society, 1965).

Gooder, E., *Coventry's Town Wall*, Coventry and N. Warwickshire History Pamphlets, iv, revised and enlarged edn (1971).

Gray, H. L., 'English Foreign Trade from 1446–1482' in Eileen Power and M. M. Postan (eds.), *Studies in English Trade in the Fifteenth Century* (London, 1933).

Green, B. and Young, R. M. R., *Norwich – the Growth of a City* (Norwich, 1964).

Hajnal, J., 'European Marriage Patterns in Perspective' in Glass and Eversley (eds.), *Population in History*.

Harley, J. B., 'Population Trends and Agricultural Developments from the Warwickshire Hundred Rolls of 1279', in Alan R. H. Baker, John D. Hamshere and John Langton (eds.), *Geographical Interpretations of Historical Sources: Readings in Historical Geography* (Newton Abbot, 1970).

Harrison, C. J., 'Grain Price Analysis and Harvest Qualities, 1465–1634', *Ag. H.R.*, xix (1971).

Harvey, P. D. A., 'Banbury', in M. D. Lobel and W. H. Johns (eds.), *Historic Towns, i*, (London and Oxford, 1969).

Harvey, P. D. A. and Thorpe, Harry *The Printed Maps of Warwickshire 1579–1800* (Warwick, 1959).

Haskins, Charles *The Ancient Trade Guilds and Companies of Salisbury* (Salisbury, 1912).

Hatcher, John *Plague, Population and the English Economy 1348–1530* (London and Basingstoke, 1977).

Heaton, H., *The Yorkshire Woollen and Worsted Industries*, 2nd edn (Oxford, 1965).

Helleiner, Karl F., 'The Population of Europe from the Black Death to the Eve of the Vital Revolution' in E. E. Rich and C. H. Wilson (eds.), *The Cambridge Economic History of Europe*, iv (1967).

Herlihy, David *Medieval and Renaissance Pistoia* (Yale, 1967).

Hill, Francis *Medieval Lincoln* (Cambridge, 1965).
Tudor and Stuart Lincoln (Cambridge, 1956).

Hilton, R. H., *A Medieval Society: the West Midlands at the End of the Thirteenth Century* (London, 1966).
The English Peasantry in the Later Middle Ages, (Oxford, 1975).

Hollingsworth, T. H., *Historical Demography* (London and Southampton, 1969).

Hoskins, W. G., *The Midland Peasant* (London, 1957).
Local History in England (London, 1959).
'The Elizabethan Merchants of Exeter' in S. T. Bindoff, J. Hurstfield and C. H. Williams (eds.), *Elizabethan Government and Society: Essays Presented to Sir John Neale* (London, 1961).
Provincial England: Essays in Social and Economic History (London, 1963).
'Harvest Fluctuations in English Economic History 1480–1619', *Ag.H.R.*, xii (1964).
The Age of Plunder: the England of Henry VIII 1500–1547 (London, 1976).

Howell, Cicely 'Peasant Inheritance Customs in the Midlands 1280–1700', in Jack Goody, Joan Thirsk and E. P. Thompson (eds.), *Family and Inheritance: Rural Society in Western Europe 1200–1800* (Cambridge, 1976).

Jones, B. C., 'The Topography of Medieval Carlisle', *Transactions of the Cumberland and Westmorland Antiquarian and Archaeological Society*, new ser., lxxvi (1976).

Jones, S. R. and Smith, J. T., 'The Wealden Houses in Warwickshire and their Significance', *B.A.S.T.*, lxxix (1960–1).

Jones, Whitney, R. D., *The Tudor Commonwealth 1529–1559* (London, 1970).

Jordan, W. K., *The Charities of London 1480–1660* (London, 1960).

Kerridge, E., 'The Returns of the Inquisition of Depopulation', *English Historical Review*, lxx (1955).

Knecht, R. J., *Francis I and Absolute Monarchy*, Historical Association pamphlet, general ser. lxxii (1969).

Lancaster, Joan C., 'Local Government and Public Services: Local Government to 1451', in *V.C.H. Warks. viii.*

'Coventry' in M. D. Lobel and W. H. Johns (eds.), *The Atlas of Historic Towns, ii, Bristol; Cambridge; Coventry; Norwich* (London, 1975).

Lancaster, Joan C. and Ellis Davidson, H. R., *Godiva of Coventry* (Coventry, 1967).

Laslett, Peter 'Size and Structure of the Household in England over Three Centuries', *Population Studies*, xiii (1969).

The World We Have Lost, 2nd edn (London, 1971).

'Mean Household Size in England Since the Sixteenth Century' in Peter Laslett assisted by Richard Wall (eds.), *Household and Family in Past Time* (Cambridge, 1972).

Lobel, M. D. and Tann, J., 'Gloucester' in *Historic Towns, i*, ed. M. D. Lobel and W. H. Johns (London and Oxford, 1969).

Luttrell, Claude 'Baiting of Bulls and Boars in the Middle English "Cleanness"', *Notes and Queries*, cxcvii (1952) and cci (1956).

MacCaffrey, W. T., *Exeter 1540–1640* (Harvard, 1958).

Macfarlane, Alan *The Family Life of Ralph Josselin* (Cambridge, 1970).

Mercer, Eric *English Art 1553–1625*, The Oxford History of English Art, 11 vols. (Oxford, 1962), vii.

Miller, E., 'Medieval York', in P. M. Tillott (ed.), *V.C.H: The City of York* (Oxford, 1961).

Mols, Roger *Introduction à la Démographie Historique des Villes d'Europe du XIVe an XVIIIe siècle*, 3 vols. (Louvain, 1955).

Mousnier, R., *Les XVIe et XVIIe Siècles* (Paris, 1961).

Neale, J. E., *The Elizabethan House of Commons* (London, 1954).

Outhwaite, R. B., *Inflation in Tudor and Early Stuart England* (London, 1969).

Palliser, D. M., 'Some Aspects of the Social and Economic History of York in the Sixteenth Century' (University of Oxford D.Phil. thesis, 1968).

'The Trade Gilds of Tudor York' in Clark and Slack (eds.), *Crisis and Order in English Towns.*

'The Boroughs of Medieval Staffordshire', *The North Staffordshire Jnl. of Field Studies*, xii (1972).

'York under the Tudors: the Trading Life of the Northern Capital' in Alan Everitt (ed.), *Perspectives in English Urban History* (London and Basingstoke, 1973).

The Staffordshire Landscape (London, 1976).

Pantin, W. A., 'Medieval English Town-house Plans', *Medieval Archaeology*, vi–vii (1962–3).

Patten, J. H. C., 'Village and Town: an Occupational Study', *Ag.H.R.*, xx (1972).

'Population Distribution in Norfolk and Suffolk during the Sixteenth and Seventeenth Centuries', *The Institute of British Geographers*, lxv (1975).

Pevsner, N. and Wedgwood, Alexandra *The Buildings of England: Warwickshire* (Harmondsworth, 1966).

Phelps Brown, E. H., and Hopkins, S. V., 'Seven Centuries of the Prices of Consumables, Compared with Builders' Wage Rates' in E. M. Carus-Wilson (ed.), *Essays in Economic History*, 3 vols. (London, 1962), ii.

Phythian-Adams, Charles 'Records of the Craft Gilds', *The Local Historian*, ix (1971).

'Ceremony and the Citizen: the Communal Year at Coventry 1450–1550' in Clark and Slack (eds.), *Crisis and Order in English Towns*.

Local History and Folklore: a New Framework, Standing Conference for Local History (London, 1975).

'The Economic and Social Stucture' in *The Fabric of the Traditional Community* (The Open University, course A 322, English Urban History 1500–1700, unit 5, 1977.)

'Urban Crisis or Urban Change?' in *The Traditional Community under Stress* (ibid., unit 9, part A).

'Jolly Cities: Goodly Towns. The Current Search for England's Urban Roots', *Urban History Yearbook 1977*.

'Urban Decay in Late Medieval England' in Philip Abrams and E. A. Wrigley, *Towns in Societies: Essays in Economic History and Historical Sociology* (Cambridge, 1978).

Pirenne, H., 'Les Dénombrements de la Population d'Ypres au XVe Siècle (1412–1506) (Contribution à la Statistique Sociale du Moyen Age)', *Vierteljahrschrift Social – und Wirtschaftsgesichte*, i (1903).

Poole, Benjamin *Coventry: its History and Antiquities* (London and Coventry, 1870).

Postan, M. M., 'Some Economic Evidence of Declining Population in the Later Middle Ages', *Econ. H.R.*, 2nd ser. ii (1950).

'Medieval Agrarian Society in its Prime: England', in M. M. Postan (ed.), *The Cambridge Economic History of Europe*, 2nd edn (Cambridge, 1966).

Pound, J. F., 'The Social and Trade Structure of Norwich 1525–1575', *Past and Present*, xxxiv (1966).

Ramsay, G. D., *The Wiltshire Woollen Industry*, 2nd edn (London, 1965).

Roberts, B. R., 'Field Systems of the West Midlands' in Baker and Butlin (eds.), *Studies of Field Systems in the British Isles*.

Rogers, Alan 'Medieval Stamford' in Alan Rogers (ed.), *The Making of Stamford* (Leicester, 1965).

Rowse, A. L., *The England of Elizabeth* (London, 1962).

Ruddock, A. A., *Italian Merchants and Shipping in Southampton 1270–1600* (Southampton Record Ser., i, 1951).

Russell, J. C., *British Medieval Population* (Albuquerque, 1948).

'Late Medieval Population Patterns', *Speculum*, xx (1945).

Scarisbrick, J. J., *Henry VIII* (London, 1976).

Schofield, R. S., 'The Geographical Distribution of Wealth in England 1334–1649', *Econ. H.R.*, 2nd ser., xviii (1965).

Sheail, J. D., 'The Regional Distribution of Wealth in England as Indicated in the Lay Subsidy Returns of 1524/5' (University of London Ph.D. thesis, 1968).

Shrewsbury, J. F. D., *A History of Bubonic Plague in the British Isles* (Cambridge, 1970).

Skipp, V. H. T., 'Economic and Social Change in the Forest of Arden, 1530–1649' in Joan Thirsk (ed.), *Land, Church and People: Essays Presented to Professor H. P. R. Finberg, Ag.H.R.*, xviii (1970), Supplement.

Slack, Paul 'Poverty and Politics in Salisbury 1597–1666', in Clark and Slack (eds.), *Crisis and Order in English Towns.*

'A Brief Comment' in *The Traditional Community Under Stress* (The Open University, course A 322, 1977), unit 9, part B.

Smith, C. T., 'Population' in *V. C. H. Leicestershire*, iii, ed. W. G. Hoskins and R. A. McKinley (Oxford, 1955).

Stephens, W. B. (ed.) *The City of Coventry and Borough of Warwick, V.C.H. Warks.*, viii (London, 1969).

Stone, Laurence 'The Political Programme of Thomas Cromwell', *Bulletin of the Instit. of Historical Research*, xxiv (1951).

Stow, John *The Annals of England . . . until this Present Year of 1601* (London, 1601).

Supple, B. E., *Commercial Crisis and Change in England, 1600–1642* (Cambridge, 1964).

Thirsk, Joan *Economic Policy and Projects: The Development of a Consumer Society in Early Modern England* (Oxford, 1978).

Thomas, Keith *Religion and the Decline of Magic: Studies in Popular Beliefs in Sixteenth and Seventeenth Century England* (London, 1971).

Age and Authority in Early Modern England, Proceedings of the British Academy, lxii (1976).

Thorold Rogers, J. E., *A History of Agriculture and Prices in England*, 8 vols. (Oxford, 1866–1902), iv.

Thrupp, Sylvia L., *The Merchant Class of Medieval London 1300–1500* (Michigan, 1962).

Townsend, Peter *The Family Life of Old People* (Harmondsworth, 1963).

Verlinden, C., 'Crises Économiques et Sociales à l'Époque de Charles-Quint', in *Charles-Quint et Son Temps* (Paris, 1959).

Wall, Richard 'Mean Household Size in England from Printed Sources', in Peter Laslett, assisted by Richard Wall (eds.), *Household and Family in Past Time* (Cambridge, 1972).

Whitcombe, Norma R., *The Medieval Floor-Tiles of Leicestershire*, Leicestershire Archaeological and Historical Society (1956).

Whitley, T. W., *Parliamentary Representation of the City of Coventry* (Coventry, 1894).

Willan, T. S., *River Navigation in England 1600–1700* (Oxford, 1936).

Williams, W. M., *A West Country Village: Ashworthy* (London, 1963).

Wilson, K. P., 'The Port of Chester in the Fifteenth Century', *Transactions of the Historic Society of Lancashire and Cheshire*, cxvii (1965).

Wright, Louis B., *Middle Class Culture in Elizabethan England* (London, 1958).

Wrigley, E. A., *Population and History* (London, 1969).

Index

administrative centre, 162
adolescence, 81–4
'Adylton', 29
age-grades, 81–93, 114–15, 122, 180, 270, 272–4
Alcester, 58
Aldermen, 77, 79, 88, 93, 122, 123, 124, 146, 158 (*see also* ex-mayors)
ale-houses, 79, 88, 95–6, 219–20
alms, monastic, 136 n. 30 (*see also*, mendivants, gild)
Alvechurch, 25
Amicable Grant, the, 63, 254
Antwerp, 61
Appleby, 9
apprentices, apprenticeships, 45, 62, 66, 83–4, 87, 105, 214–15, 273–4, 281 n. 2, 306–7
Arden, forest of, 24, 25, 26 n. 50, 27, 57 n. 26, 58
Ariès, P., 82
armoury, the, 162
Armstrong, Clement, 286
Astley, Warks., 256
Astleyn, Thomas (mayor, 1529), 116 n. 104
Aston, 25
Aston, Robert, 155
Aston, William, 155
Atherstone, 28
Attleborough, 25
Avon, River, 25, 26, 58

Bablake (*see also* Bonde's hospital; St John), 84 n. 23
Bacon, Francis, 252
Baginton (Warks.), 49, 109, 143, 154
Bailey Lane, 160, 162, 191, 323
Baltic, the, 20, 27, 58
Banbury, 24 n. 45, 28, 30
Banwell, Joan, 151, 166 n. 33
Banwell, Thomas (mayor, 1524), 61 n. 51, 149, 152, 252
Barkers' Butts, 111, 161
Bars, the 174
Bartelot, R., 291
Basle (Switzerland), 199
Beccles, 12

Bedford, 9, 10, 17
beggars, 64, 66, 135–6, 295 (*see also* vagrants)
Berkley, Lady Isabel, 100
Berkswell, 25
Bethnal Green, 152
Beverley, 16
Birmingham, 8, 19, 20, 25, 28, 29, 30, 139, 181, 214
Birmingham plateau, 24, 25, 28, 282
Bishop of Coventry and Lichfield, 138, 182, 259
    palace of, 21, 219, 162 (*see also* Coventry and Lichfield, diocese of)
Bishop Gate, 176
Bishop Street, 159 n. 8, 324
Black Prince, the, 140, 173
Bodmin, 9, 12, 15
Boleyn, Anne, 259
Bolton, D., 172
Bonde, Dorothy, 154
Bonde, John (mayor, 1520), 57, 143, 149, 150, 154, 266 n. 47, 251
Bonde, Thomas (mayor, 1498), 143, 149, 150, 151
Bonde, Thomas, 147
Bonde, Winifred, 149
Bonde's hospital, 135, 190
Boston, 8, 13 n. 12, 16, 20, 139, 276 n. 3
Bowden, P., 55 n. 19, 60
Bradford, Samuel, 323
Bradgate, Leics., 255
Bridbury, A. R., 42
Bridgnorth, 8, 17
Bridgwater, 8, 14, 17, 286
Bridport, 286
Bristol, 11, 12, 15, 17, 20, 21, 28, 30, 58, 61, 139, 140, 149, 217, 266 n. 47, 276 n. 3, 283, 284, 285, 287
Bromsgrove, 18, 26
Bromwich, Roger, 132 n. 18
Bryan, Sir Francis, 259
bull-baiting, 77
Bull ring, the, 77 n. 36
Buckingham, 9
Buckinghamshire, 24 n. 45, 27